Tadi
dadi da

藤崎　竜

I sometimes think about material for
a different manga even on holiday.
I wanna be lazy! I wanna live my life
singing and dancing! That's what I
think, but I guess it's the sad habits
of a mangaka that've stuck with me.

Ryu Fujisaki

Ryu Fujisaki's *Worlds* came in second place for the
prestigious 40th Tezuka Award. His *Psycho +*, *Wāqwāq* and
Hoshin Engi have all run in *Weekly Shonen Jump* magazine,
and the *Hoshin Engi* anime is available on DVD in Japan
and North America. A lover of science fiction, literature
and history, Fujisaki has made *Hoshin Engi* a mix of genres
that truly showcases his amazing art and imagination.

HOSHIN ENGI VOL. 18
SHONEN JUMP Manga Edition

STORY AND ART BY RYU FUJISAKI
Based on the novel *Hoshin Engi*, translated by Tsutomu Ano,
published by Kodansha Bunko

Translation & Adaptation/Tomo Kimura
Touch-up Art & Lettering/HudsonYards
Design/Matt Hinrichs
Editor/Jonathan Tarbox

VP, Production/Alvin Lu
VP, Sales & Product Marketing/Gonzalo Ferreyra
VP, Creative/Linda Espinosa
Publisher/Hyoe Narita

Printed in Canada

Published by VIZ Media, LLC
P.O. Box 77010
San Francisco, CA 94107

10 9 8 7 6 5 4 3 2 1
First printing, April 2010

www.viz.com

THE WORLD'S MOST POPULAR MANGA
www.shonenjump.com

HOSHIN ENGI

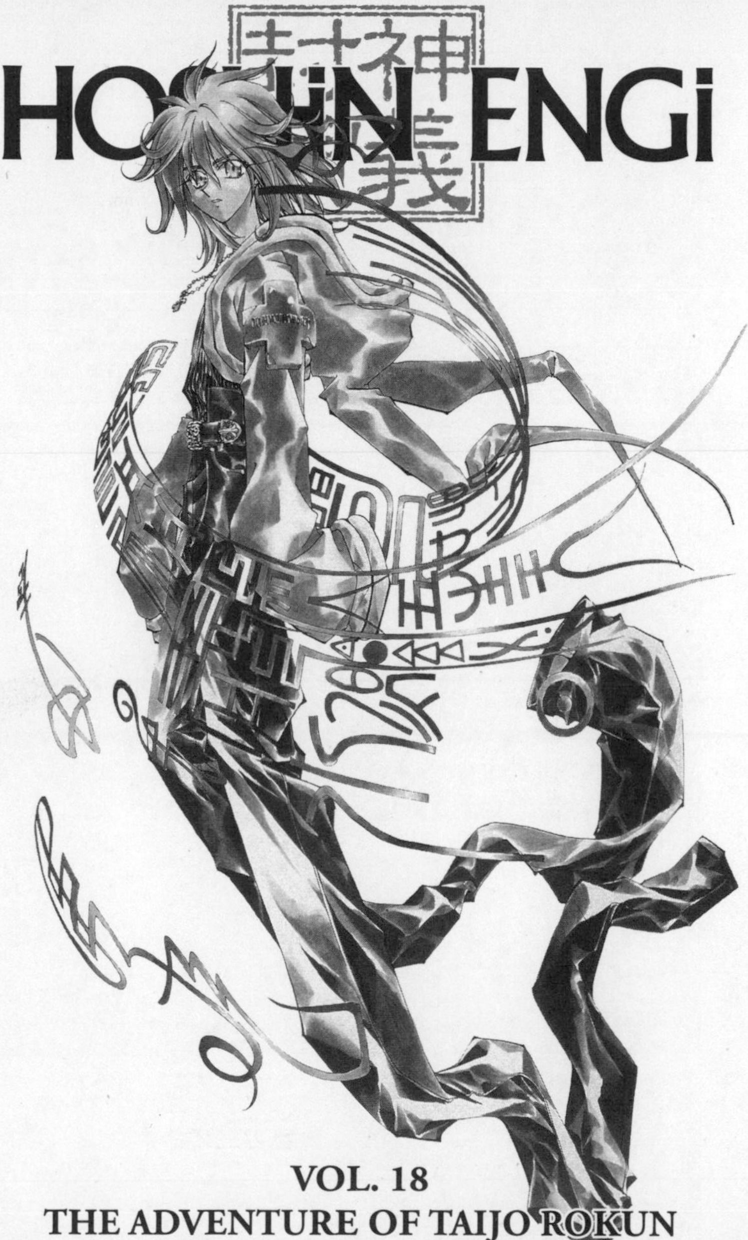

VOL. 18

THE ADVENTURE OF TAIJO ROKUN

STORY AND ART BY RYU FUJISAKI

THE CHARACTERS

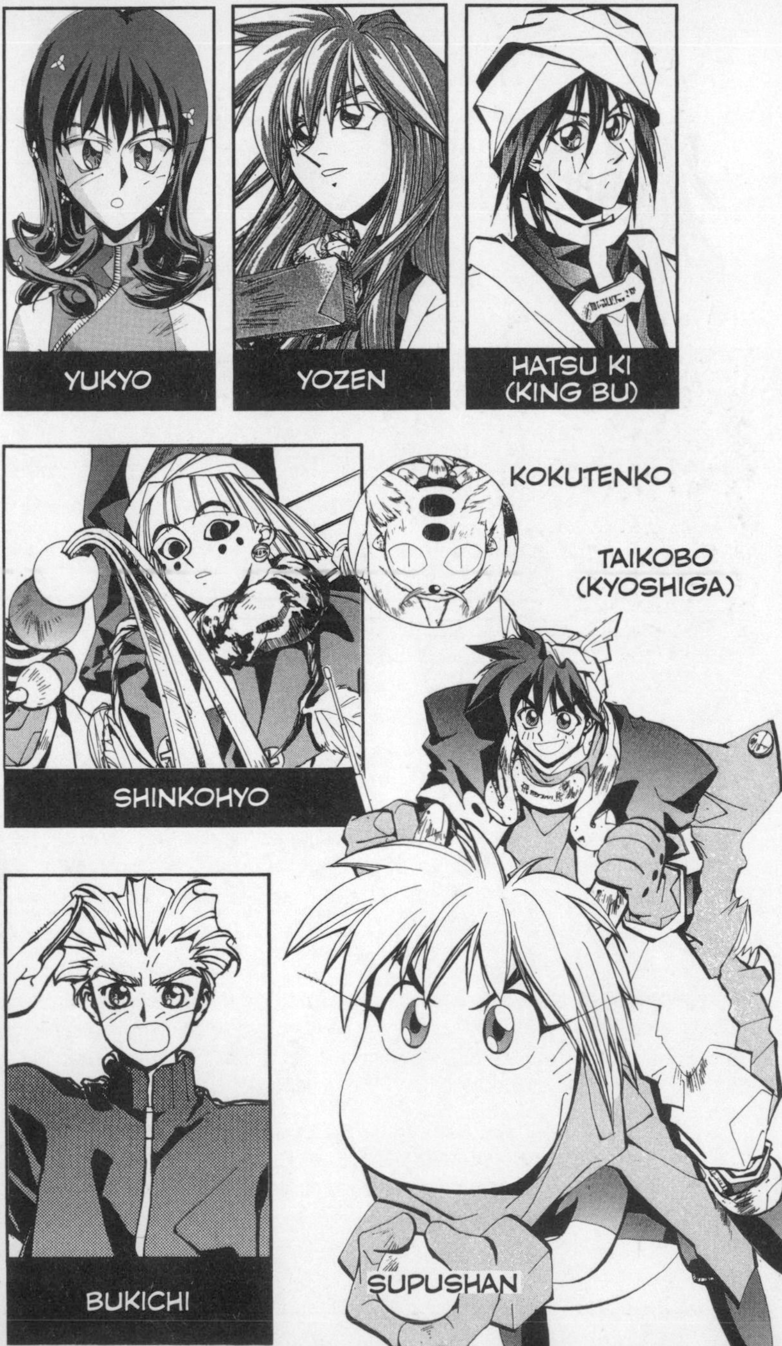
HATSU KI (KING BU)
YOZEN
YUKYO
KOKUTENKO
TAIKOBO (KYOSHIGA)
SHINKOHYO
SUPUSHAN
BUKICHI

KING CHU

BUNCHU

DAKKI

OKIJIN

KOKIBI

The Story Thus Far

Ancient China, over 3,000 years ago. It is the era of the Yin Dynasty.

After King Chu, the emperor, married the beautiful Dakki, the good king was no longer himself and became an unmanly and foolish ruler. Dakki, a *Sennyo* with a wicked heart, took control of Yin, and the country fell into chaos.

To save the human world, the Hoshin Project was put into action. The project will seal evil Sennin and Doshi into the Shinkai and cause Seihakuko Sho Ki to set up a new dynasty to replace Yin. Taikobo, who was chosen to execute this project, acts to install Sho Ki's heir Hatsu Ki as the next king.

The intense battles become an all-out war between Mount Kongrong and Kingo Island. Taikobo and his comrades seal one Juttenkun after another and finally settle the battle with Bunchu, but they suffer heavy casualties. The survivors return to Zhou. And Taikobo sets off on a journey to look for Taijo Rokun, one of the three great Sennin for the coming battle against Dakki.

HOSHIN ENGI

VOL. 18
THE ADVENTURE OF TAIJO ROKUN

CONTENTS

Chapter 152

THE ADVENTURE OF TAIJO ROKUN, PART 4
TAIKOBO GETS MACHO

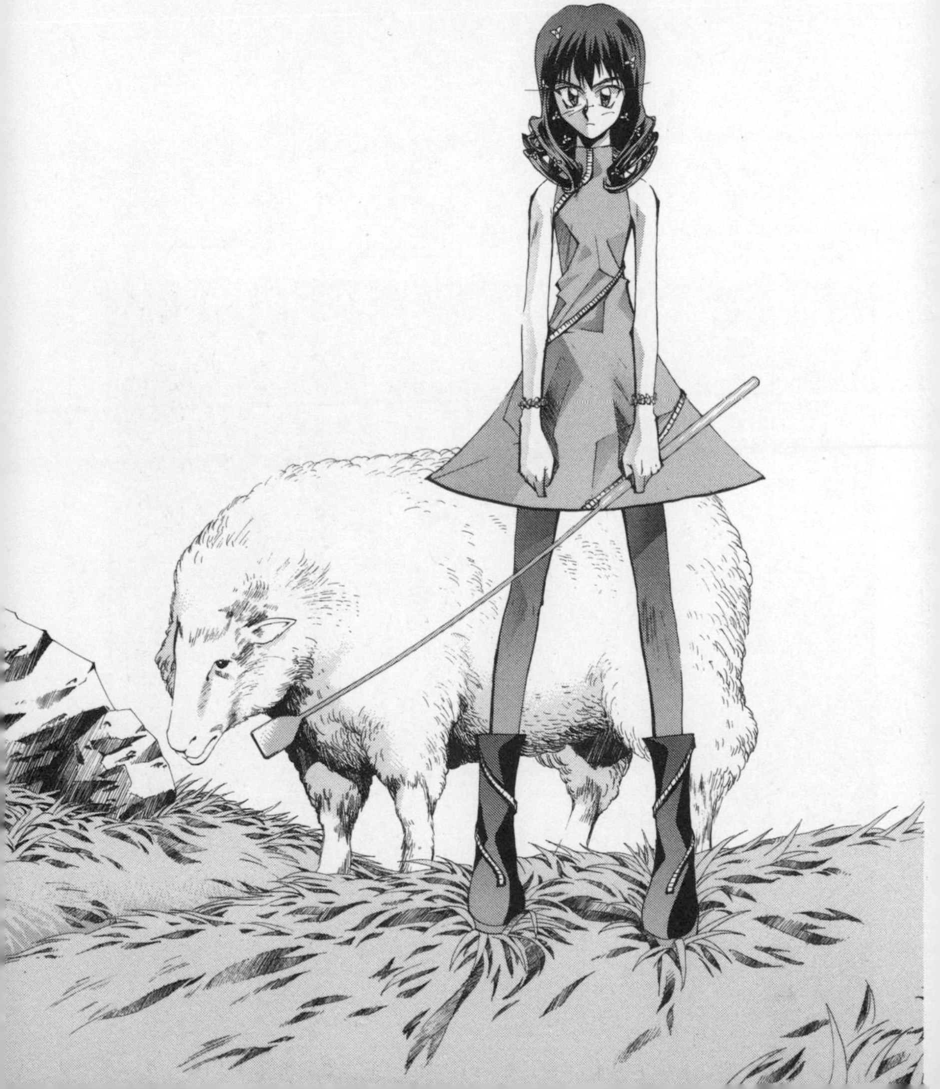

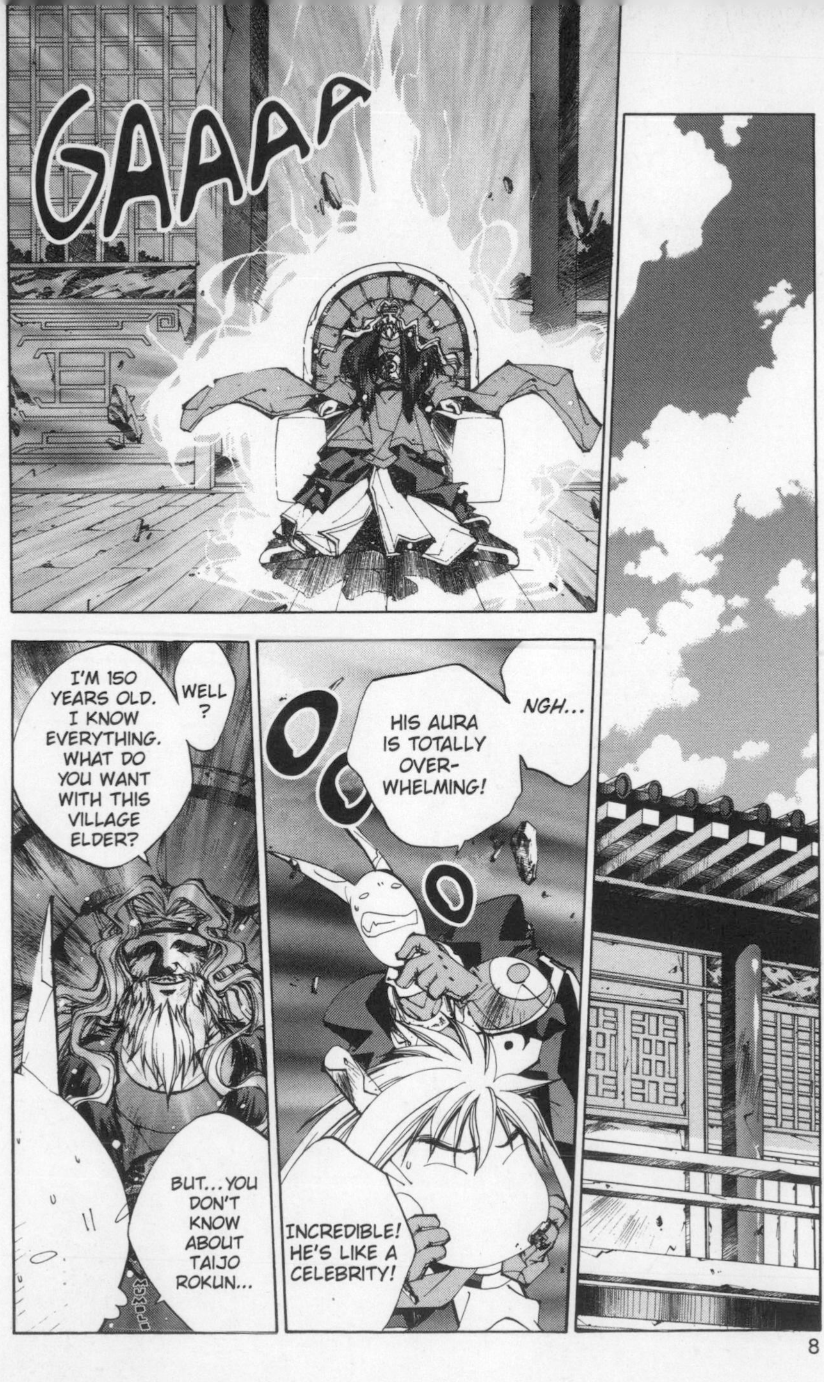
GAAAA
NGH...
HIS AURA IS TOTALLY OVER-WHELMING!
OOO
INCREDIBLE! HE'S LIKE A CELEBRITY!
WELL?
I'M 150 YEARS OLD. I KNOW EVERYTHING. WHAT DO YOU WANT WITH THIS VILLAGE ELDER?
BUT...YOU DON'T KNOW ABOUT TAIJO ROKUN...
MUMBLE

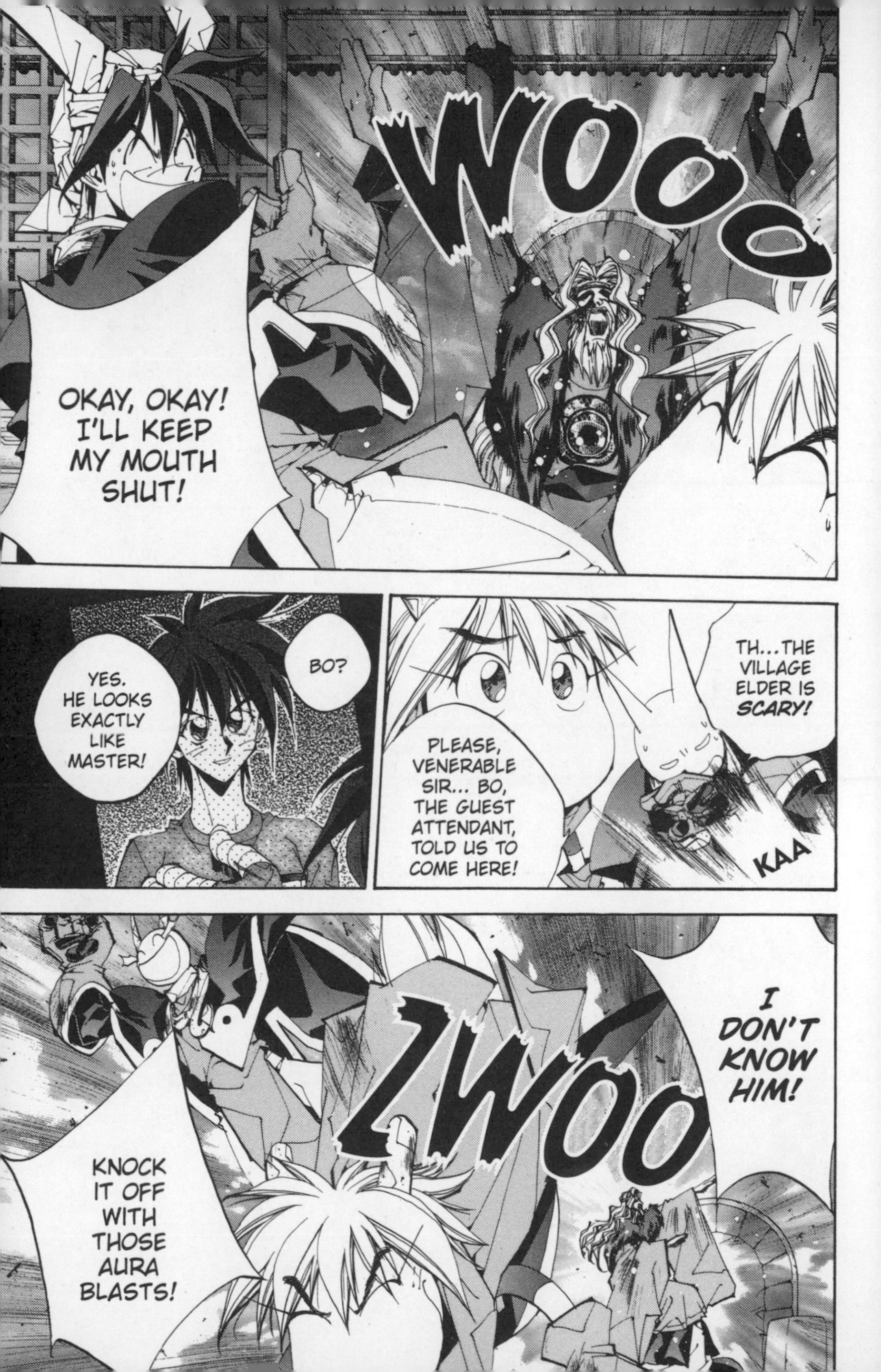
WOOOO
OKAY, OKAY! I'LL KEEP MY MOUTH SHUT!
TH...THE VILLAGE ELDER IS *SCARY!*
PLEASE, VENERABLE SIR... BO, THE GUEST ATTENDANT, TOLD US TO COME HERE!
KAA
BO?
YES. HE LOOKS EXACTLY LIKE MASTER!
I DON'T KNOW HIM!
ZWOO
KNOCK IT OFF WITH THOSE AURA BLASTS!

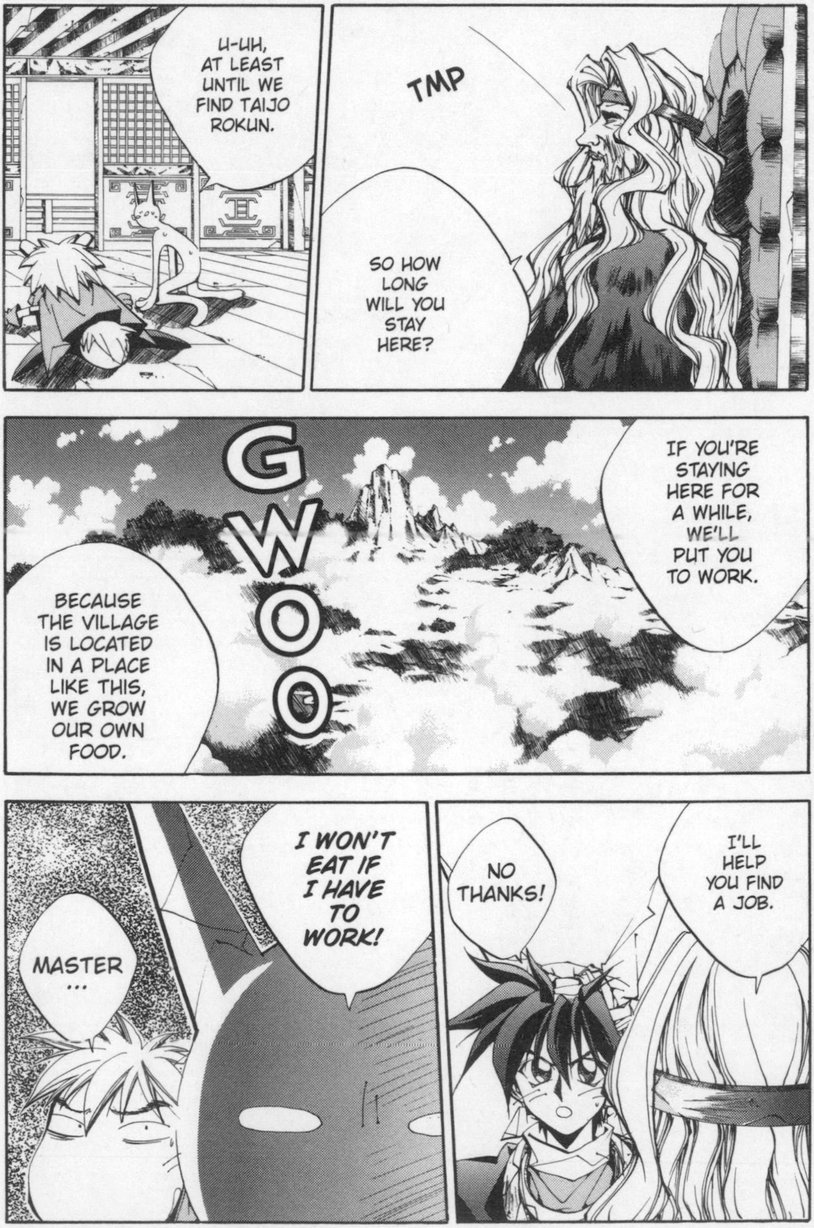
TMP
SO HOW LONG WILL YOU STAY HERE?
U-UH, AT LEAST UNTIL WE FIND TAIJO ROKUN.
IF YOU'RE STAYING HERE FOR A WHILE, WE'LL PUT YOU TO WORK.
GWOO
BECAUSE THE VILLAGE IS LOCATED IN A PLACE LIKE THIS, WE GROW OUR OWN FOOD.
I'LL HELP YOU FIND A JOB.
NO THANKS!
I WON'T EAT IF I HAVE TO WORK!
MASTER ...

READ THIS WAY

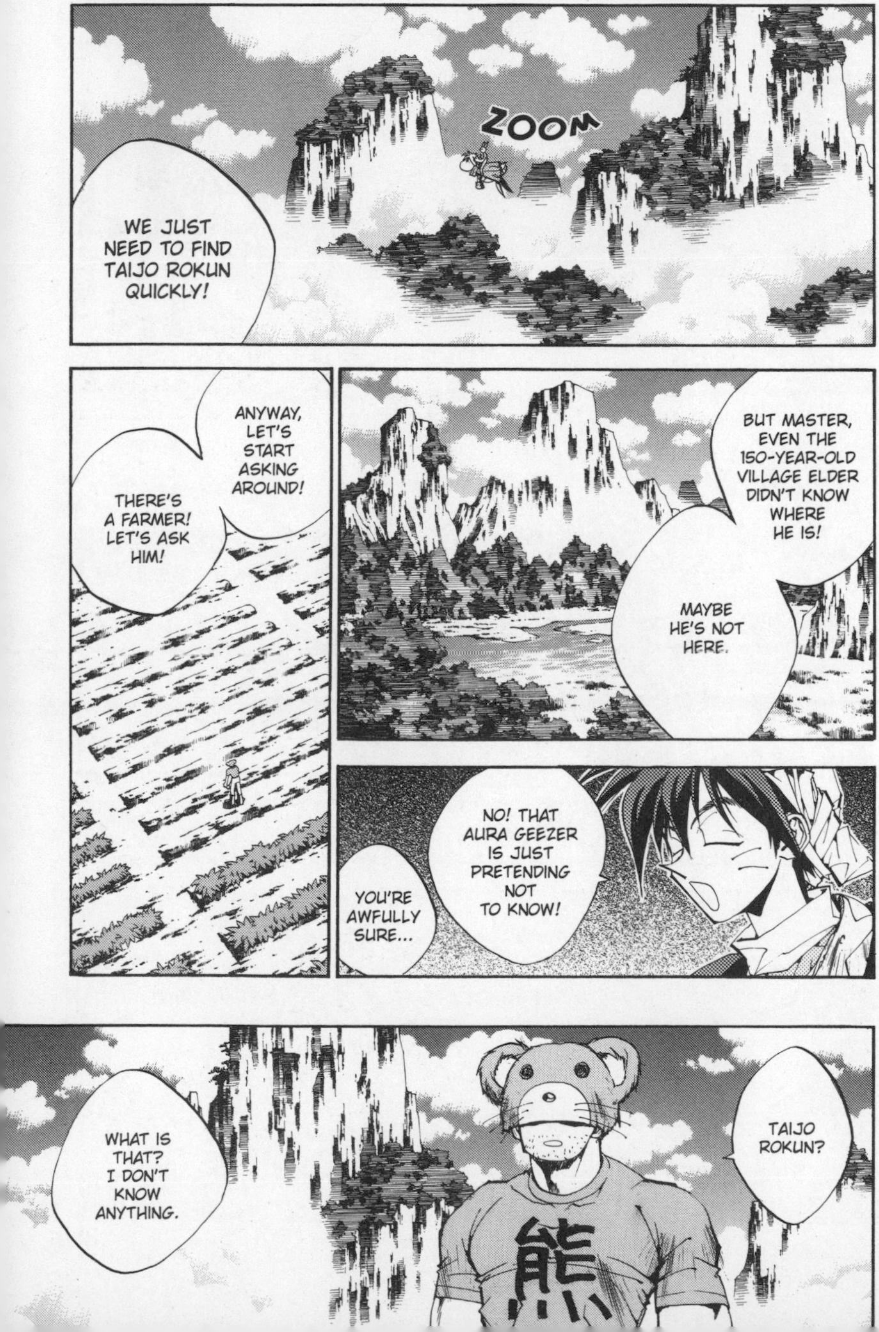
ZOOM
WE JUST NEED TO FIND TAIJO ROKUN QUICKLY!
BUT MASTER, EVEN THE 150-YEAR-OLD VILLAGE ELDER DIDN'T KNOW WHERE HE IS!
MAYBE HE'S NOT HERE.
NO! THAT AURA GEEZER IS JUST PRETENDING NOT TO KNOW!
YOU'RE AWFULLY SURE...
ANYWAY, LET'S START ASKING AROUND!
THERE'S A FARMER! LET'S ASK HIM!
TAIJO ROKUN?
WHAT IS THAT? I DON'T KNOW ANYTHING.
熊

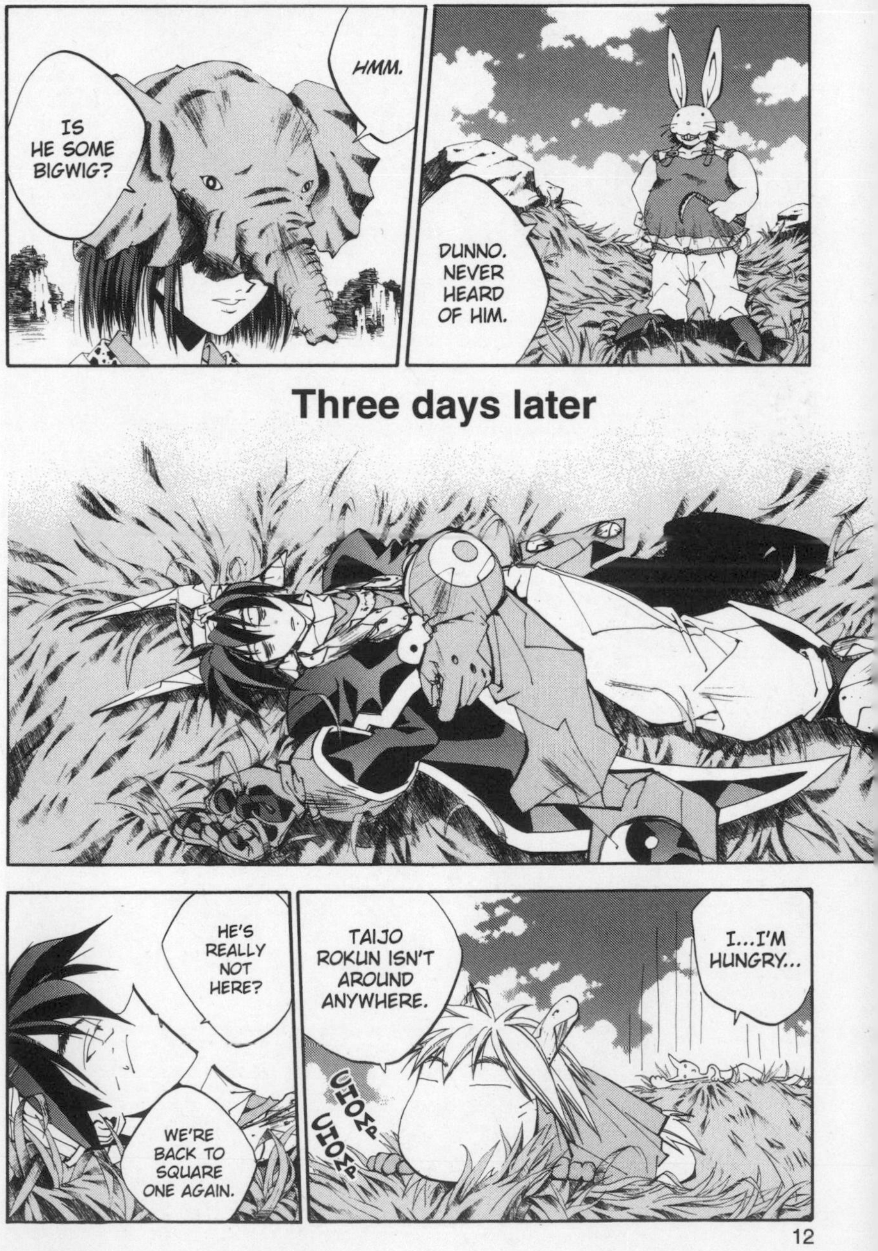
DUNNO. NEVER HEARD OF HIM.
HMM.
IS HE SOME BIGWIG?
Three days later
I...I'M HUNGRY...
TAIJO ROKUN ISN'T AROUND ANYWHERE.
CHOMP
CHOMP
HE'S REALLY NOT HERE?
WE'RE BACK TO SQUARE ONE AGAIN.

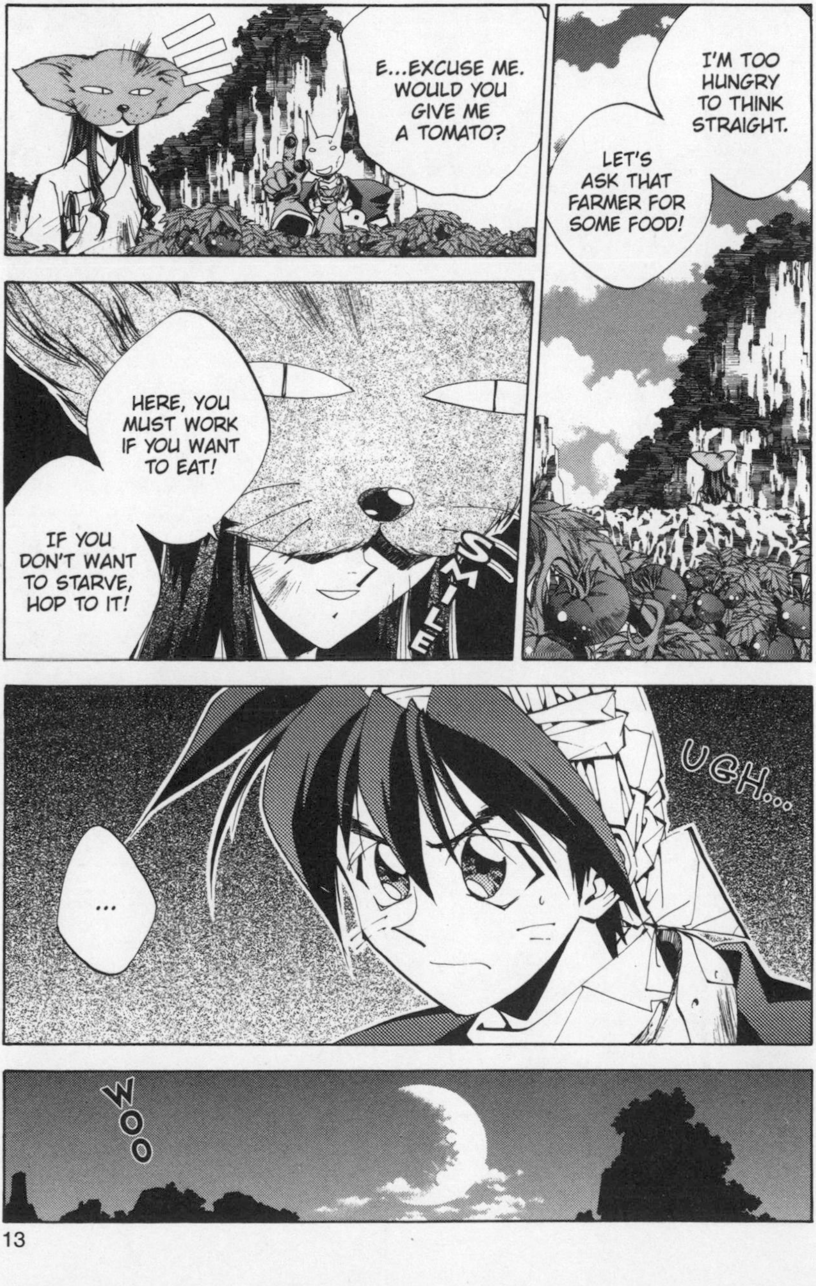
I'M TOO HUNGRY TO THINK STRAIGHT.
LET'S ASK THAT FARMER FOR SOME FOOD!
E...EXCUSE ME. WOULD YOU GIVE ME A TOMATO?
HERE, YOU MUST WORK IF YOU WANT TO EAT!
SMILE
IF YOU DON'T WANT TO STARVE, HOP TO IT!
UGH...
...
WOO

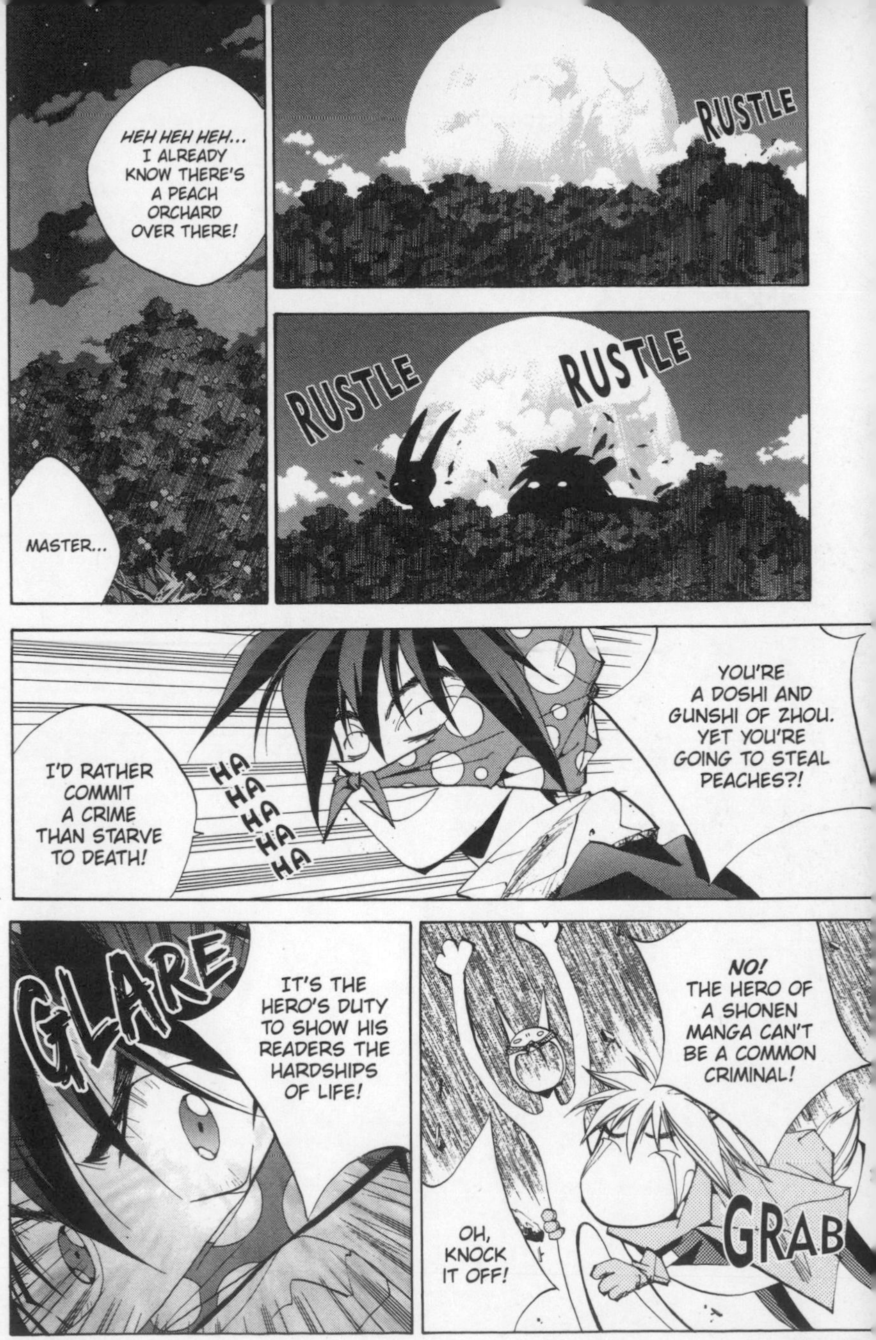
RUSTLE
RUSTLE
RUSTLE
HEH HEH HEH... I ALREADY KNOW THERE'S A PEACH ORCHARD OVER THERE!
MASTER...
YOU'RE A DOSHI AND GUNSHI OF ZHOU. YET YOU'RE GOING TO STEAL PEACHES?!
HA HA HA HA HA HA
I'D RATHER COMMIT A CRIME THAN STARVE TO DEATH!
NO! THE HERO OF A SHONEN MANGA CAN'T BE A COMMON CRIMINAL!
GRAB
OH, KNOCK IT OFF!
IT'S THE HERO'S DUTY TO SHOW HIS READERS THE HARDSHIPS OF LIFE!
GLARE

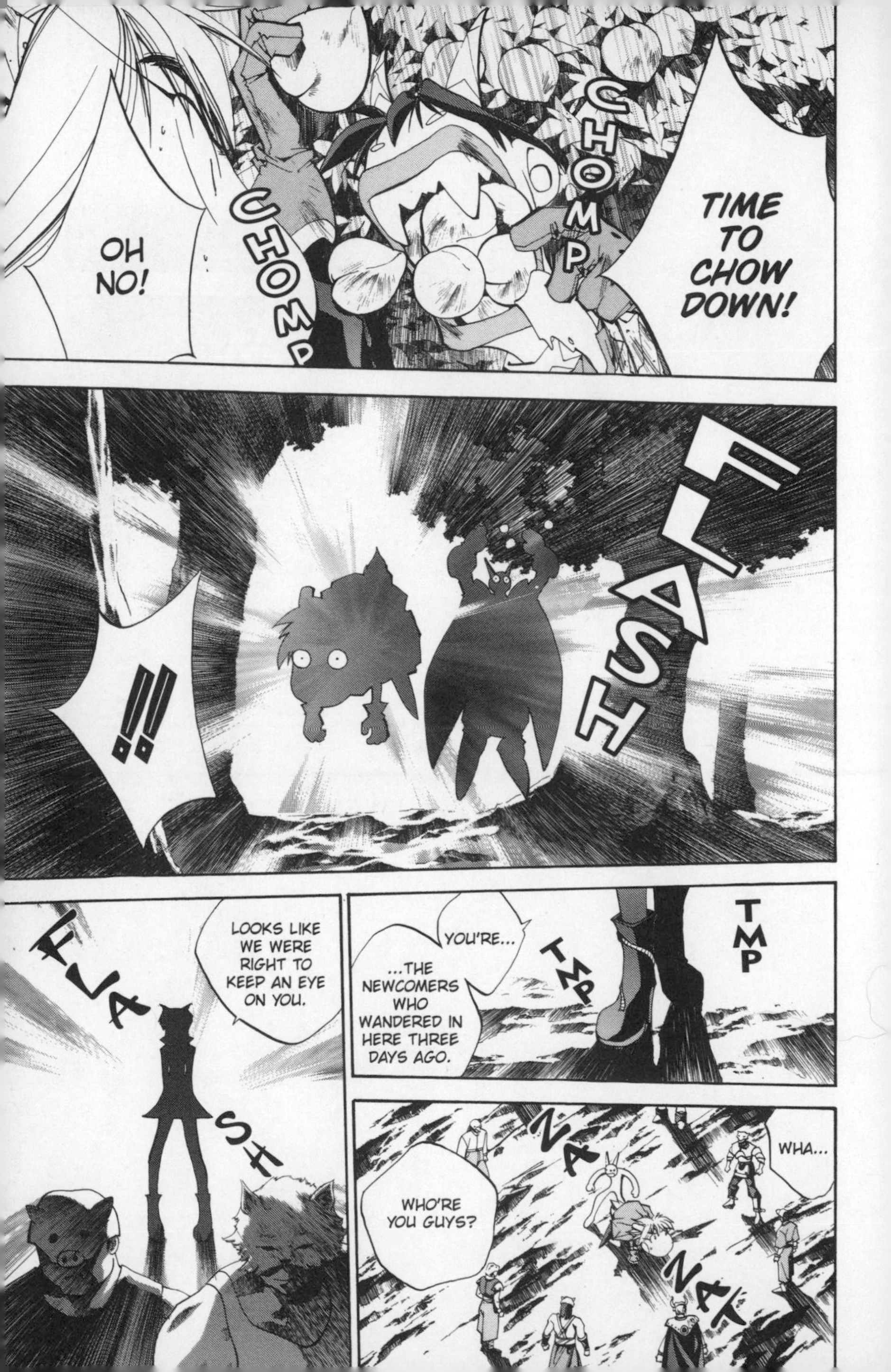
TIME TO CHOW DOWN!
CHOMP
CHOMP
OH NO!
FLASH
!!
TMP
TMP
YOU'RE...
...THE NEWCOMERS WHO WANDERED IN HERE THREE DAYS AGO.
WHA...
NA
NA
WHO'RE YOU GUYS?
LOOKS LIKE WE WERE RIGHT TO KEEP AN EYE ON YOU.
FWASH

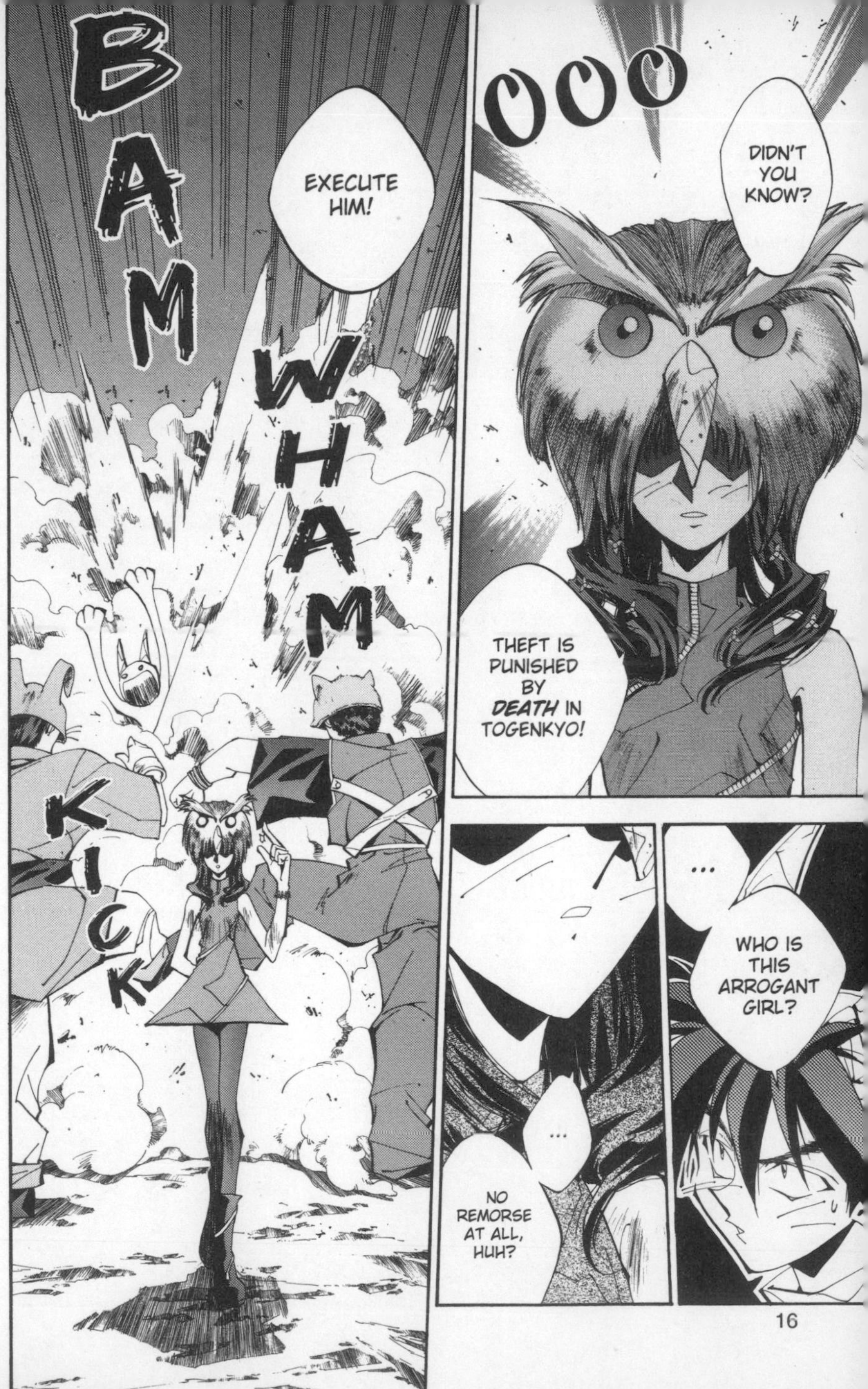
OOO
DIDN'T YOU KNOW?
THEFT IS PUNISHED BY *DEATH* IN TOGENKYO!
...
WHO IS THIS ARROGANT GIRL?
...
NO REMORSE AT ALL, HUH?
BAM
EXECUTE HIM!
WHAM
KICK

READ THIS WAY

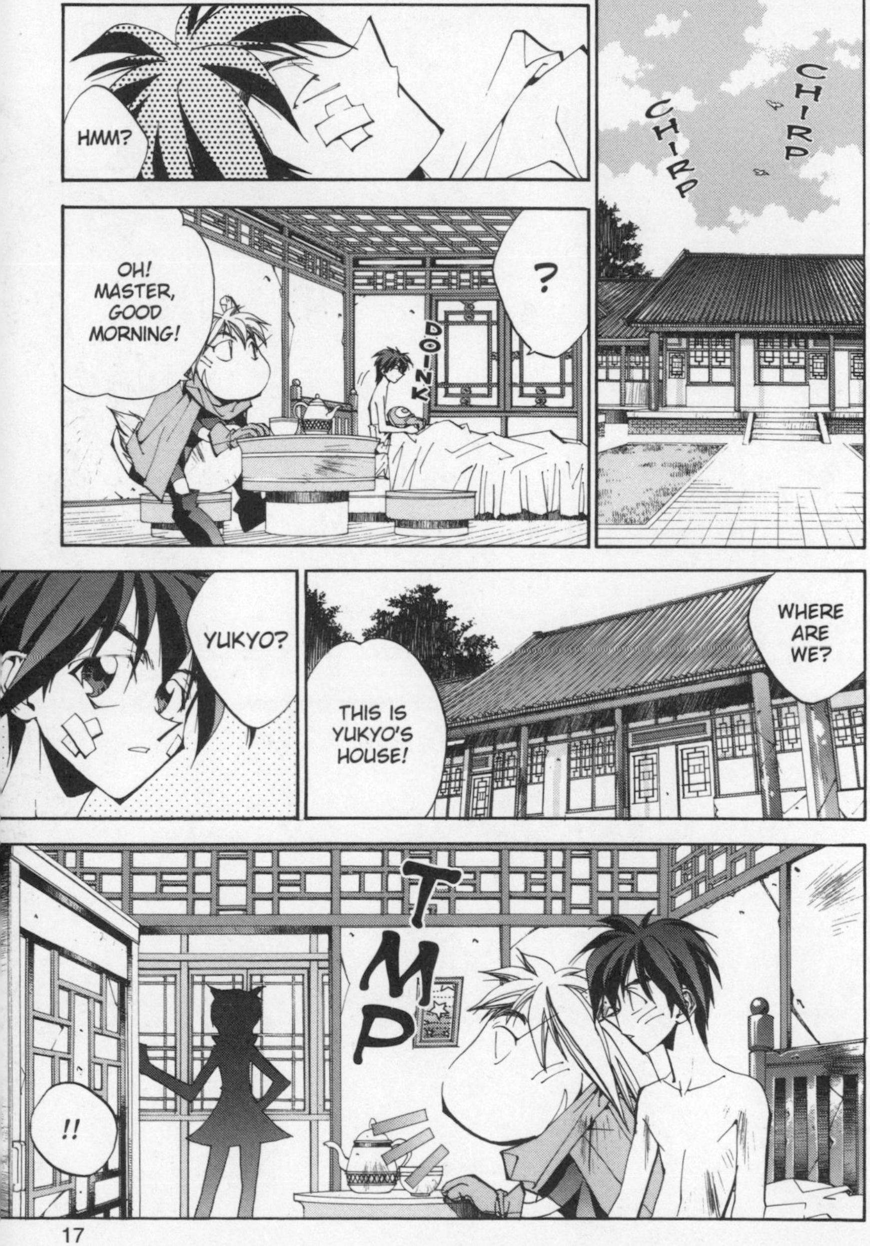

CHIRP
CHIRP
HMM?
?
DOINK
OH! MASTER, GOOD MORNING!
WHERE ARE WE?
THIS IS YUKYO'S HOUSE!
YUKYO?
TMP
!!

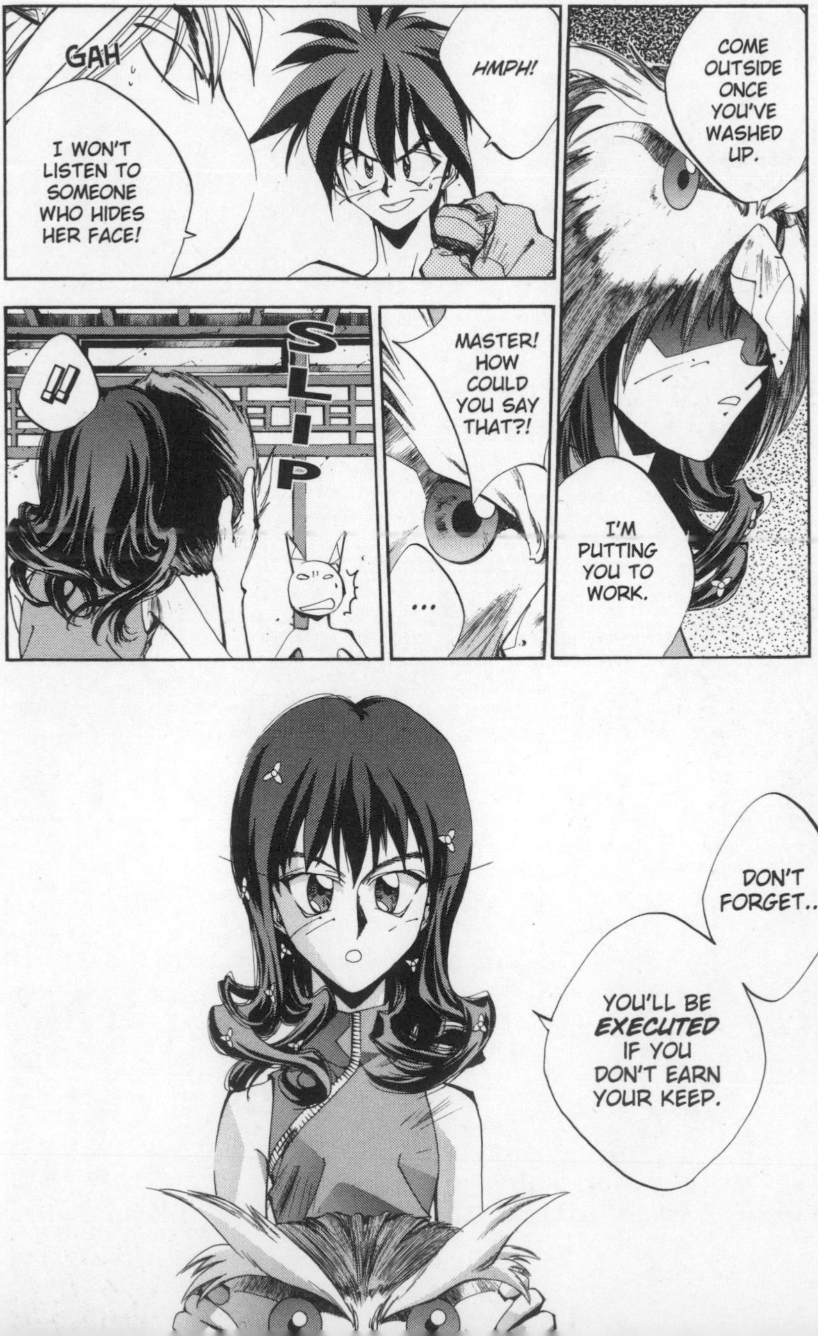
COME OUTSIDE ONCE YOU'VE WASHED UP.
I'M PUTTING YOU TO WORK.
HMPH!
GAH
I WON'T LISTEN TO SOMEONE WHO HIDES HER FACE!
MASTER! HOW COULD YOU SAY THAT?!
...
SLIP
!!
DON'T FORGET...
YOU'LL BE ***EXECUTED*** IF YOU DON'T EARN YOUR KEEP.

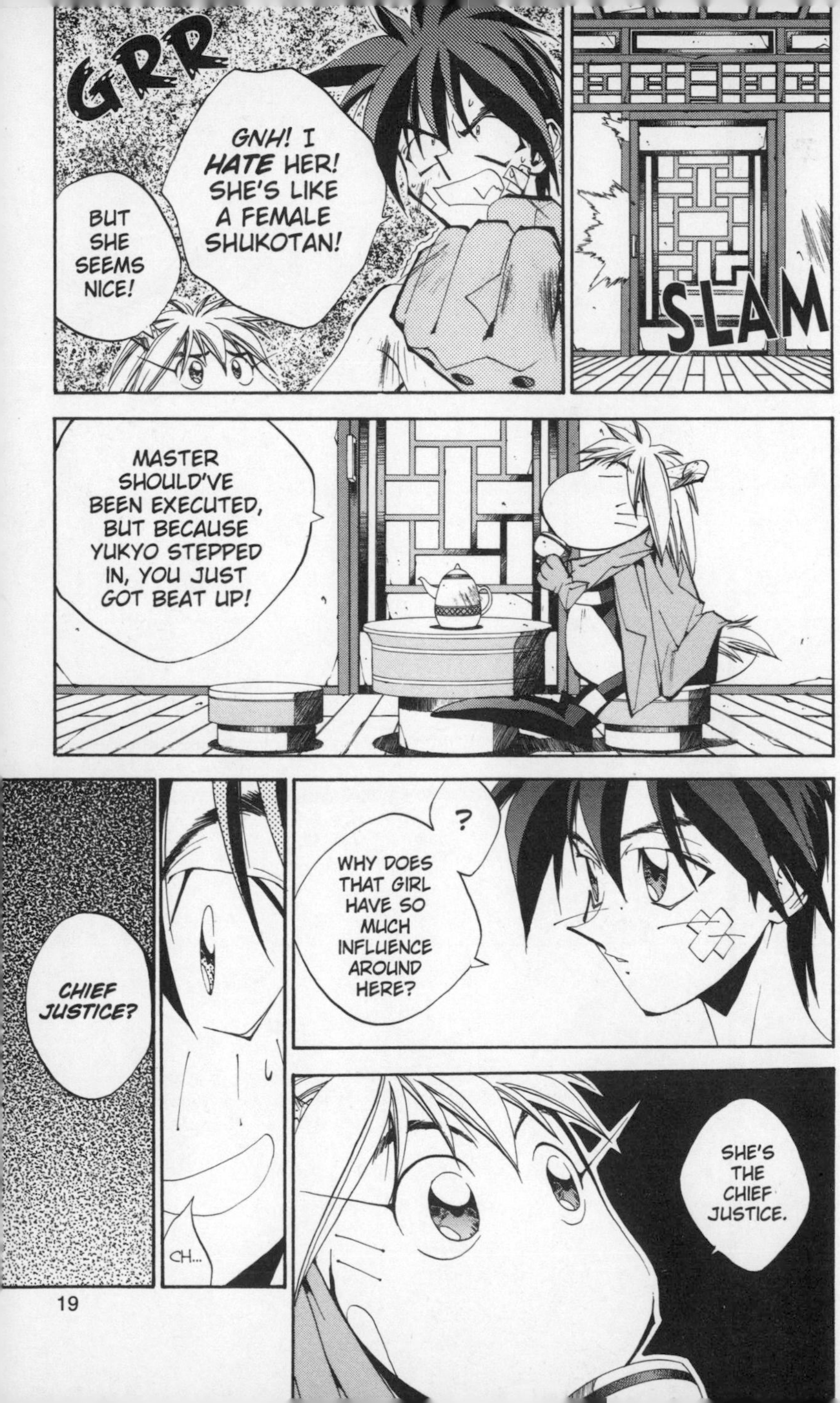

SLAM
GRR
GNH! I HATE HER! SHE'S LIKE A FEMALE SHUKOTAN!
BUT SHE SEEMS NICE!
MASTER SHOULD'VE BEEN EXECUTED, BUT BECAUSE YUKYO STEPPED IN, YOU JUST GOT BEAT UP!
?
WHY DOES THAT GIRL HAVE SO MUCH INFLUENCE AROUND HERE?
SHE'S THE CHIEF JUSTICE.
CH...
CHIEF JUSTICE?

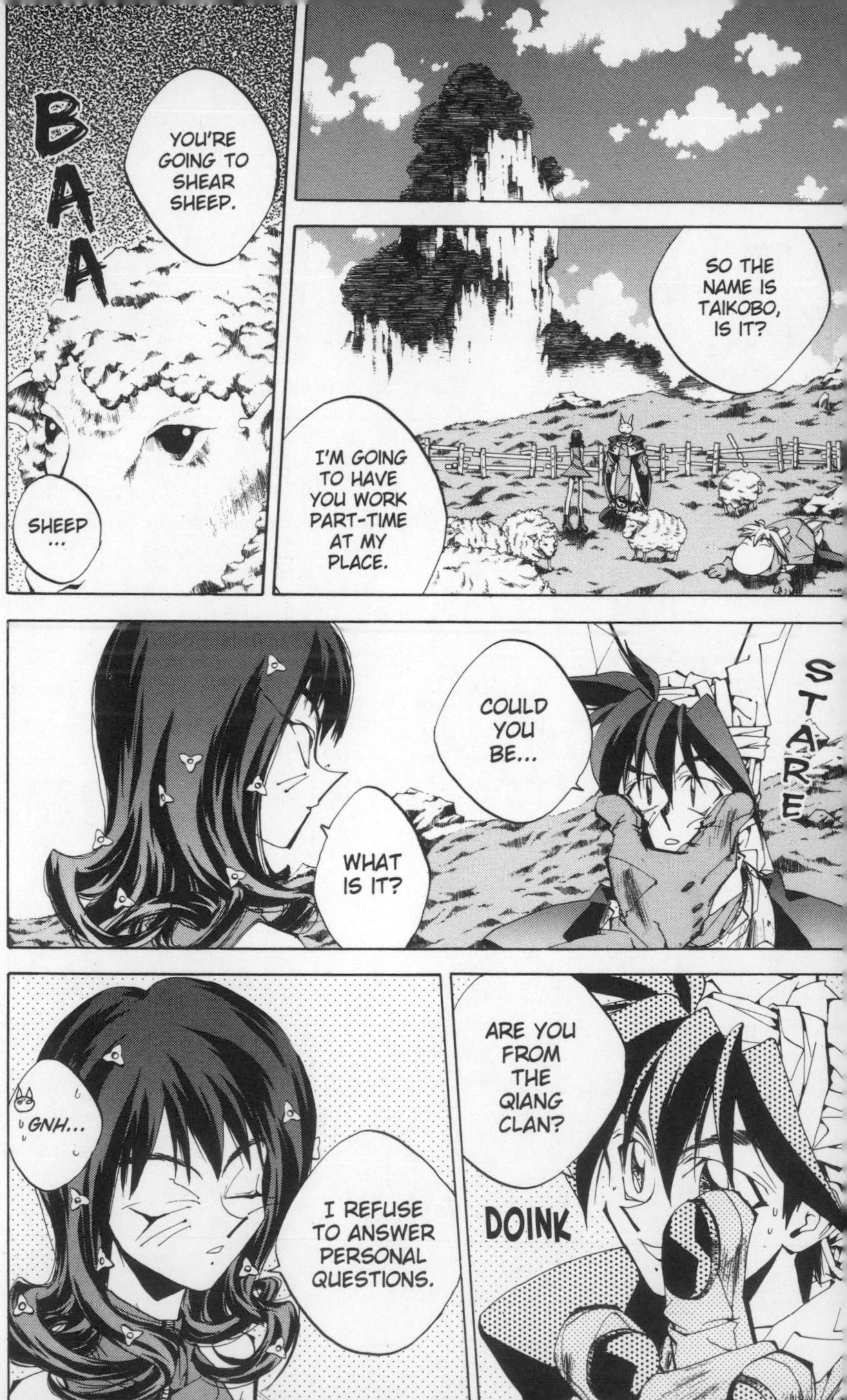
SO THE NAME IS TAIKOBO, IS IT?
I'M GOING TO HAVE YOU WORK PART-TIME AT MY PLACE.
YOU'RE GOING TO SHEAR SHEEP.
BAA
SHEEP...
STARE
COULD YOU BE...
WHAT IS IT?
ARE YOU FROM THE QIANG CLAN?
DOINK
GNH...
I REFUSE TO ANSWER PERSONAL QUESTIONS.

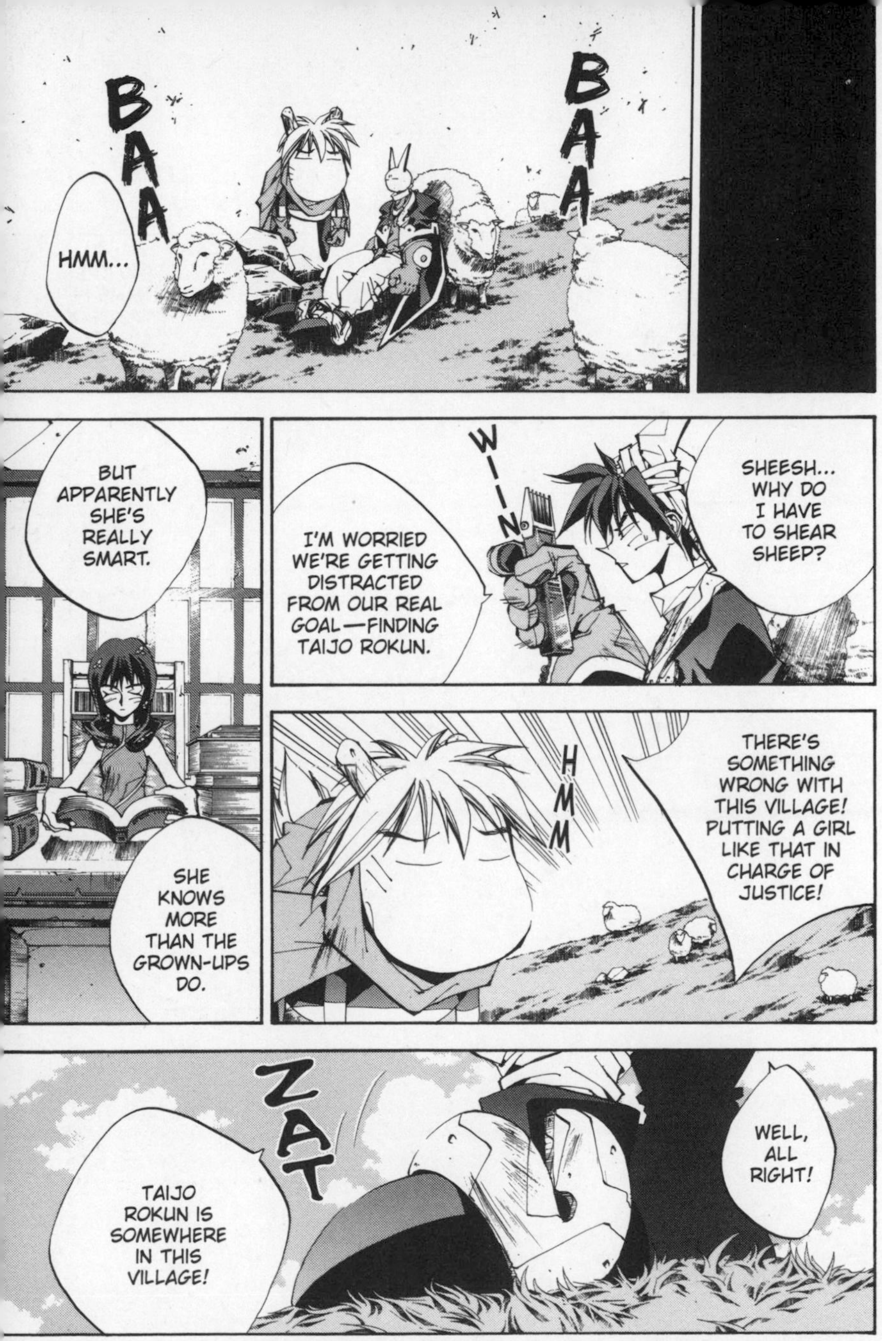
BAA
BAA
HMM...
SHEESH... WHY DO I HAVE TO SHEAR SHEEP?
WIIN
I'M WORRIED WE'RE GETTING DISTRACTED FROM OUR REAL GOAL—FINDING TAIJO ROKUN.
THERE'S SOMETHING WRONG WITH THIS VILLAGE! PUTTING A GIRL LIKE THAT IN CHARGE OF JUSTICE!
HMM
BUT APPARENTLY SHE'S REALLY SMART.
SHE KNOWS MORE THAN THE GROWN-UPS DO.
WELL, ALL RIGHT!
ZAT
TAIJO ROKUN IS SOMEWHERE IN THIS VILLAGE!

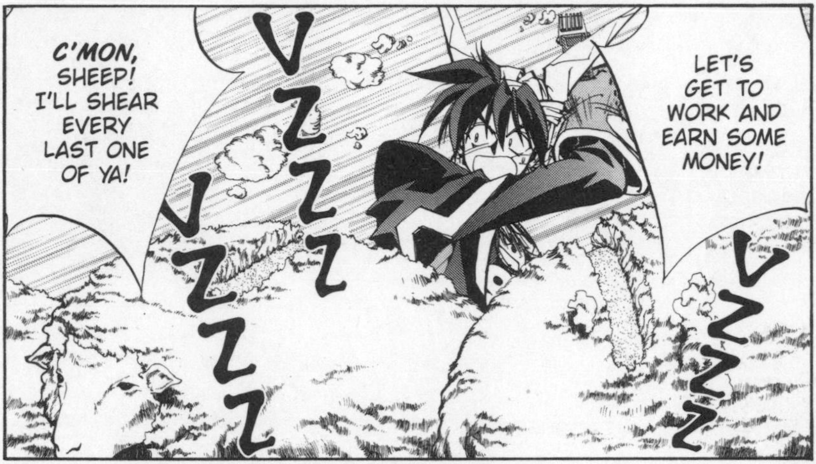
LET'S GET TO WORK AND EARN SOME MONEY!
VZZZZ
VZZZ
C'MON, SHEEP! I'LL SHEAR EVERY LAST ONE OF YA!
VZZZZ

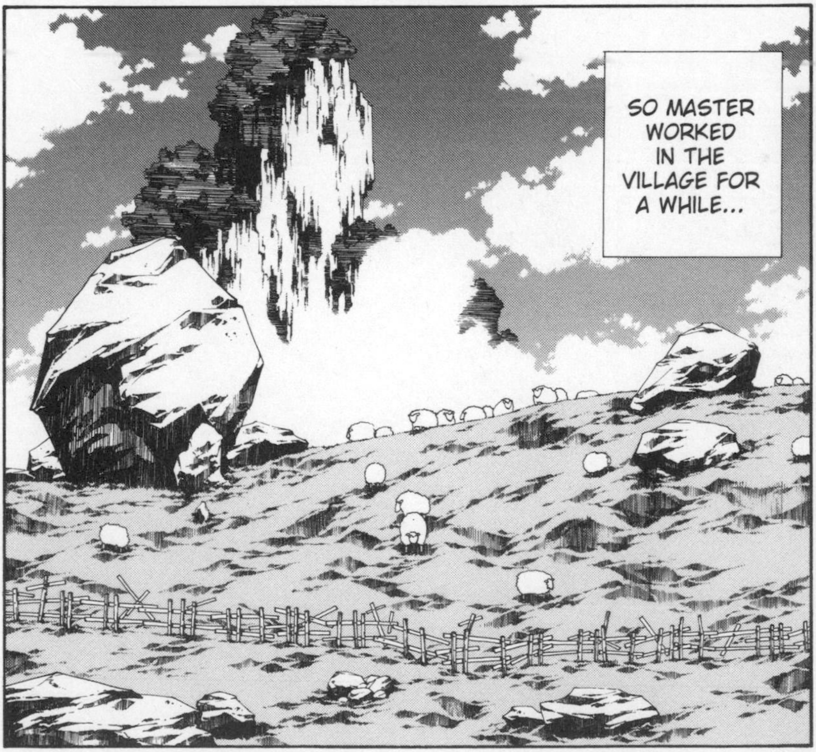
SO MASTER WORKED IN THE VILLAGE FOR A WHILE...

READ THIS WAY

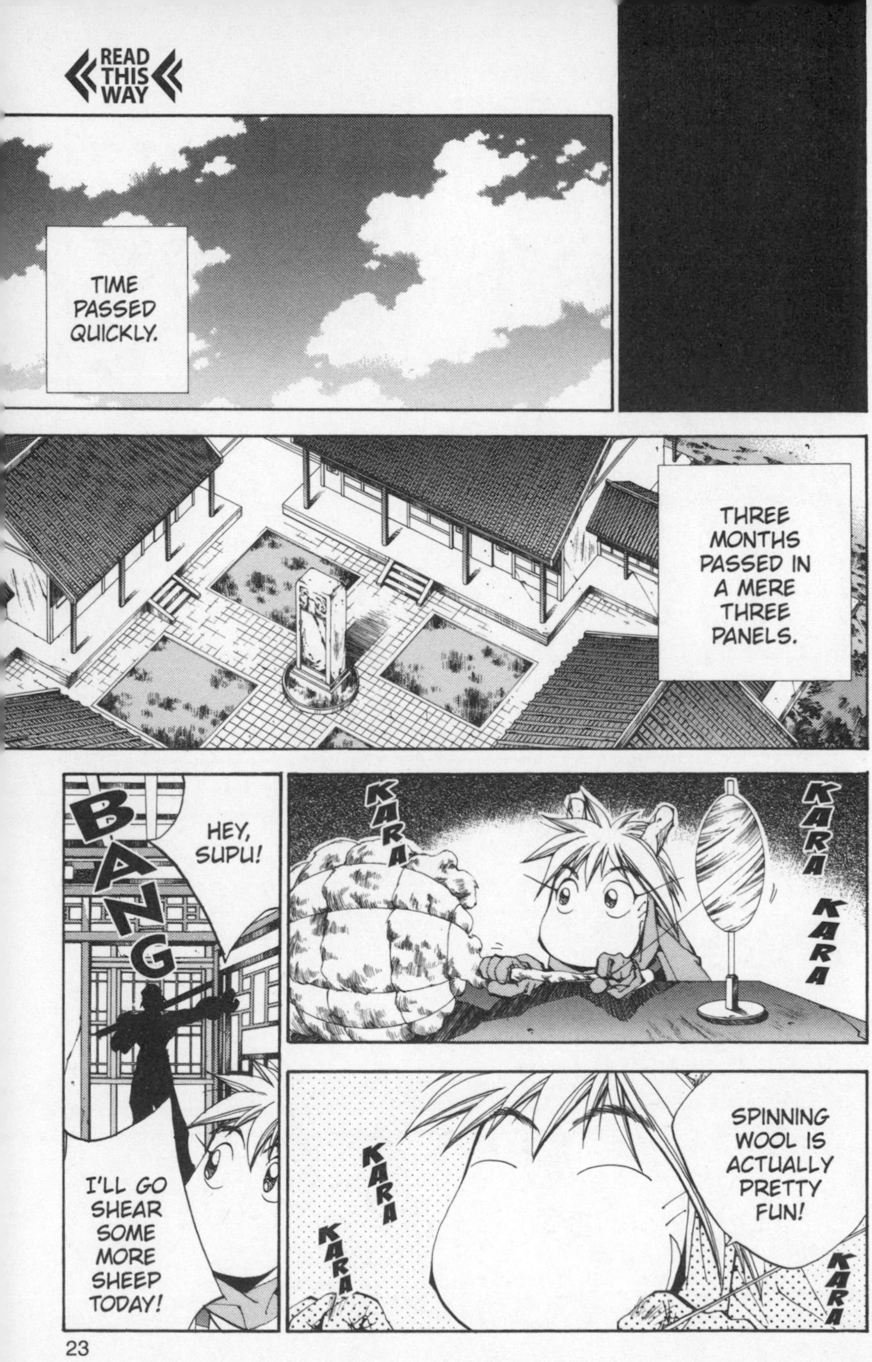

TIME PASSED QUICKLY.
THREE MONTHS PASSED IN A MERE THREE PANELS.
KARA
KARA KARA KARA
SPINNING WOOL IS ACTUALLY PRETTY FUN!
KARA
KARA
KARA
BANG
HEY, SUPU!
I'LL GO SHEAR SOME MORE SHEEP TODAY!

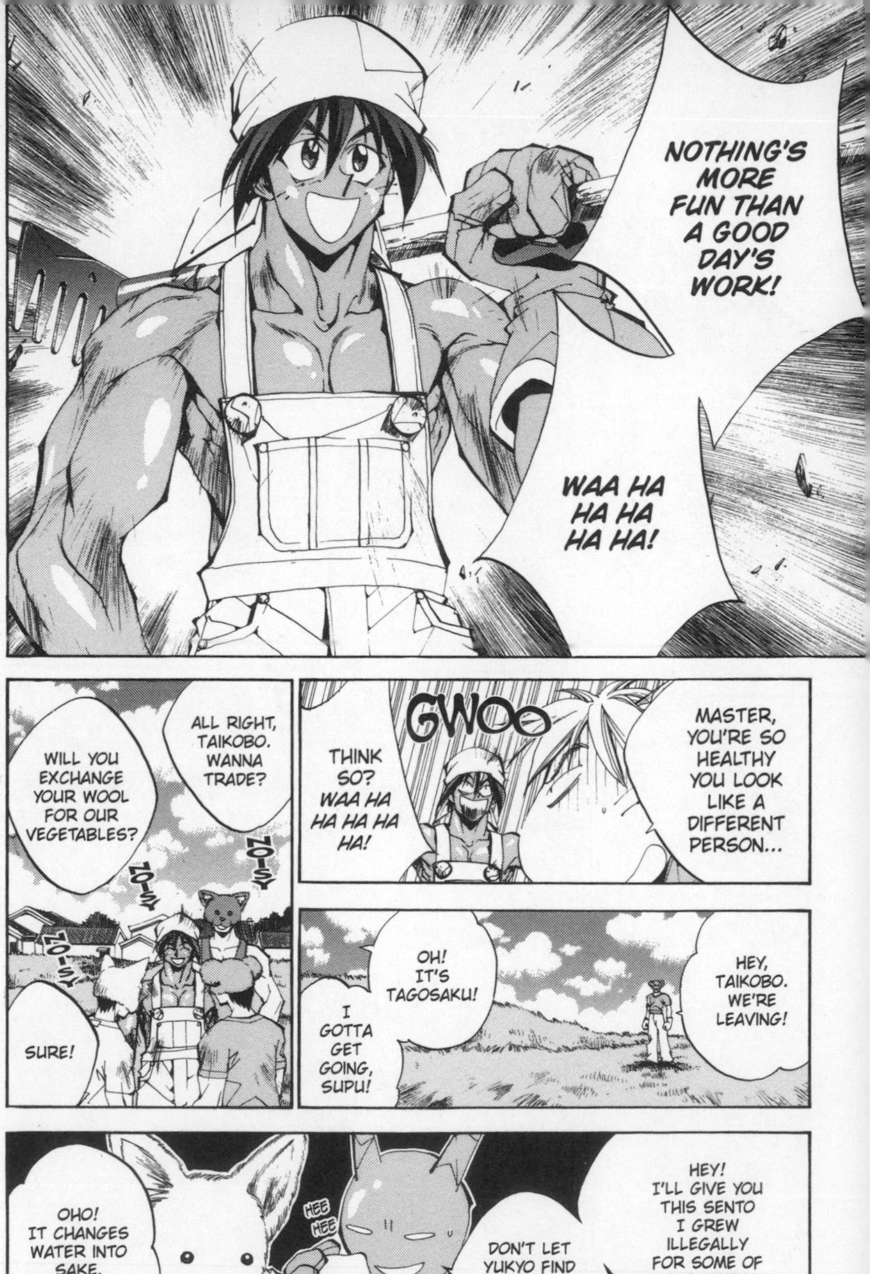
NOTHING'S MORE FUN THAN A GOOD DAY'S WORK!
WAA HA HA HA HA HA!
MASTER, YOU'RE SO HEALTHY YOU LOOK LIKE A DIFFERENT PERSON...
GWOO
THINK SO? WAA HA HA HA HA HA!
HEY, TAIKOBO. WE'RE LEAVING!
OH! IT'S TAGOSAKU!
I GOTTA GET GOING, SUPU!
ALL RIGHT, TAIKOBO. WANNA TRADE?
WILL YOU EXCHANGE YOUR WOOL FOR OUR VEGETABLES?
NOISY
NOISY
NOISY
SURE!
HEY! I'LL GIVE YOU THIS SENTO I GREW ILLEGALLY FOR SOME OF YOUR WHEAT.
DON'T LET YUKYO FIND OUT ABOUT IT!
HEE HEE
OHO! IT CHANGES WATER INTO SAKE, RIGHT?

READ THIS WAY

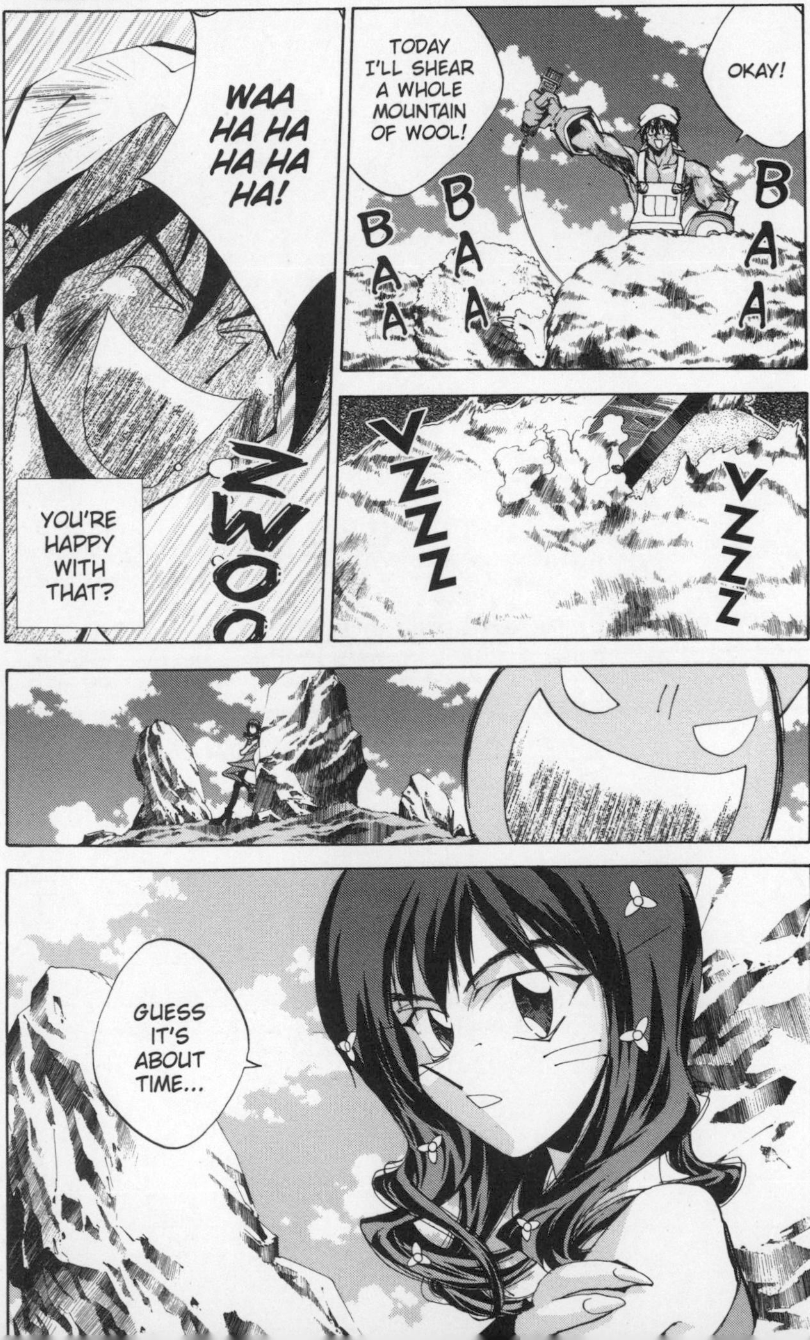
OKAY!
BAA
TODAY I'LL SHEAR A WHOLE MOUNTAIN OF WOOL!
BAA
BAA
VZZZ
VZZZ
WAA HA HA HA HA HA HA!
ZWOO
YOU'RE HAPPY WITH THAT?
GUESS IT'S ABOUT TIME...

封神演義

Chapter 153

THE ADVENTURE OF TAIJO ROKUN, PART 5
LAO-TZU

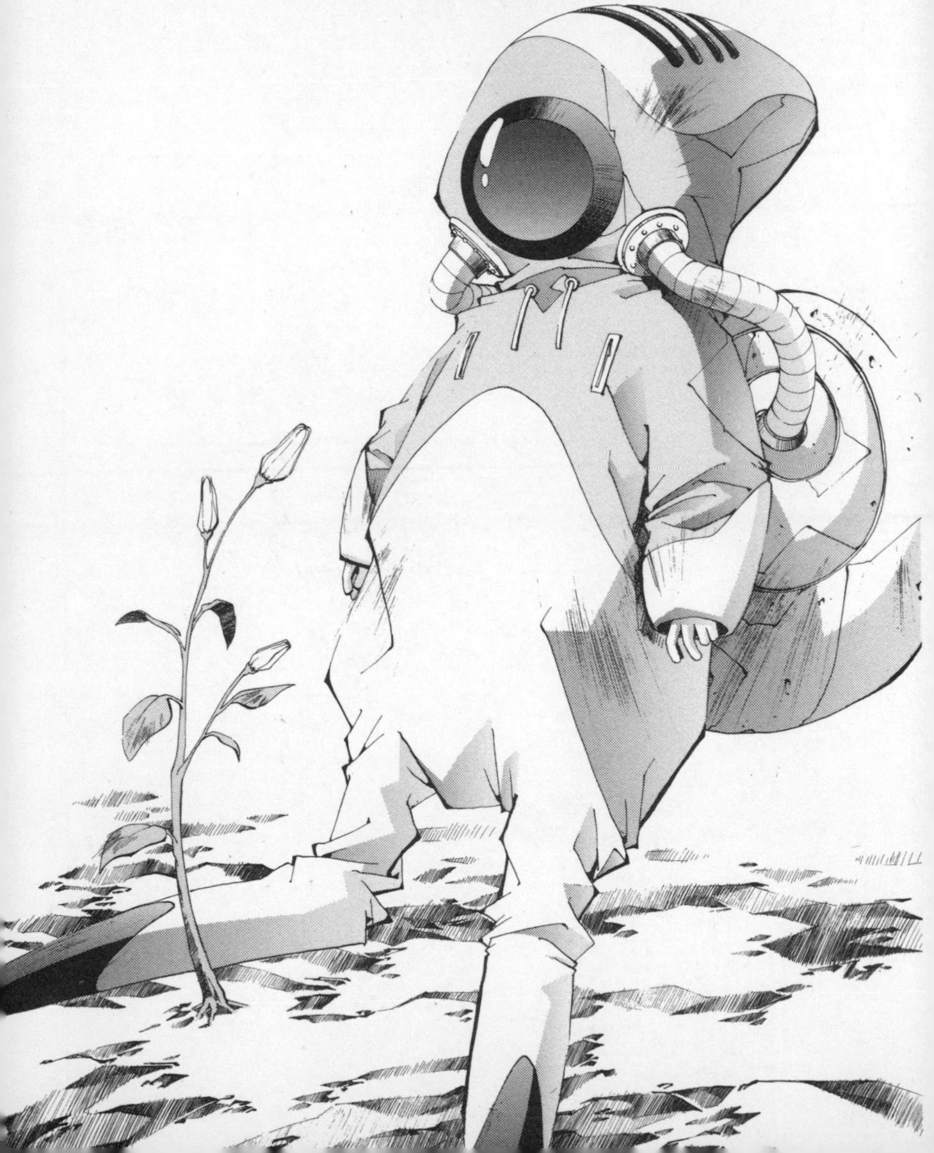

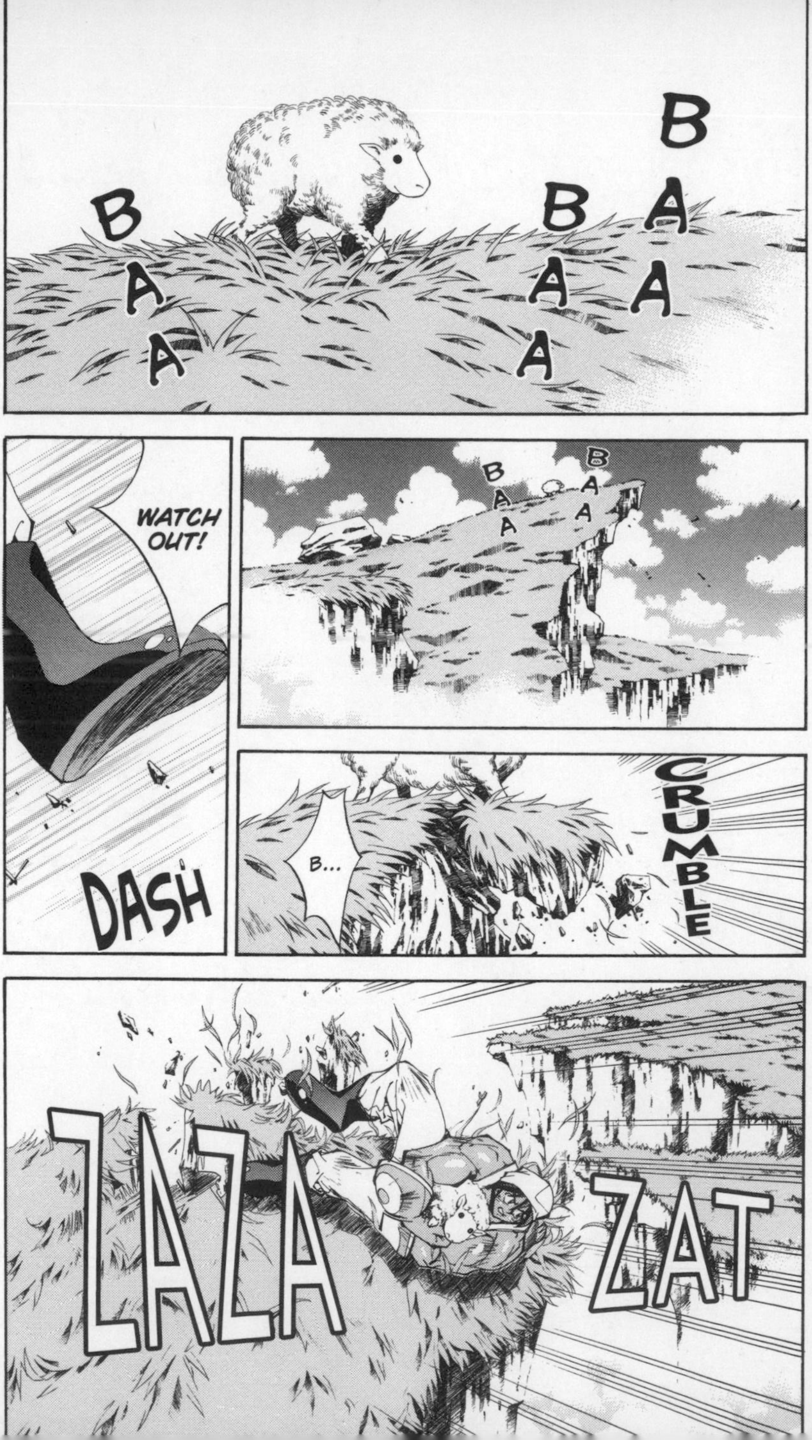
BAA
BAA
BAA
BAA
BAA
B...
CRUMBLE
WATCH OUT!
DASH
ZAT
LAZA

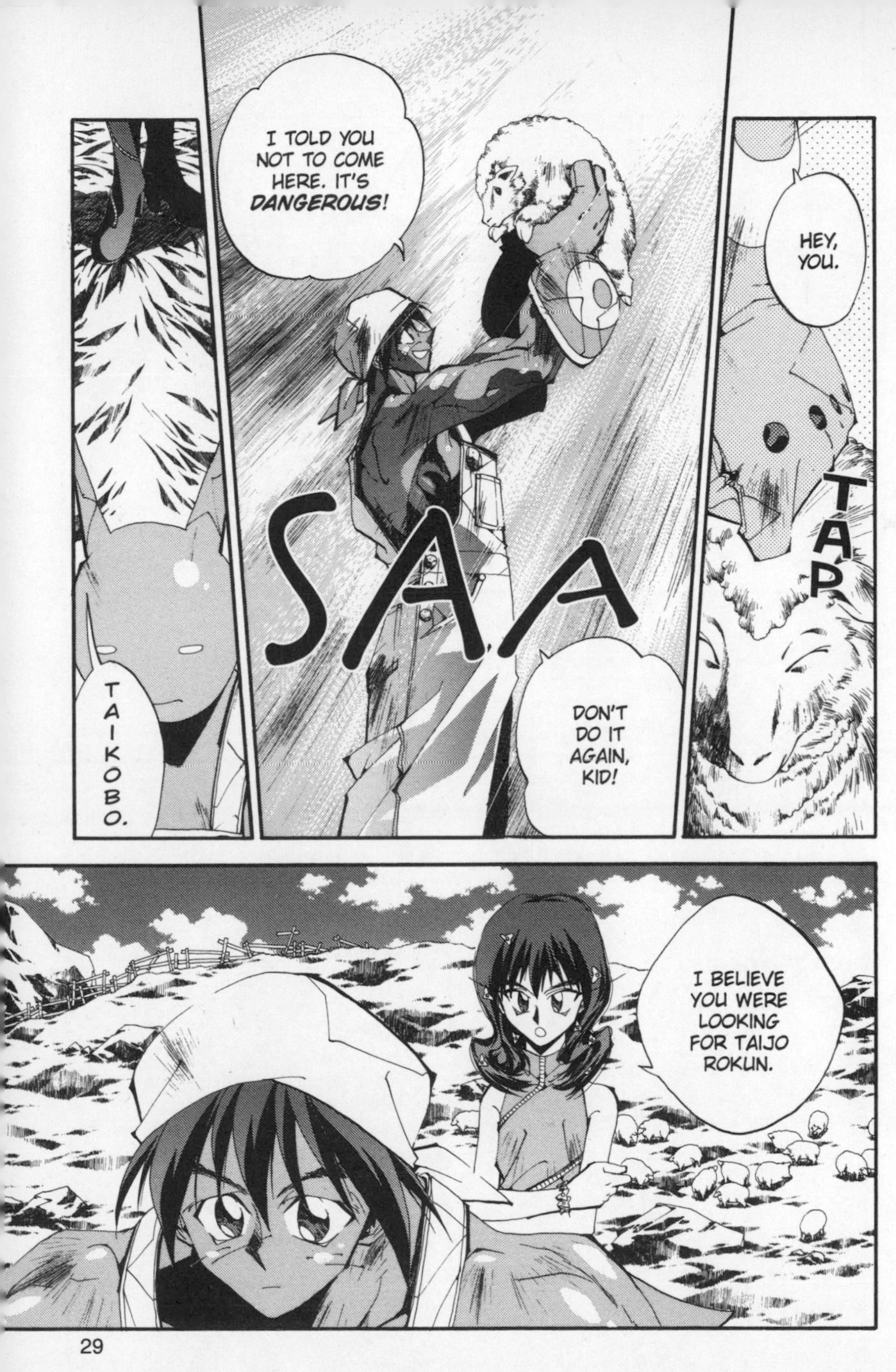
HEY, YOU.
TAP
I TOLD YOU NOT TO COME HERE. IT'S *DANGEROUS*!
SAA
DON'T DO IT AGAIN, KID!
TAIKOBO.
I BELIEVE YOU WERE LOOKING FOR TAIJO ROKUN.

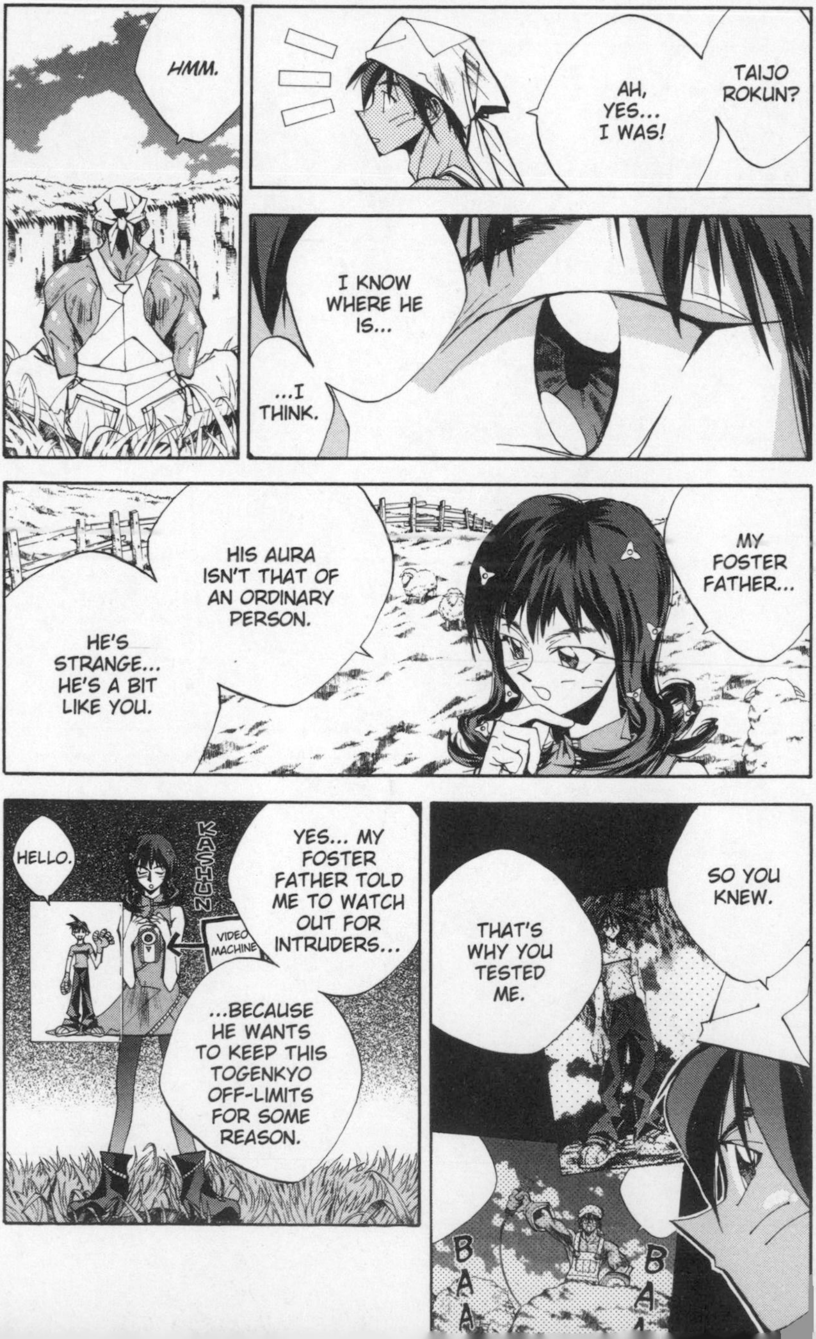
TAIJO ROKUN?
AH, YES... I WAS!
I KNOW WHERE HE IS...
...I THINK.
HMM.
MY FOSTER FATHER...
HIS AURA ISN'T THAT OF AN ORDINARY PERSON.
HE'S STRANGE... HE'S A BIT LIKE YOU.
SO YOU KNEW.
THAT'S WHY YOU TESTED ME.
BAA
BAA
YES... MY FOSTER FATHER TOLD ME TO WATCH OUT FOR INTRUDERS...
...BECAUSE HE WANTS TO KEEP THIS TOGENKYO OFF-LIMITS FOR SOME REASON.
KASHUN
HELLO.
VIDEO MACHINE

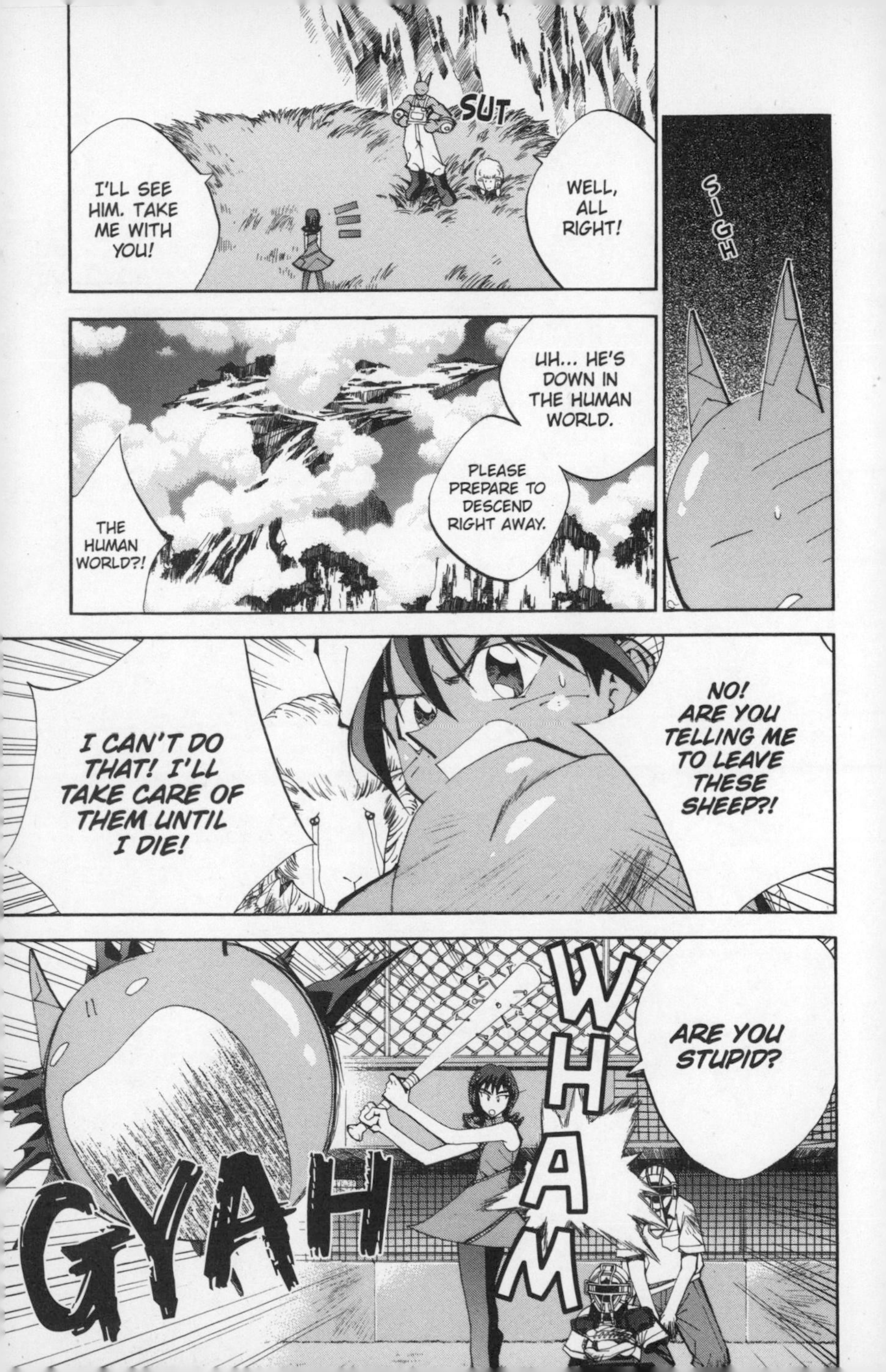
SIGH
WELL, ALL RIGHT!
SUT
I'LL SEE HIM. TAKE ME WITH YOU!
UH... HE'S DOWN IN THE HUMAN WORLD.
PLEASE PREPARE TO DESCEND RIGHT AWAY.
THE HUMAN WORLD?!
NO! ARE YOU TELLING ME TO LEAVE THESE SHEEP?!
I CAN'T DO THAT! I'LL TAKE CARE OF THEM UNTIL I DIE!
ARE YOU STUPID?
WHAM
GYAH

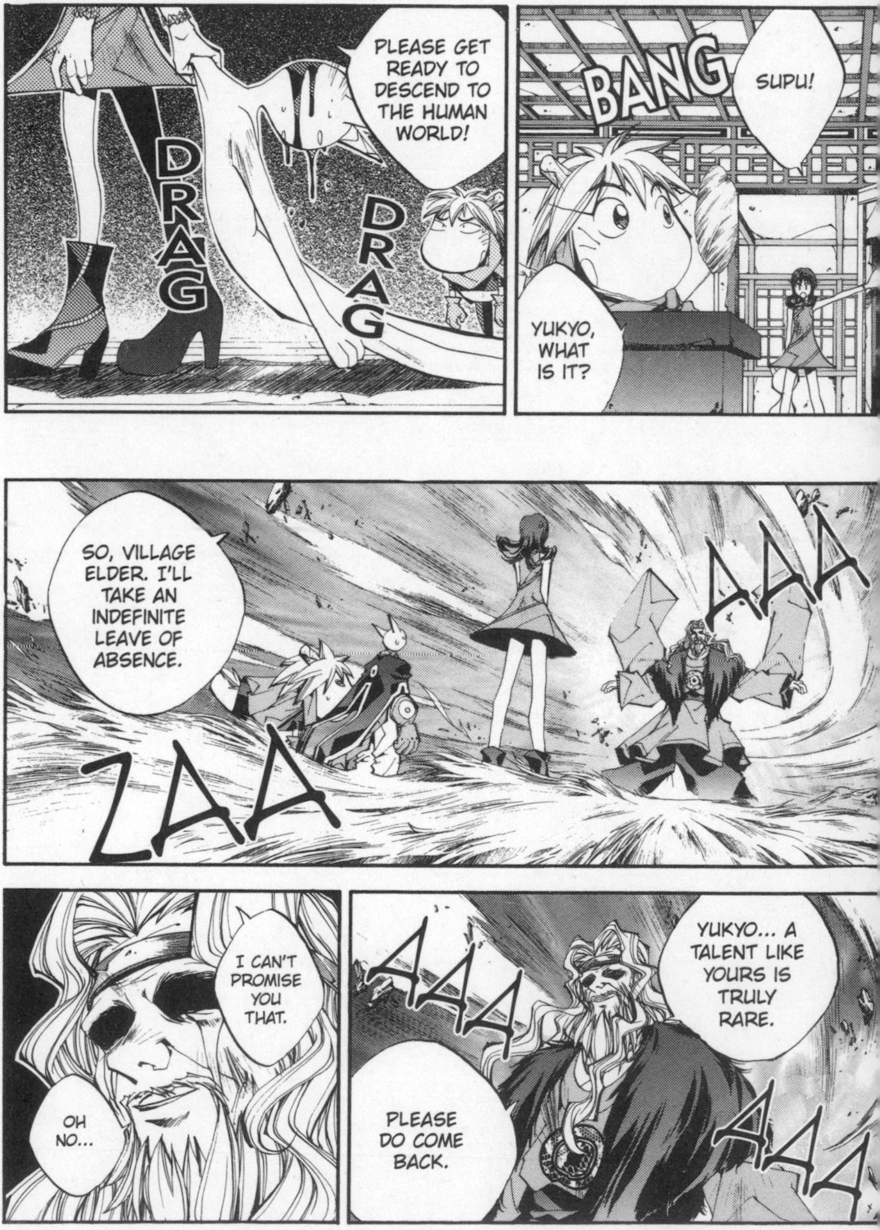
SUPU!
BANG
YUKYO, WHAT IS IT?
PLEASE GET READY TO DESCEND TO THE HUMAN WORLD!
DRAG
DRAG
AAA
SO, VILLAGE ELDER. I'LL TAKE AN INDEFINITE LEAVE OF ABSENCE.
ZAA
YUKYO... A TALENT LIKE YOURS IS TRULY RARE.
AAA
PLEASE DO COME BACK.
AAA
I CAN'T PROMISE YOU THAT.
OH NO...

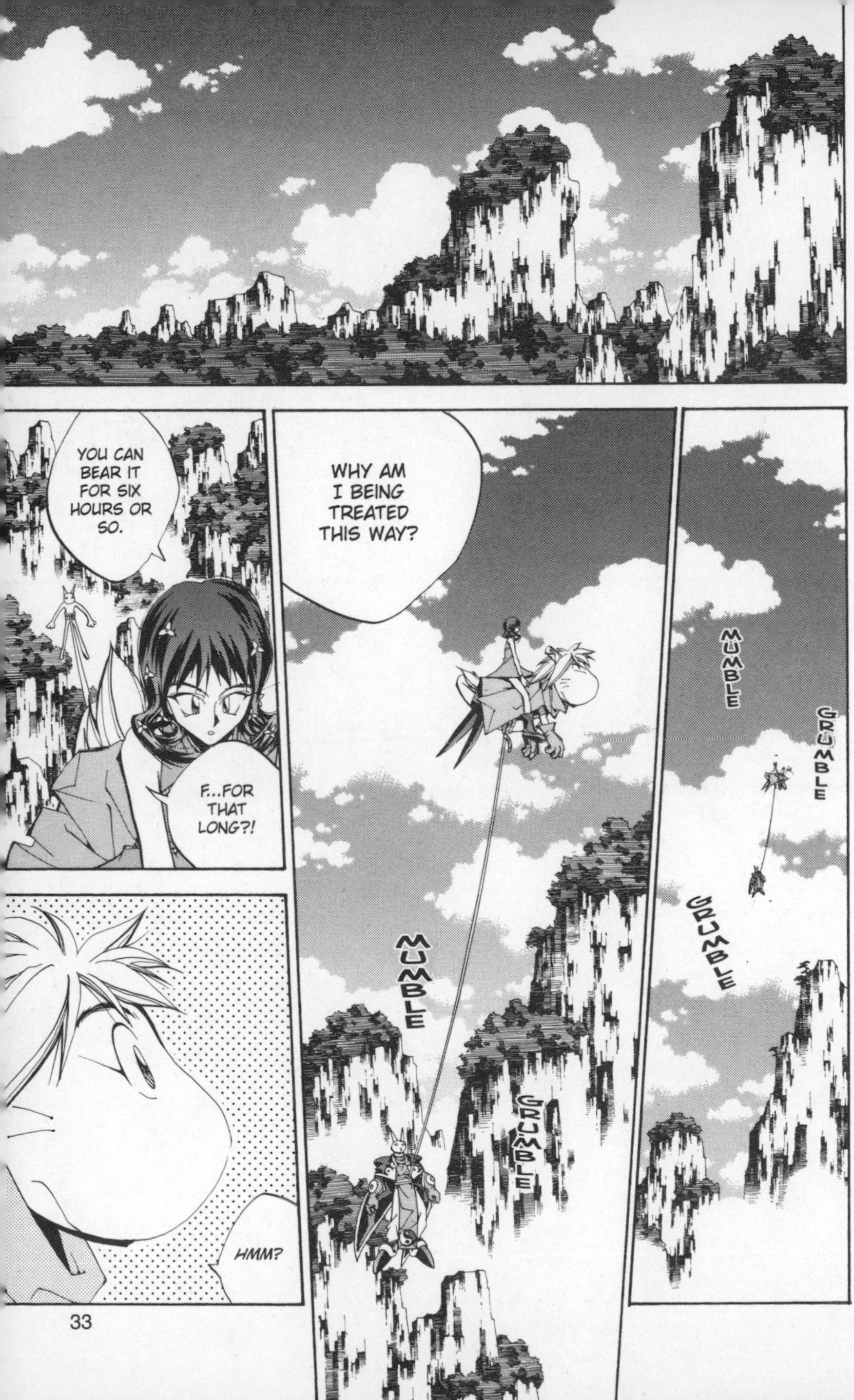
GRUMBLE
MUMBLE
GRUMBLE
WHY AM I BEING TREATED THIS WAY?
MUMBLE
GRUMBLE
YOU CAN BEAR IT FOR SIX HOURS OR SO.
F...FOR THAT LONG?!
HMM?

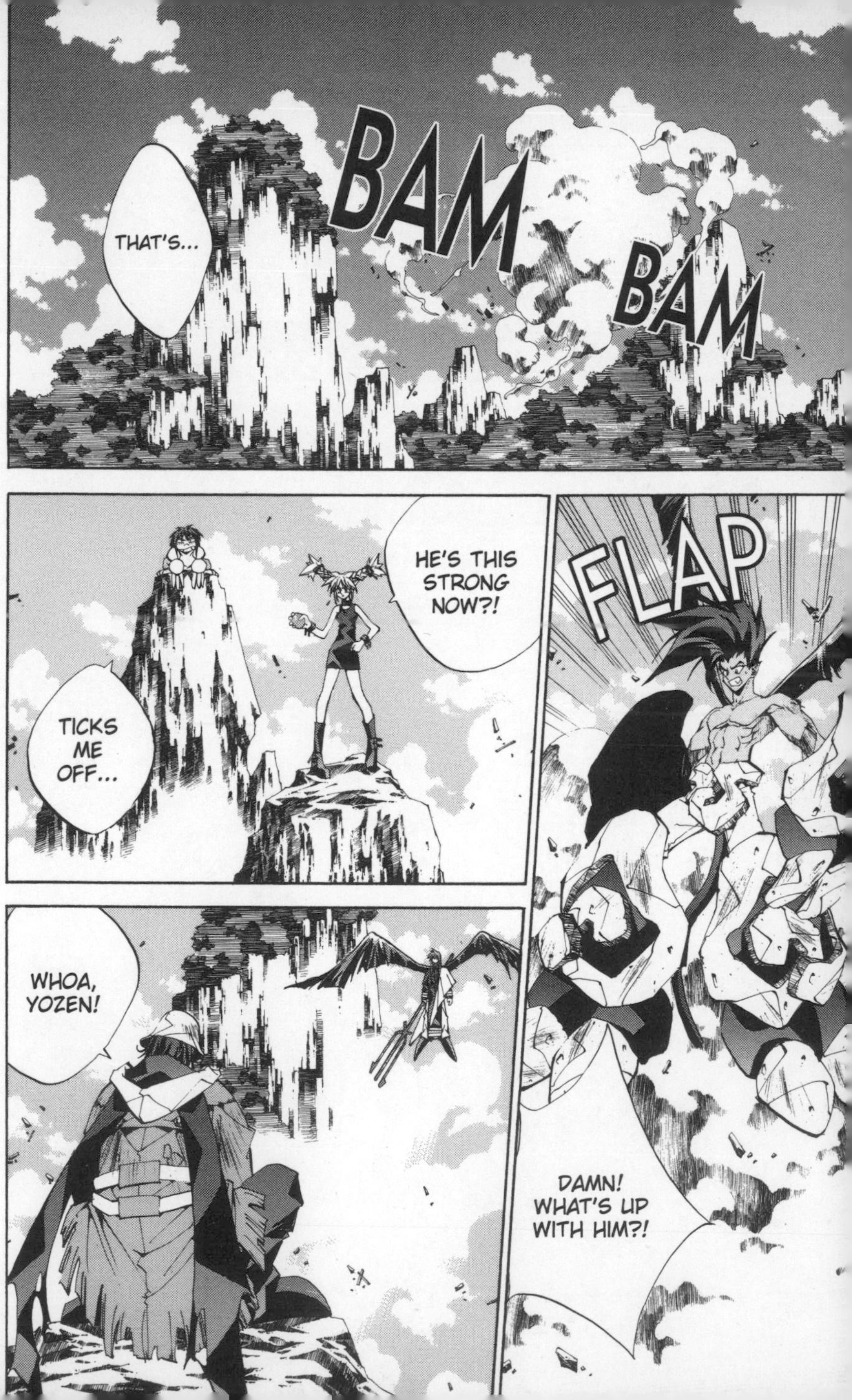
BAM
BAM
THAT'S...
FLAP
DAMN! WHAT'S UP WITH HIM?!
HE'S THIS STRONG NOW?!
TICKS ME OFF...
WHOA, YOZEN!

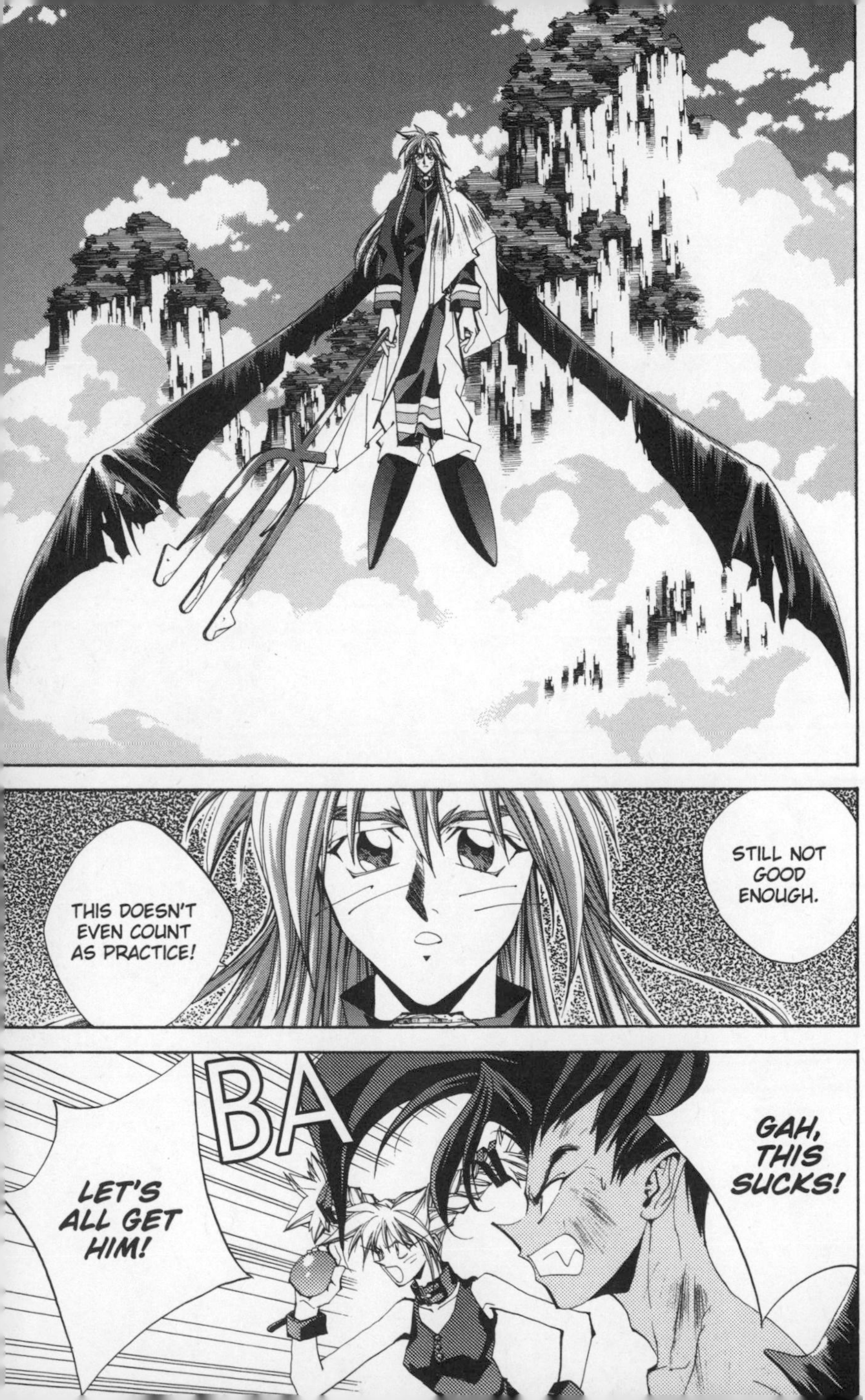
STILL NOT GOOD ENOUGH.
THIS DOESN'T EVEN COUNT AS PRACTICE!
GAH, THIS SUCKS!
BA
LET'S ALL GET HIM!

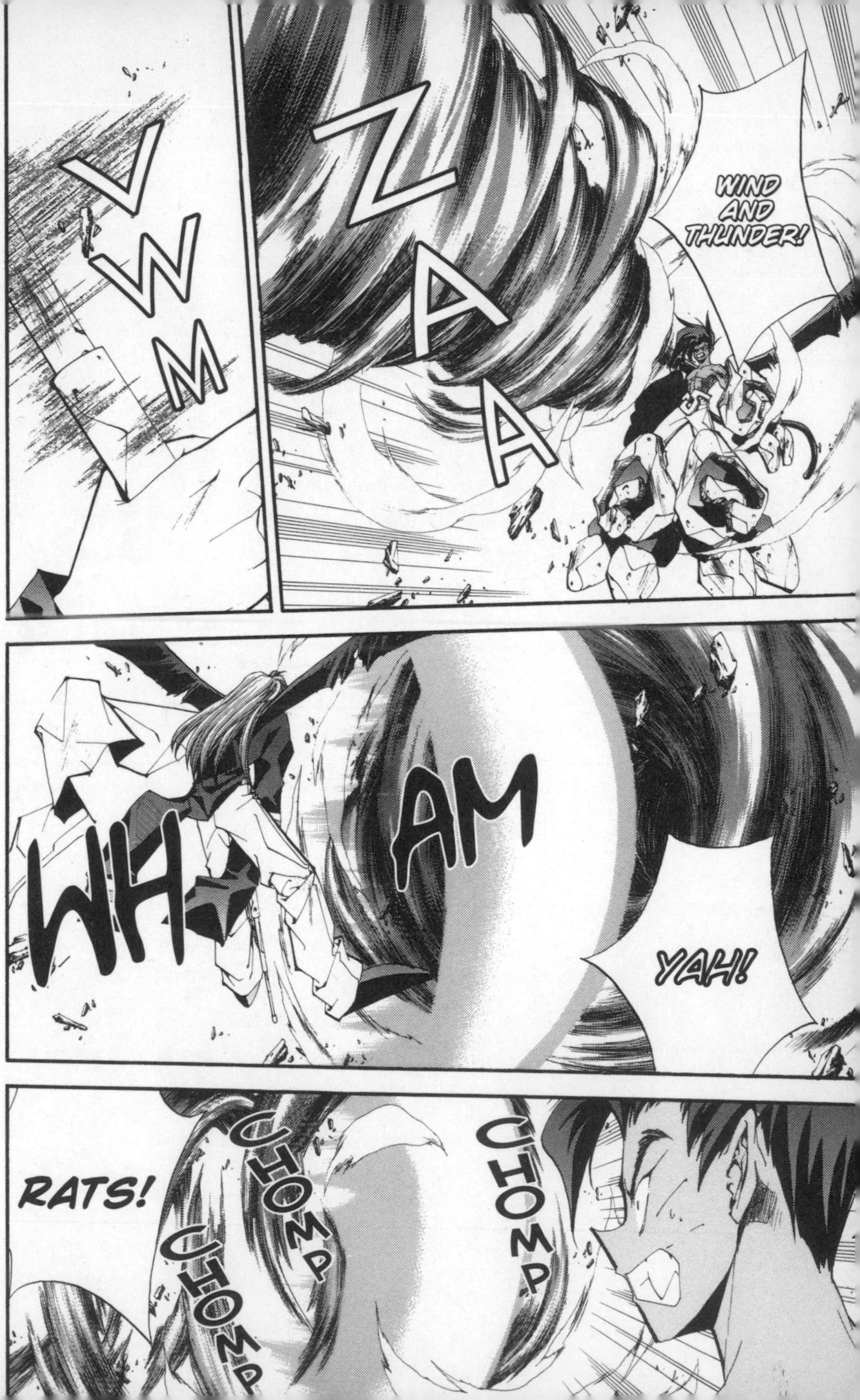
WIND AND THUNDER!
ZAA
VWM
YAH!
WHAM
CHOMP
CHOMP
CHOMP
RATS!

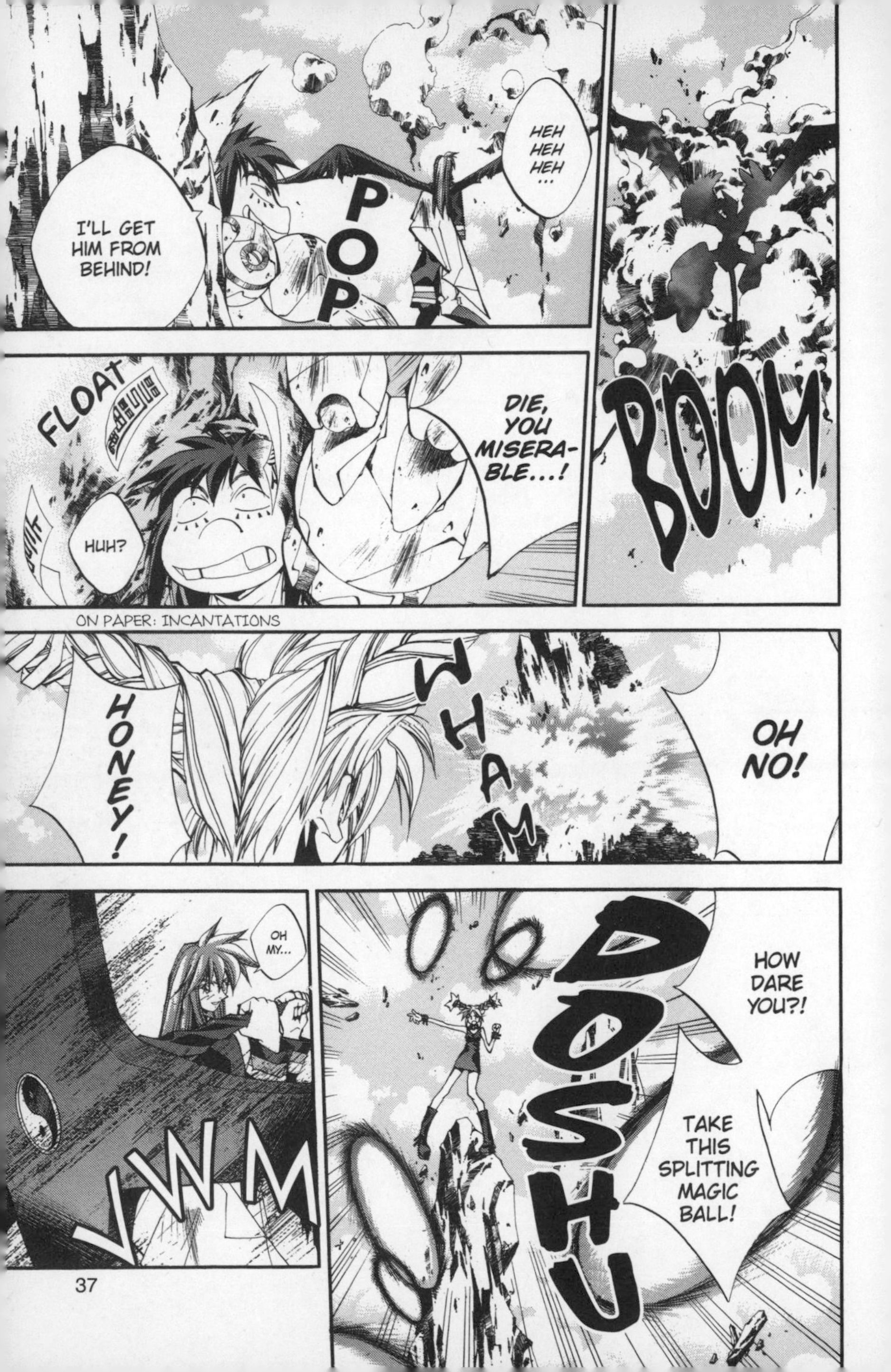
BOOM
HEH HEH HEH...
POP
I'LL GET HIM FROM BEHIND!
DIE, YOU MISERA-BLE...!
FLOAT
HUH?
ON PAPER: INCANTATIONS
OH NO!
WHAM
HONEY!
HOW DARE YOU?!
TAKE THIS SPLITTING MAGIC BALL!
DOSHU
OH MY...
VWM

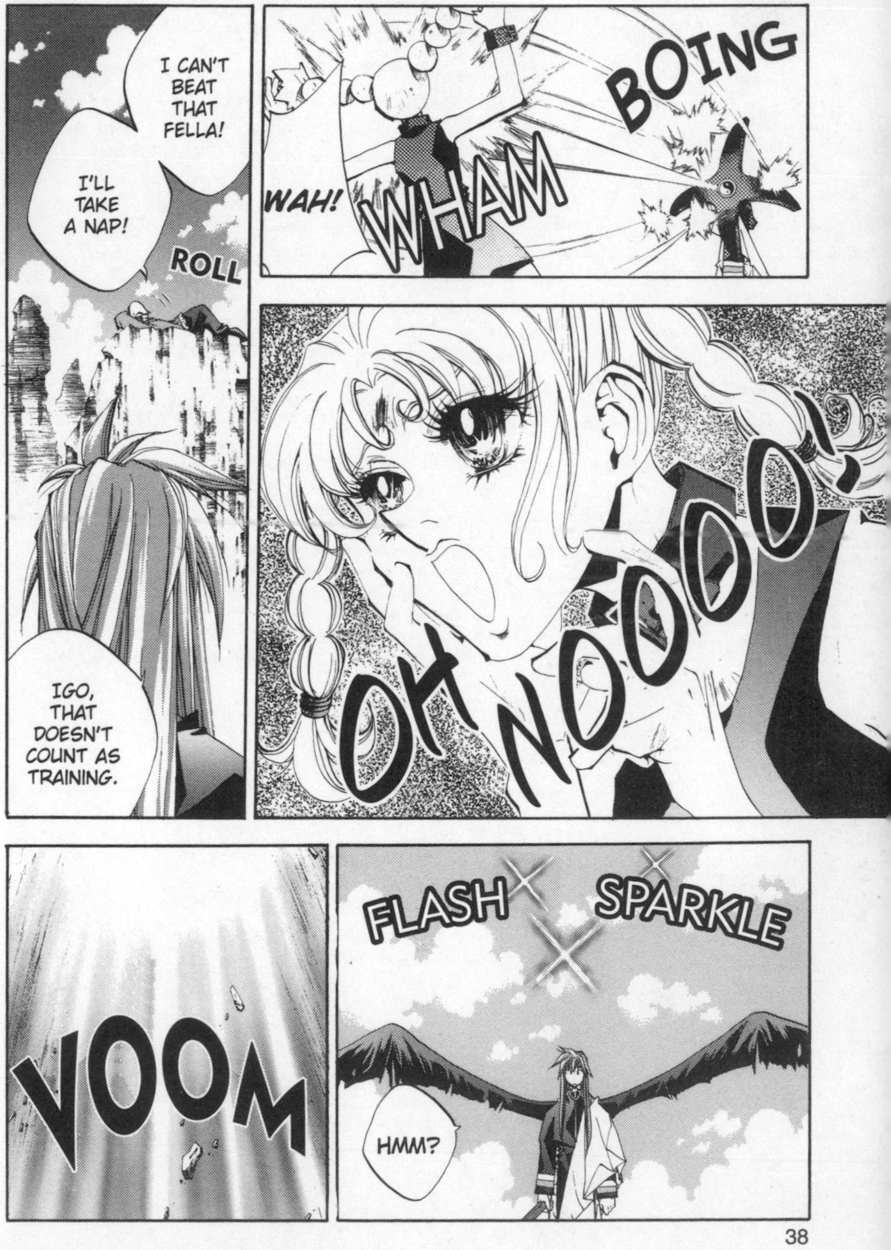
BOING
WHAM
WAH!
OH NOOOOO!
I CAN'T BEAT THAT FELLA!
I'LL TAKE A NAP!
ROLL
IGO, THAT DOESN'T COUNT AS TRAINING.
SPARKLE
FLASH
HMM?
VOOM

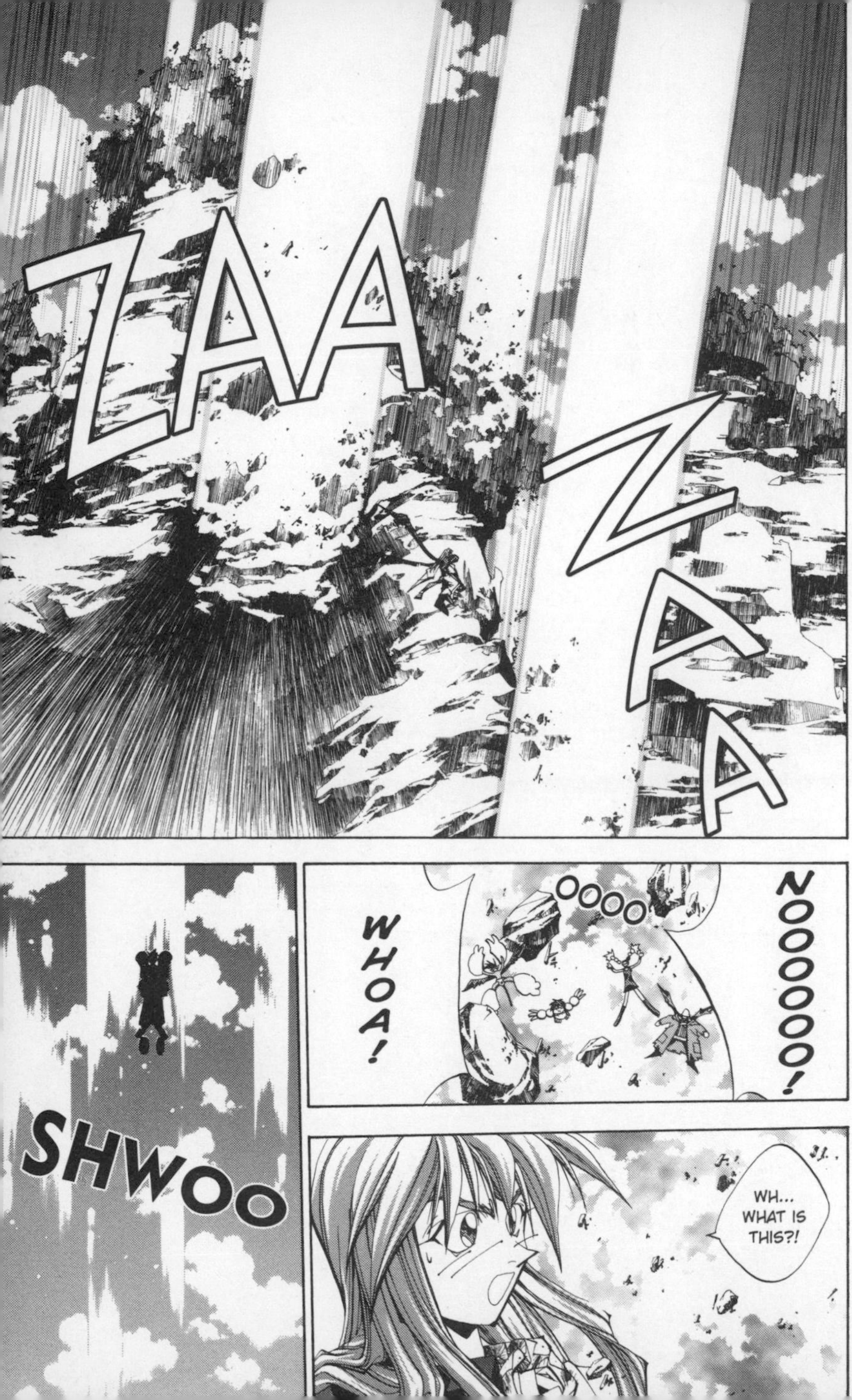
ZAANAA
NOOOOOO!
OOOO
WHOA!
WH... WHAT IS THIS?!
SHWOO

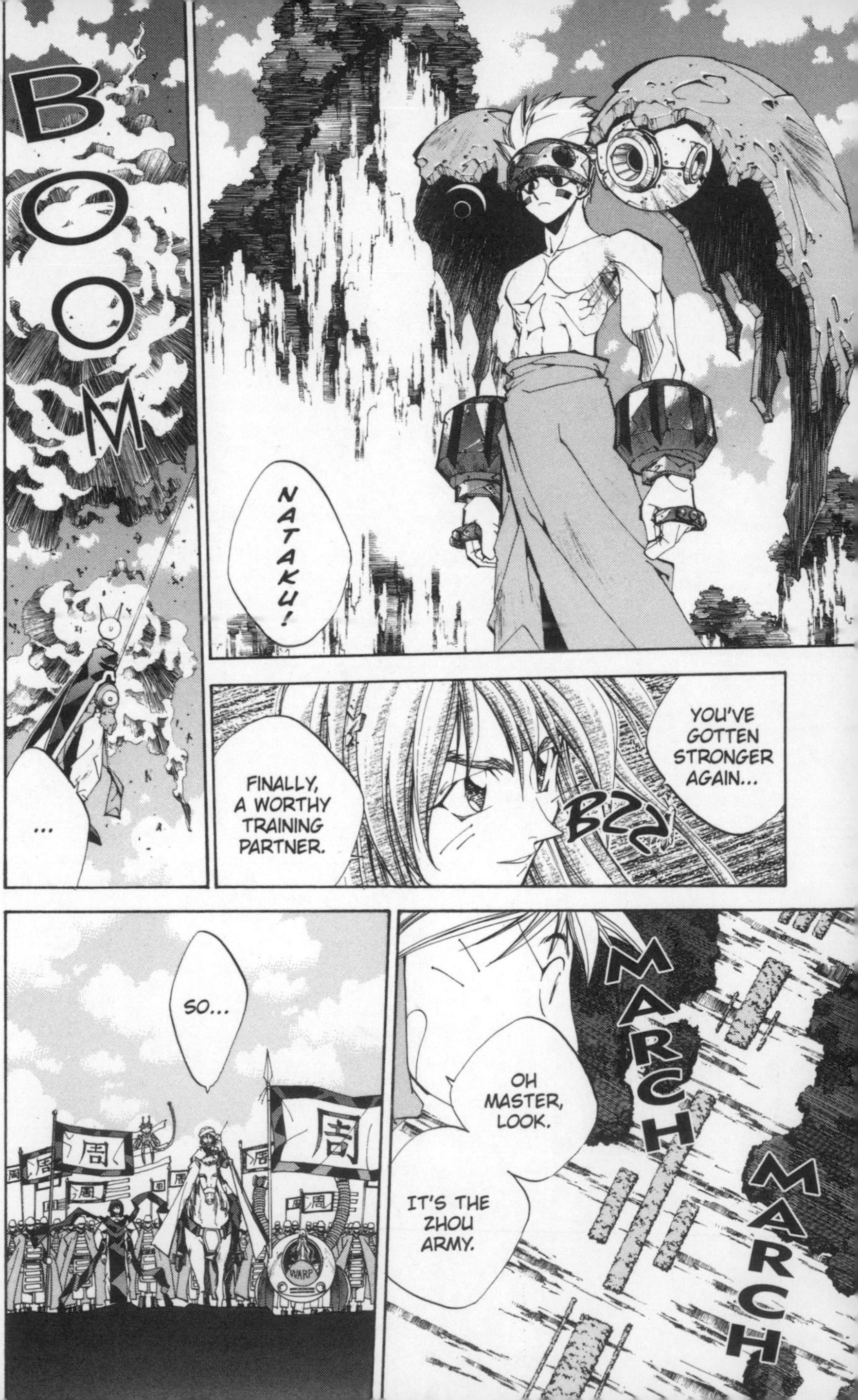
NATAKU!
YOU'VE GOTTEN STRONGER AGAIN...
BZZ
FINALLY, A WORTHY TRAINING PARTNER.
BOOM
...
MARCH
MARCH
OH MASTER, LOOK.
IT'S THE ZHOU ARMY.
SO...

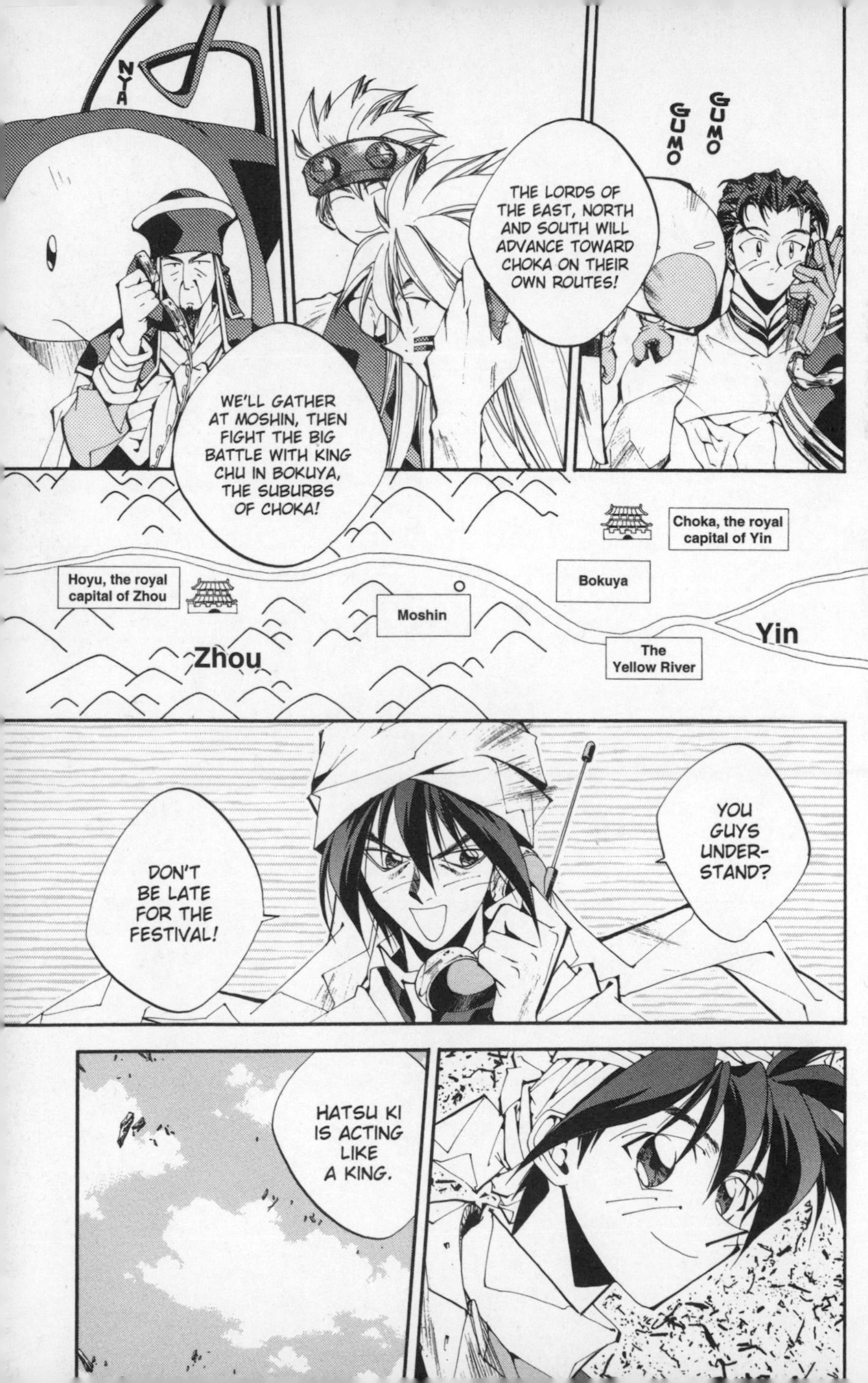
GUMO GUMO
THE LORDS OF THE EAST, NORTH AND SOUTH WILL ADVANCE TOWARD CHOKA ON THEIR OWN ROUTES!
NYA
WE'LL GATHER AT MOSHIN, THEN FIGHT THE BIG BATTLE WITH KING CHU IN BOKUYA, THE SUBURBS OF CHOKA!
Choka, the royal capital of Yin
Bokuya
Yin
The Yellow River
Moshin
Hoyu, the royal capital of Zhou
Zhou
YOU GUYS UNDER-STAND?
DON'T BE LATE FOR THE FESTIVAL!
HATSU KI IS ACTING LIKE A KING.

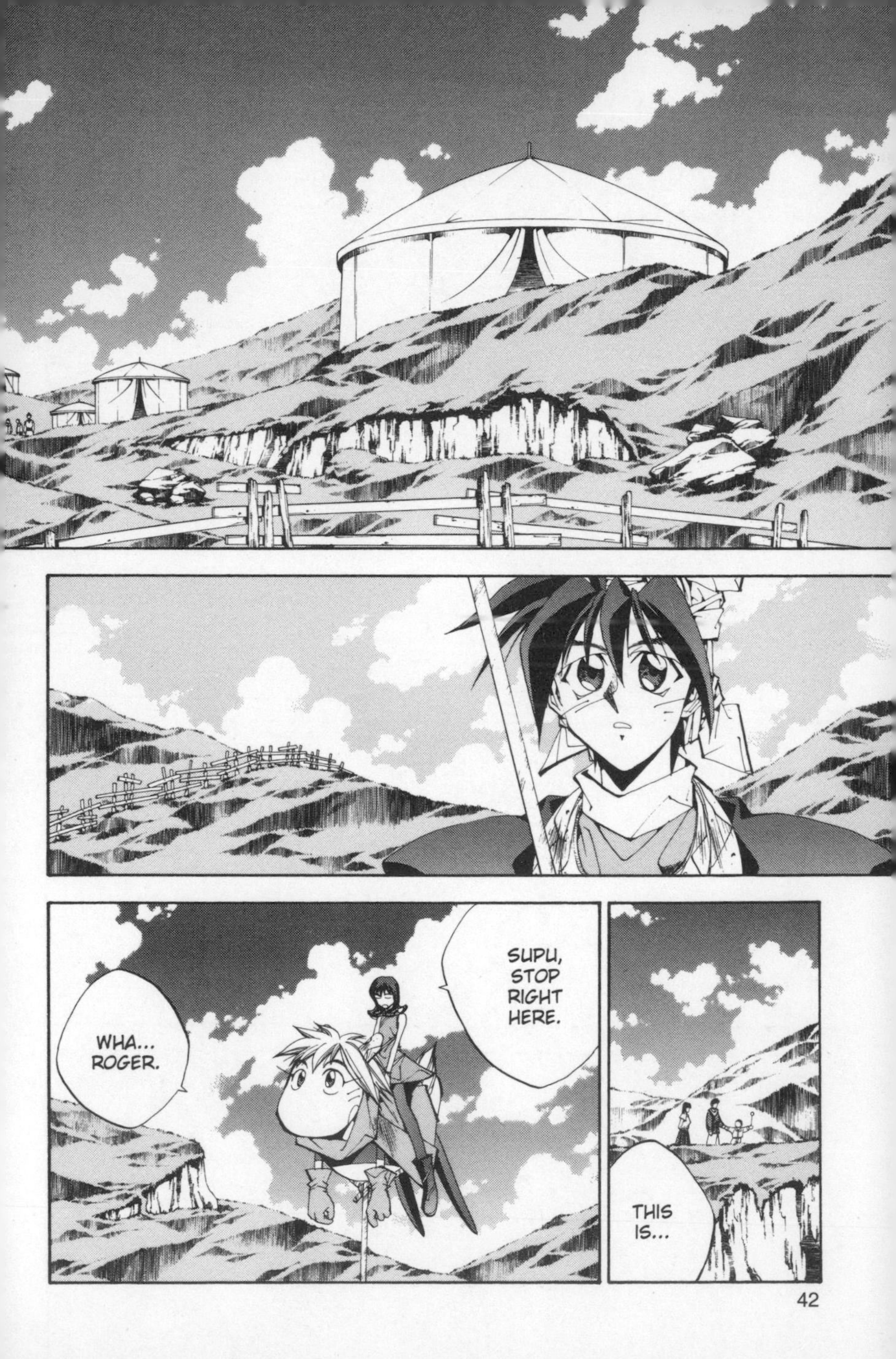
THIS IS...
SUPU, STOP RIGHT HERE.
WHA... ROGER.

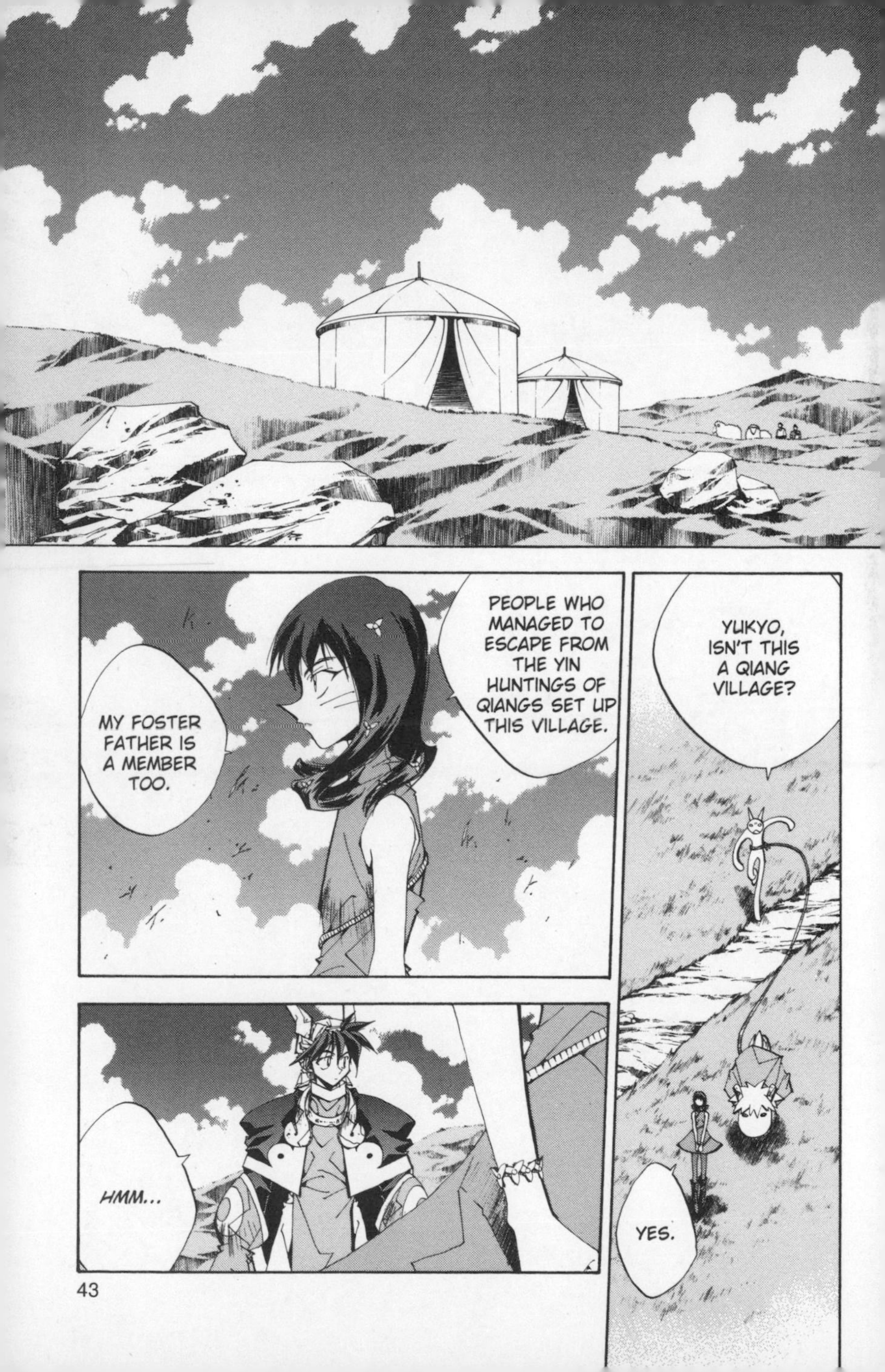
YUKYO, ISN'T THIS A QIANG VILLAGE?
YES.
PEOPLE WHO MANAGED TO ESCAPE FROM THE YIN HUNTINGS OF QIANGS SET UP THIS VILLAGE.
MY FOSTER FATHER IS A MEMBER TOO.
HMM...

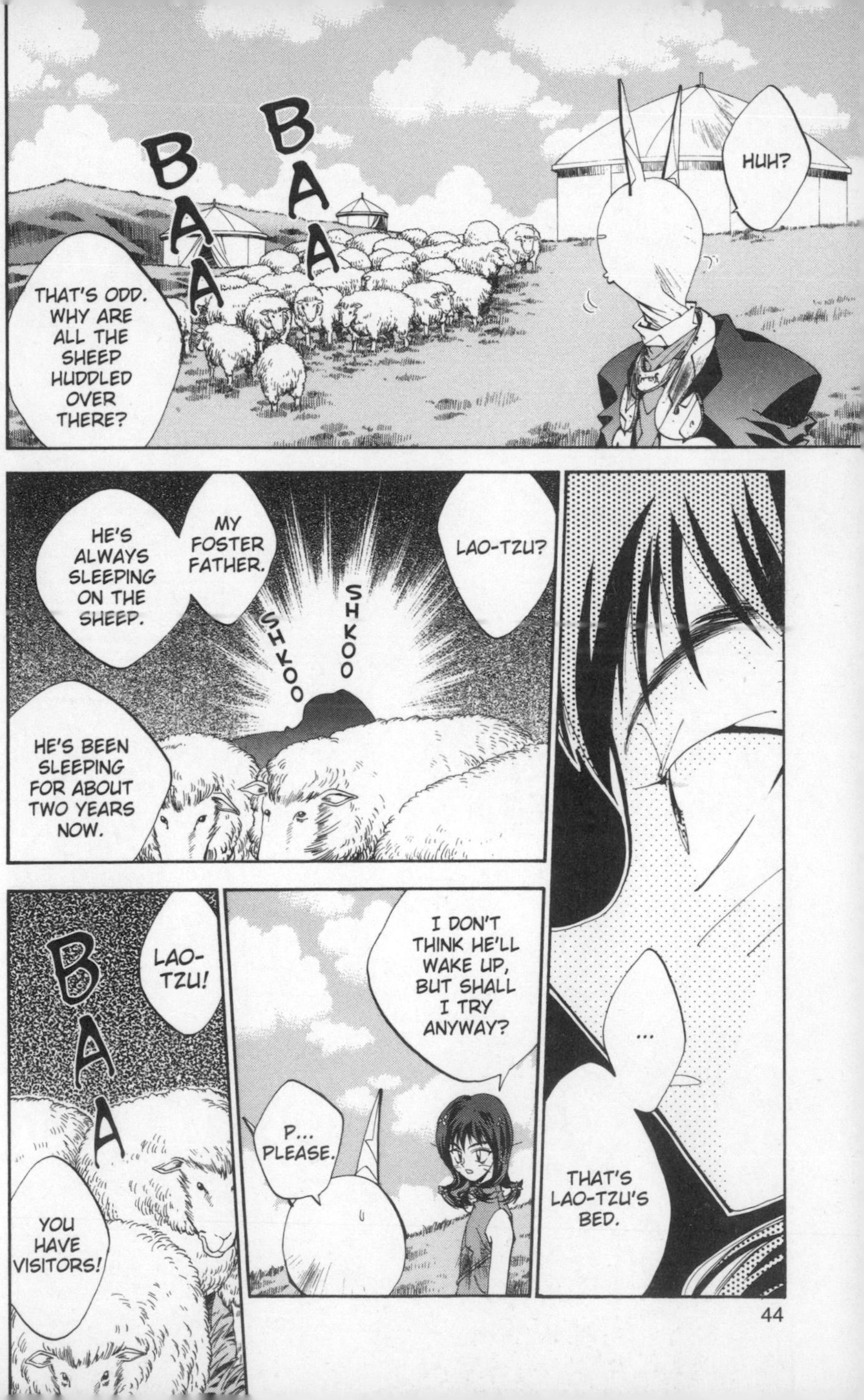
HUH?
BAA
BAA
THAT'S ODD. WHY ARE ALL THE SHEEP HUDDLED OVER THERE?
...
THAT'S LAO-TZU'S BED.
LAO-TZU?
SHKOO
SHKOO
MY FOSTER FATHER.
HE'S ALWAYS SLEEPING ON THE SHEEP.
HE'S BEEN SLEEPING FOR ABOUT TWO YEARS NOW.
I DON'T THINK HE'LL WAKE UP, BUT SHALL I TRY ANYWAY?
P... PLEASE.
LAO-TZU!
BAA
YOU HAVE VISITORS!

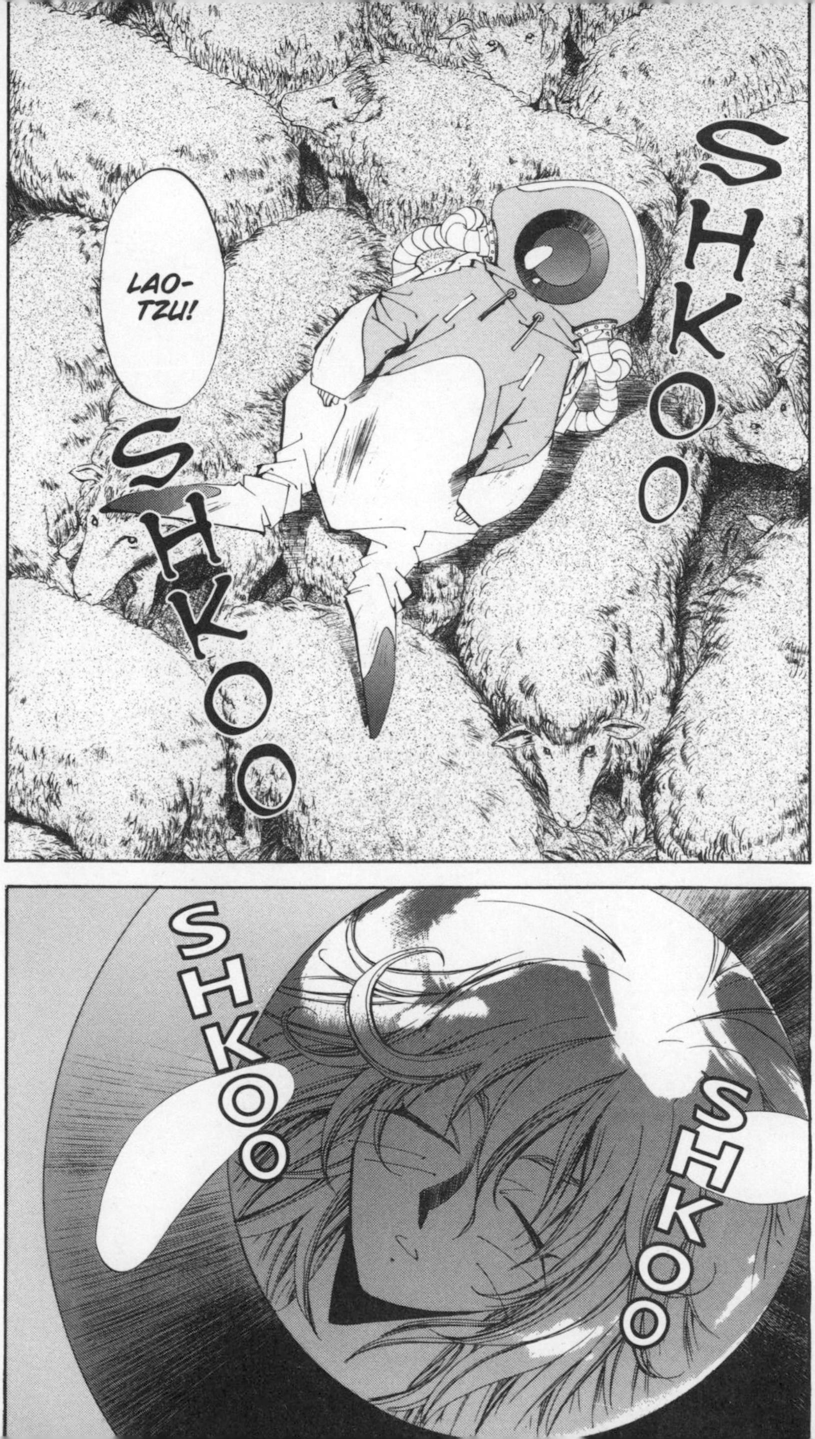
SHKOO
LAO-TZU!
SHKOO
SHKOO
SHKOO

封神演義

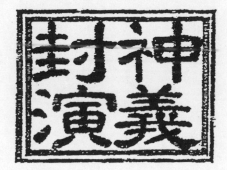

Chapter 154

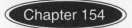

THE ADVENTURE OF TAIJO ROKUN, PART 6
SLEEP

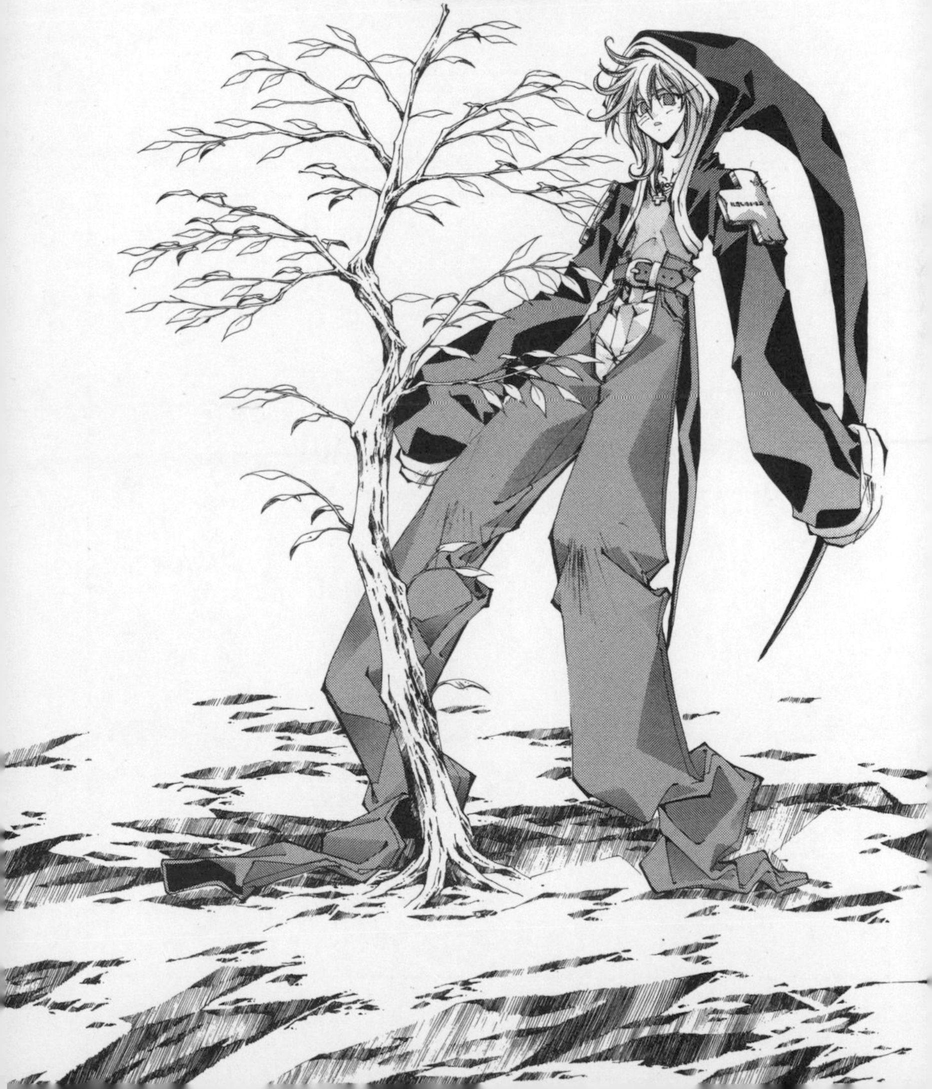

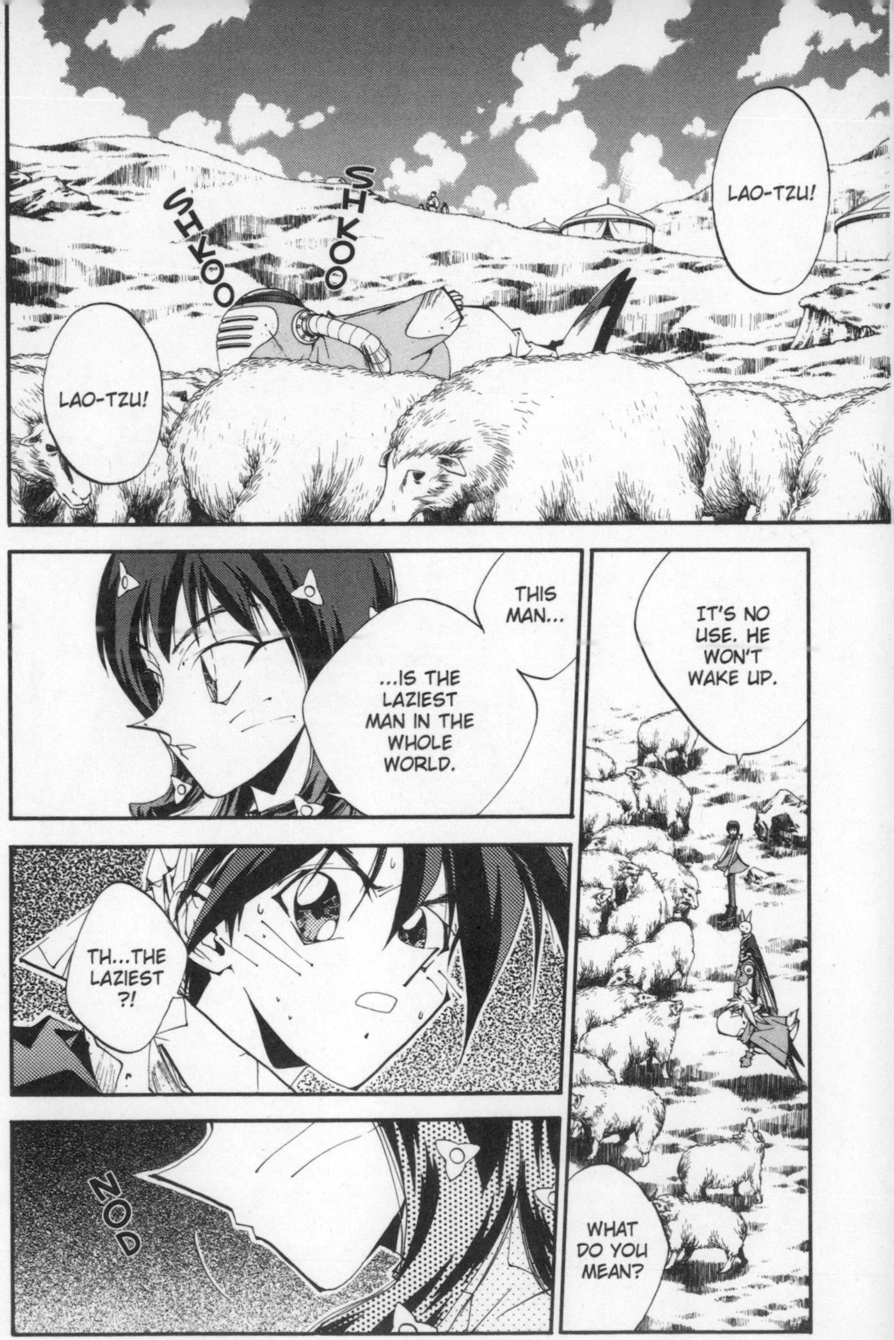
LAO-TZU!
SHKOO
SHKOO
LAO-TZU!
IT'S NO USE. HE WON'T WAKE UP.
WHAT DO YOU MEAN?
THIS MAN...
...IS THE LAZIEST MAN IN THE WHOLE WORLD.
TH...THE LAZIEST?!
NOD

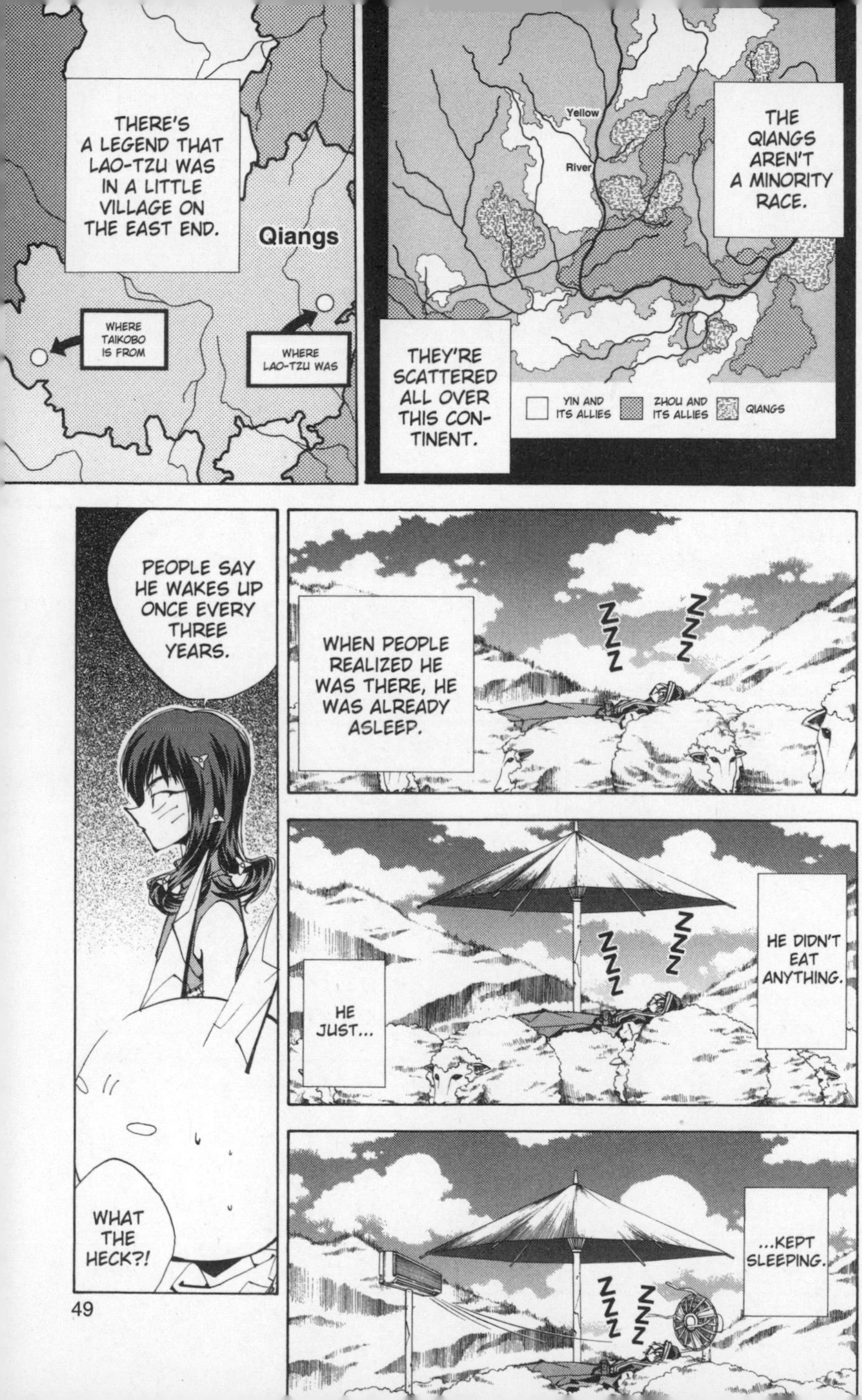
THE QIANGS AREN'T A MINORITY RACE.
Yellow
River
THEY'RE SCATTERED ALL OVER THIS CON-TINENT.
YIN AND ITS ALLIES
ZHOU AND ITS ALLIES
QIANGS
THERE'S A LEGEND THAT LAO-TZU WAS IN A LITTLE VILLAGE ON THE EAST END.
Qiangs
WHERE LAO-TZU WAS
WHERE TAIKOBO IS FROM
WHEN PEOPLE REALIZED HE WAS THERE, HE WAS ALREADY ASLEEP.
ZZZ
ZZZ
HE DIDN'T EAT ANYTHING.
HE JUST...
ZZZ
ZZZ
...KEPT SLEEPING.
ZZZ
ZZZ
PEOPLE SAY HE WAKES UP ONCE EVERY THREE YEARS.
WHAT THE HECK?!

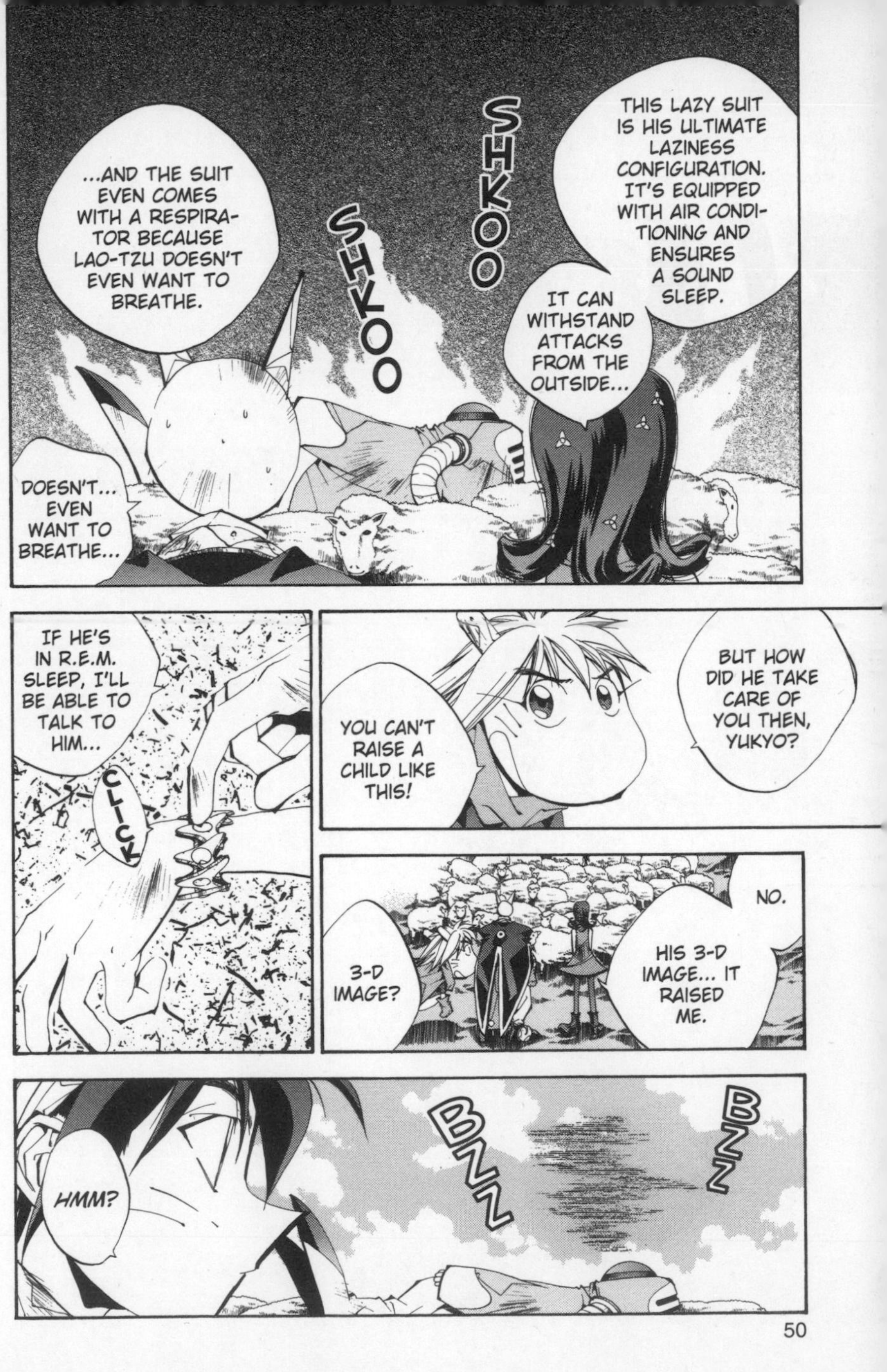
THIS LAZY SUIT IS HIS ULTIMATE LAZINESS CONFIGURATION. IT'S EQUIPPED WITH AIR CONDITIONING AND ENSURES A SOUND SLEEP.
SHKOO
SHKOO
IT CAN WITHSTAND ATTACKS FROM THE OUTSIDE...
...AND THE SUIT EVEN COMES WITH A RESPIRATOR BECAUSE LAO-TZU DOESN'T EVEN WANT TO BREATHE.
DOESN'T... EVEN WANT TO BREATHE...
BUT HOW DID HE TAKE CARE OF YOU THEN, YUKYO?
YOU CAN'T RAISE A CHILD LIKE THIS!
NO.
HIS 3-D IMAGE... IT RAISED ME.
3-D IMAGE?
IF HE'S IN R.E.M. SLEEP, I'LL BE ABLE TO TALK TO HIM...
CLICK
BZZ
BZZ
HMM?

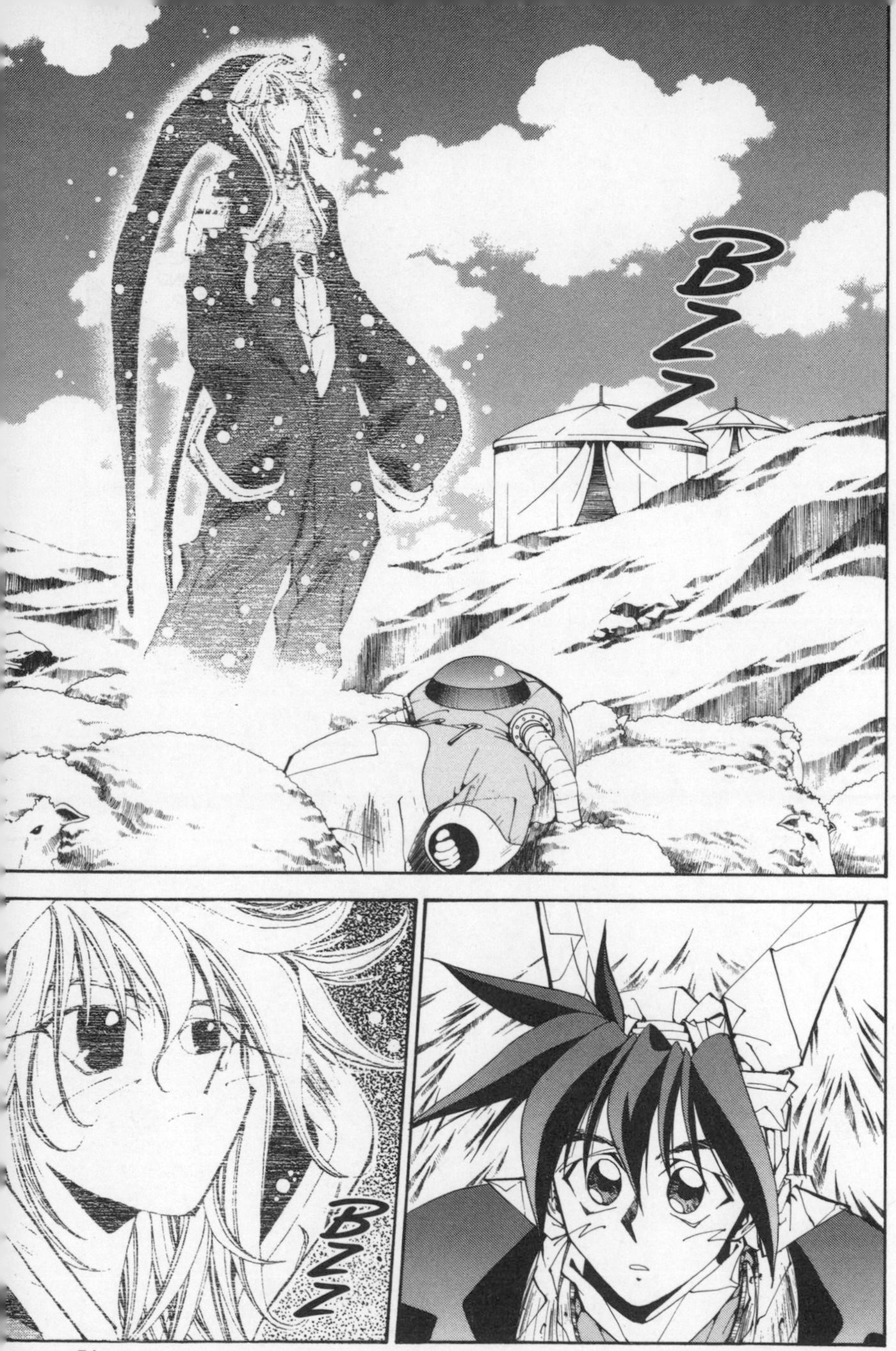
BZZ
BZZ

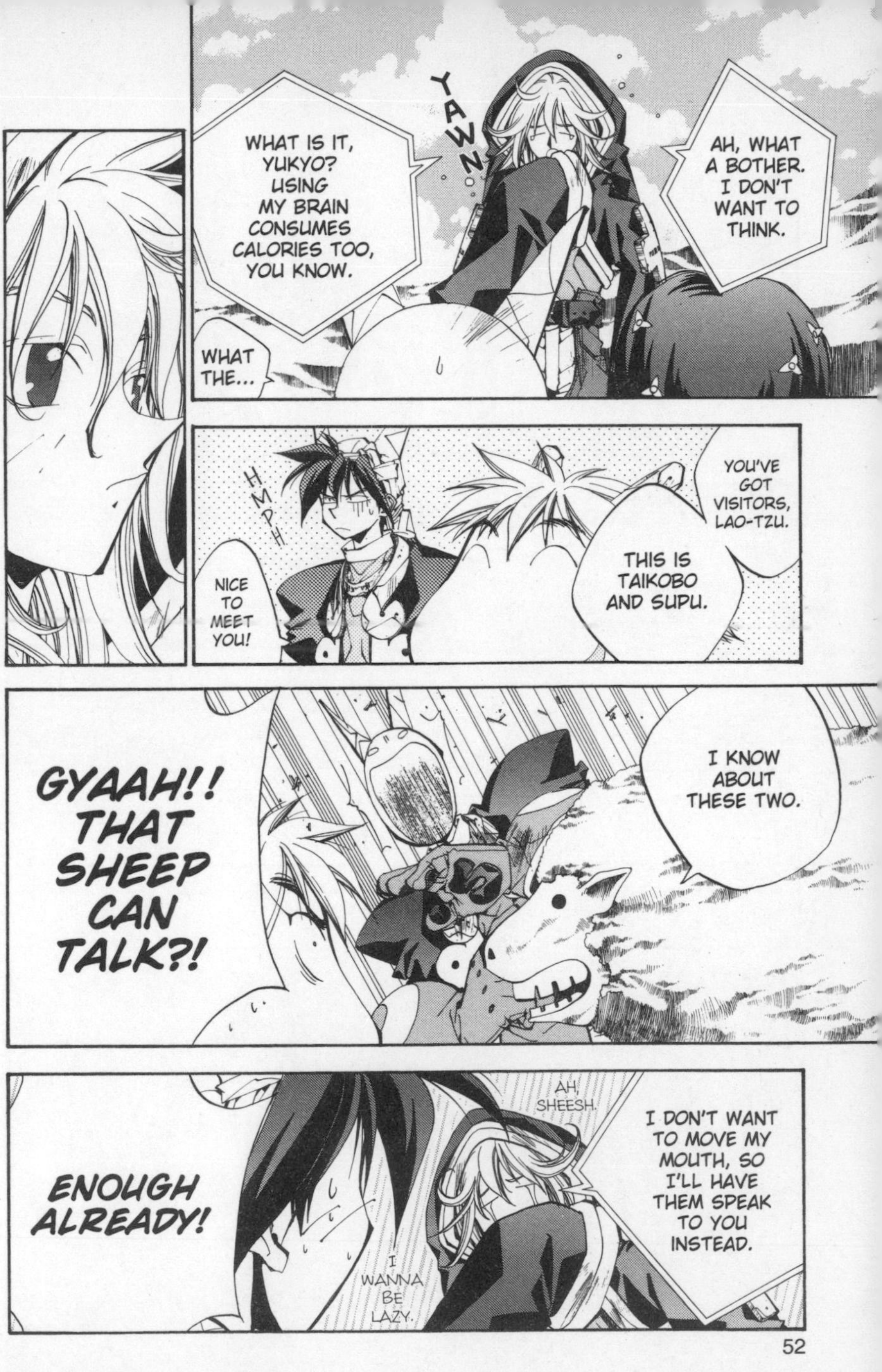
AH, WHAT A BOTHER. I DON'T WANT TO THINK.
YAWN
WHAT IS IT, YUKYO? USING MY BRAIN CONSUMES CALORIES TOO, YOU KNOW.
WHAT THE...
YOU'VE GOT VISITORS, LAO-TZU.
THIS IS TAIKOBO AND SUPU.
HMPH
NICE TO MEET YOU!
I KNOW ABOUT THESE TWO.
GYAAH!! THAT SHEEP CAN TALK?!
AH, SHEESH.
I DON'T WANT TO MOVE MY MOUTH, SO I'LL HAVE THEM SPEAK TO YOU INSTEAD.
I WANNA BE LAZY.
ENOUGH ALREADY!

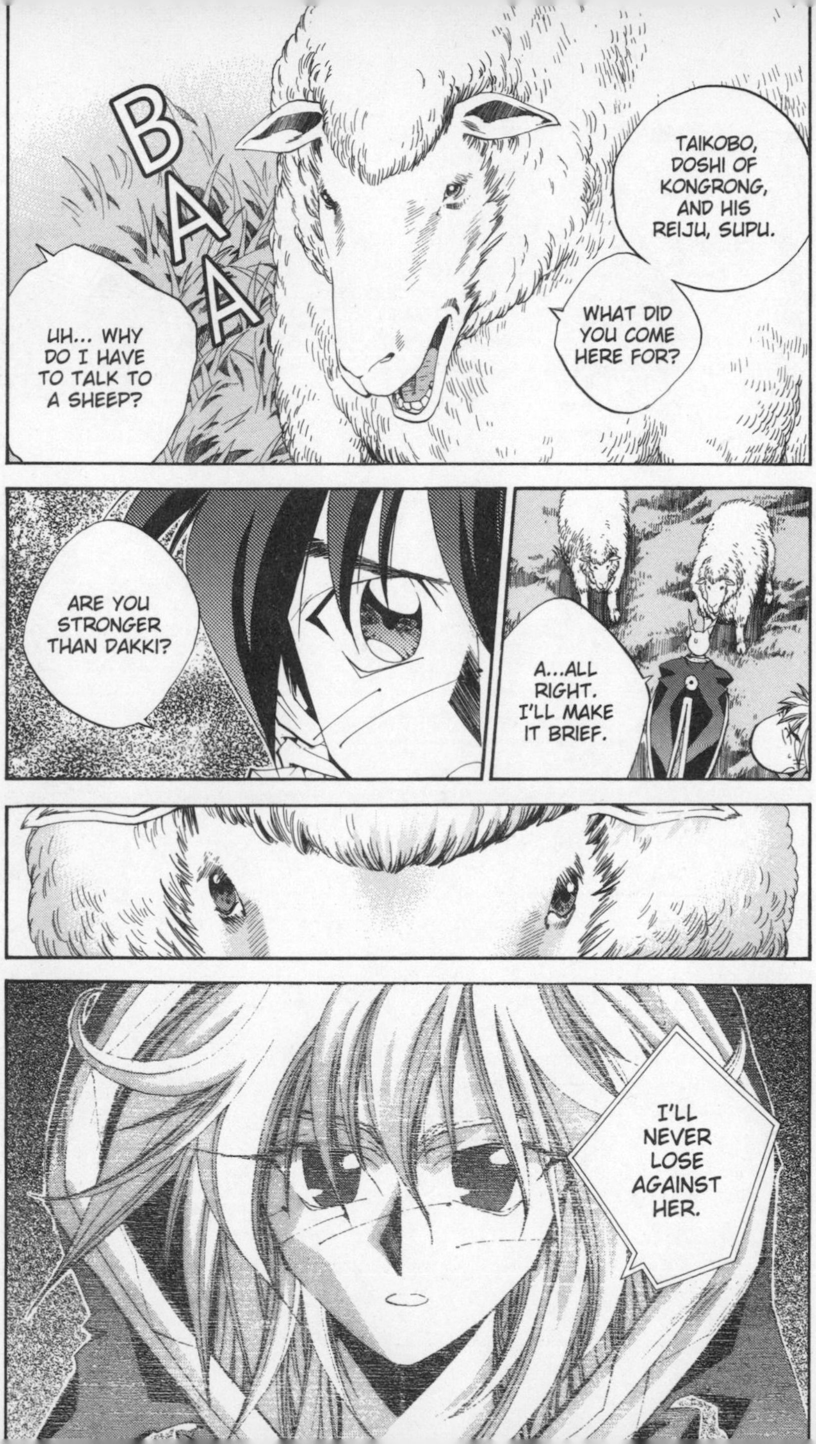
TAIKOBO, DOSHI OF KONGRONG, AND HIS REIJU, SUPU.
WHAT DID YOU COME HERE FOR?
BAA
UH... WHY DO I HAVE TO TALK TO A SHEEP?
A...ALL RIGHT. I'LL MAKE IT BRIEF.
ARE YOU STRONGER THAN DAKKI?
I'LL NEVER LOSE AGAINST HER.

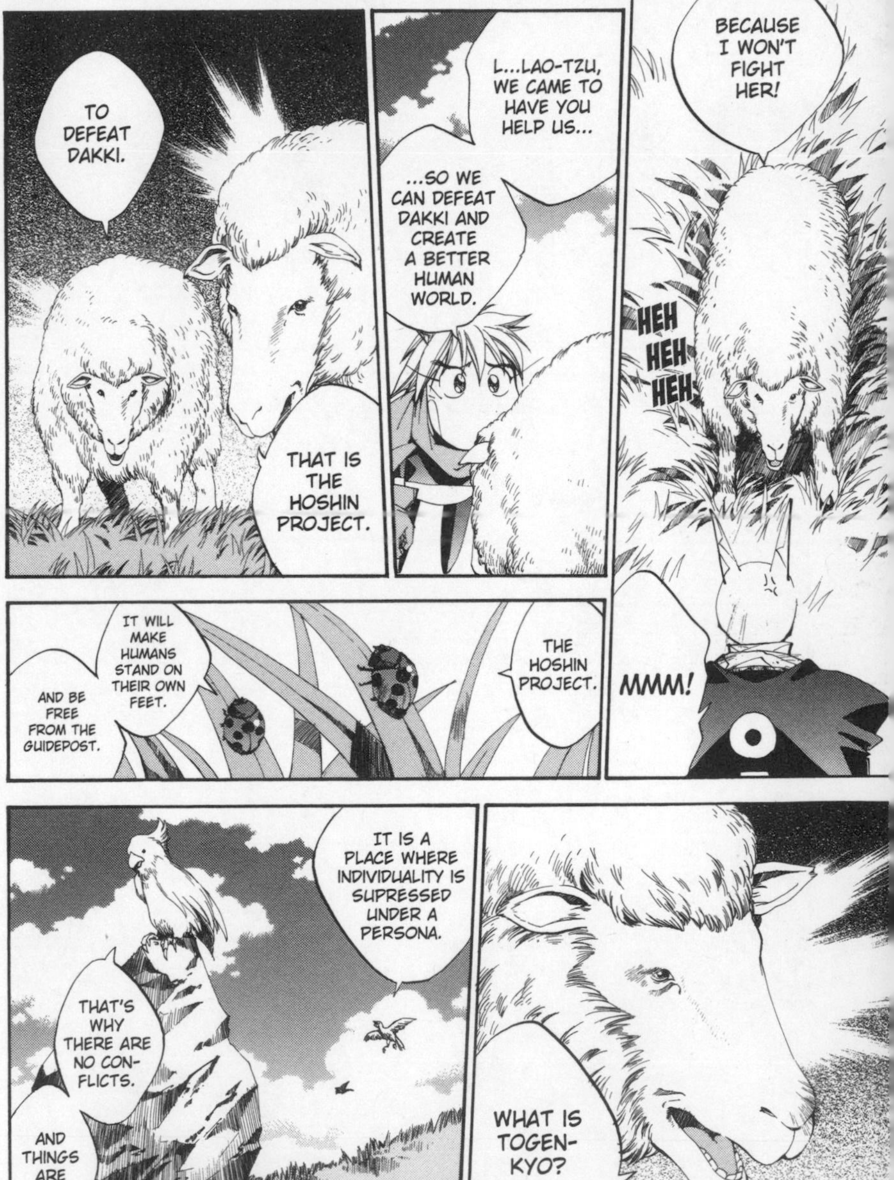
BECAUSE I WON'T FIGHT HER!
HEH HEH HEH
MMM!
L...LAO-TZU, WE CAME TO HAVE YOU HELP US...
...SO WE CAN DEFEAT DAKKI AND CREATE A BETTER HUMAN WORLD.
TO DEFEAT DAKKI.
THAT IS THE HOSHIN PROJECT.
THE HOSHIN PROJECT.
IT WILL MAKE HUMANS STAND ON THEIR OWN FEET.
AND BE FREE FROM THE GUIDEPOST.
WHAT IS TOGEN-KYO?
IT IS A PLACE WHERE INDIVIDUALITY IS SUPRESSED UNDER A PERSONA.
THAT'S WHY THERE ARE NO CON-FLICTS.
AND THINGS ARE FAIR.

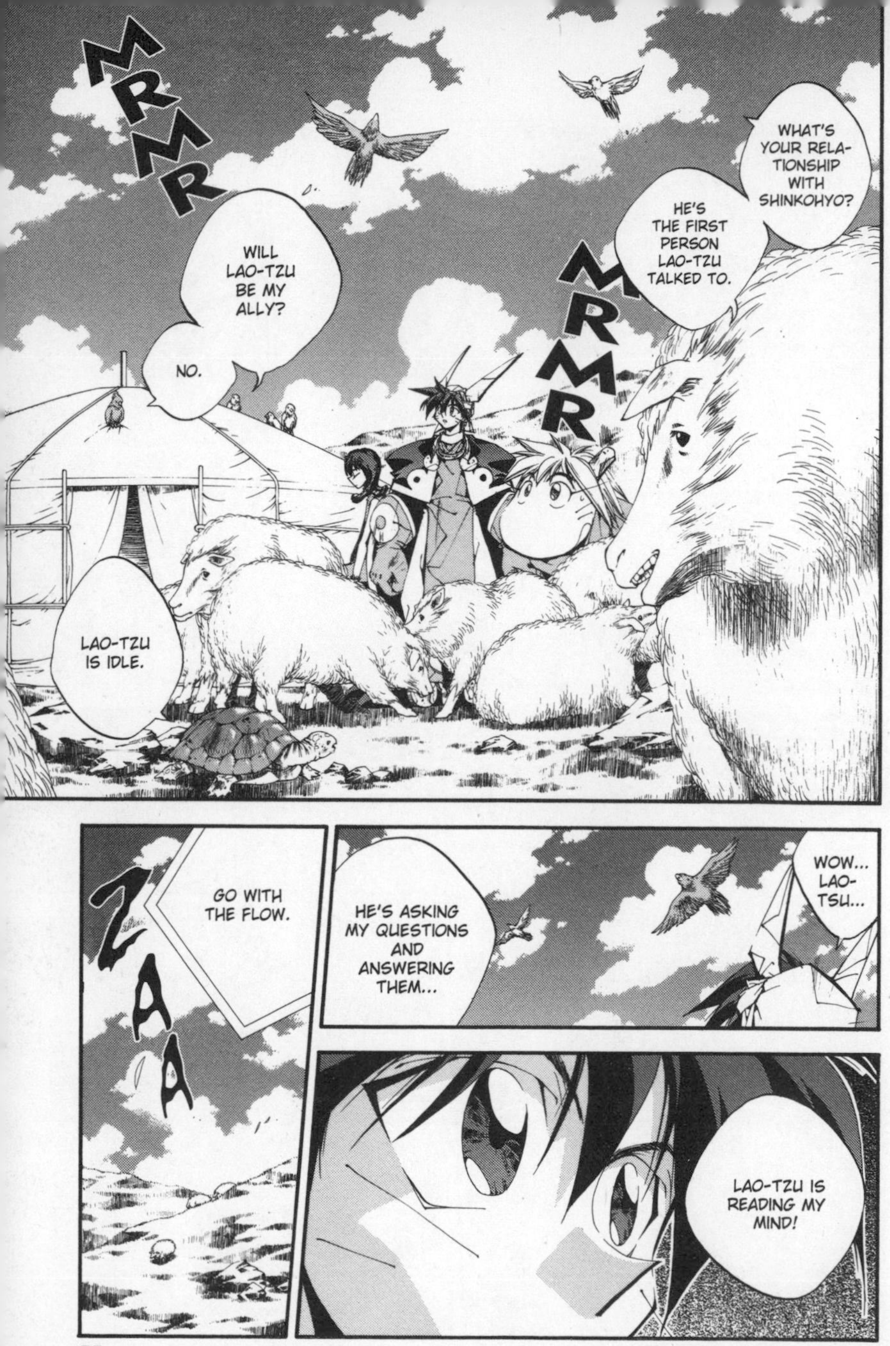
WHAT'S YOUR RELATIONSHIP WITH SHINKOHYO?
HE'S THE FIRST PERSON LAO-TZU TALKED TO.
MRMR
WILL LAO-TZU BE MY ALLY?
NO.
MRMR
LAO-TZU IS IDLE.
WOW... LAO-TSU...
HE'S ASKING MY QUESTIONS AND ANSWERING THEM...
LAO-TZU IS READING MY MIND!
GO WITH THE FLOW.
ZAA

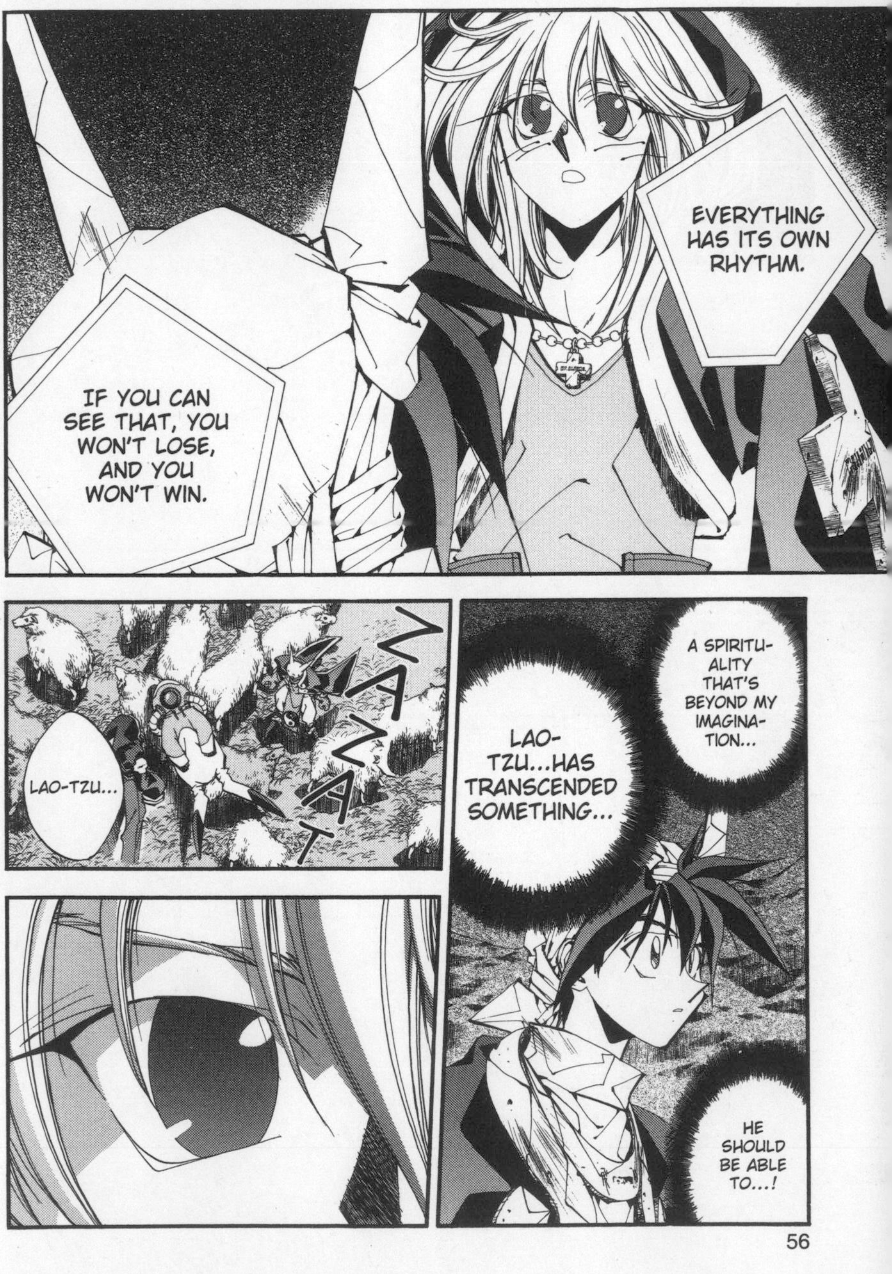
EVERYTHING HAS ITS OWN RHYTHM.
IF YOU CAN SEE THAT, YOU WON'T LOSE, AND YOU WON'T WIN.
A SPIRITU-ALITY THAT'S BEYOND MY IMAGINA-TION...
LAO-TZU...HAS TRANSCENDED SOMETHING...
HE SHOULD BE ABLE TO...!
ZAZAT
LAO-TZU...

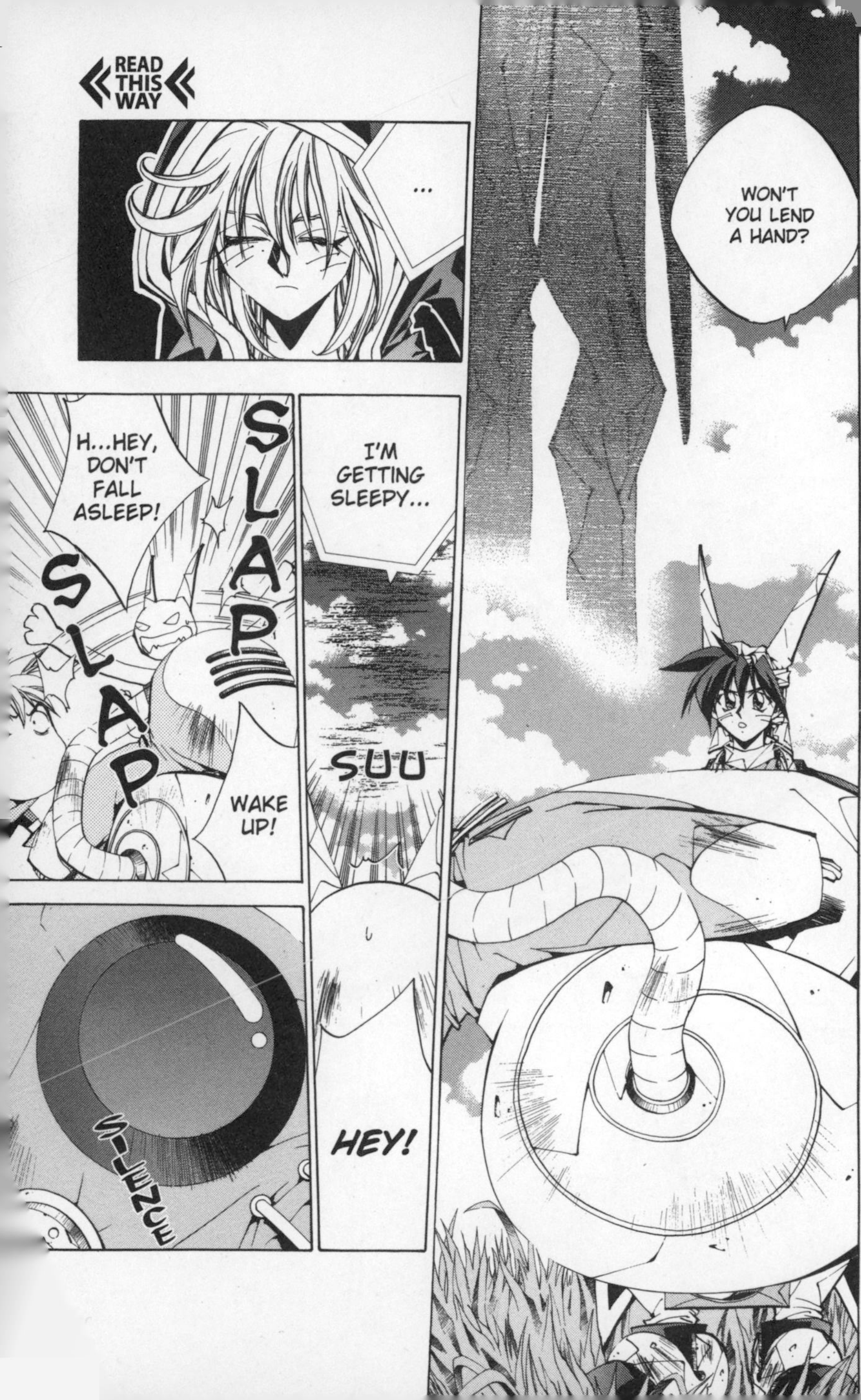
READ THIS WAY
WON'T YOU LEND A HAND?
...
I'M GETTING SLEEPY...
SUU
H...HEY, DON'T FALL ASLEEP!
SLAP
SLAP
WAKE UP!
HEY!
SILENCE

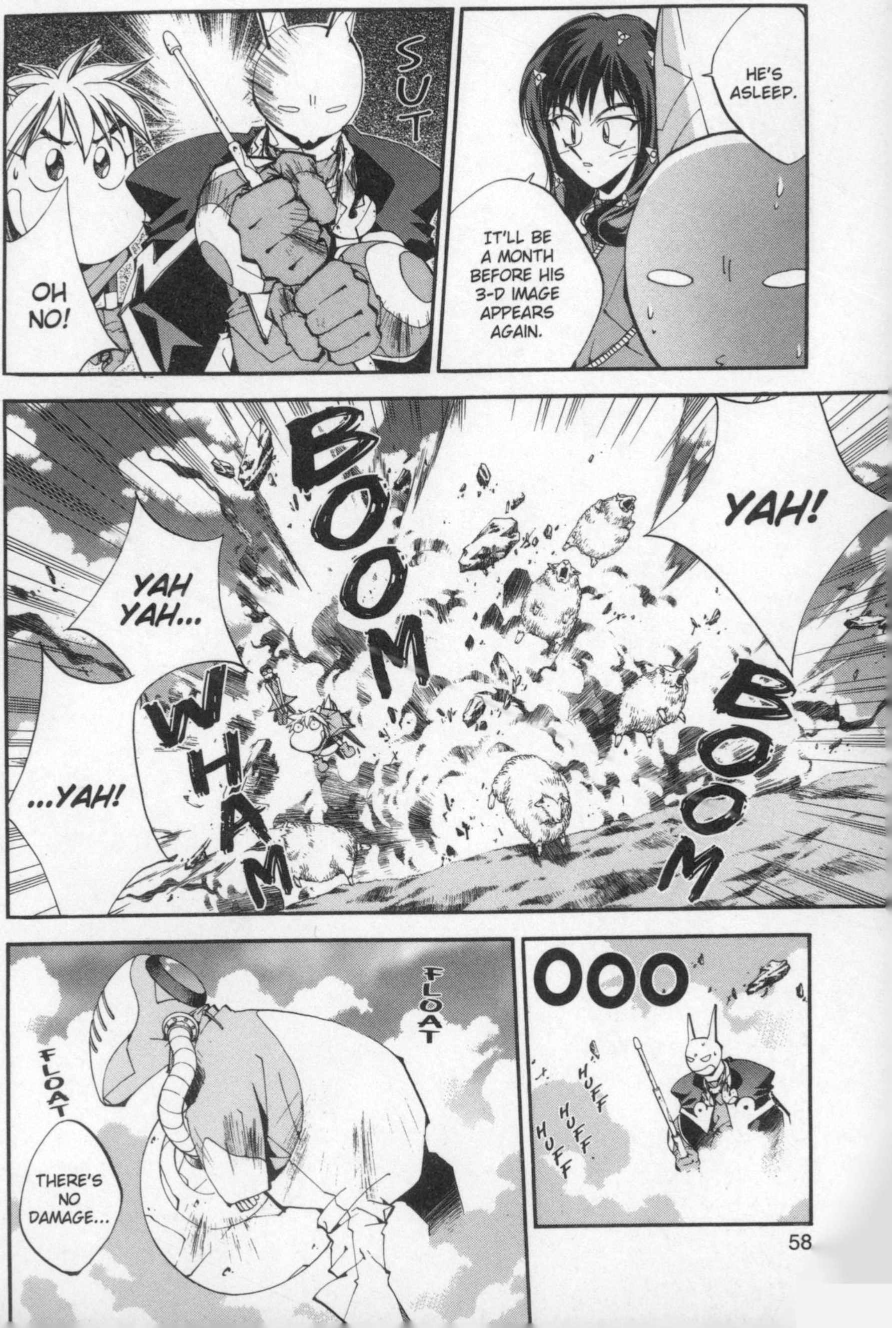
HE'S ASLEEP.
IT'LL BE A MONTH BEFORE HIS 3-D IMAGE APPEARS AGAIN.
SUT
OH NO!
YAH!
BOOM
BOOM
YAH YAH...
WHAM
...YAH!
OOO
HUFF
HUFF
HUFF
FLOAT
FLOAT
THERE'S NO DAMAGE...

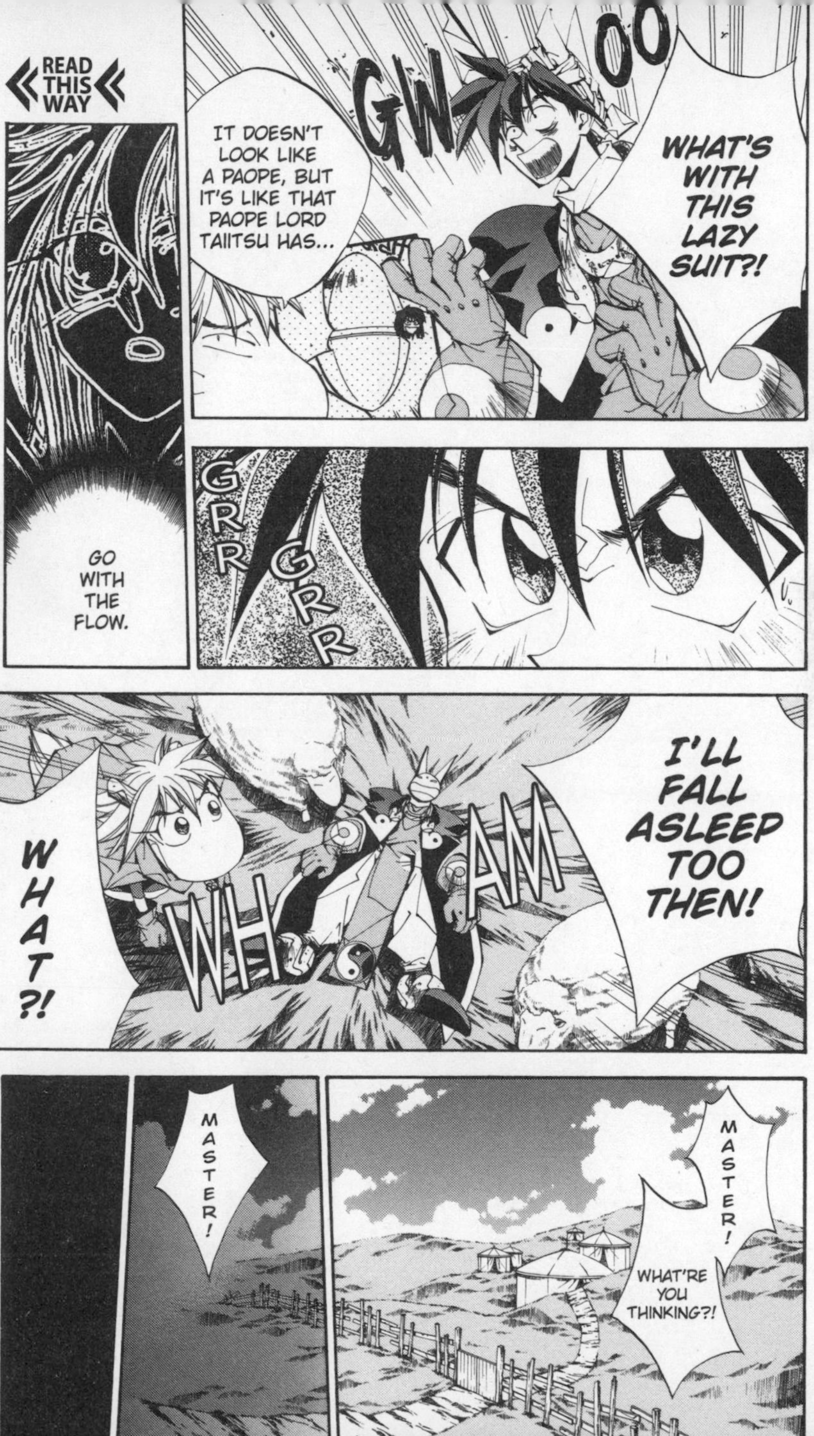
READ THIS WAY
GWOO
WHAT'S WITH THIS LAZY SUIT?!
IT DOESN'T LOOK LIKE A PAOPE, BUT IT'S LIKE THAT PAOPE LORD TAIITSU HAS...
GRRR GRRR
GO WITH THE FLOW.
I'LL FALL ASLEEP TOO THEN!
WHAM
WHAT?!
MASTER!
WHAT'RE YOU THINKING?!
MASTER!

THE OLD MAN SAID...

...THAT WE CAN'T BE HAPPY UNLESS WE CAN CHANGE THE WHOLE WORLD.

THAT WAS MY BEGINNING.

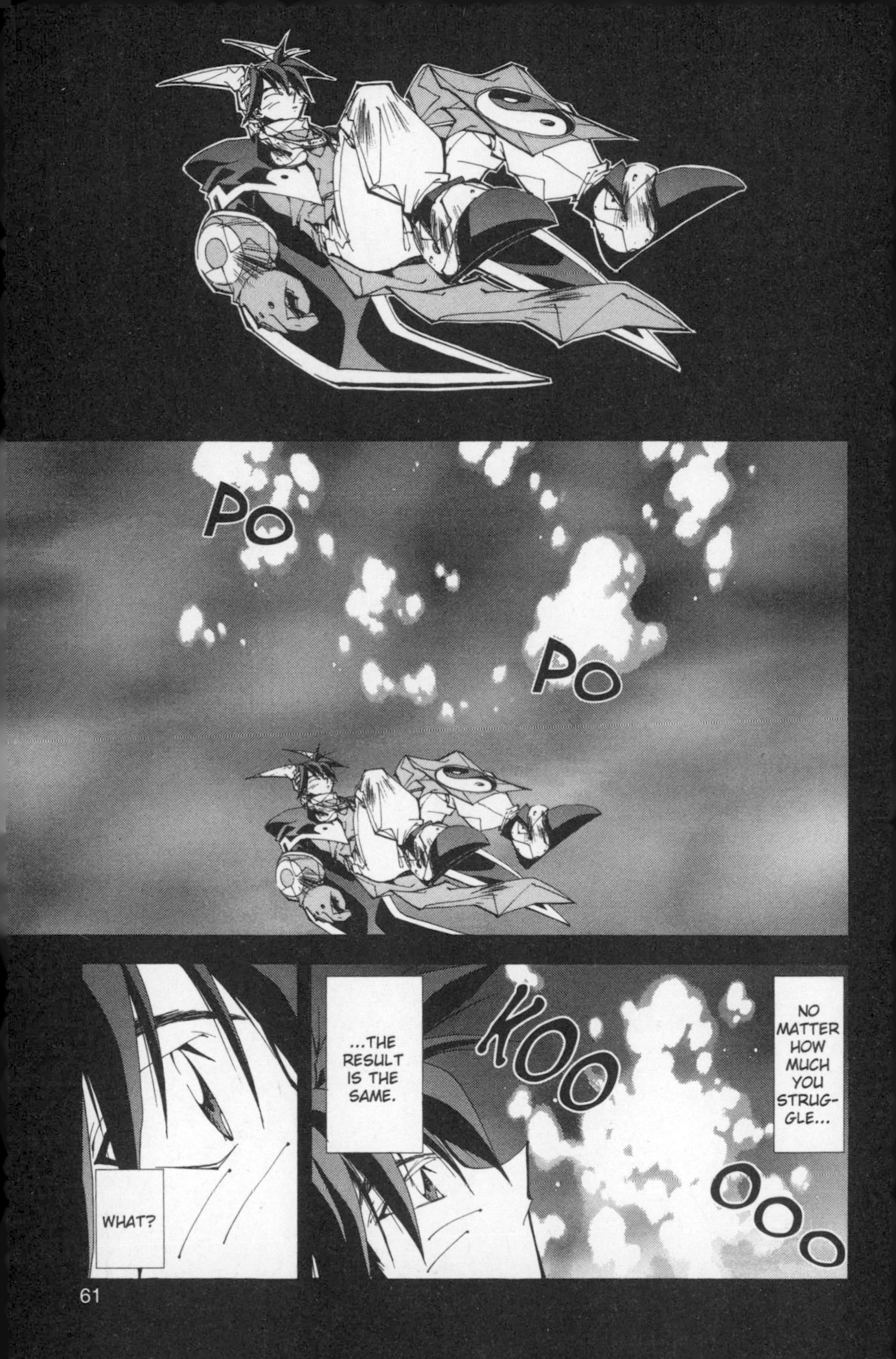
PO
PO
NO MATTER HOW MUCH YOU STRUG-GLE...
KOOOOOO
...THE RESULT IS THE SAME.
WHAT?

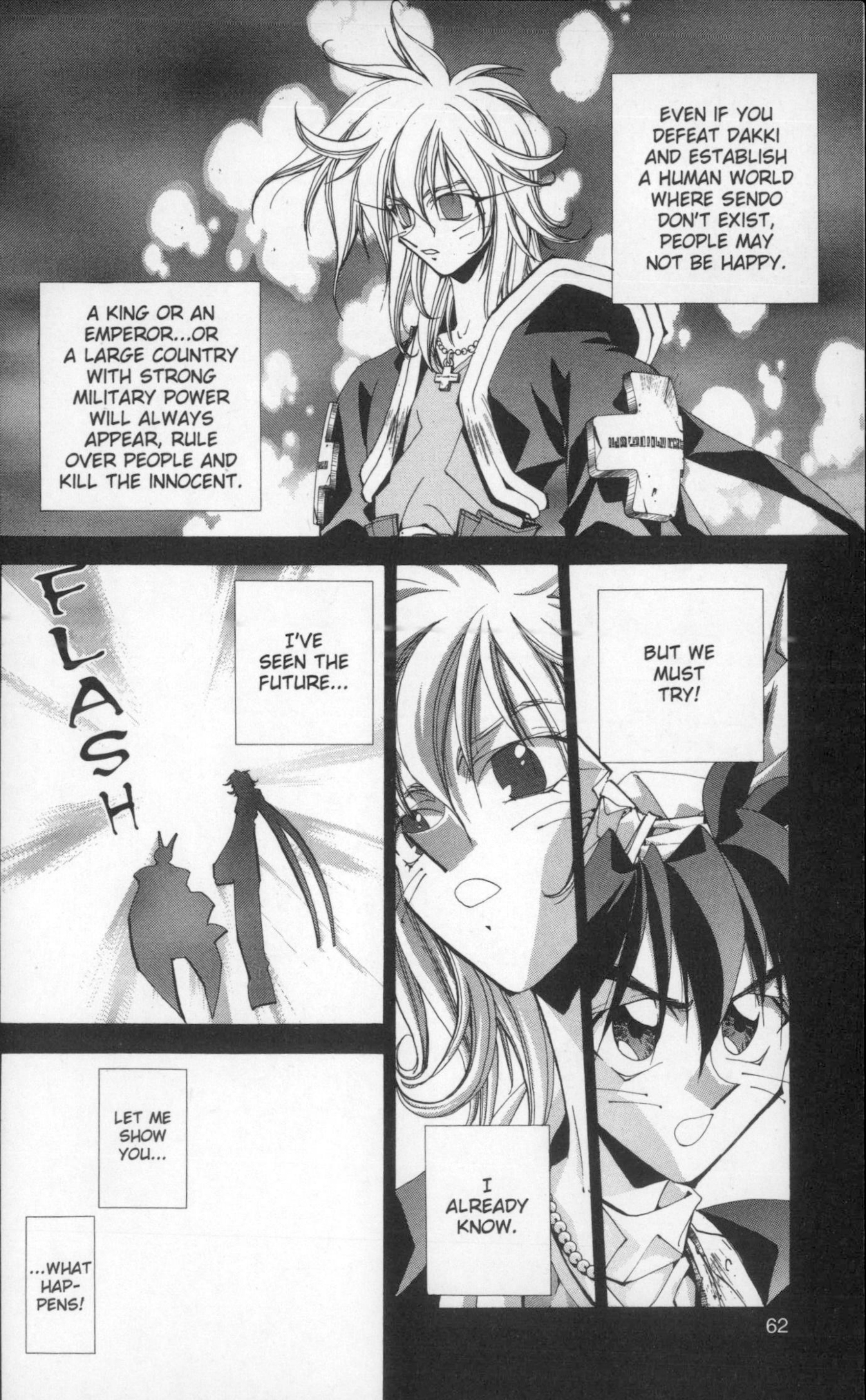
EVEN IF YOU DEFEAT DAKKI AND ESTABLISH A HUMAN WORLD WHERE SENDO DON'T EXIST, PEOPLE MAY NOT BE HAPPY.
A KING OR AN EMPEROR...OR A LARGE COUNTRY WITH STRONG MILITARY POWER WILL ALWAYS APPEAR, RULE OVER PEOPLE AND KILL THE INNOCENT.
BUT WE MUST TRY!
I ALREADY KNOW.
I'VE SEEN THE FUTURE...
FLASH
LET ME SHOW YOU...
...WHAT HAP-PENS!

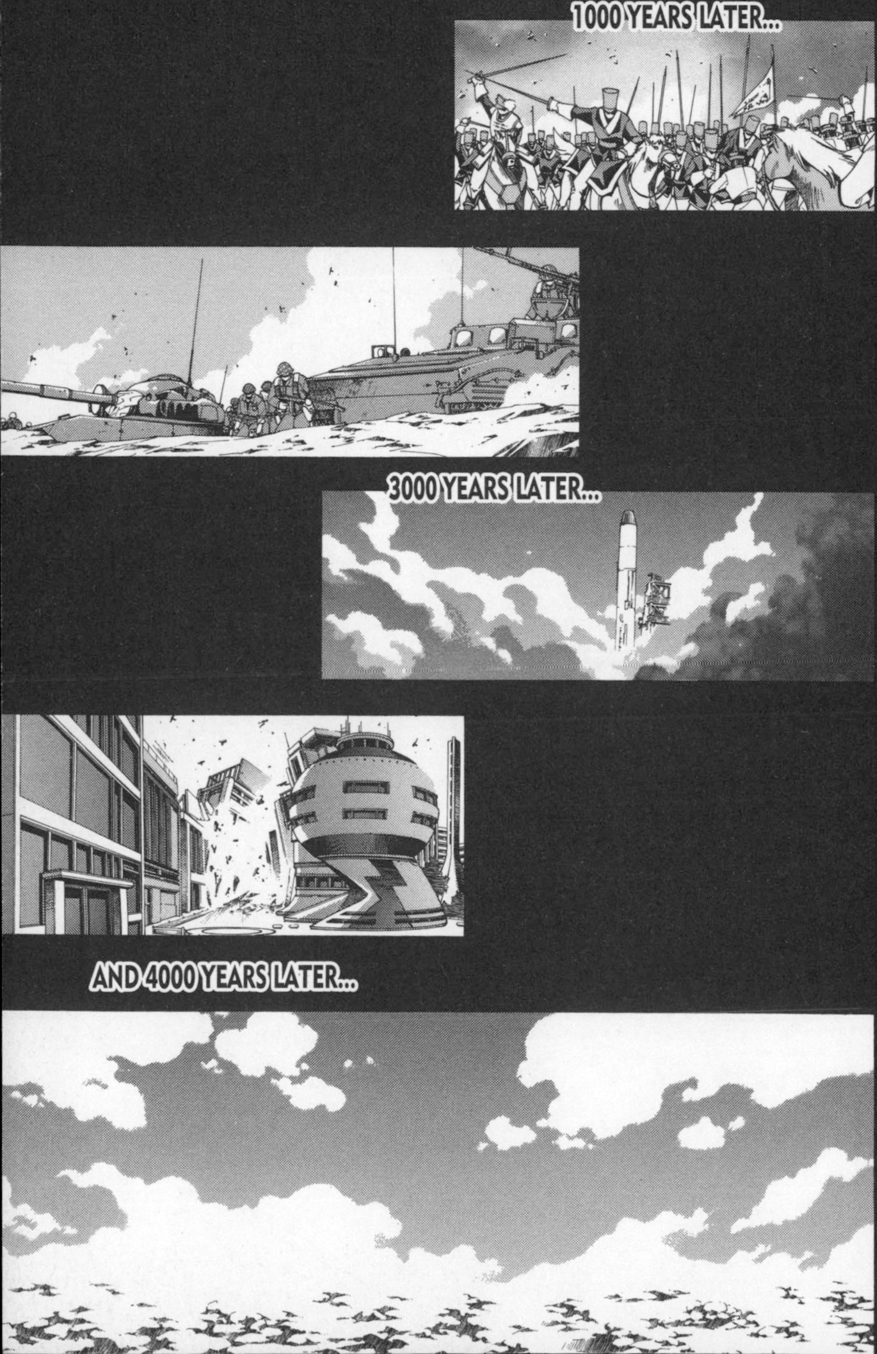
1000 YEARS LATER...
3000 YEARS LATER...
AND 4000 YEARS LATER...

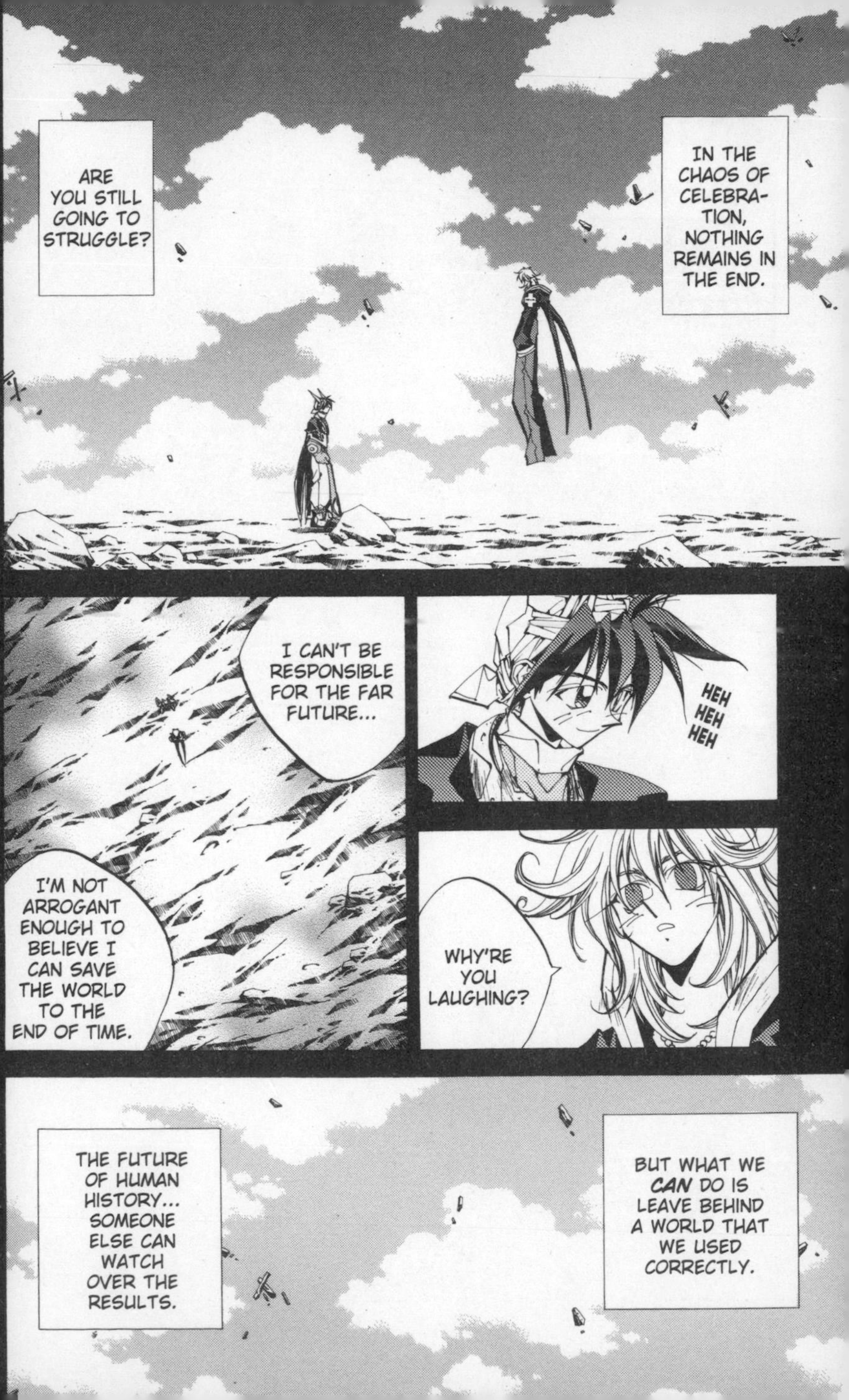
IN THE CHAOS OF CELEBRATION, NOTHING REMAINS IN THE END.
ARE YOU STILL GOING TO STRUGGLE?
HEH HEH HEH
WHY'RE YOU LAUGHING?
I CAN'T BE RESPONSIBLE FOR THE FAR FUTURE...
I'M NOT ARROGANT ENOUGH TO BELIEVE I CAN SAVE THE WORLD TO THE END OF TIME.
BUT WHAT WE *CAN* DO IS LEAVE BEHIND A WORLD THAT WE USED CORRECTLY.
THE FUTURE OF HUMAN HISTORY... SOMEONE ELSE CAN WATCH OVER THE RESULTS.

READ THIS WAY

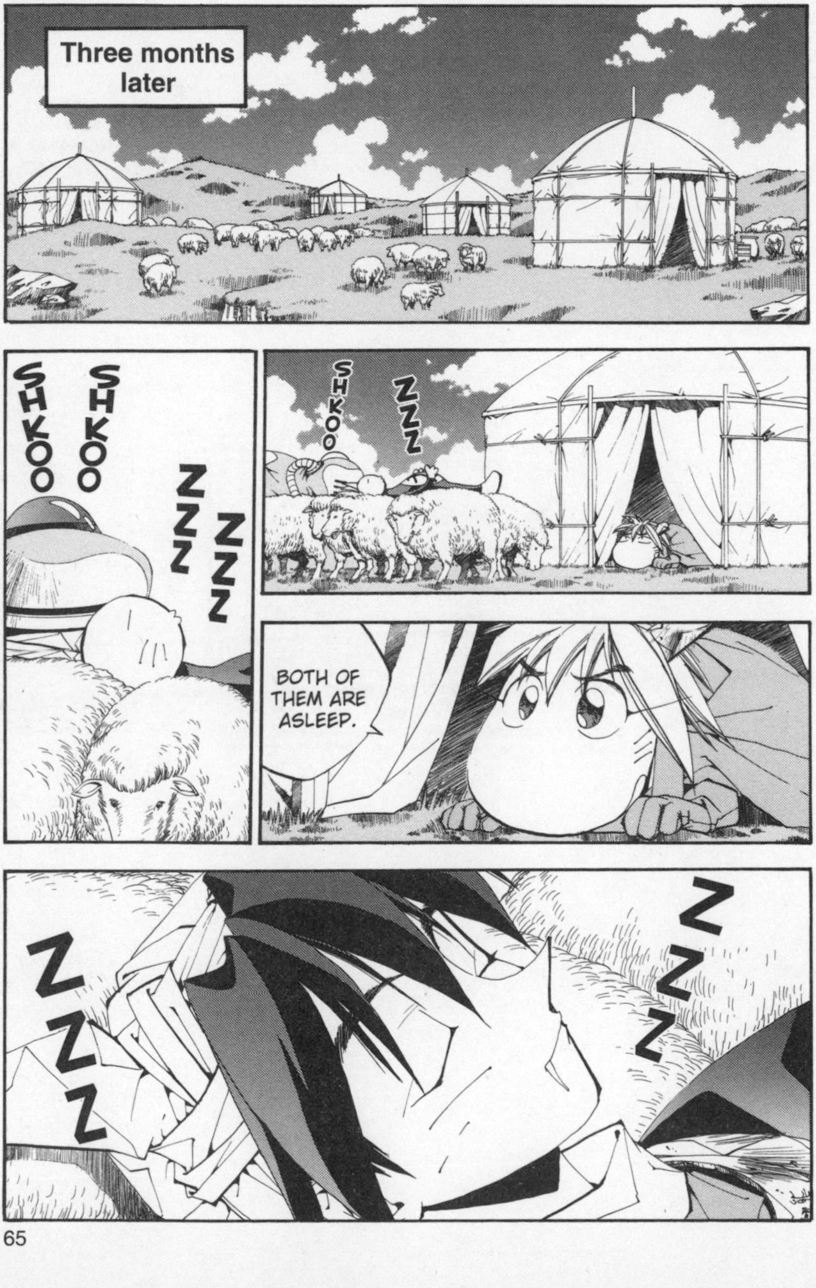
Three months later
SHKOO
ZZZ
BOTH OF THEM ARE ASLEEP.
SHKOO SHKOO
ZZZ ZZZ
ZZZ
ZZZ

封神演義

Chapter 155

THE ADVENTURE OF TAIJO ROKUN, PART 7
TAIKOBO RESORTS TO EXTORTION

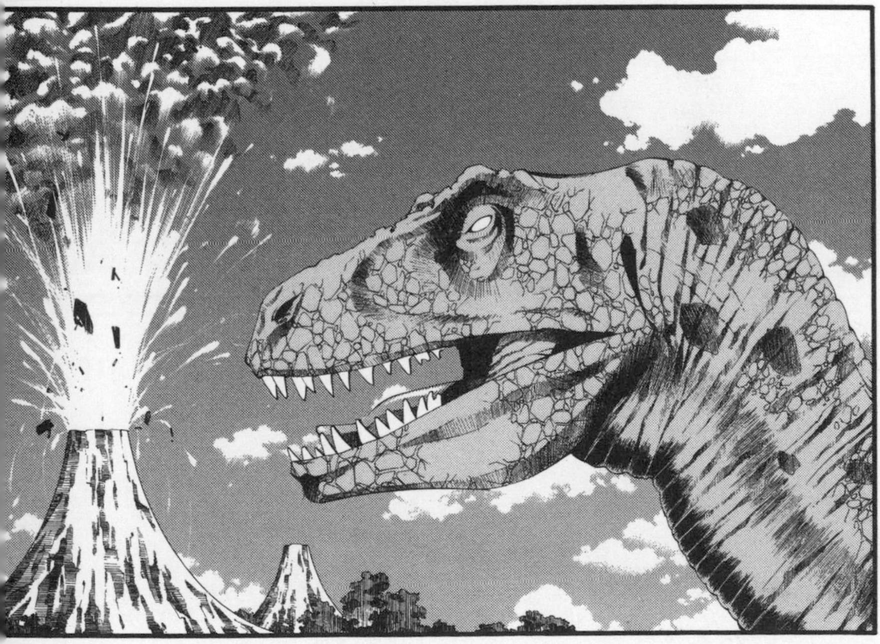

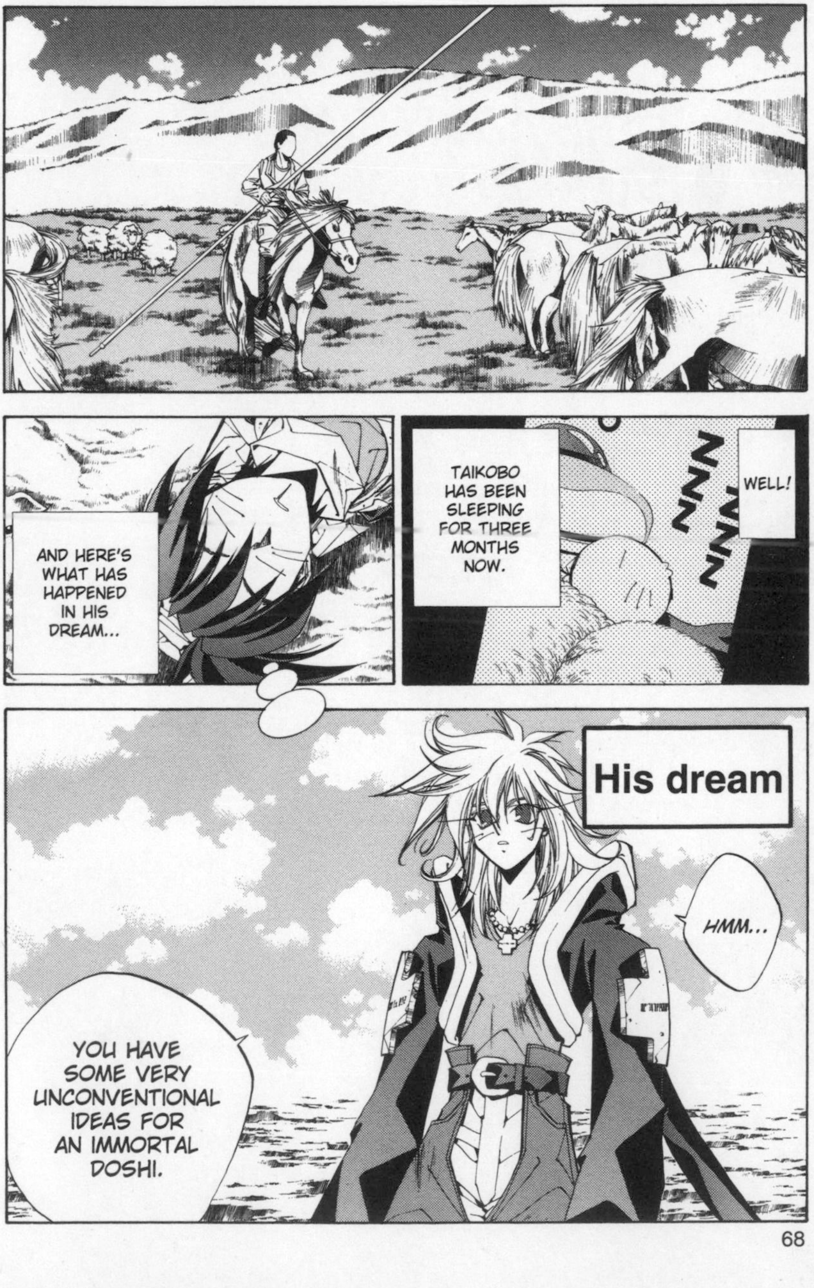
WELL!
NNN NNN
TAIKOBO HAS BEEN SLEEPING FOR THREE MONTHS NOW.
AND HERE'S WHAT HAS HAPPENED IN HIS DREAM...
His dream
HMM...
YOU HAVE SOME VERY UNCONVENTIONAL IDEAS FOR AN IMMORTAL DOSHI.

READ THIS WAY

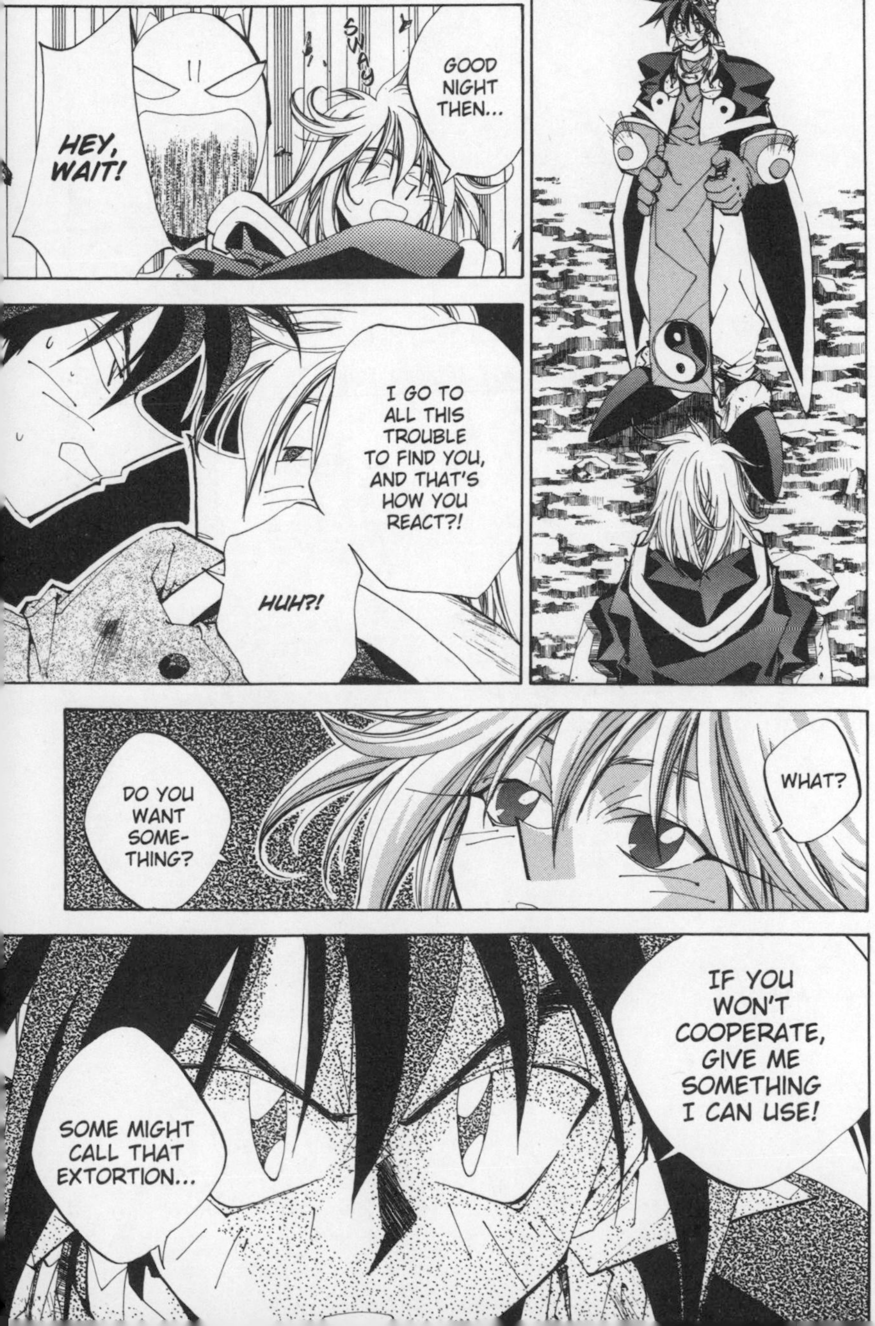
SWAY
GOOD NIGHT THEN...
HEY, WAIT!
I GO TO ALL THIS TROUBLE TO FIND YOU, AND THAT'S HOW YOU REACT?!
HUH?!
WHAT?
DO YOU WANT SOME-THING?
IF YOU WON'T COOPERATE, GIVE ME SOMETHING I CAN USE!
SOME MIGHT CALL THAT EXTORTION...

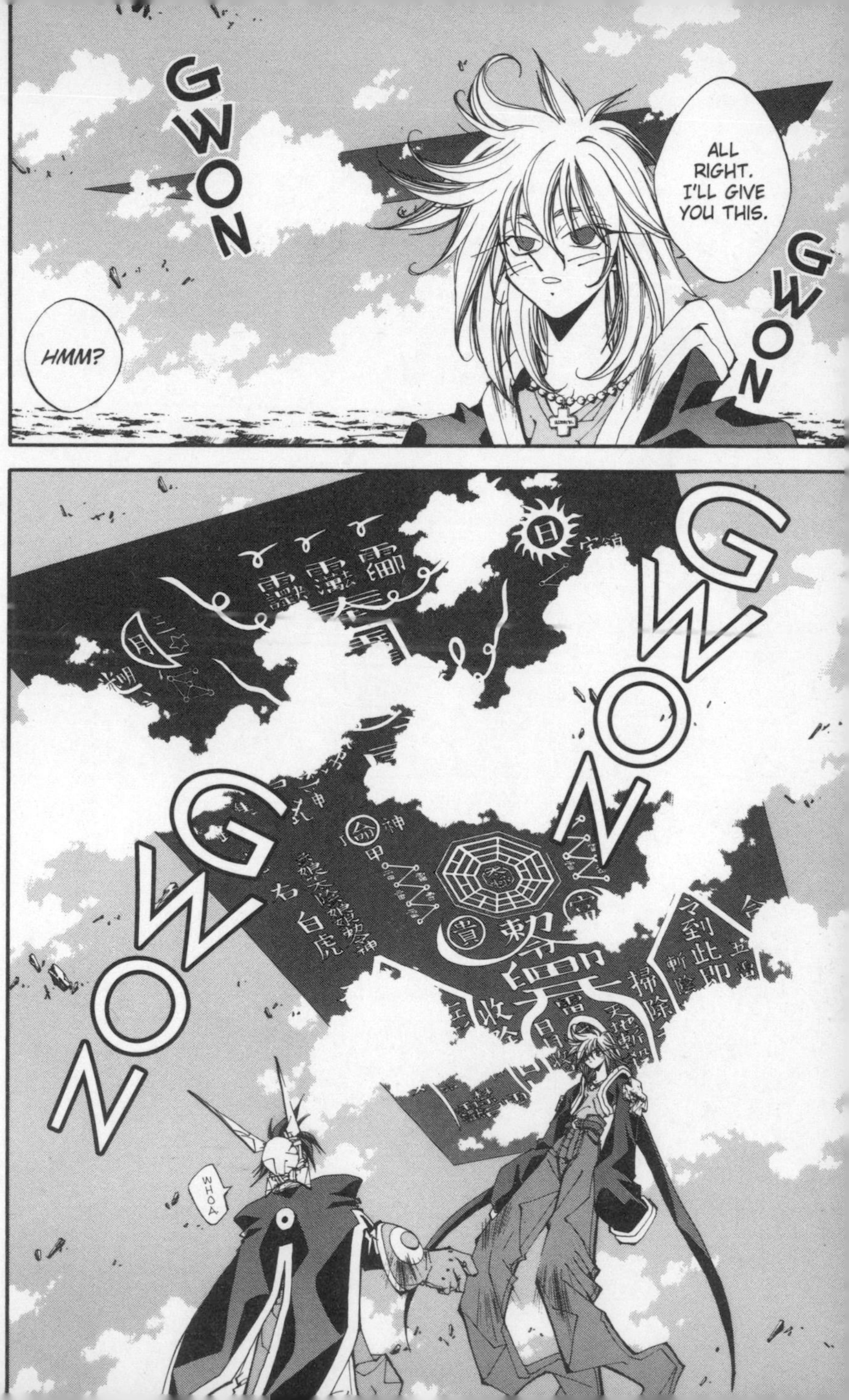
ALL RIGHT. I'LL GIVE YOU THIS.
GWON
GWON
HMM?
GWON
GWON
WHOA

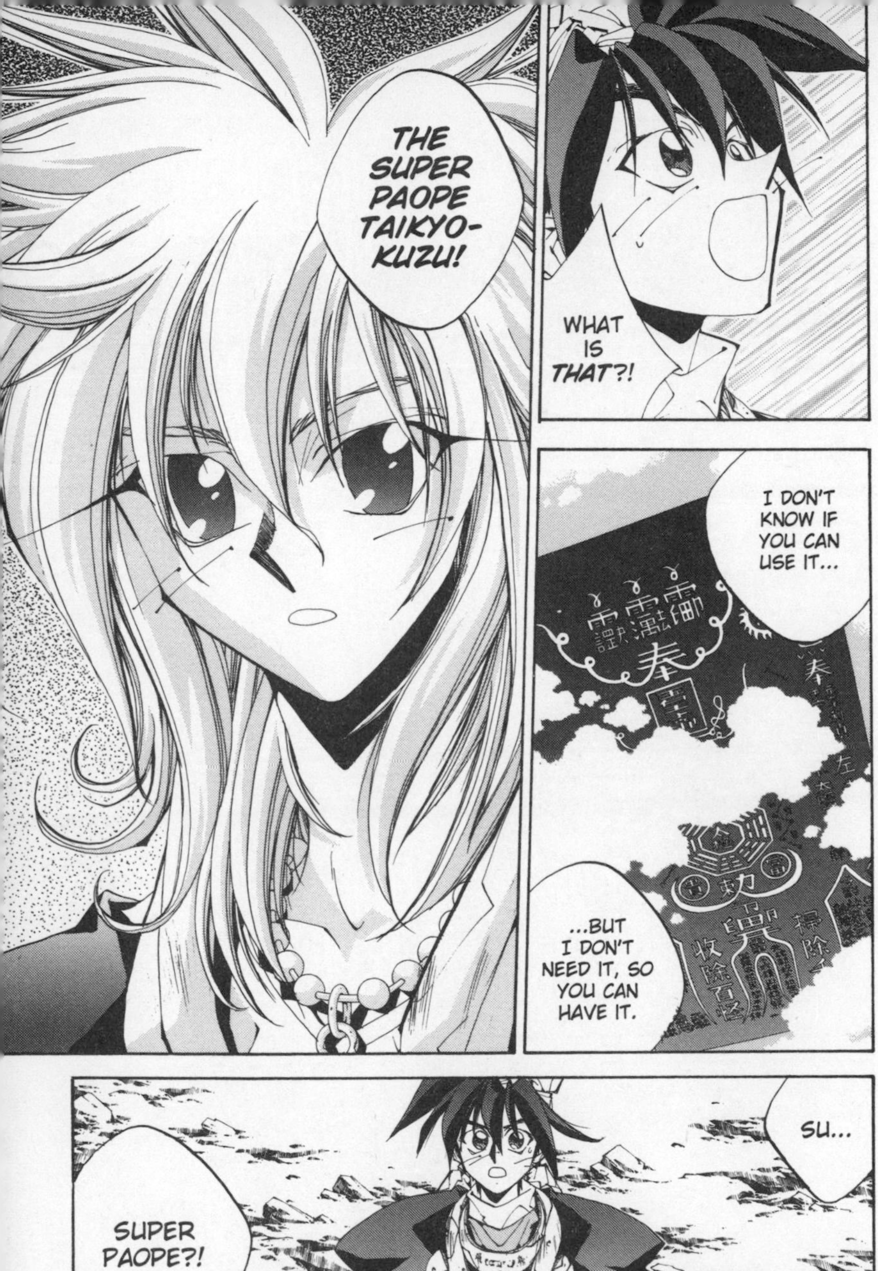
WHAT IS THAT?!
I DON'T KNOW IF YOU CAN USE IT...
...BUT I DON'T NEED IT, SO YOU CAN HAVE IT.
THE SUPER PAOPE TAIKYO-KUZU!
SU...
SUPER PAOPE?!

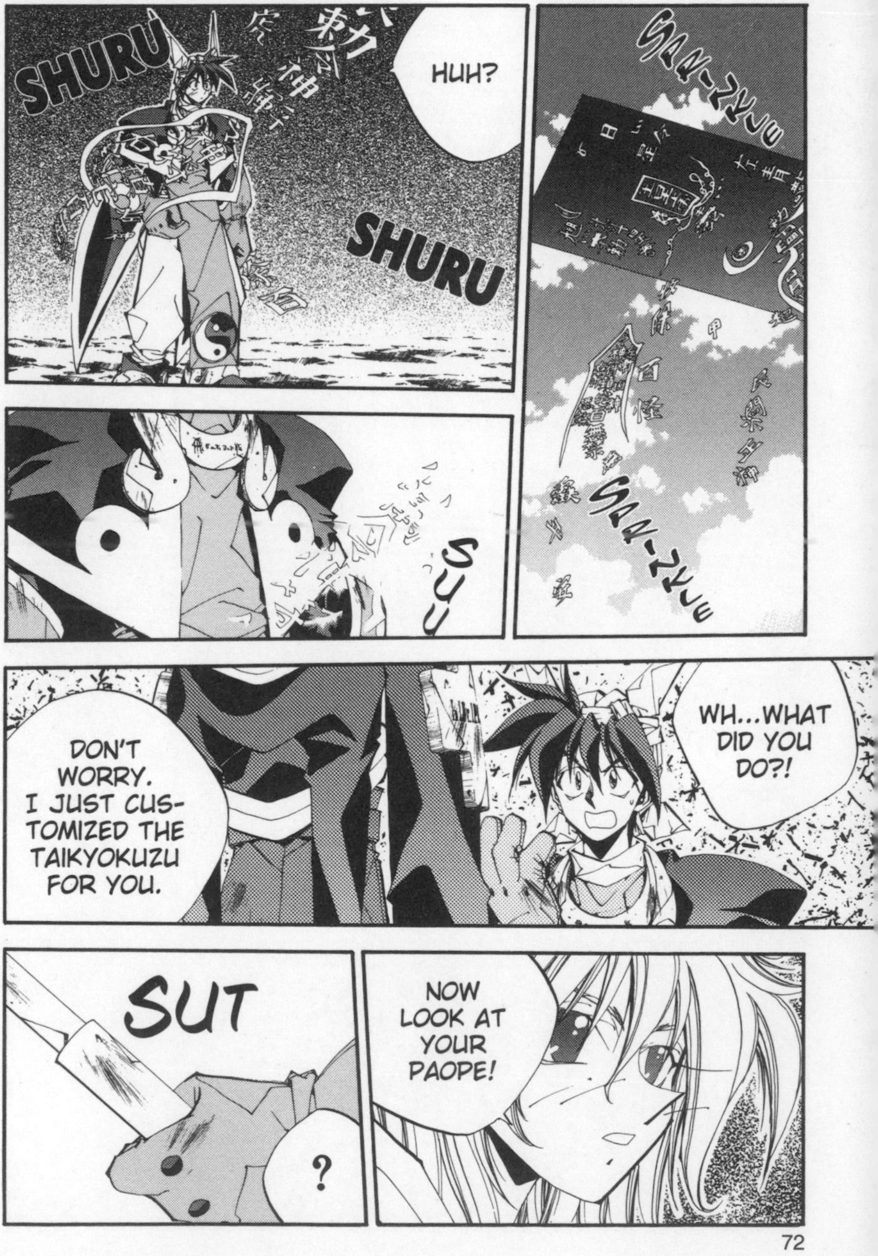
SAA-ZKLE
SAA-ZKLE
HUH?
SHURU
SHURU
SUU
WH...WHAT DID YOU DO?!
DON'T WORRY. I JUST CUS-TOMIZED THE TAIKYOKUZU FOR YOU.
NOW LOOK AT YOUR PAOPE!
SUT
?

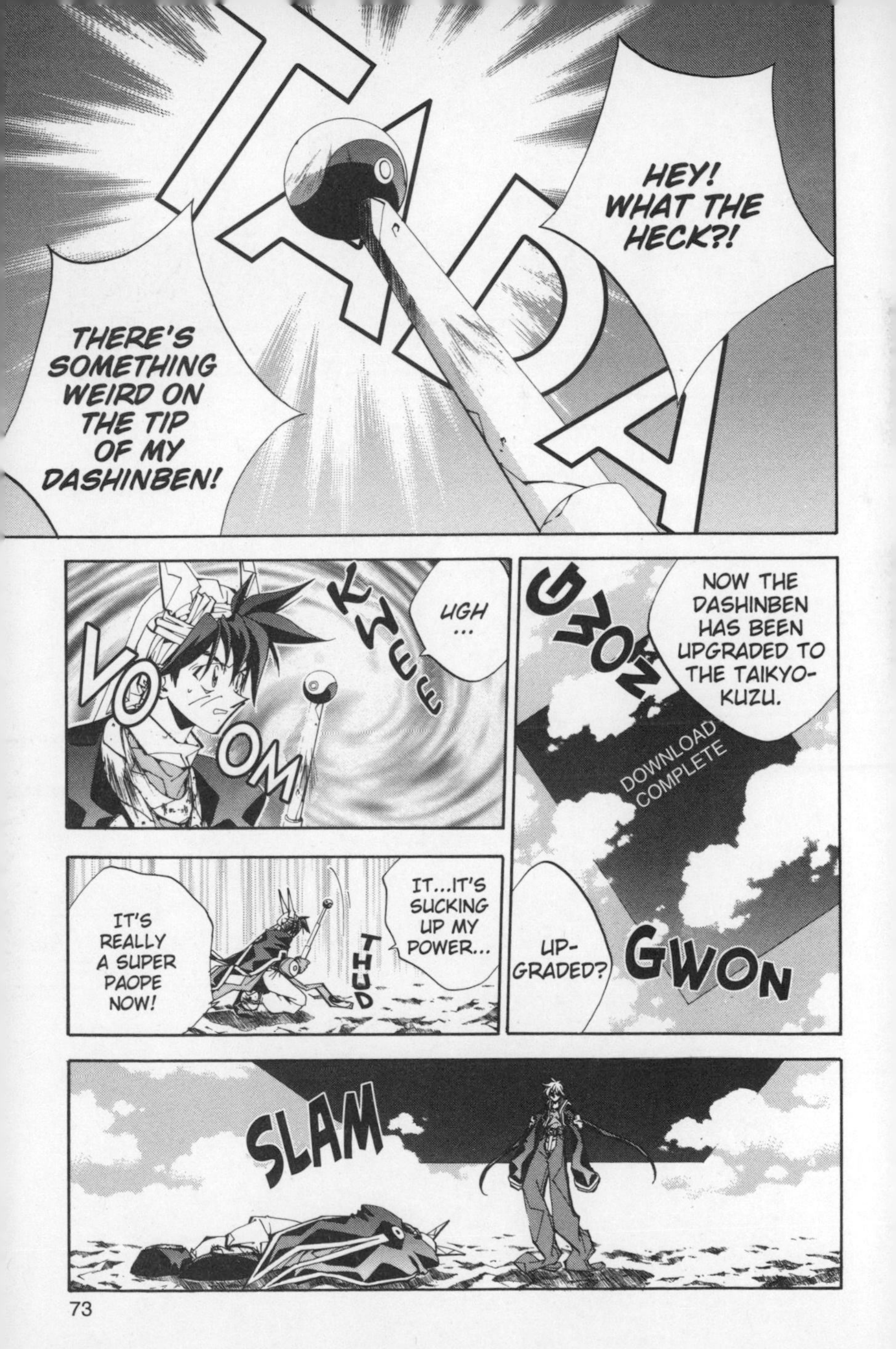
HEY! WHAT THE HECK?!
TADA
THERE'S SOMETHING WEIRD ON THE TIP OF MY DASHINBEN!
GWOON
NOW THE DASHINBEN HAS BEEN UPGRADED TO THE TAIKYO-KUZU.
DOWNLOAD COMPLETE
UP-GRADED?
GWON
KWEEE
UGH ...
VOOOM
IT...IT'S SUCKING UP MY POWER...
THUD
IT'S REALLY A SUPER PAOPE NOW!
SLAM

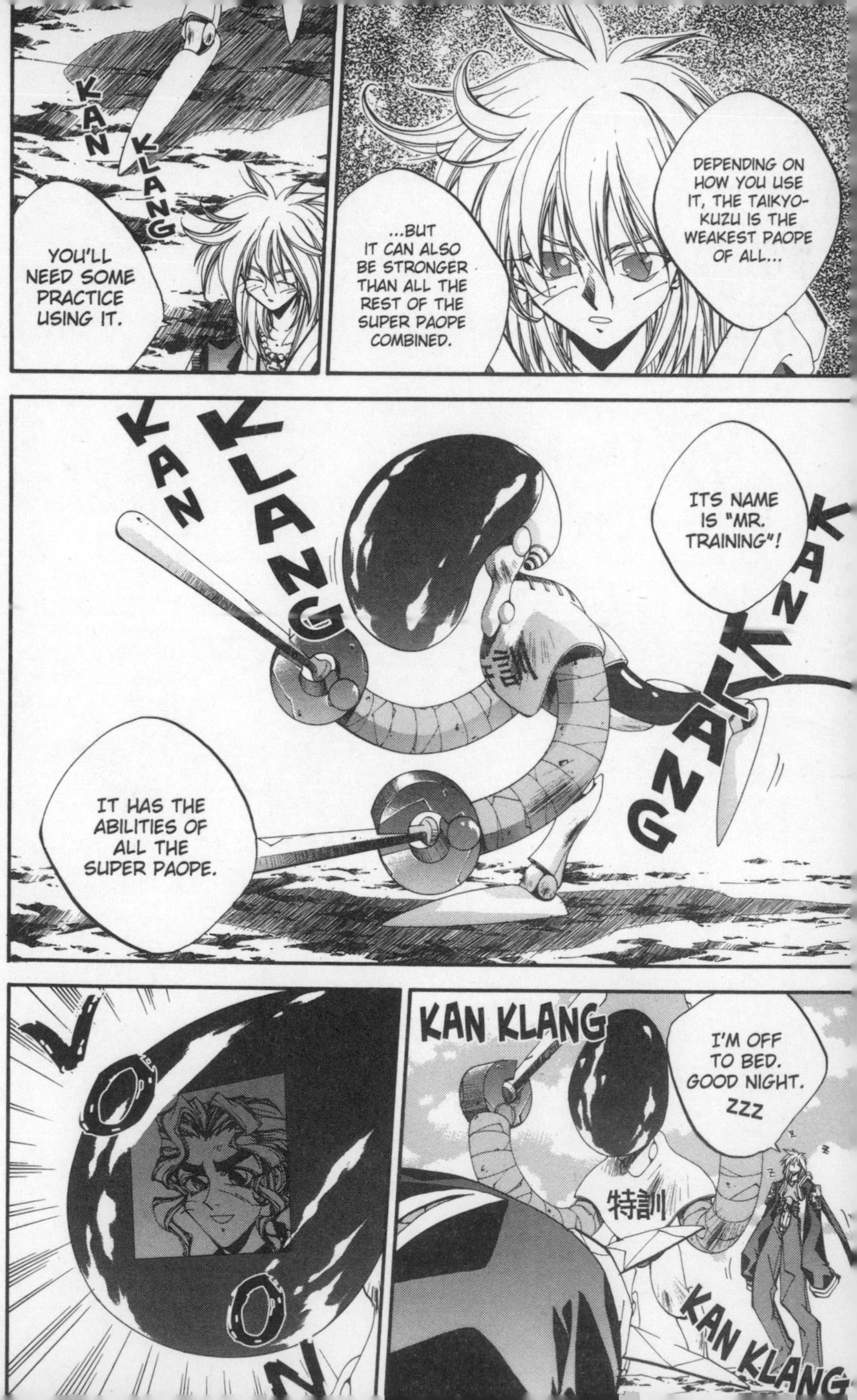
DEPENDING ON HOW YOU USE IT, THE TAIKYO-KUZU IS THE WEAKEST PAOPE OF ALL...
...BUT IT CAN ALSO BE STRONGER THAN ALL THE REST OF THE SUPER PAOPE COMBINED.
KAN KLANG
YOU'LL NEED SOME PRACTICE USING IT.
ITS NAME IS "MR. TRAINING"!
KAN KLANG
KAN KLANG
IT HAS THE ABILITIES OF ALL THE SUPER PAOPE.
I'M OFF TO BED. GOOD NIGHT. ZZZ
KAN KLANG
特訓
KAN KLANG
VOON

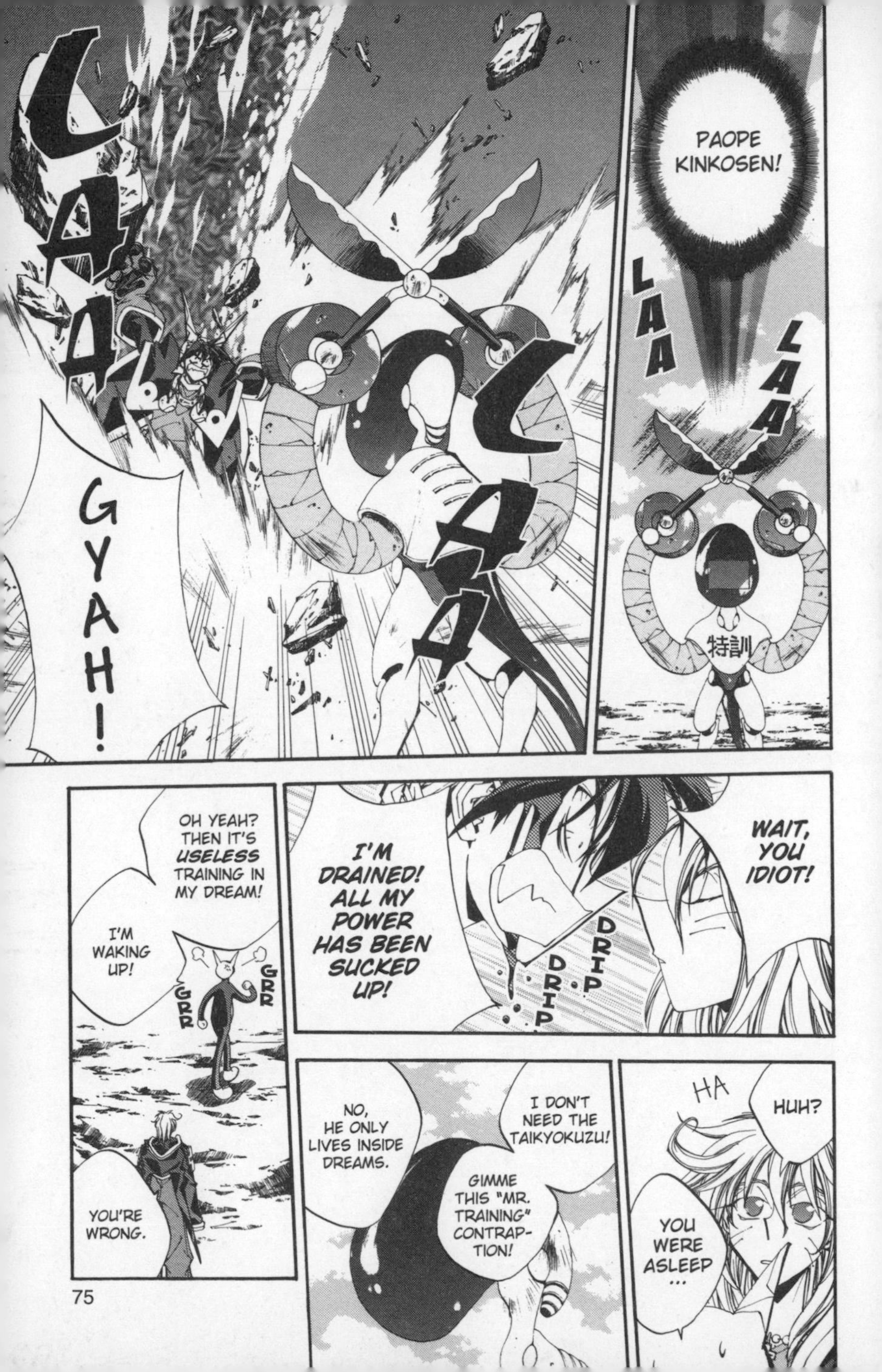

PAOPE KINKOSEN!
LAA
LAA
特訓
LAAA
GYAH!
LAAA
WAIT, YOU IDIOT!
I'M DRAINED! ALL MY POWER HAS BEEN SUCKED UP!
DRIP
DRIP
HA
HUH?
YOU WERE ASLEEP...
I DON'T NEED THE TAIKYOKUZU!
NO, HE ONLY LIVES INSIDE DREAMS.
GIMME THIS "MR. TRAINING" CONTRAPTION!
OH YEAH? THEN IT'S *USELESS* TRAINING IN MY DREAM!
I'M WAKING UP!
GRR
GRR
YOU'RE WRONG.

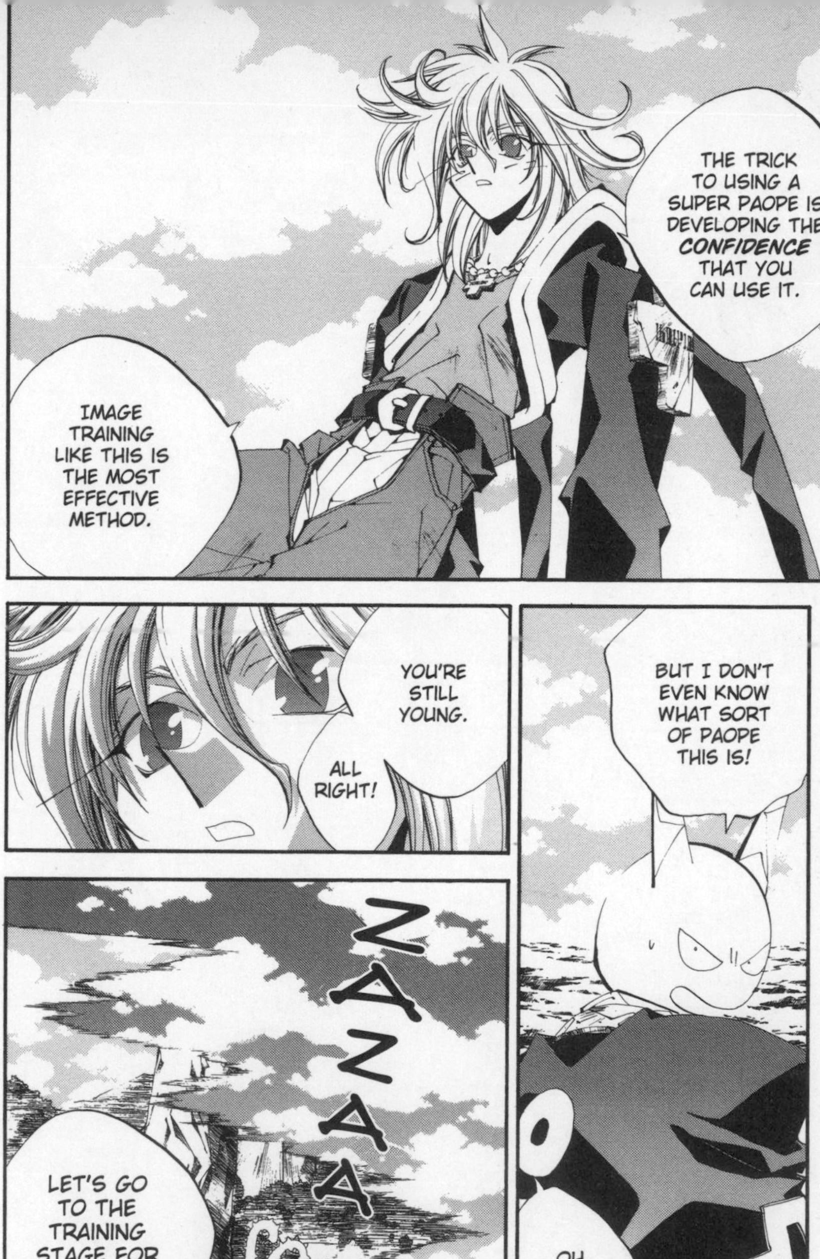
THE TRICK TO USING A SUPER PAOPE IS DEVELOPING THE ***CONFIDENCE*** THAT YOU CAN USE IT.
IMAGE TRAINING LIKE THIS IS THE MOST EFFECTIVE METHOD.
BUT I DON'T EVEN KNOW WHAT SORT OF PAOPE THIS IS!
OH, SORRY.
YOU'RE STILL YOUNG.
ALL RIGHT!
ZAZAA
LET'S GO TO THE TRAINING STAGE FOR BEGINNERS!

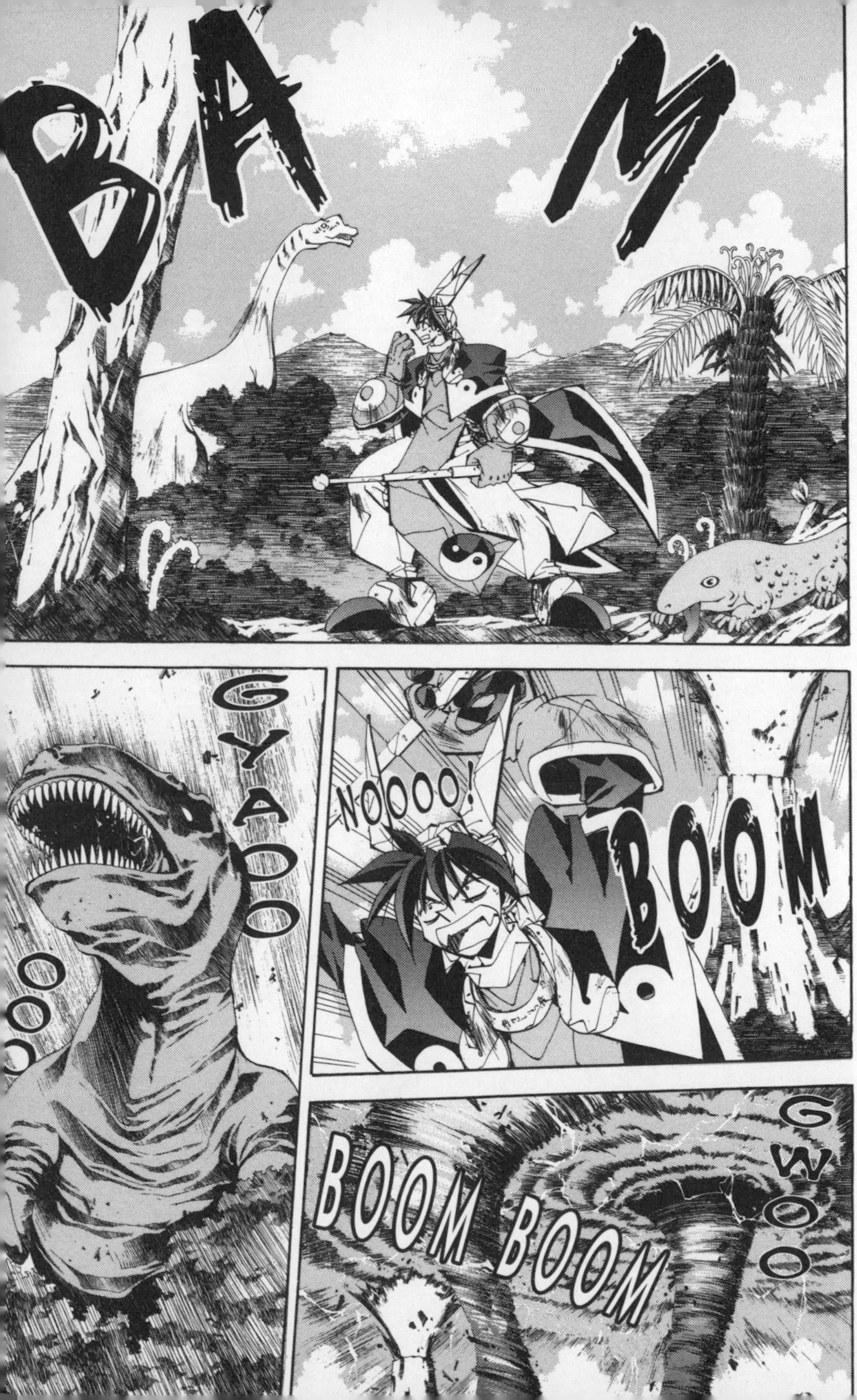
BAM
NOOOO!
BOOM
GWOO
BOOM BOOM
GYAOOO
OOOO

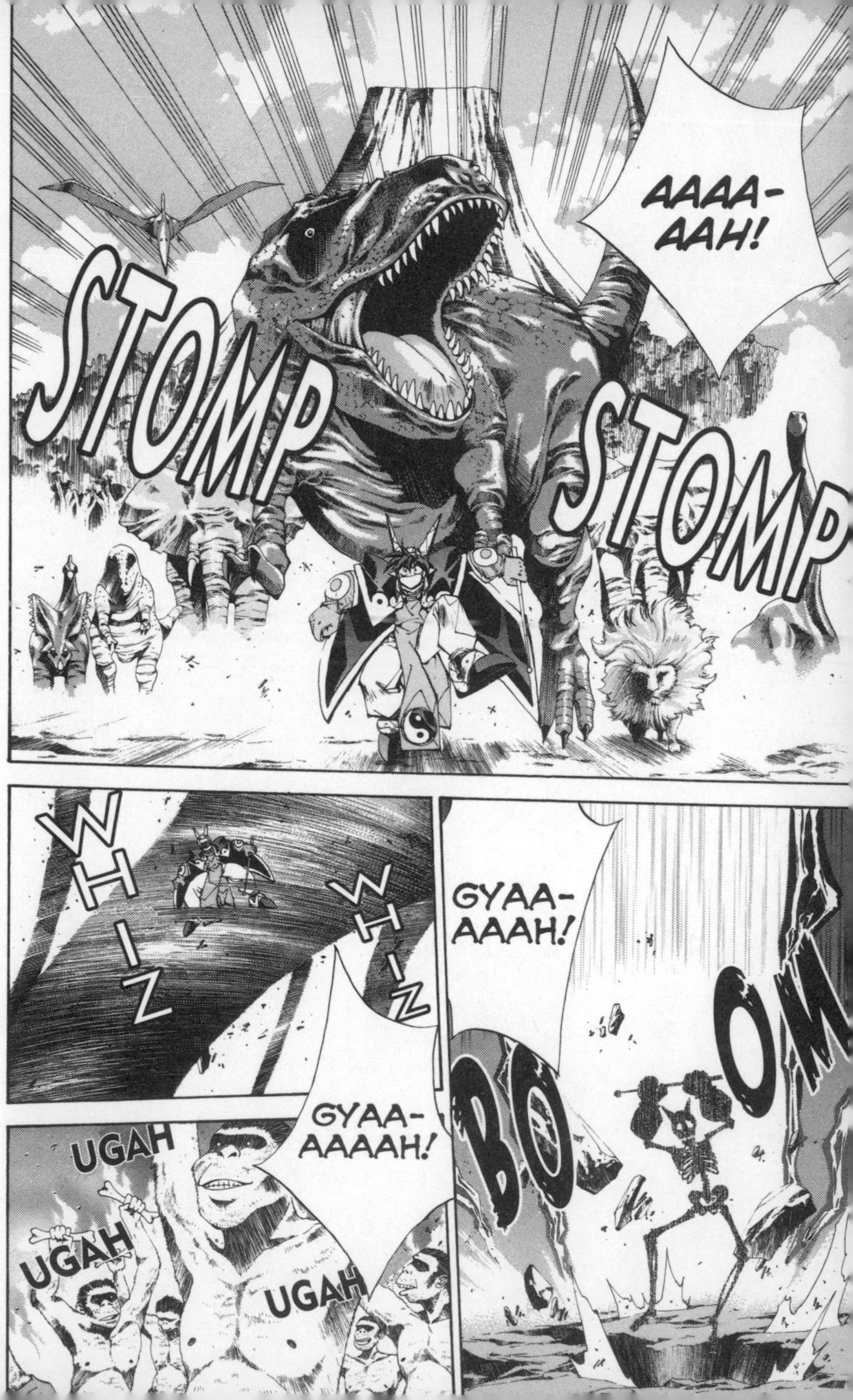
AAAA-
AAH!
STOMP
STOMP
GYAA-
AAAH!
BOOM
WHIZ
WHIZ
GYAA-
AAAAH!
UGAH
UGAH
UGAH

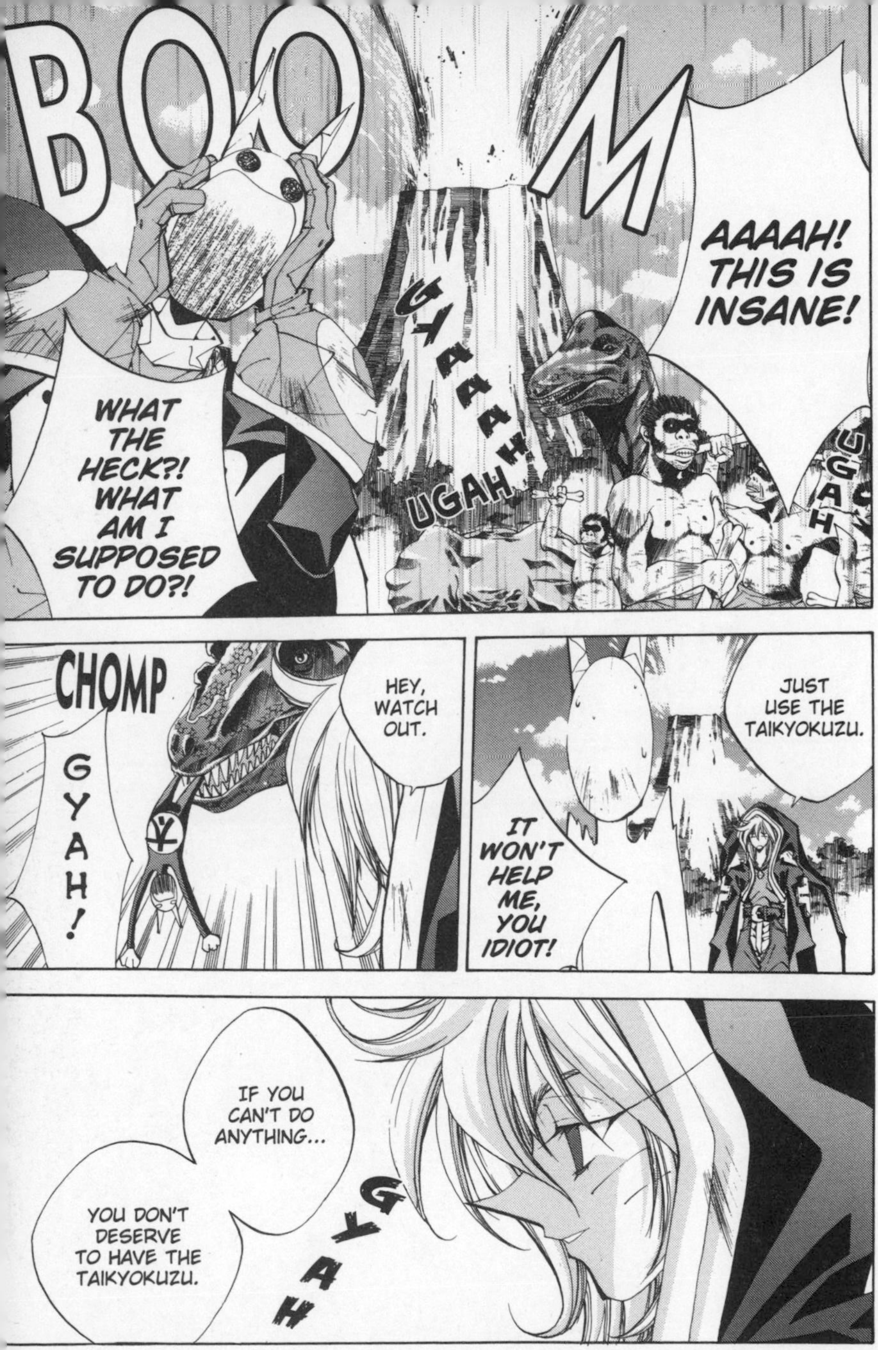
BOOM
AAAAH! THIS IS INSANE!
UGAH
GYAAAH
UGAH
WHAT THE HECK?! WHAT AM I SUPPOSED TO DO?!
JUST USE THE TAIKYOKUZU.
IT WON'T HELP ME, YOU IDIOT!
HEY, WATCH OUT.
CHOMP
GYAH!
IF YOU CAN'T DO ANYTHING...
GYAH
YOU DON'T DESERVE TO HAVE THE TAIKYOKUZU.

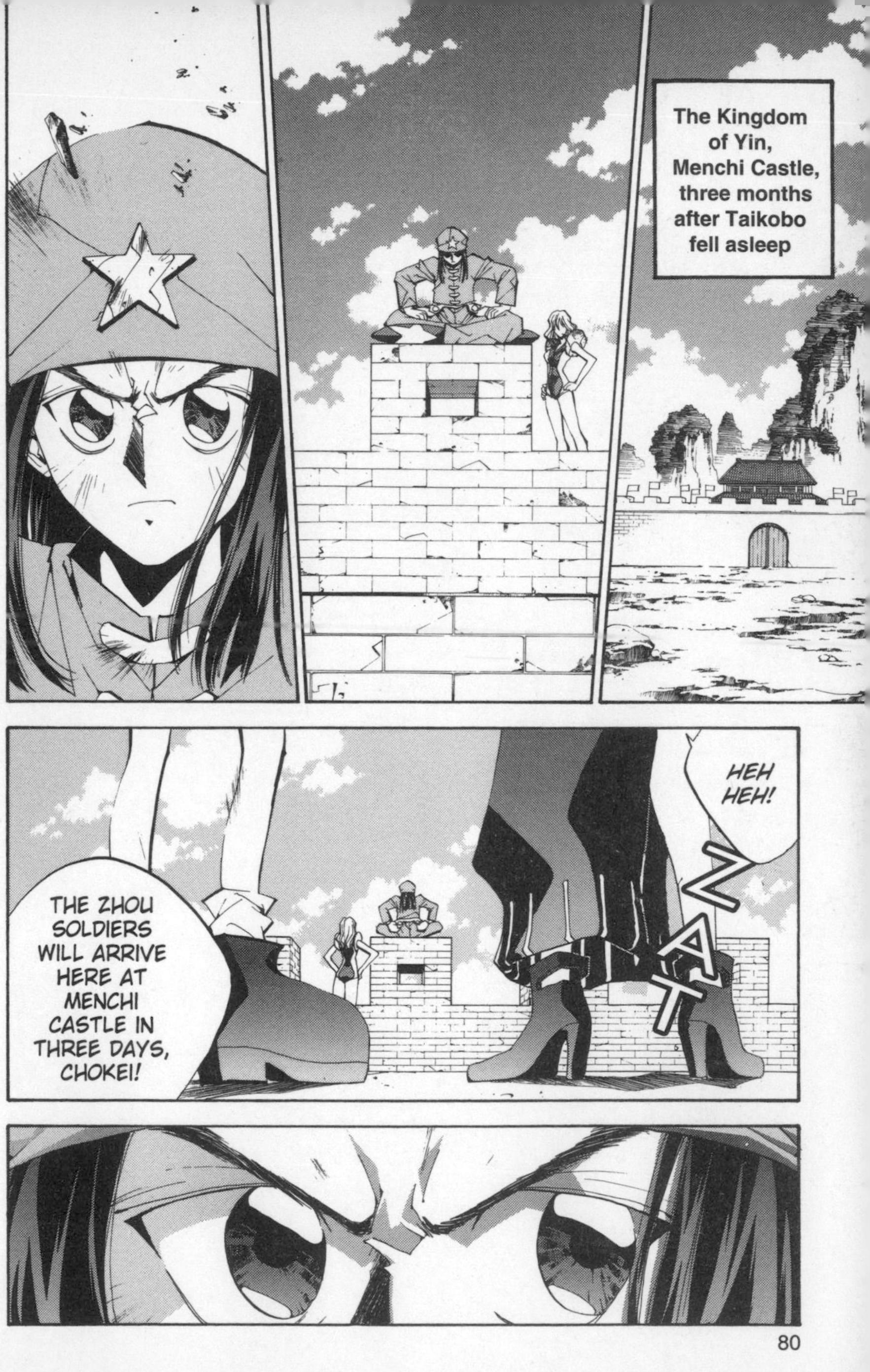
The Kingdom of Yin, Menchi Castle, three months after Taikobo fell asleep
HEH HEH!
ZAT
THE ZHOU SOLDIERS WILL ARRIVE HERE AT MENCHI CASTLE IN THREE DAYS, CHOKEI!

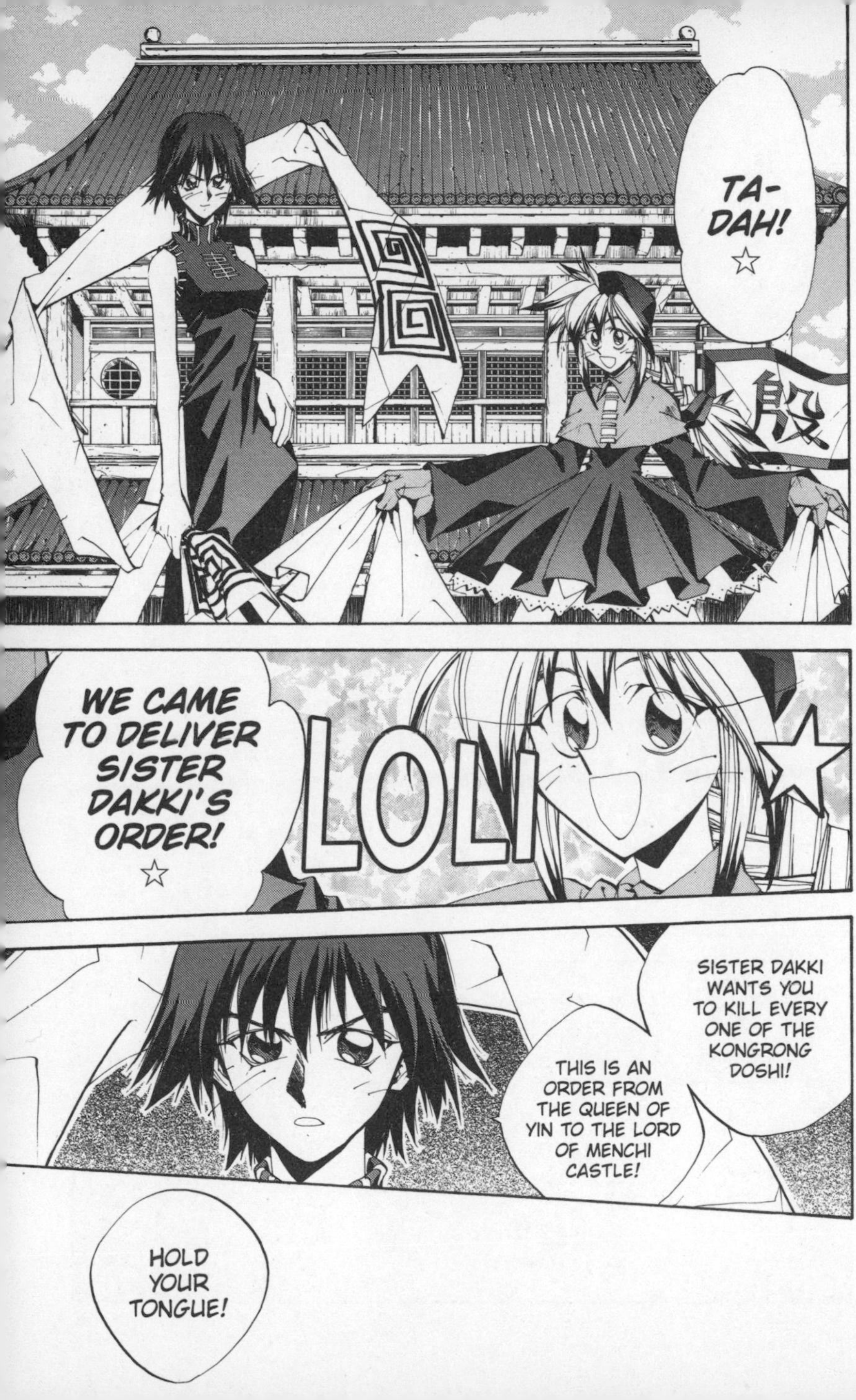
TA-DAH! ☆
殷
LOLI
WE CAME TO DELIVER SISTER DAKKI'S ORDER! ☆
SISTER DAKKI WANTS YOU TO KILL EVERY ONE OF THE KONGRONG DOSHI!
THIS IS AN ORDER FROM THE QUEEN OF YIN TO THE LORD OF MENCHI CASTLE!
HOLD YOUR TONGUE!

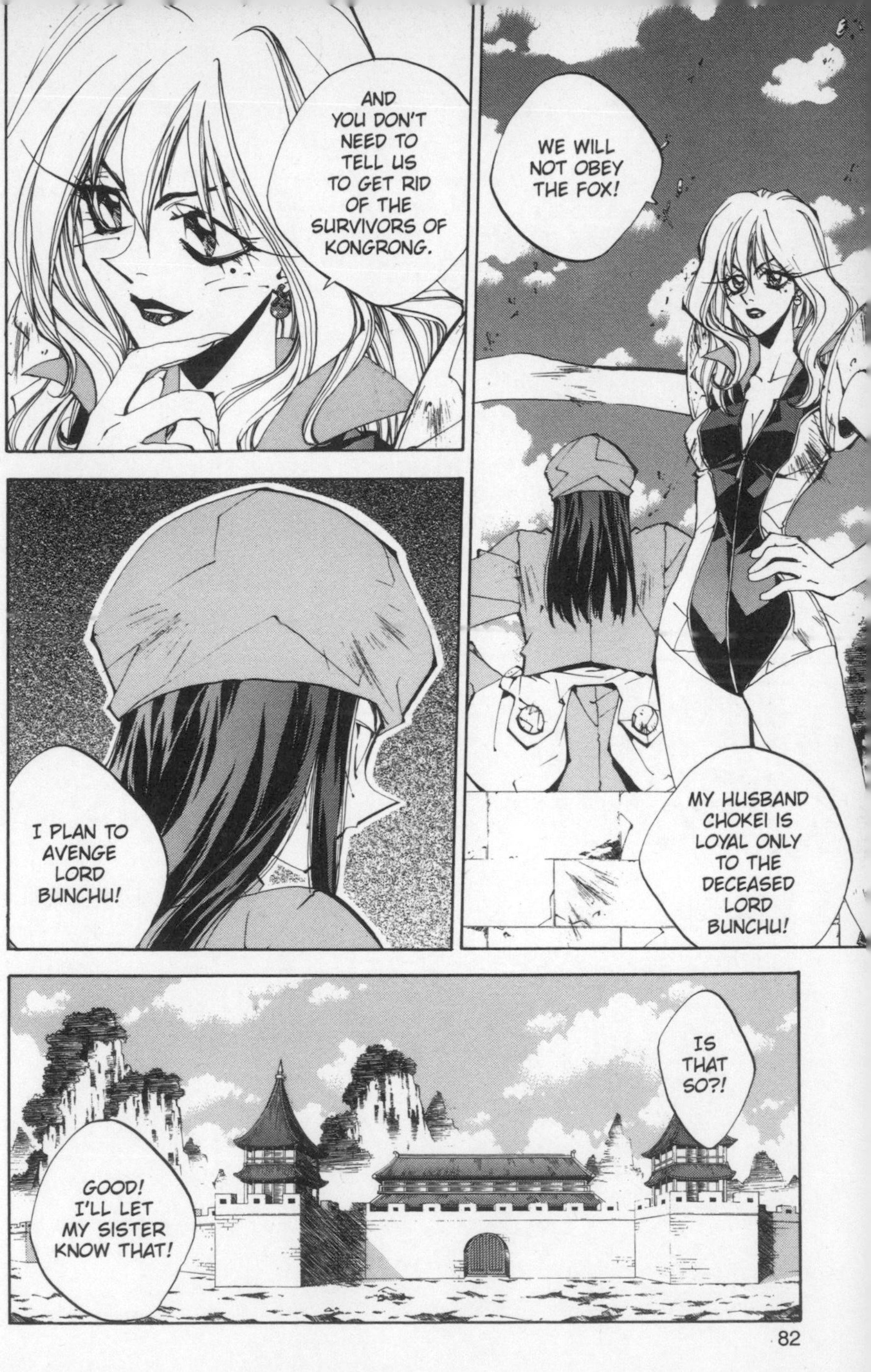
WE WILL NOT OBEY THE FOX!
MY HUSBAND CHOKEI IS LOYAL ONLY TO THE DECEASED LORD BUNCHU!
AND YOU DON'T NEED TO TELL US TO GET RID OF THE SURVIVORS OF KONGRONG.
I PLAN TO AVENGE LORD BUNCHU!
IS THAT SO?!
GOOD! I'LL LET MY SISTER KNOW THAT!

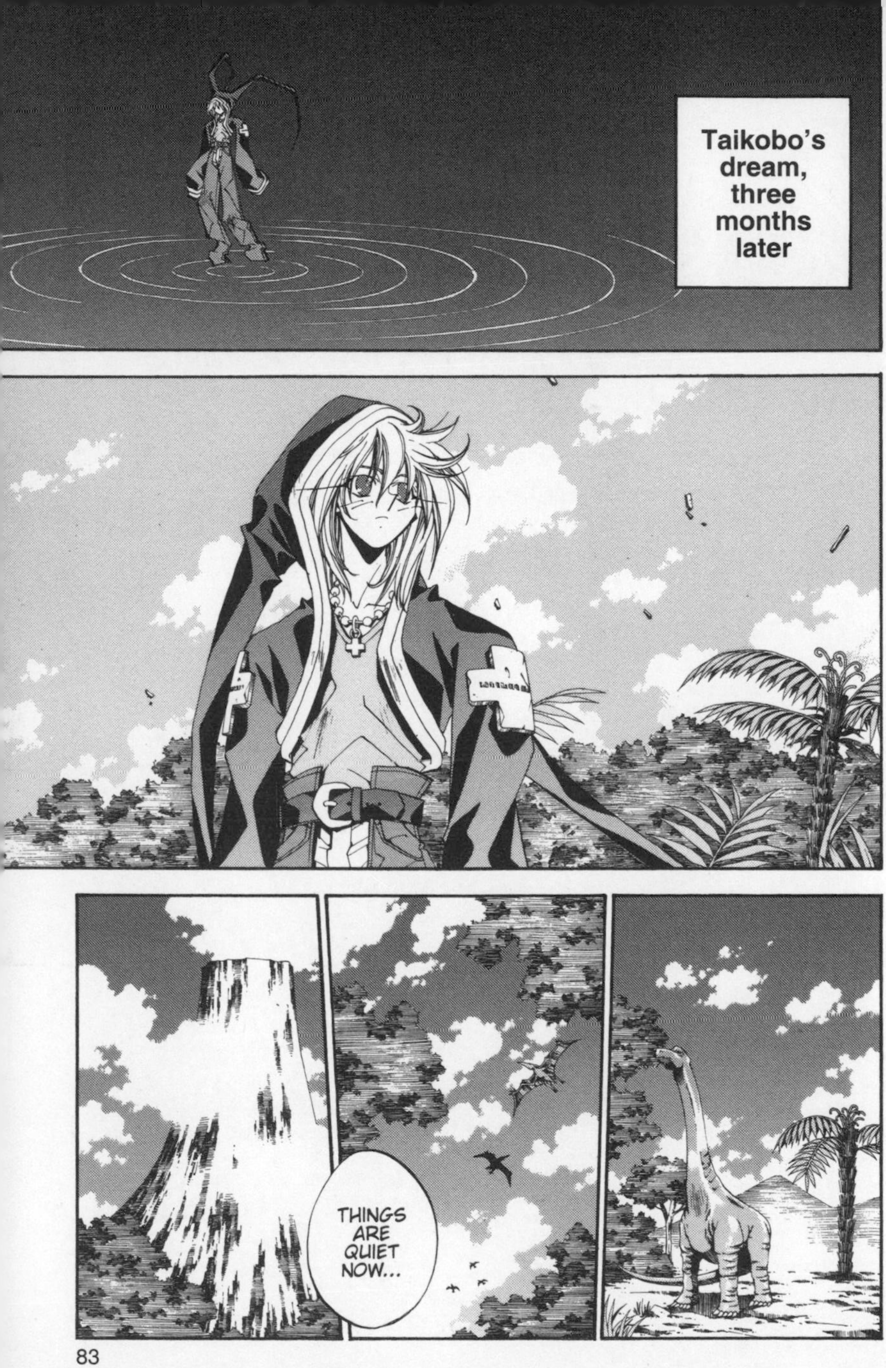
Taikobo's dream, three months later
THINGS ARE QUIET NOW...

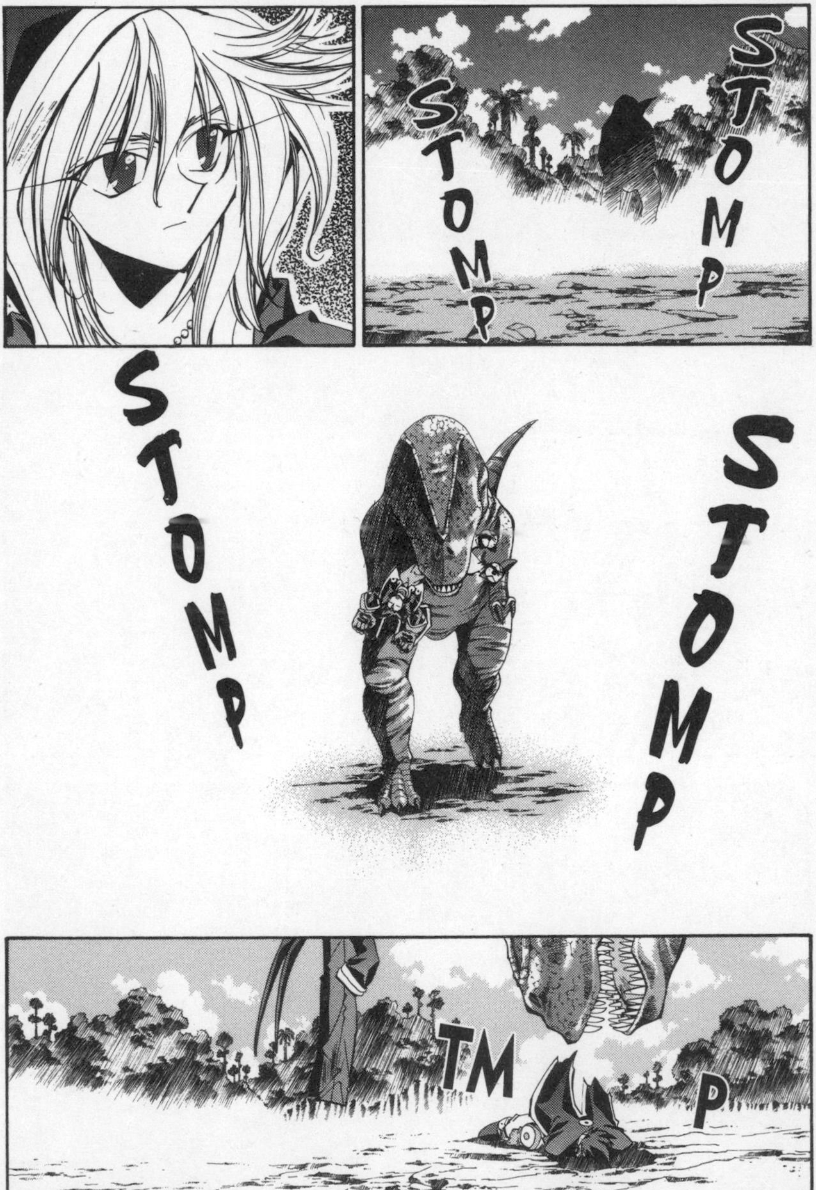
STOMP
STOMP
STOMP
STOMP
TM P

READ THIS WAY

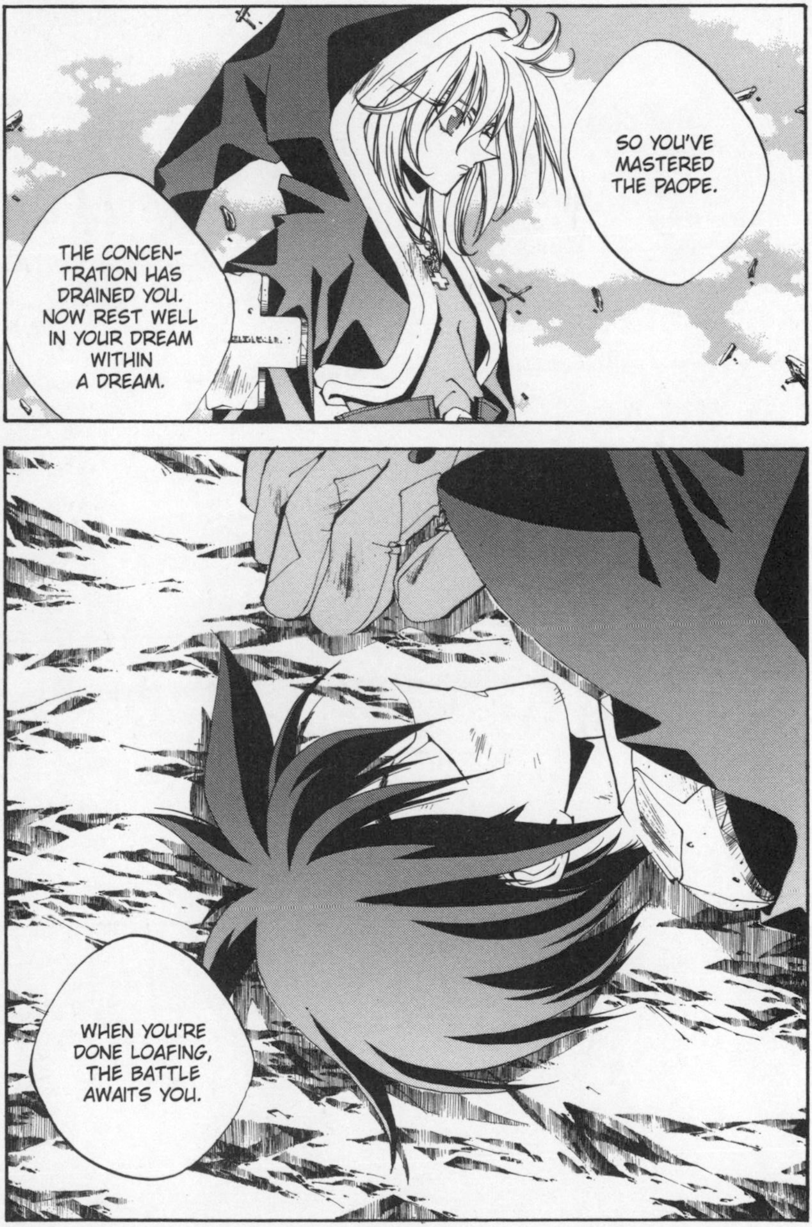
SO YOU'VE MASTERED THE PAOPE.
THE CONCEN-TRATION HAS DRAINED YOU. NOW REST WELL IN YOUR DREAM WITHIN A DREAM.
WHEN YOU'RE DONE LOAFING, THE BATTLE AWAITS YOU.

封神演義

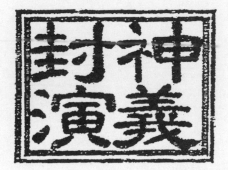

Chapter 156

THE ADVENTURE OF TAIJO ROKUN, PART 8
AWAKENING

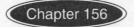

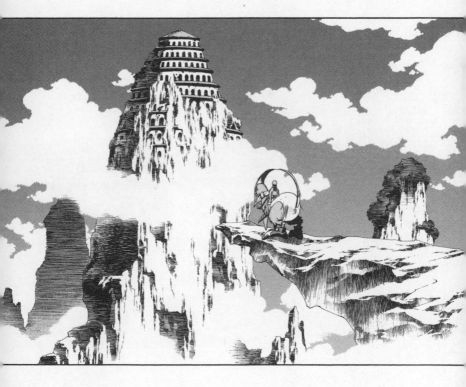

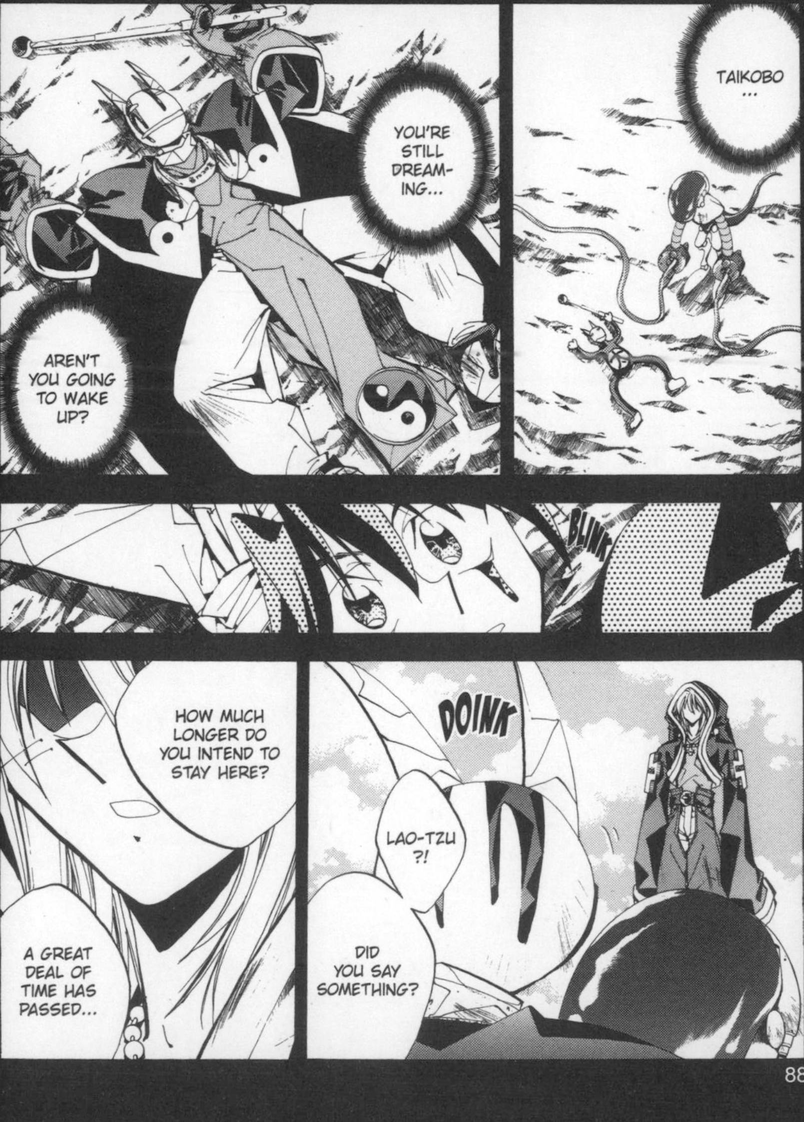
TAIKOBO...
YOU'RE STILL DREAMING...
AREN'T YOU GOING TO WAKE UP?
BLINK
DOINK
LAO-TZU?!
DID YOU SAY SOMETHING?
HOW MUCH LONGER DO YOU INTEND TO STAY HERE?
A GREAT DEAL OF TIME HAS PASSED...

READ THIS WAY

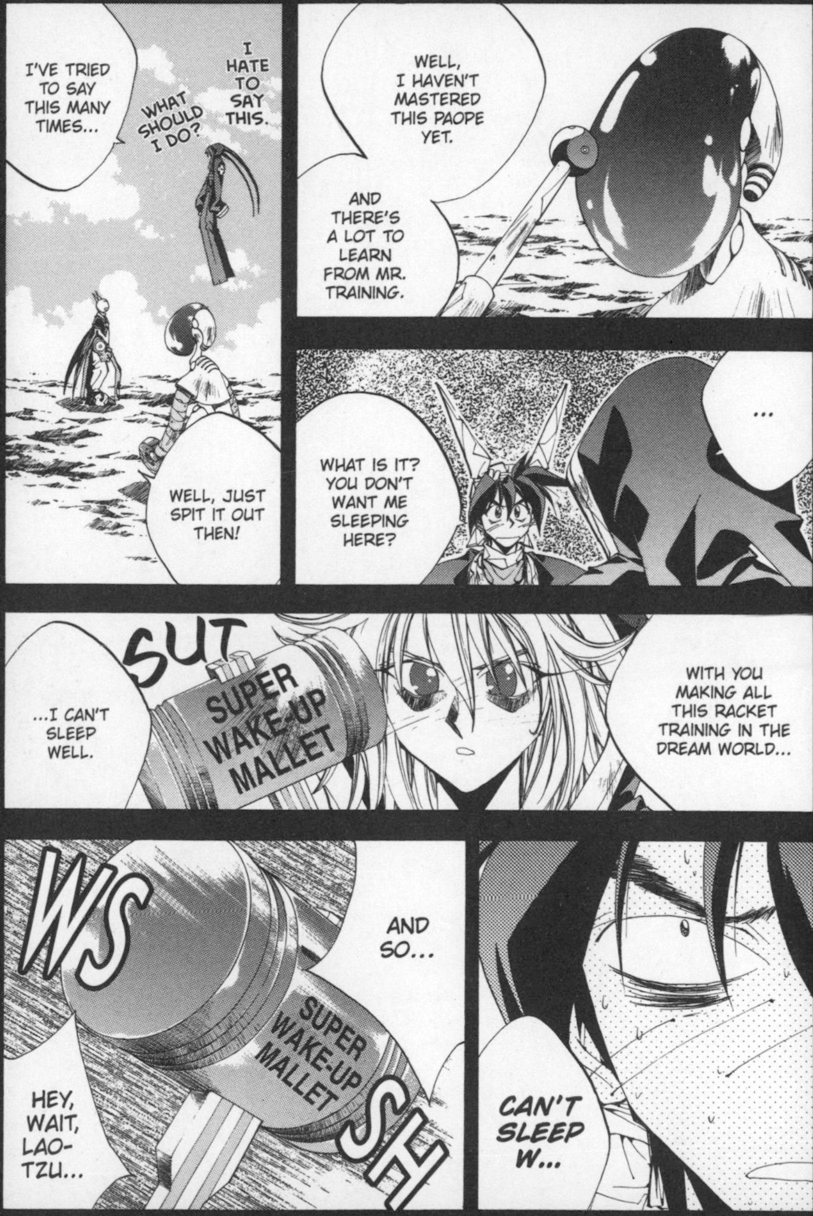

WELL, I HAVEN'T MASTERED THIS PAOPE YET.
AND THERE'S A LOT TO LEARN FROM MR. TRAINING.
...
WHAT IS IT? YOU DON'T WANT ME SLEEPING HERE?
I HATE TO SAY THIS.
WHAT SHOULD I DO?
I'VE TRIED TO SAY THIS MANY TIMES...
WELL, JUST SPIT IT OUT THEN!
WITH YOU MAKING ALL THIS RACKET TRAINING IN THE DREAM WORLD...
SUT
SUPER WAKE-UP MALLET
...I CAN'T SLEEP WELL.
CAN'T SLEEP W...
AND SO...
WS
SUPER WAKE-UP MALLET
SH
HEY, WAIT, LAO-TZU...

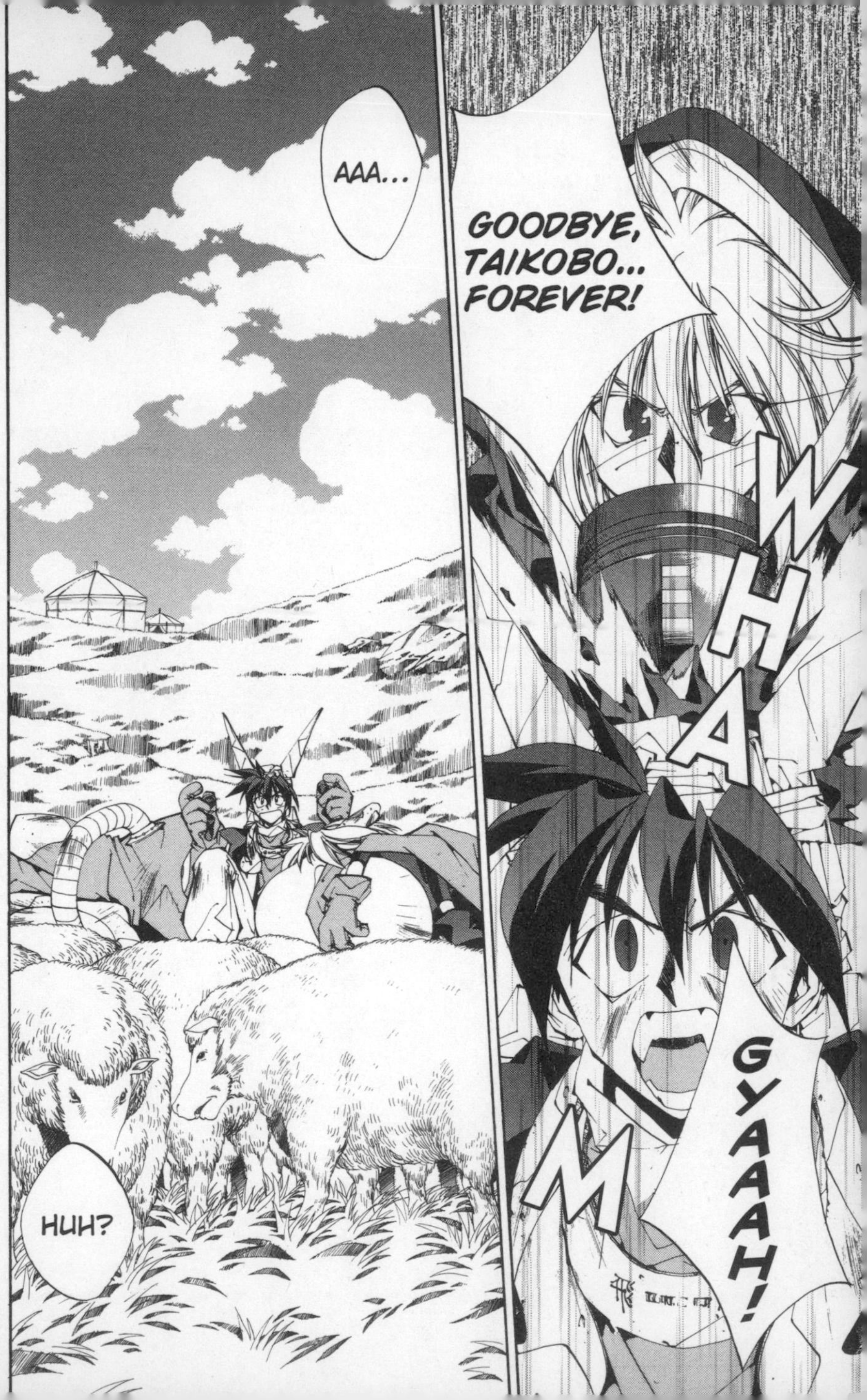
GOODBYE, TAIKOBO... FOREVER!
WHAM
GYAAAH!
AAA...
HUH?

READ THIS WAY

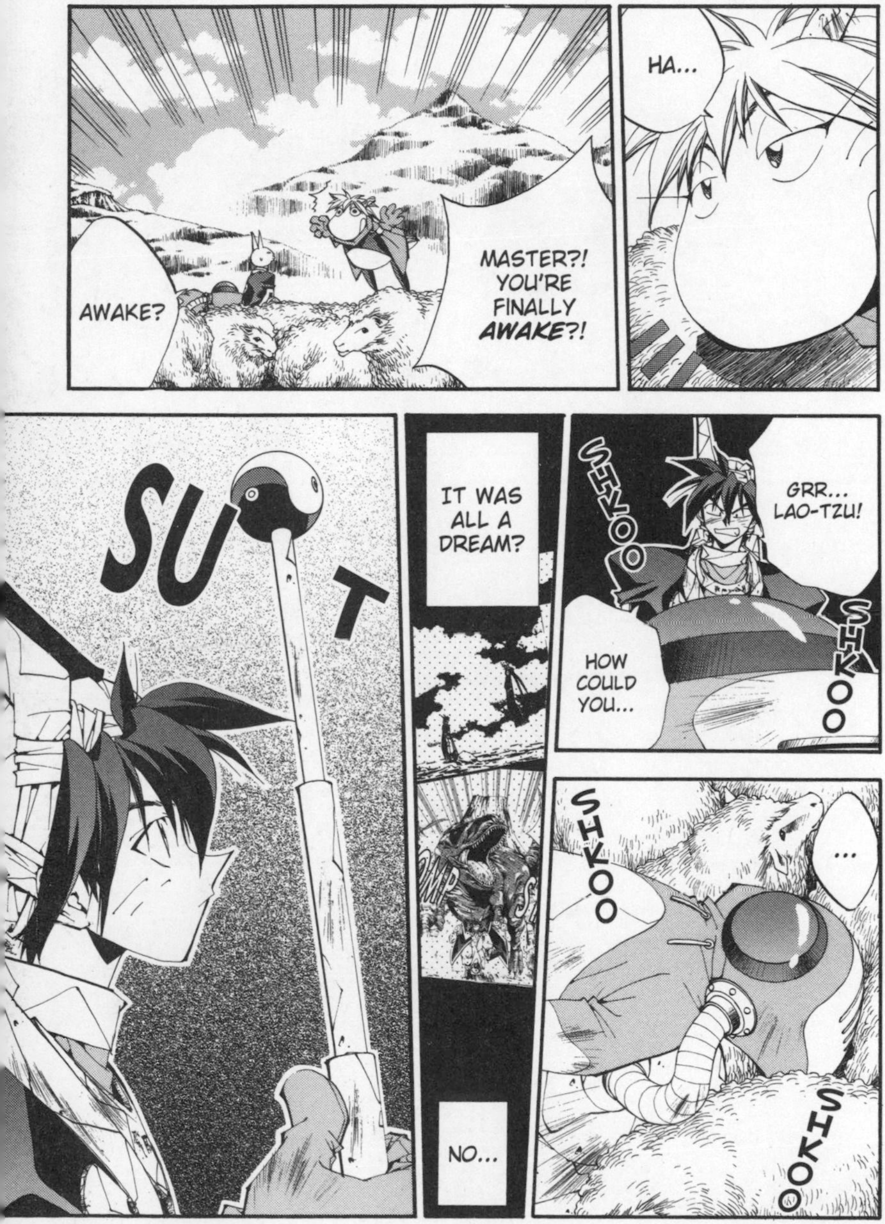
HA...
MASTER?! YOU'RE FINALLY **AWAKE**?!
AWAKE?
SHKOO
GRR... LAO-TZU!
HOW COULD YOU...
SHKOO
SHKOO
...
SHKOO
IT WAS ALL A DREAM?
NO...
SUT

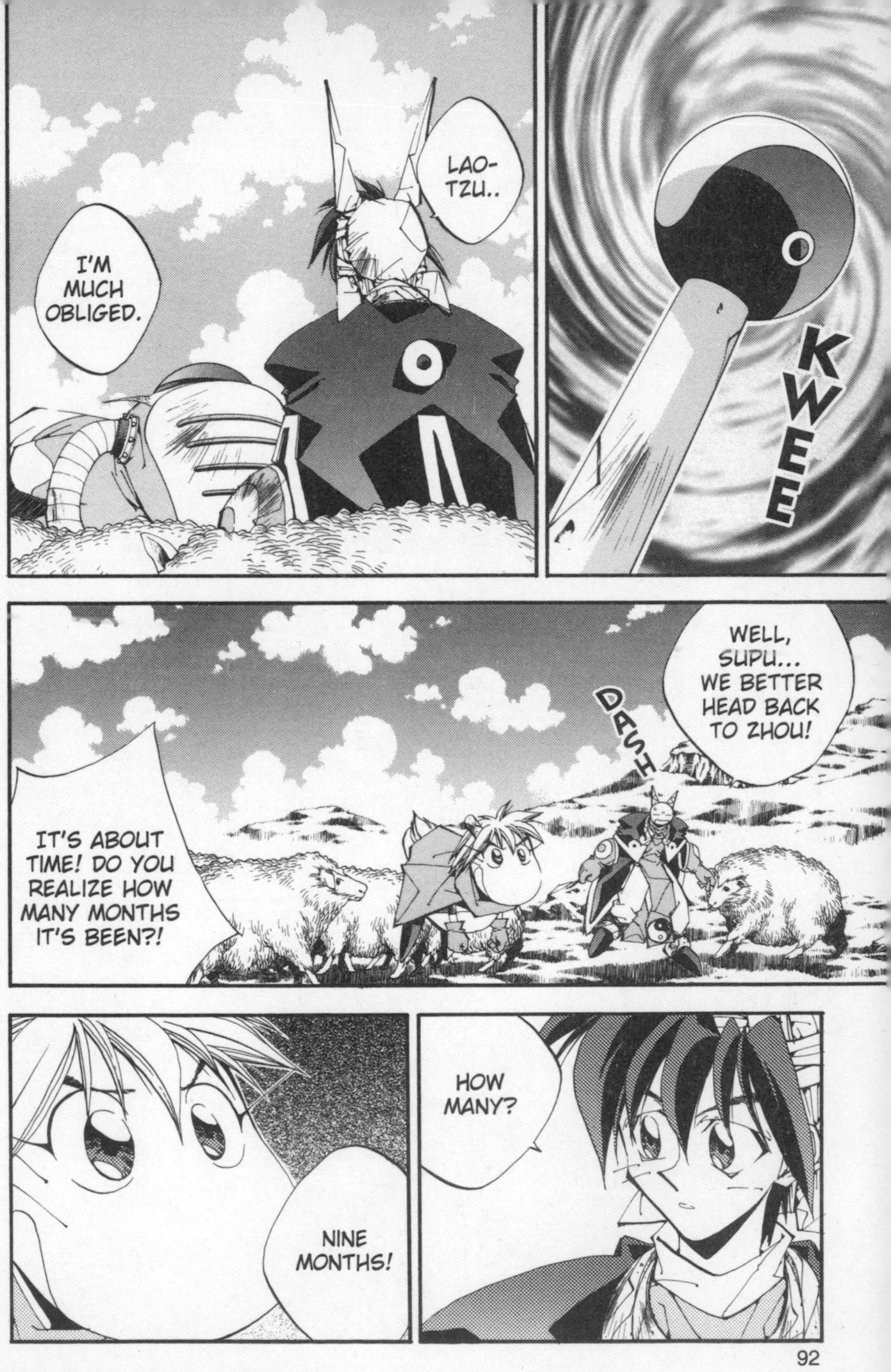
KWEE
LAO-TZU..
I'M MUCH OBLIGED.
WELL, SUPU... WE BETTER HEAD BACK TO ZHOU!
DASH
IT'S ABOUT TIME! DO YOU REALIZE HOW MANY MONTHS IT'S BEEN?!
HOW MANY?
NINE MONTHS!

READ THIS WAY

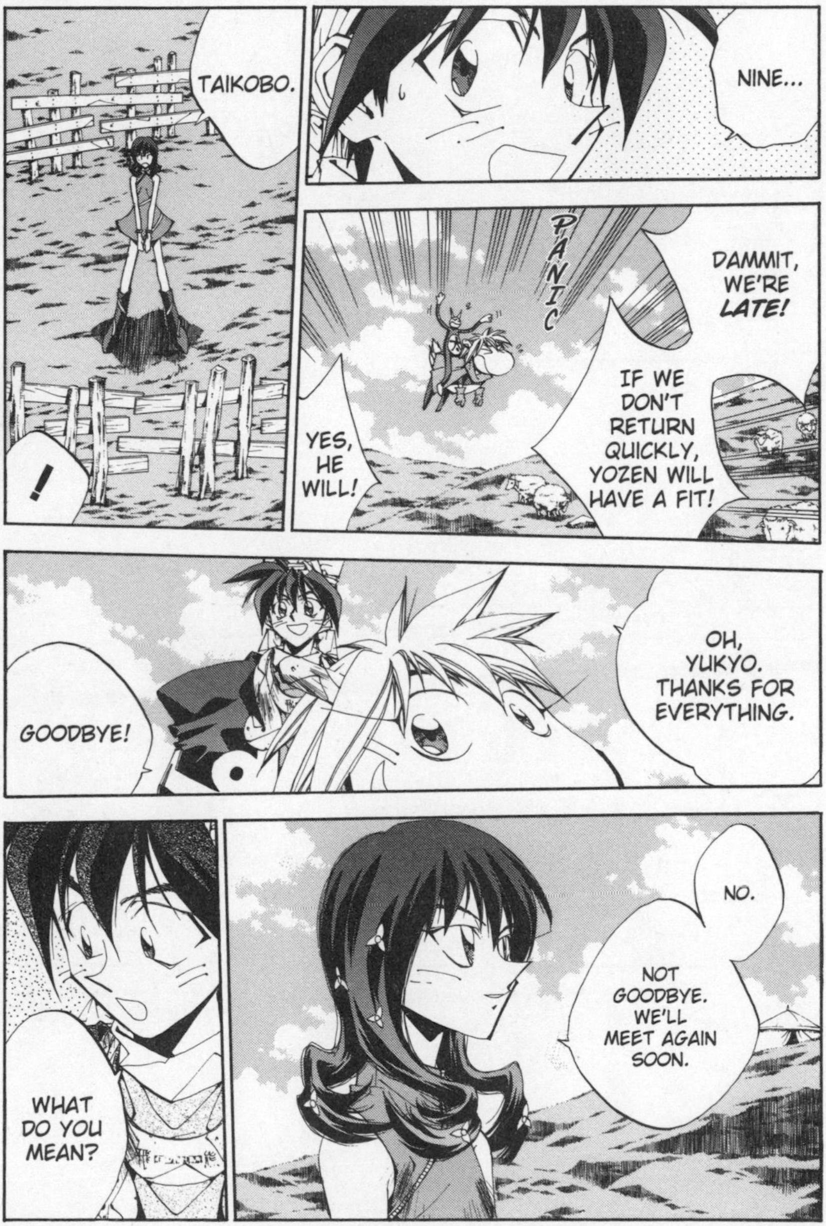
NINE...
PANIC
DAMMIT, WE'RE LATE!
IF WE DON'T RETURN QUICKLY, YOZEN WILL HAVE A FIT!
YES, HE WILL!
TAIKOBO.
!
OH, YUKYO. THANKS FOR EVERYTHING.
GOODBYE!
NO.
NOT GOODBYE. WE'LL MEET AGAIN SOON.
WHAT DO YOU MEAN?

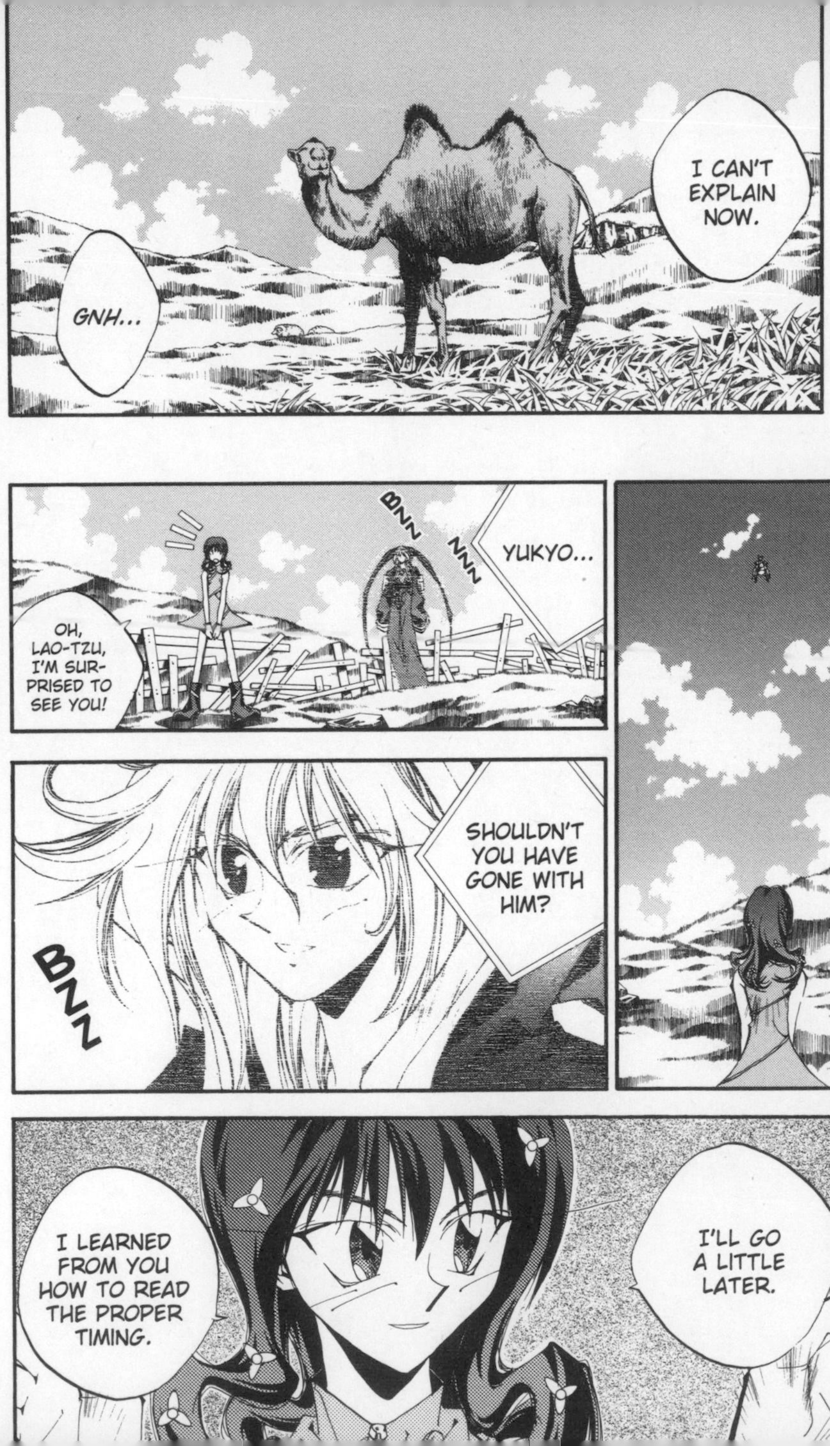
I CAN'T EXPLAIN NOW.
GNH...
YUKYO...
BNN NNN
OH, LAO-TZU, I'M SUR-PRISED TO SEE YOU!
SHOULDN'T YOU HAVE GONE WITH HIM?
BZZ
I'LL GO A LITTLE LATER.
I LEARNED FROM YOU HOW TO READ THE PROPER TIMING.

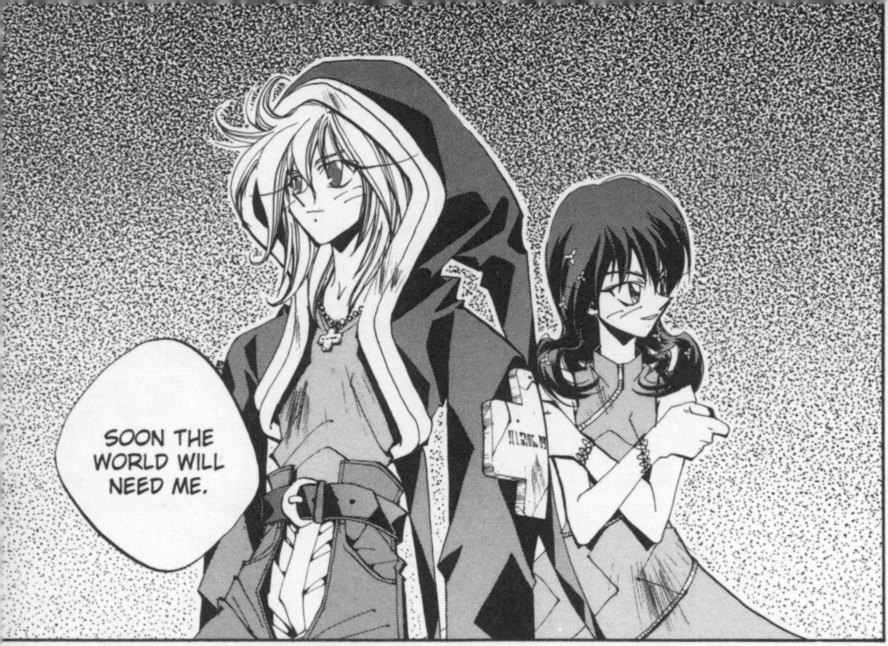
SOON THE WORLD WILL NEED ME.

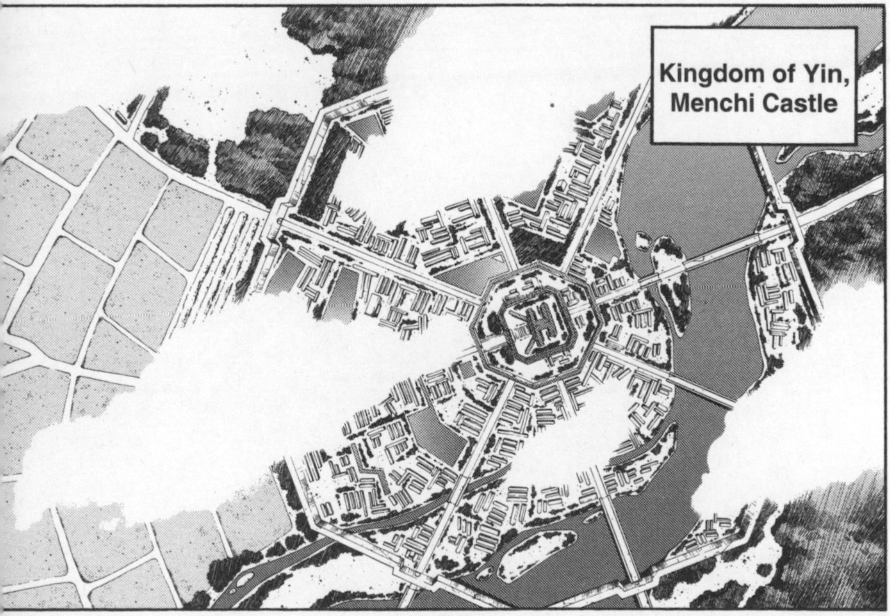
Kingdom of Yin, Menchi Castle

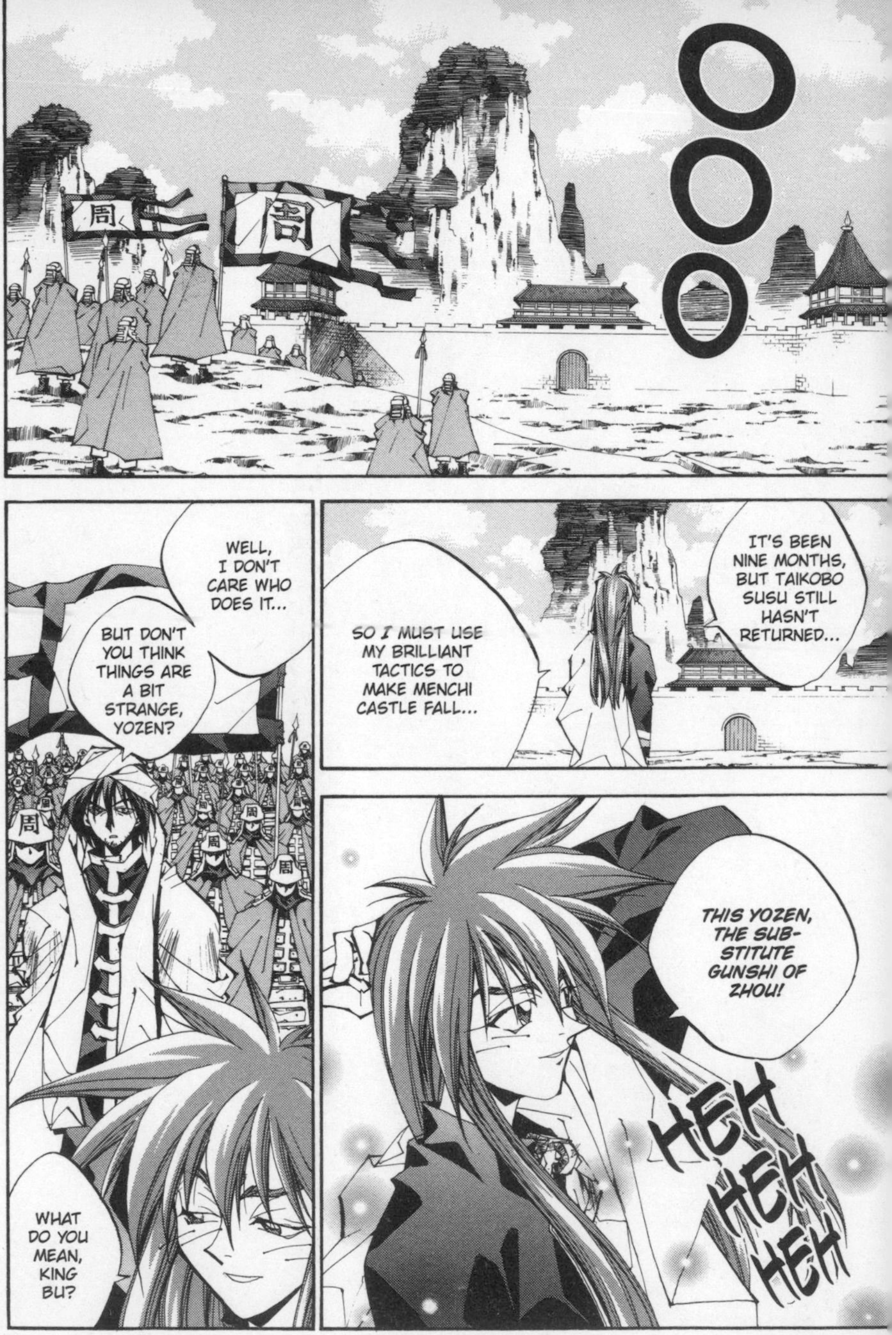
OOO
IT'S BEEN NINE MONTHS, BUT TAIKOBO SUSU STILL HASN'T RETURNED...
SO I MUST USE MY BRILLIANT TACTICS TO MAKE MENCHI CASTLE FALL...
THIS YOZEN, THE SUB-STITUTE GUNSHI OF ZHOU!
HEH HEH HEH
WELL, I DON'T CARE WHO DOES IT...
BUT DON'T YOU THINK THINGS ARE A BIT STRANGE, YOZEN?
WHAT DO YOU MEAN, KING BU?

READ THIS WAY

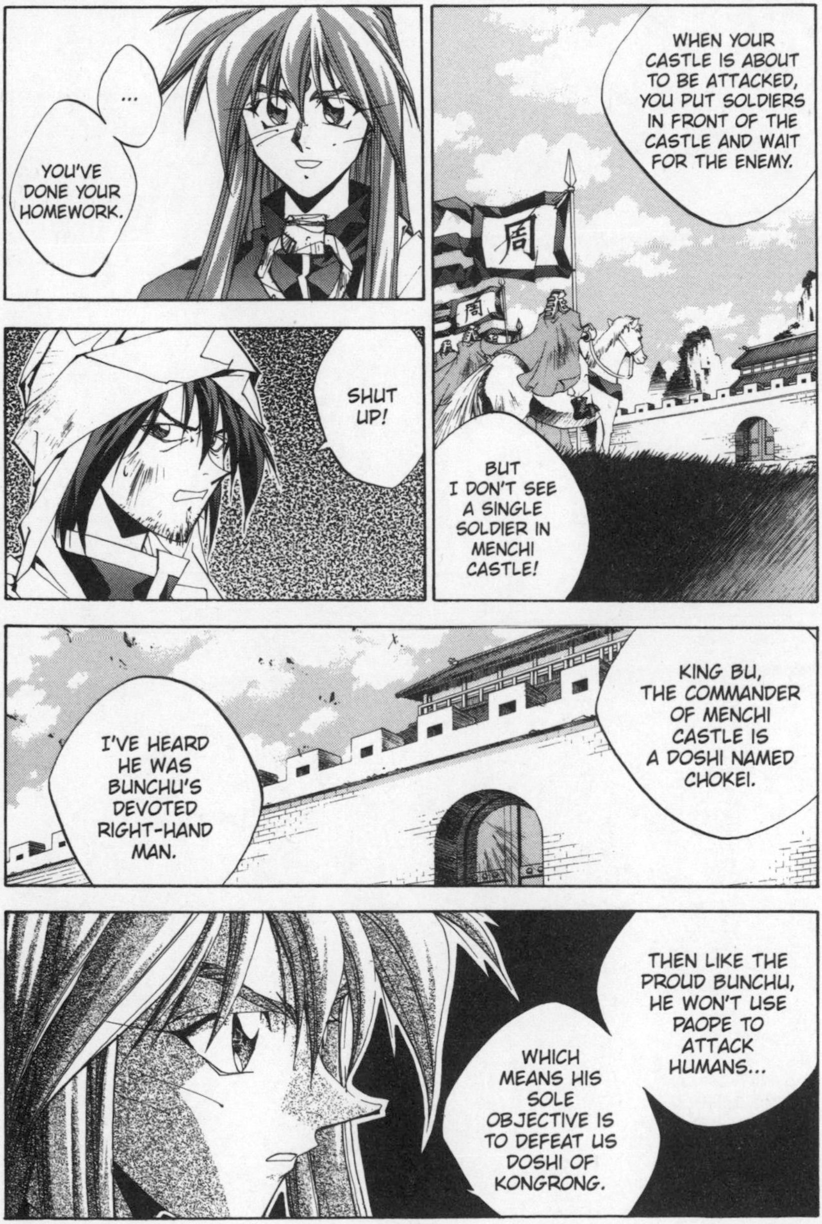

WHEN YOUR CASTLE IS ABOUT TO BE ATTACKED, YOU PUT SOLDIERS IN FRONT OF THE CASTLE AND WAIT FOR THE ENEMY.
BUT I DON'T SEE A SINGLE SOLDIER IN MENCHI CASTLE!
...
YOU'VE DONE YOUR HOMEWORK.
SHUT UP!
KING BU, THE COMMANDER OF MENCHI CASTLE IS A DOSHI NAMED CHOKEI.
I'VE HEARD HE WAS BUNCHU'S DEVOTED RIGHT-HAND MAN.
THEN LIKE THE PROUD BUNCHU, HE WON'T USE PAOPE TO ATTACK HUMANS...
WHICH MEANS HIS SOLE OBJECTIVE IS TO DEFEAT US DOSHI OF KONGRONG.

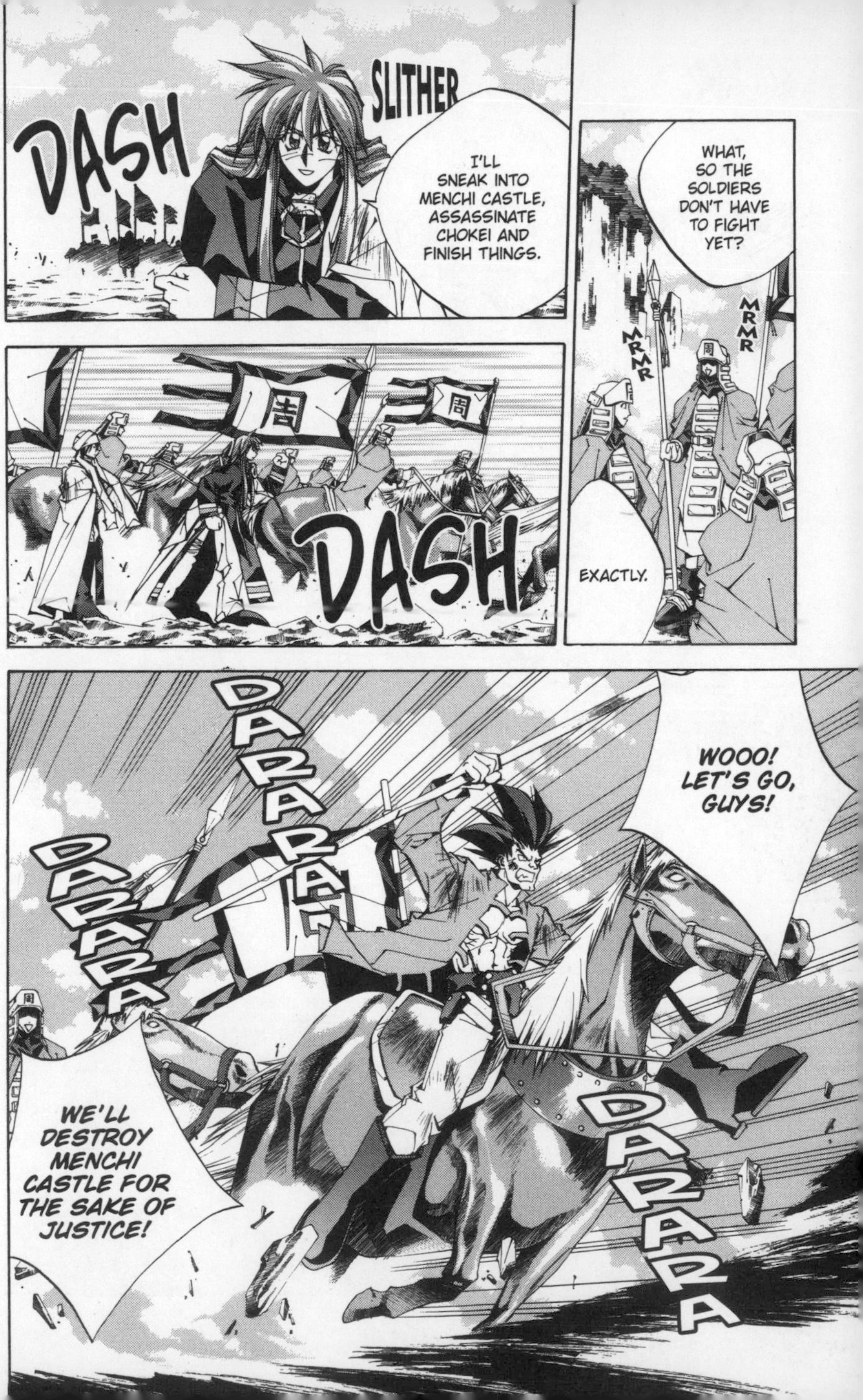
SLITHER
DASH
I'LL SNEAK INTO MENCHI CASTLE, ASSASSINATE CHOKEI AND FINISH THINGS.
DASH
WHAT, SO THE SOLDIERS DON'T HAVE TO FIGHT YET?
MRMR
MRMR
EXACTLY.
WOOO! LET'S GO, GUYS!
DARARA
DARARA
WE'LL DESTROY MENCHI CASTLE FOR THE SAKE OF JUSTICE!
DARARA

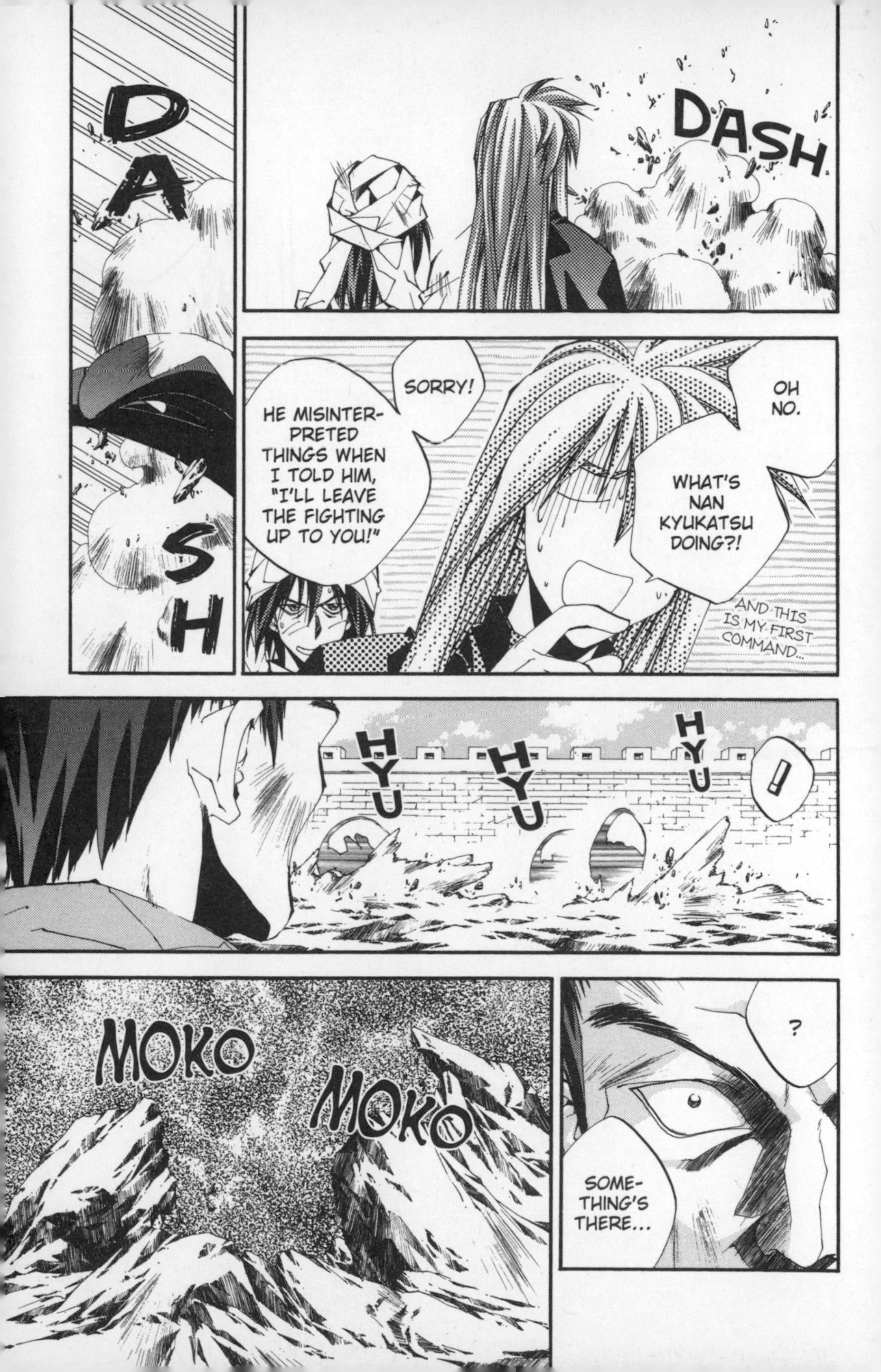
DASH
DASH
OH NO.
WHAT'S NAN KYUKATSU DOING?!
AND THIS IS MY FIRST COMMAND...
SORRY!
HE MISINTER-PRETED THINGS WHEN I TOLD HIM, "I'LL LEAVE THE FIGHTING UP TO YOU!"
HYU
HYU
HYU
!
?
SOME-THING'S THERE...
MOKO
MOKO

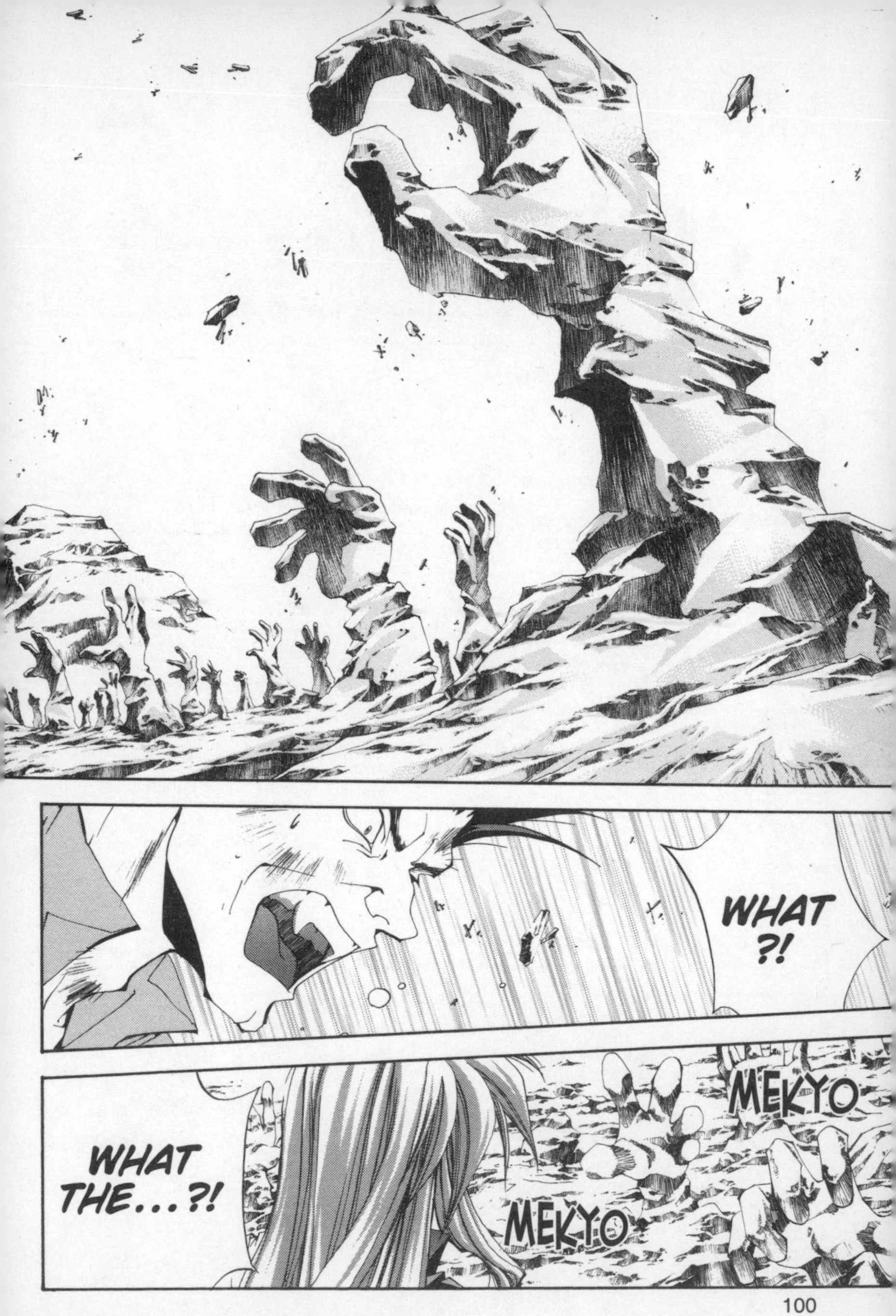
WHAT ?!
MEKYO
MEKYO
WHAT THE...?!

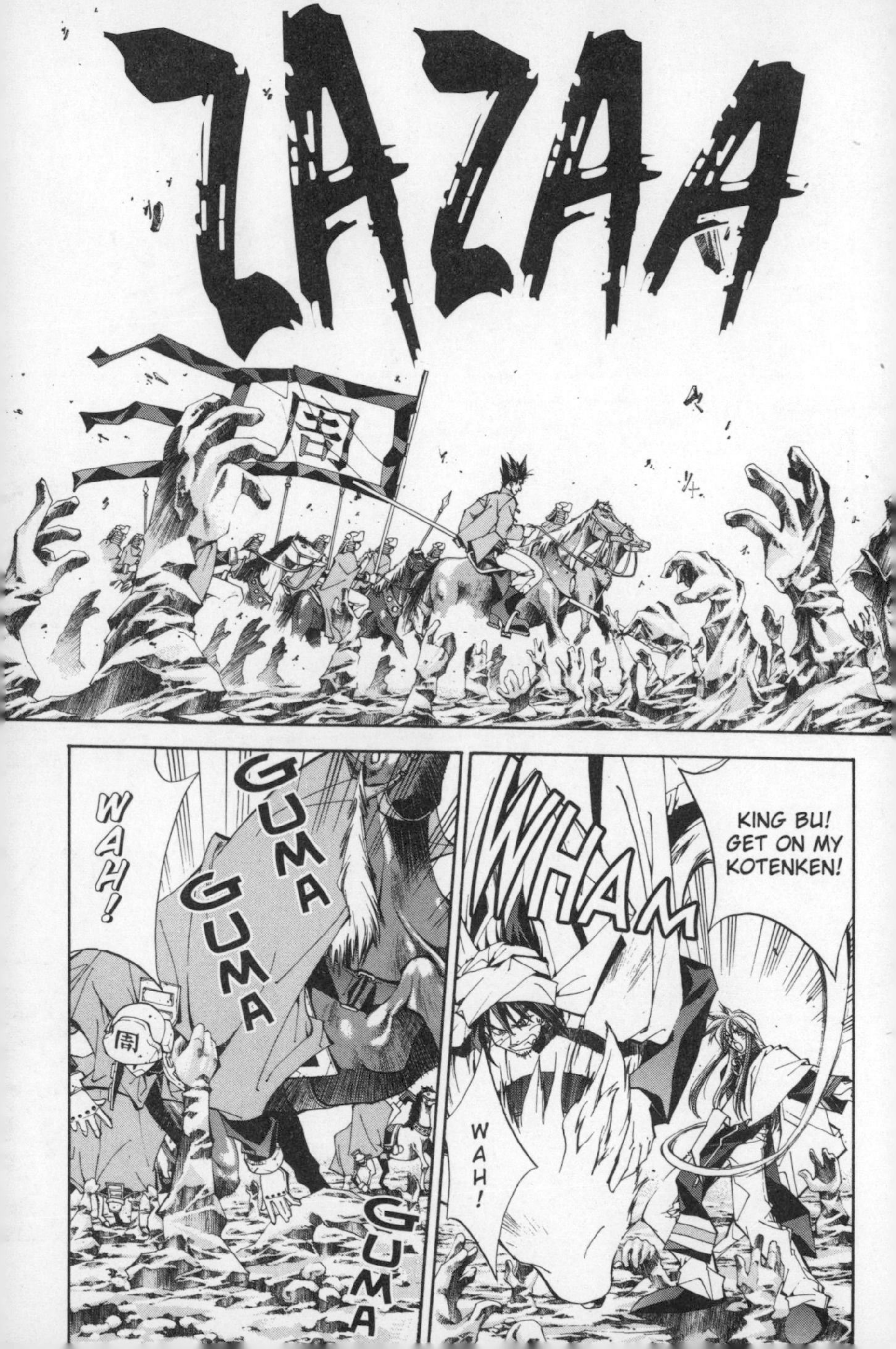
ZAZAA
KING BU! GET ON MY KOTENKEN!
WHAM
WAH!
GUMA GUMA
WAH!
GUMA GUMA
GUMA

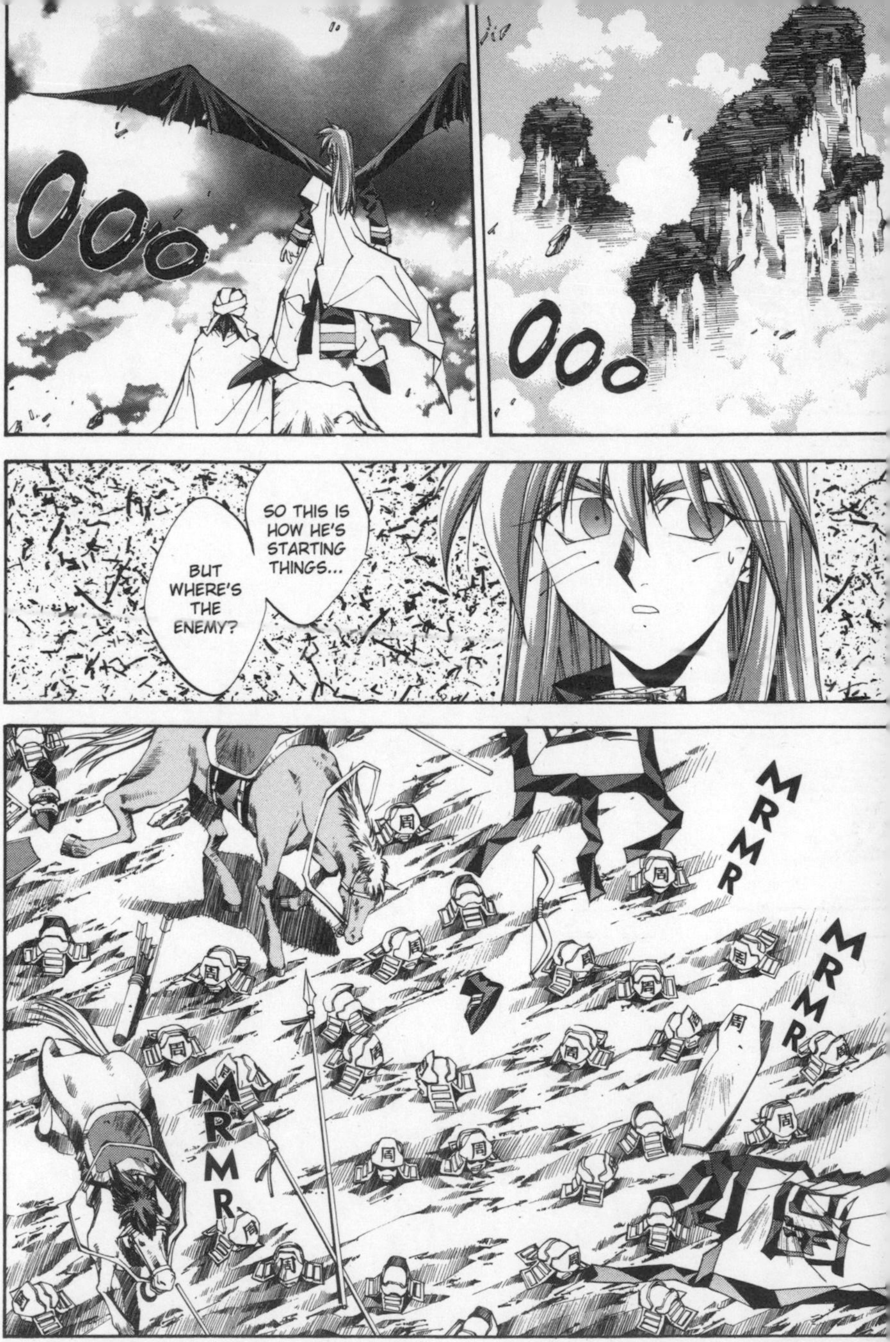
OOO
OOO
SO THIS IS HOW HE'S STARTING THINGS...
BUT WHERE'S THE ENEMY?
MRMR
MRMR
MRMR

READ THIS WAY

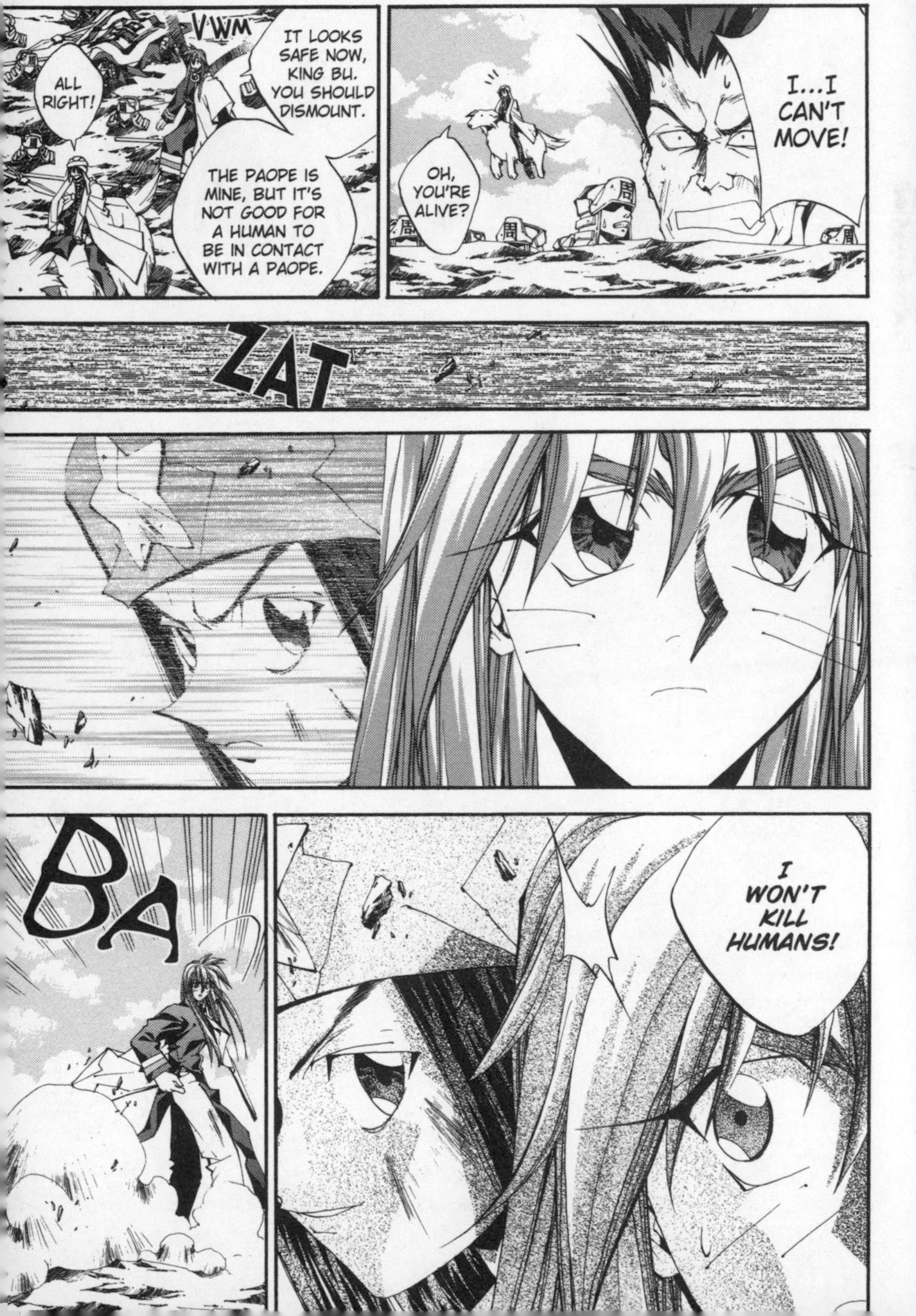
I...I CAN'T MOVE!
OH, YOU'RE ALIVE?
IT LOOKS SAFE NOW, KING BU. YOU SHOULD DISMOUNT.
VWM
ALL RIGHT!
THE PAOPE IS MINE, BUT IT'S NOT GOOD FOR A HUMAN TO BE IN CONTACT WITH A PAOPE.
ZAT
I WON'T KILL HUMANS!
BA

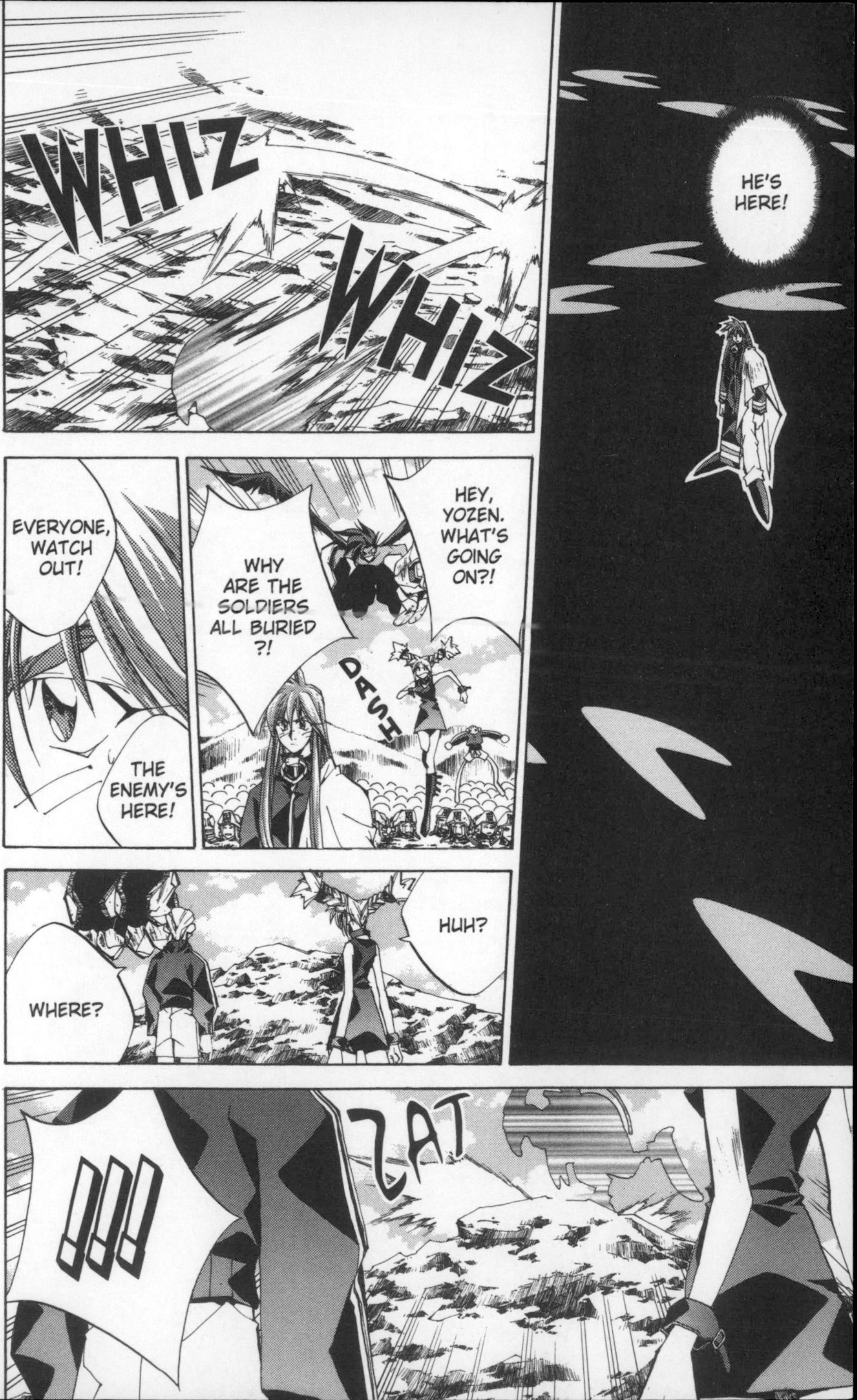
HE'S HERE!
WHIZ
WHIZ
HEY, YOZEN. WHAT'S GOING ON?!
WHY ARE THE SOLDIERS ALL BURIED?!
DASH
EVERYONE, WATCH OUT!
THE ENEMY'S HERE!
HUH?
WHERE?
ZAT
!!!

READ THIS WAY

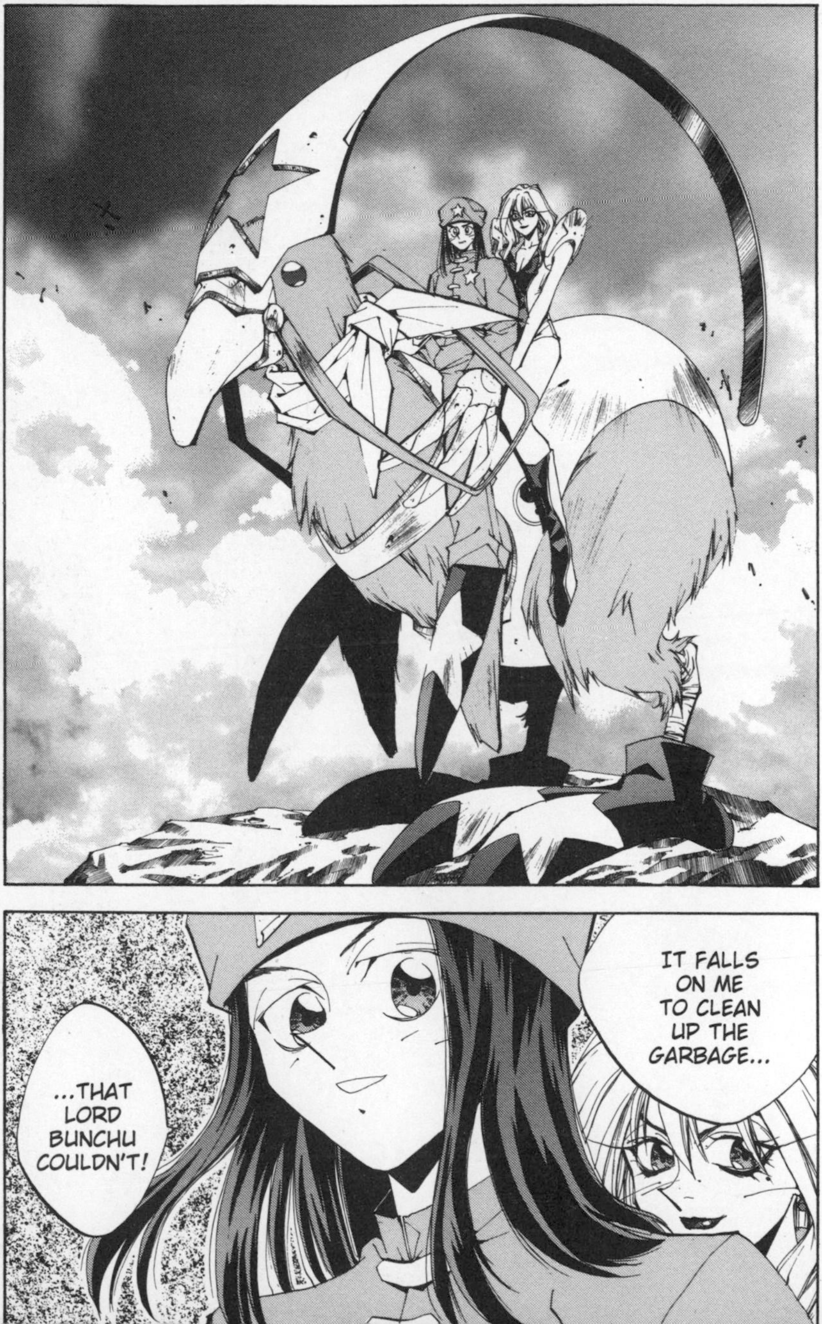
IT FALLS ON ME TO CLEAN UP THE GARBAGE...
...THAT LORD BUNCHU COULDN'T!

封神演義

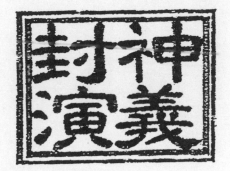

Chapter 157

THE BATTLE OF MENCHI CASTLE, PART 1
CHOKEI AND HIS POWER TEAM!

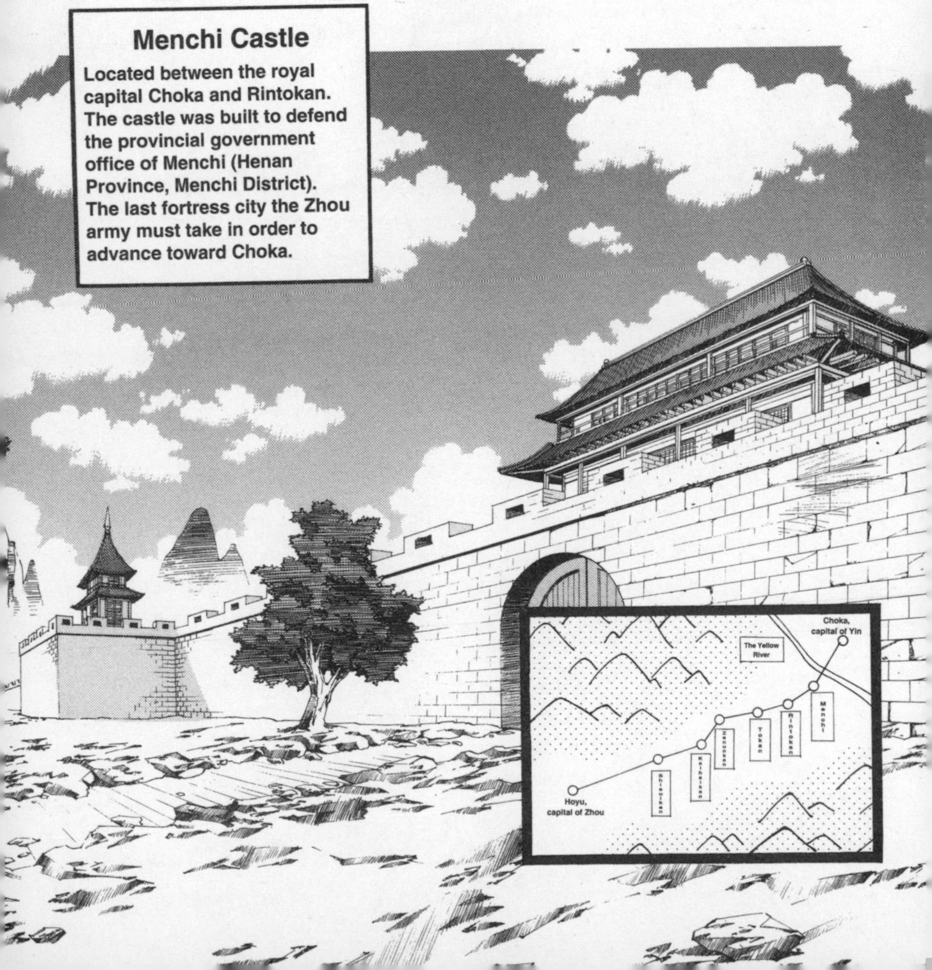
Menchi Castle
Located between the royal capital Choka and Rintokan. The castle was built to defend the provincial government office of Menchi (Henan Province, Menchi District). The last fortress city the Zhou army must take in order to advance toward Choka.
Choka, capital of Yin
The Yellow River
Menchi
Rintokan
Tokan
Zenunkan
Kaiheikan
Shisuikan
Hoyu, capital of Zhou

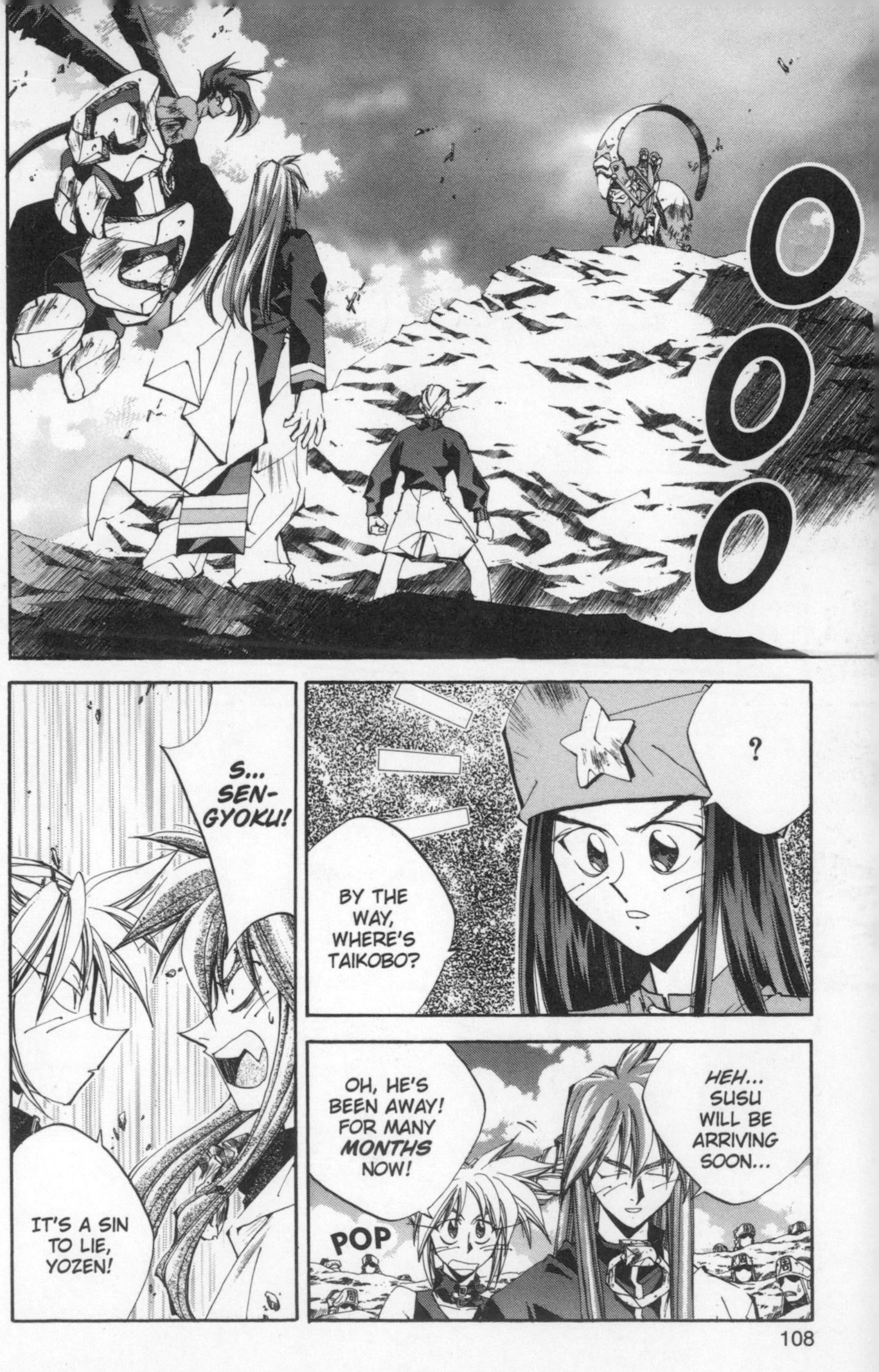
?
BY THE WAY, WHERE'S TAIKOBO?
HEH... SUSU WILL BE ARRIVING SOON...
OH, HE'S BEEN AWAY! FOR MANY MONTHS NOW!
POP
S... SEN-GYOKU!
IT'S A SIN TO LIE, YOZEN!

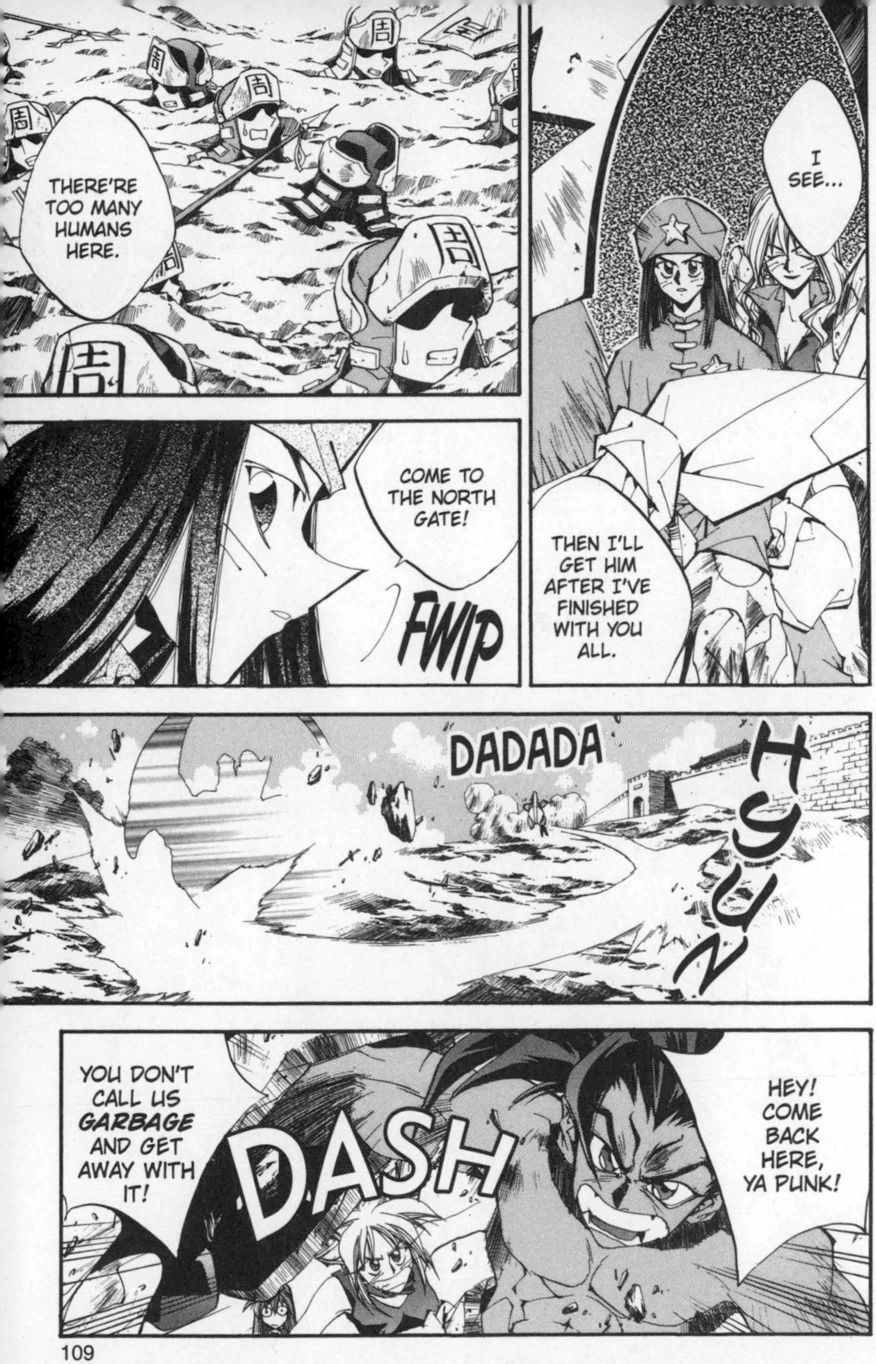

I SEE...
THEN I'LL GET HIM AFTER I'VE FINISHED WITH YOU ALL.
THERE'RE TOO MANY HUMANS HERE.
COME TO THE NORTH GATE!
FWIP
HYUN
DADADA
HEY! COME BACK HERE, YA PUNK!
DASH
YOU DON'T CALL US GARBAGE AND GET AWAY WITH IT!

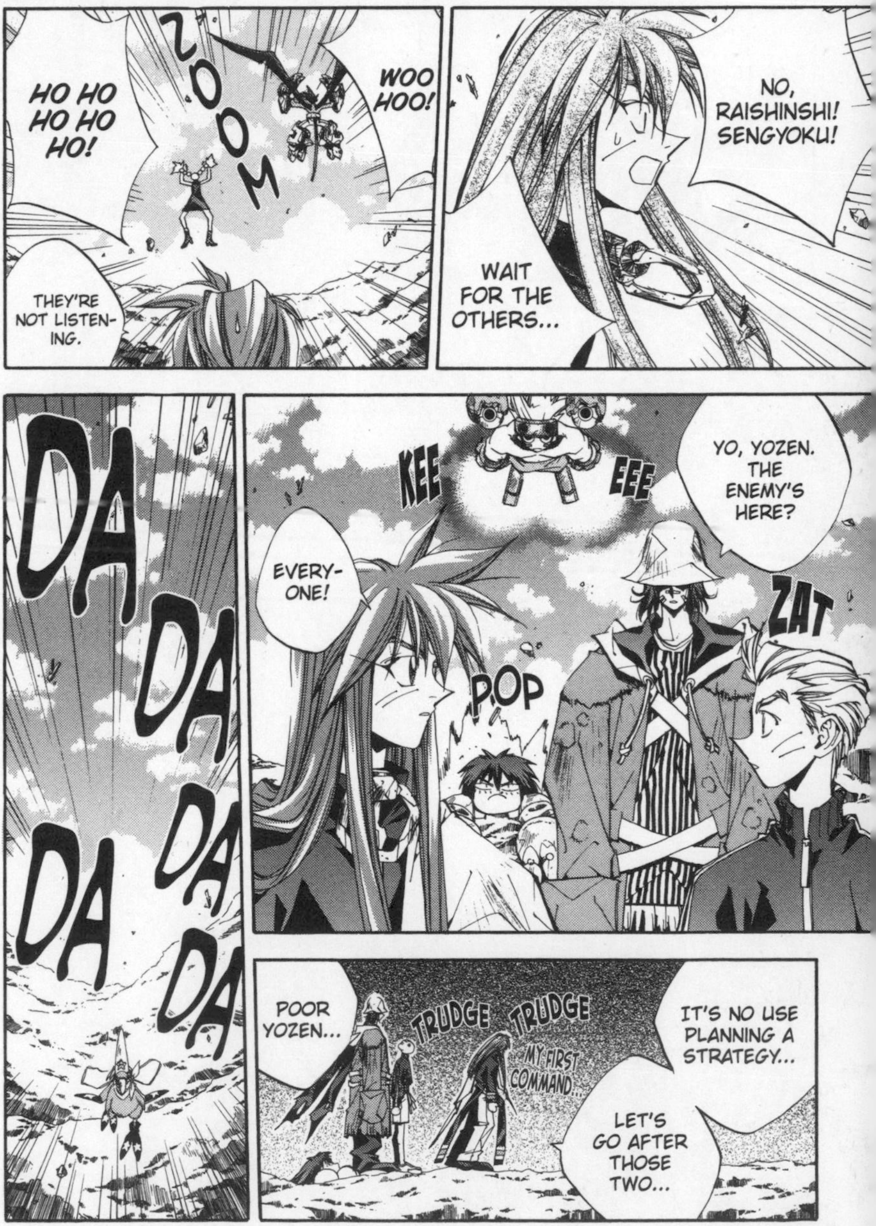
NO, RAISHINSHI! SENGYOKU!
WAIT FOR THE OTHERS...
WOO HOO!
ZOOM
HO HO HO HO HO!
THEY'RE NOT LISTEN-ING.
YO, YOZEN. THE ENEMY'S HERE?
KEE
EEE
EVERY-ONE!
ZAT
POP
IT'S NO USE PLANNING A STRATEGY...
LET'S GO AFTER THOSE TWO...
TRUDGE
TRUDGE
MY FIRST COMMAND...
POOR YOZEN...
DA
DA
DA
DA
DA
DA

READ THIS WAY

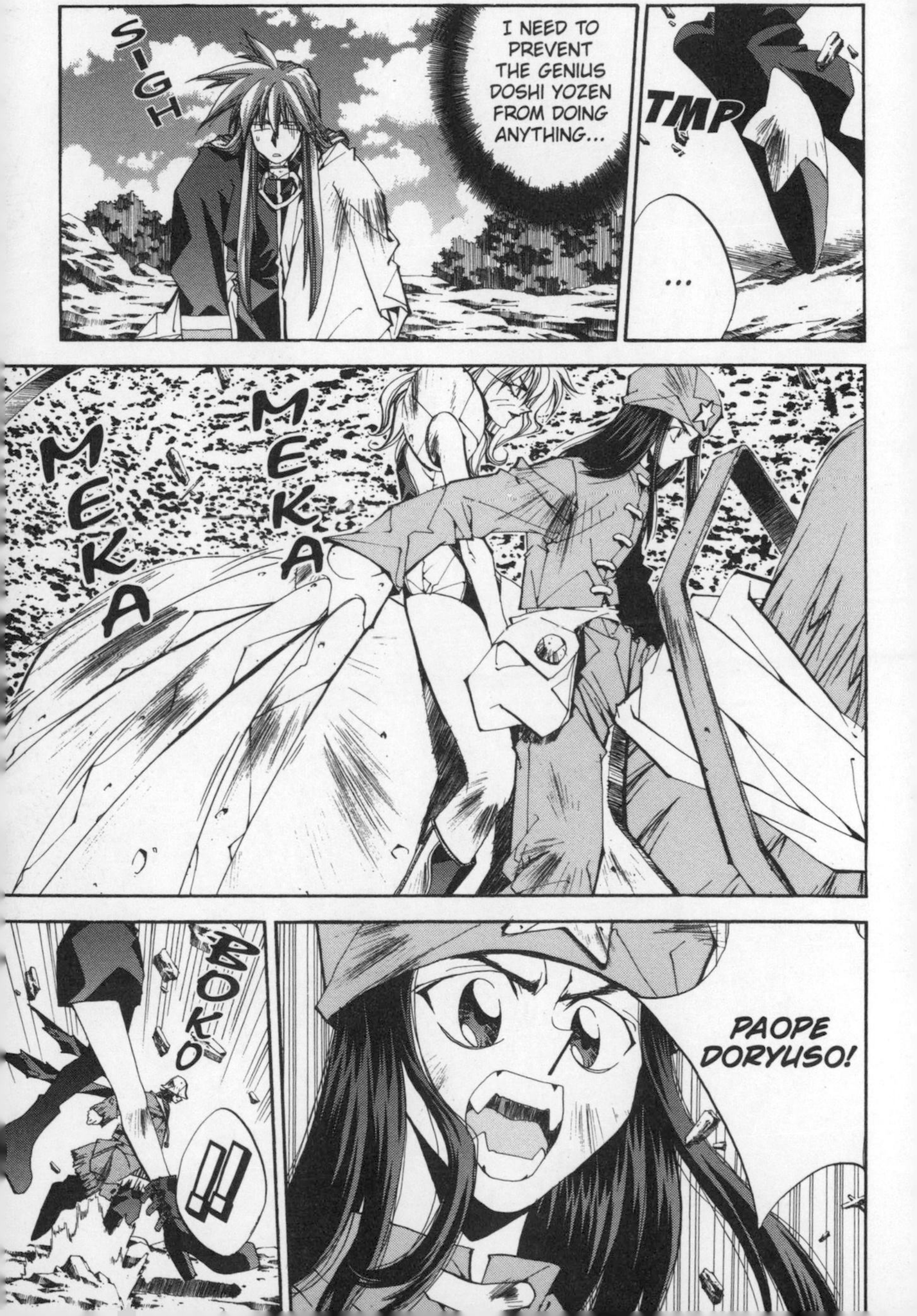
TMP
...
I NEED TO PREVENT THE GENIUS DOSHI YOZEN FROM DOING ANYTHING...
SIGH
MEKA
MEKA
PAOPE DORYUSO!
BOKO
!!

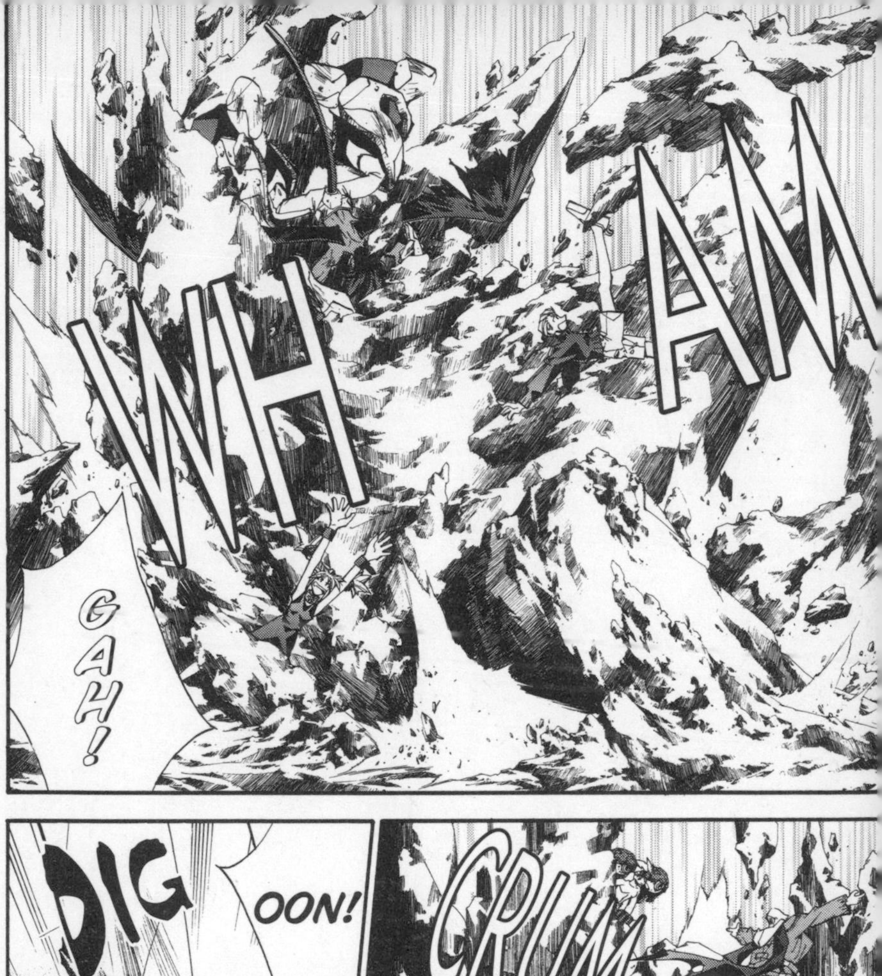
WHAM
GAH!

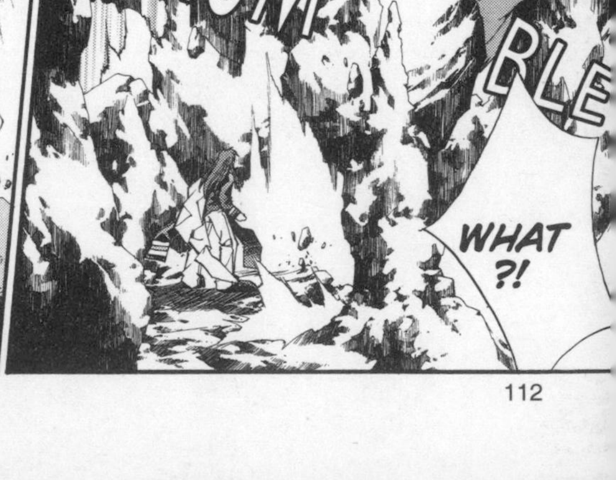
CRUMBLE
WHAT ?!

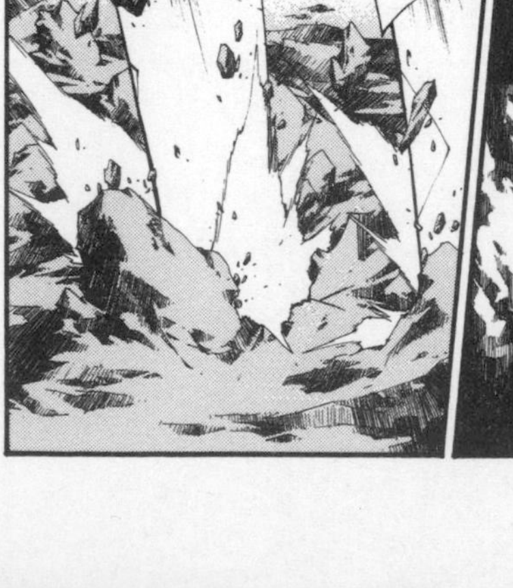
DIG
OON!

READ THIS WAY

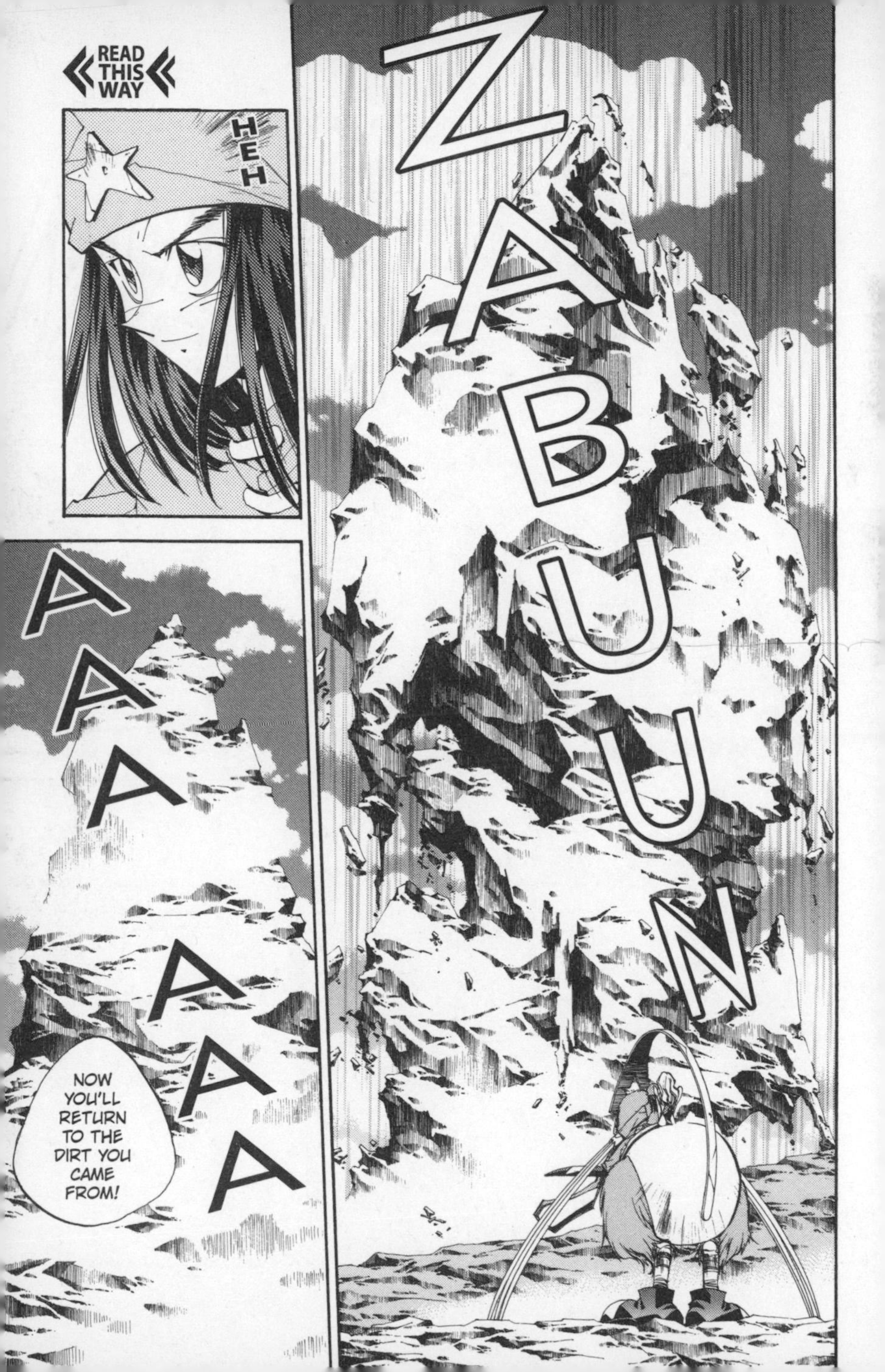
ZABUUN
HEH
AAAAAA
NOW YOU'LL RETURN TO THE DIRT YOU CAME FROM!

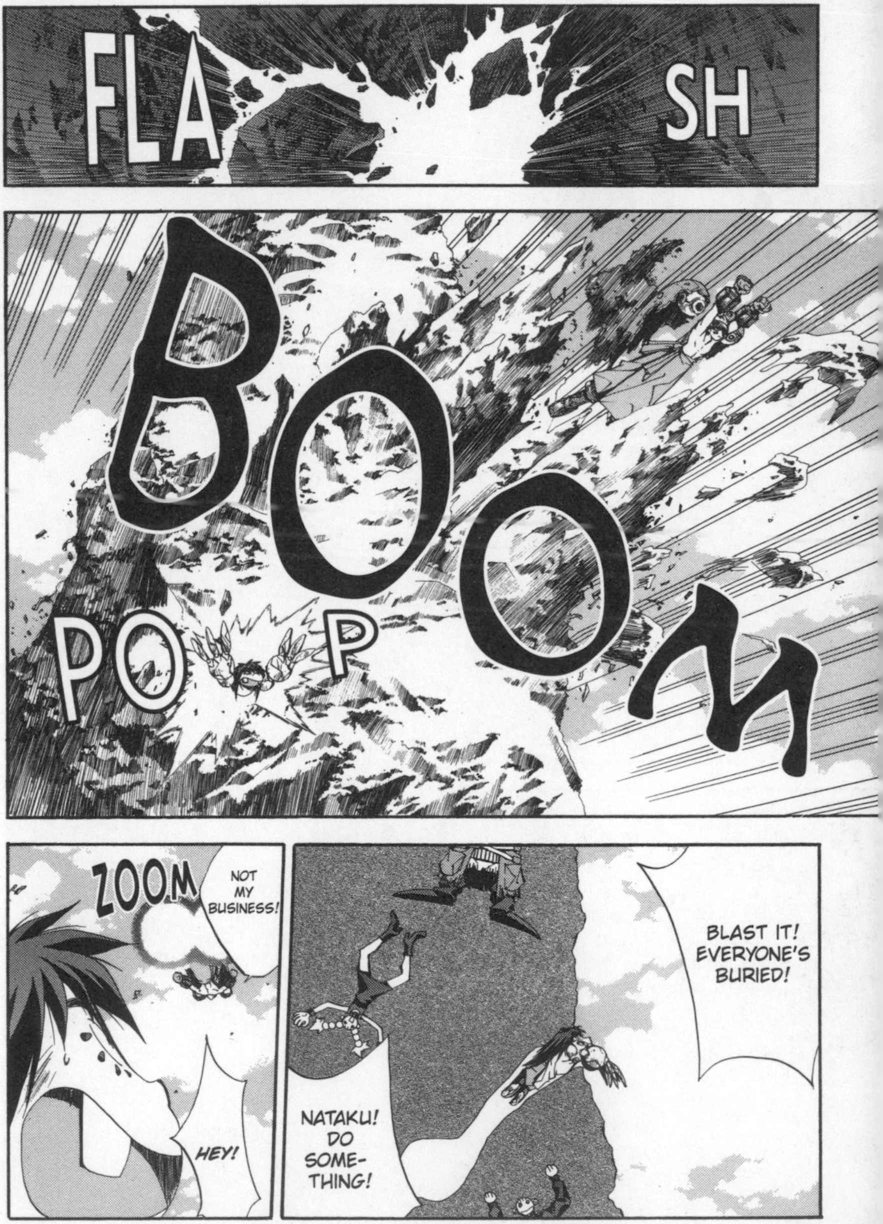
FLASH
BOOOM
POP
BLAST IT! EVERYONE'S BURIED!
NATAKU! DO SOMETHING!
NOT MY BUSINESS!
ZOOM
HEY!

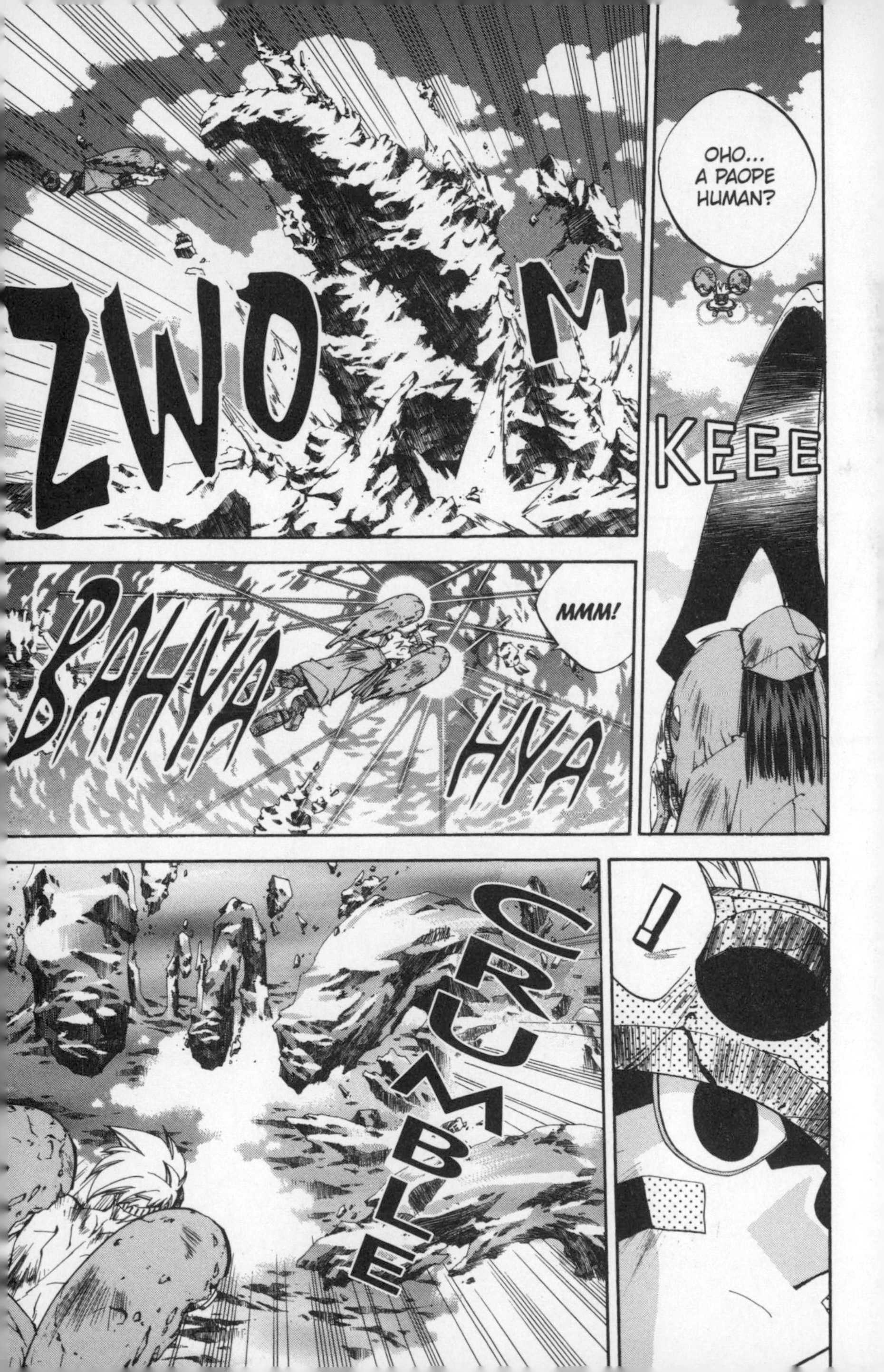
OHO... A PAOPE HUMAN?
KEEE
ZWOM
MMM!
BAHYA
HYA
!
CRUMBLE

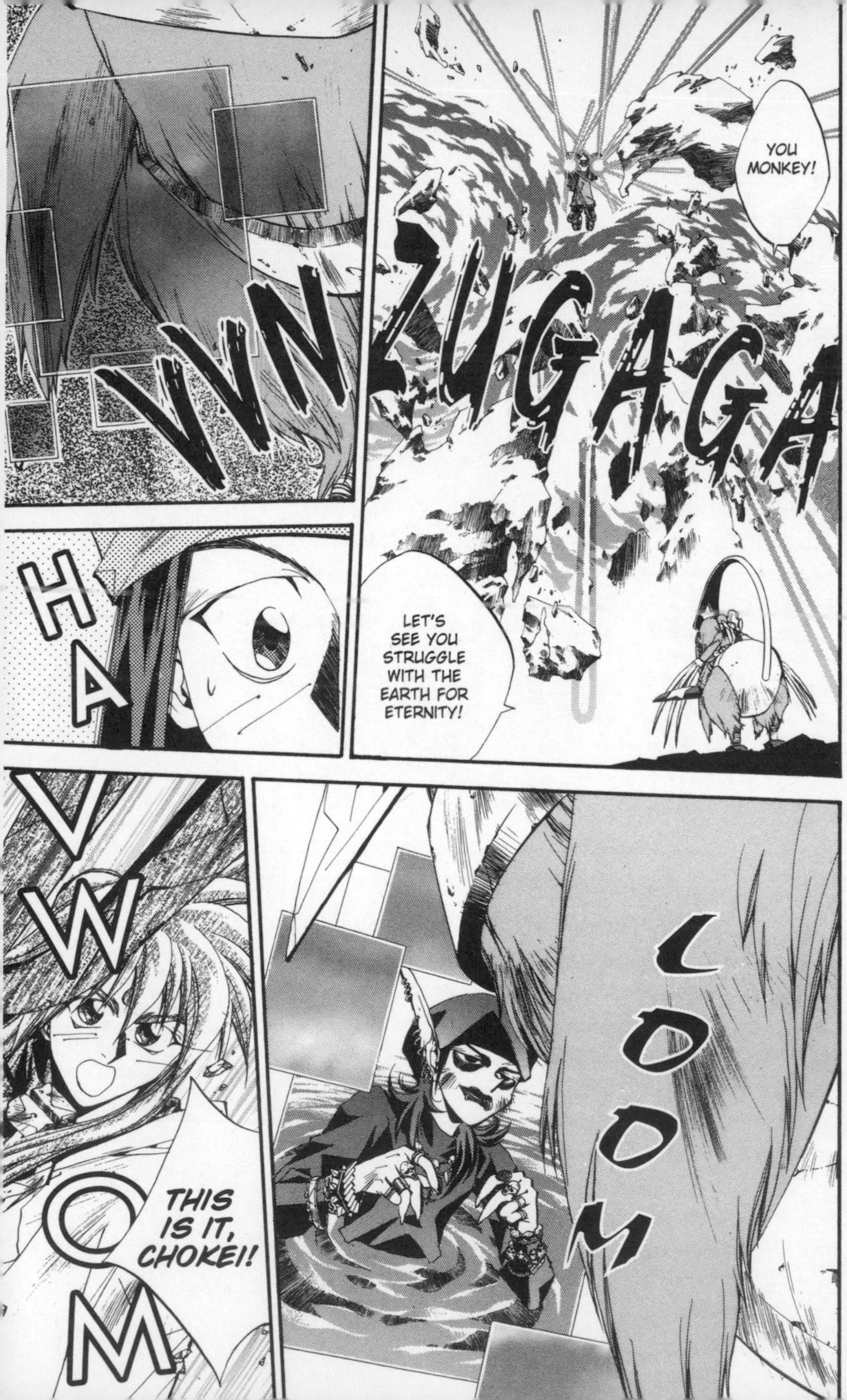
YOU MONKEY!
VVNZUGAGA
LET'S SEE YOU STRUGGLE WITH THE EARTH FOR ETERNITY!
HA
LOOM
VWOM
THIS IS IT, CHOKEI!

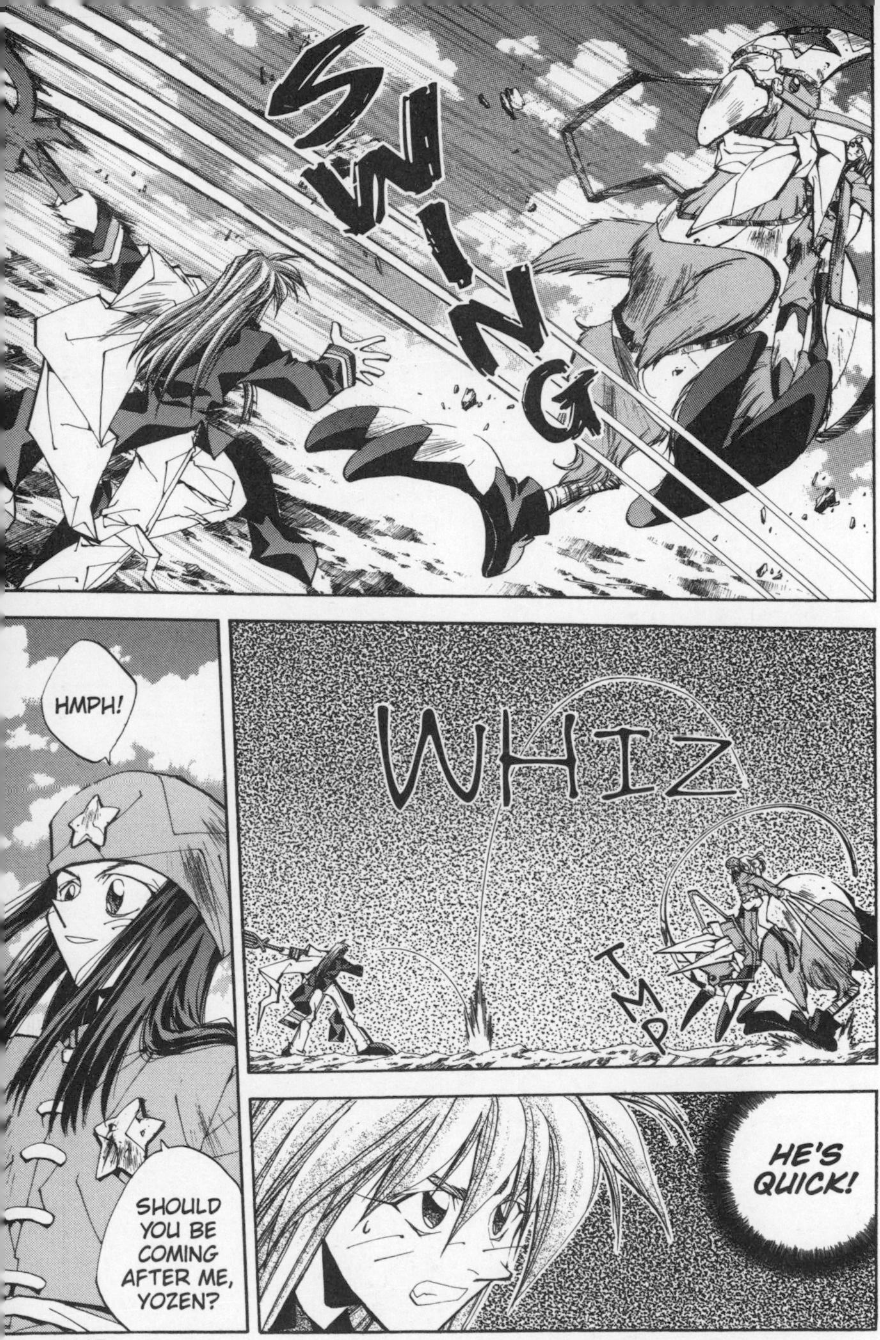
SWING
WHIZ
TMP
HE'S QUICK!
HMPH!
SHOULD YOU BE COMING AFTER ME, YOZEN?

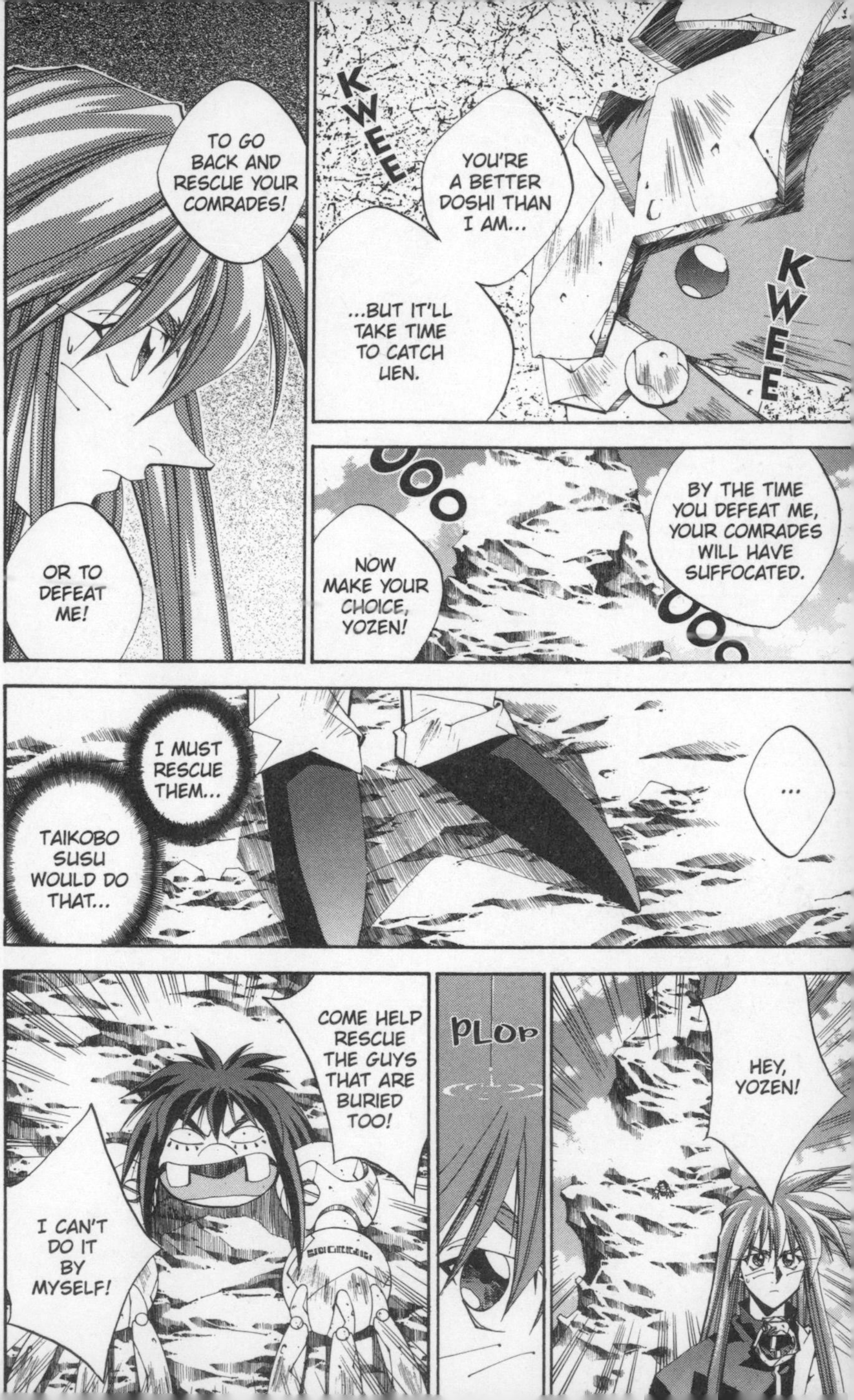
KWEE
KWEE
YOU'RE A BETTER DOSHI THAN I AM...
...BUT IT'LL TAKE TIME TO CATCH UEN.
OOOO
BY THE TIME YOU DEFEAT ME, YOUR COMRADES WILL HAVE SUFFOCATED.
OOOO
NOW MAKE YOUR CHOICE, YOZEN!
TO GO BACK AND RESCUE YOUR COMRADES!
OR TO DEFEAT ME!
...
I MUST RESCUE THEM...
TAIKOBO SUSU WOULD DO THAT...
HEY, YOZEN!
PLOP
COME HELP RESCUE THE GUYS THAT ARE BURIED TOO!
I CAN'T DO IT BY MYSELF!

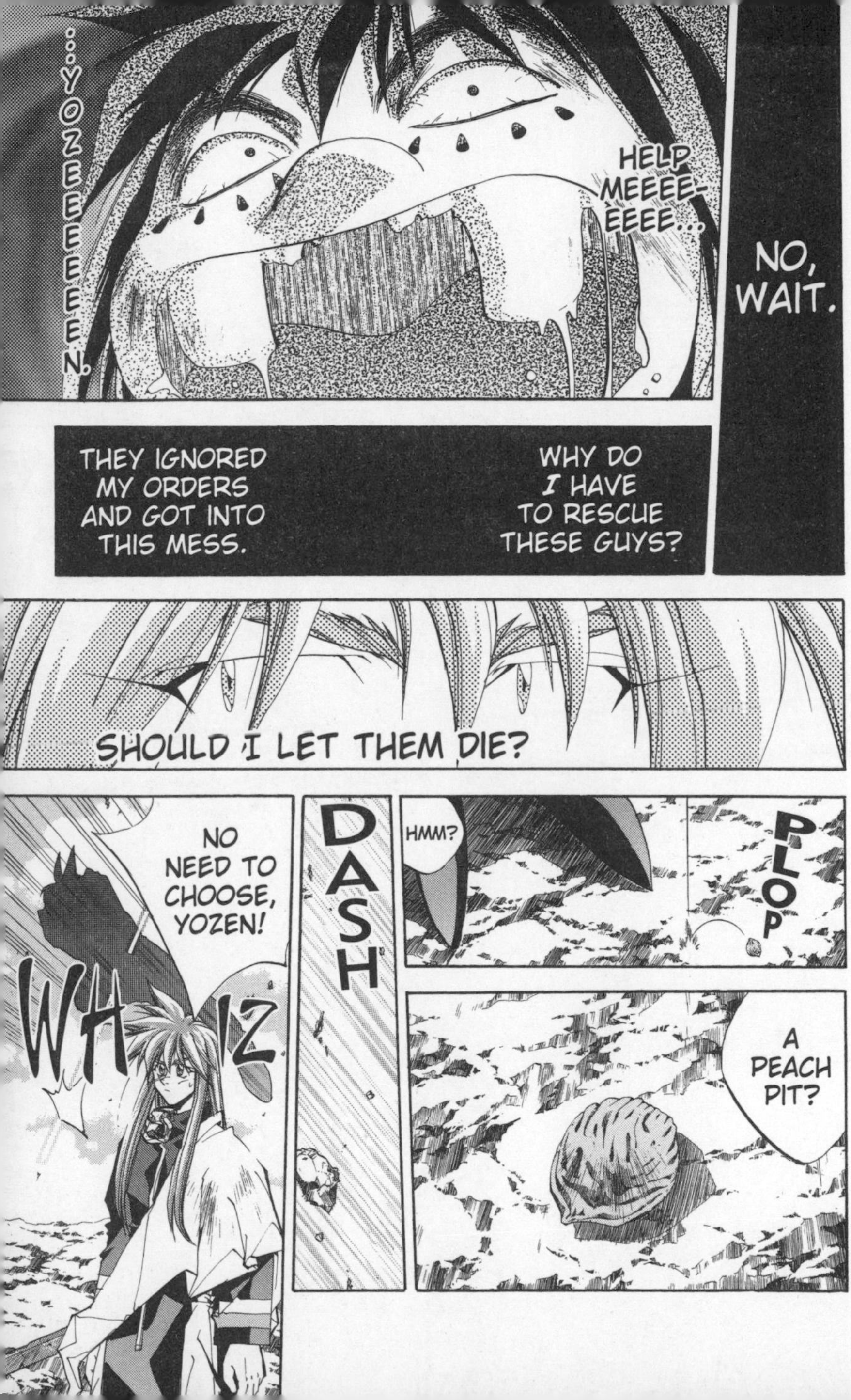
NO, WAIT.
HELP MEEEE-EEEE...
...YOZEEEEEEEEEN.
WHY DO I HAVE TO RESCUE THESE GUYS?
THEY IGNORED MY ORDERS AND GOT INTO THIS MESS.
SHOULD I LET THEM DIE?
PLOP
HMM?
A PEACH PIT?
DASH
NO NEED TO CHOOSE, YOZEN!
WHIZ

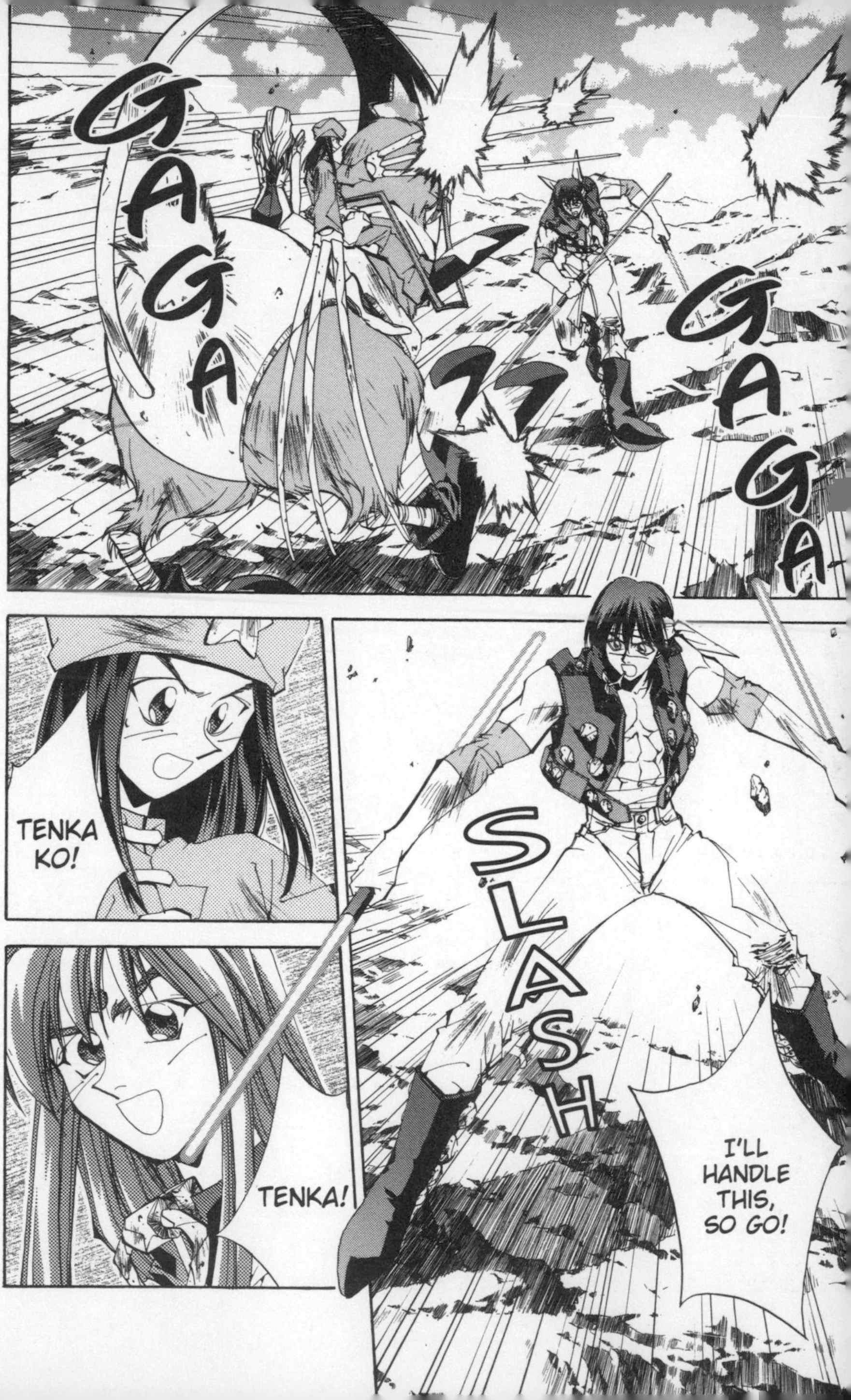
GAGA
GAGA
SLASH
I'LL HANDLE THIS, SO GO!
TENKA KO!
TENKA!

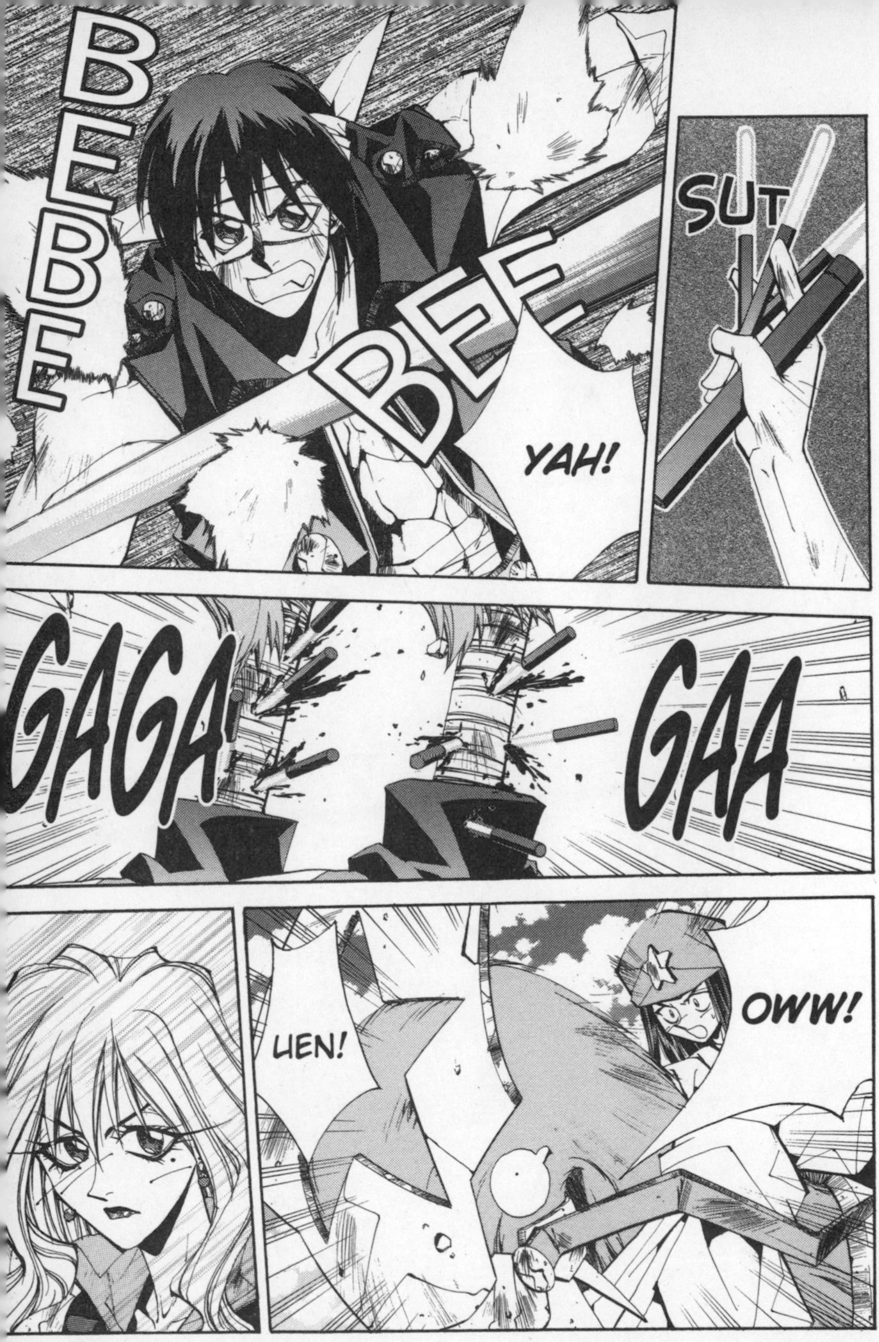
SUT
BEBE
BEE
YAH!
GAGA
GAA
OWW!
LIEN!

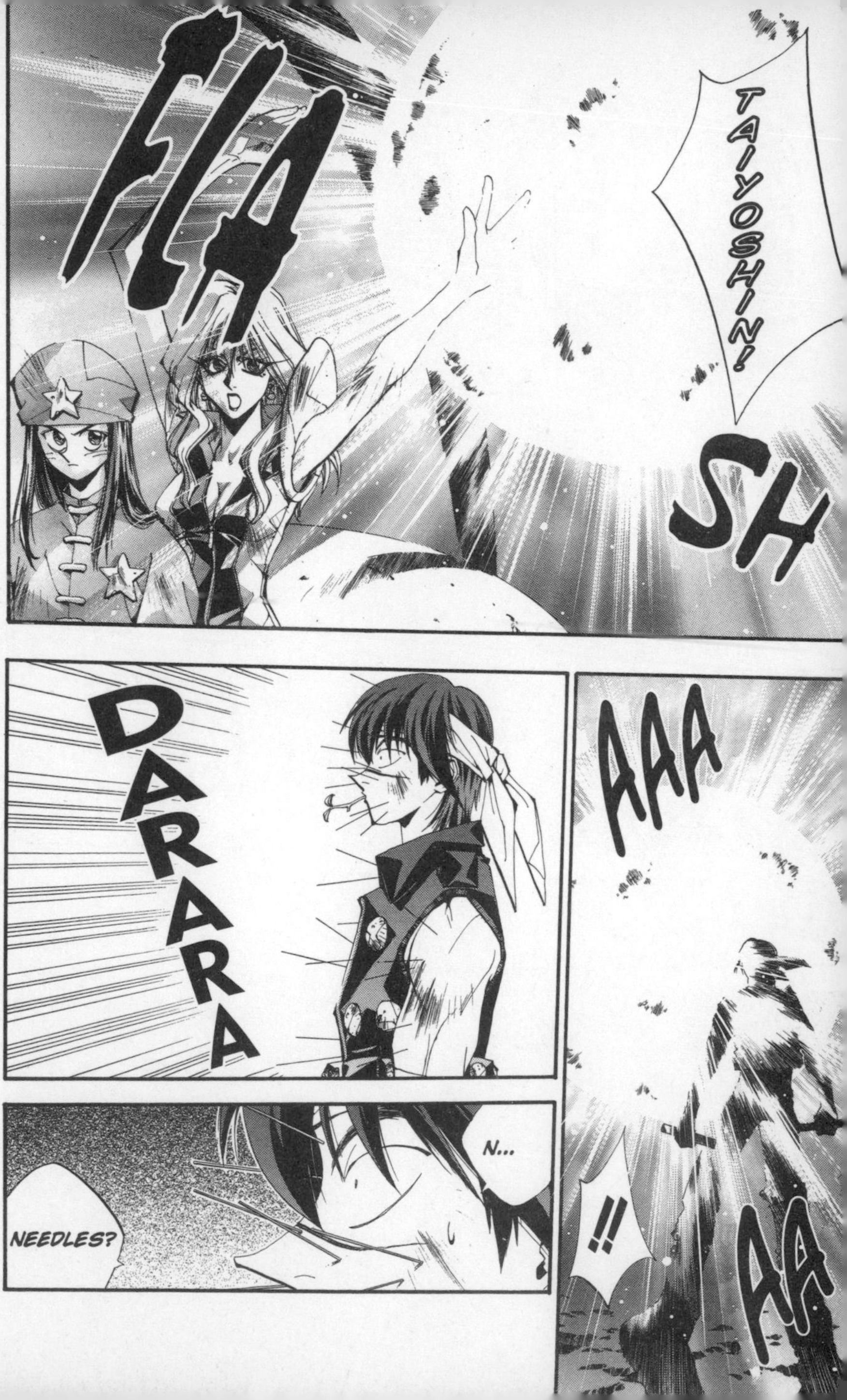
TAIYOSHIN!
SH
FLA
AAA
!!
AA
DARARA
N...
NEEDLES?

READ THIS WAY

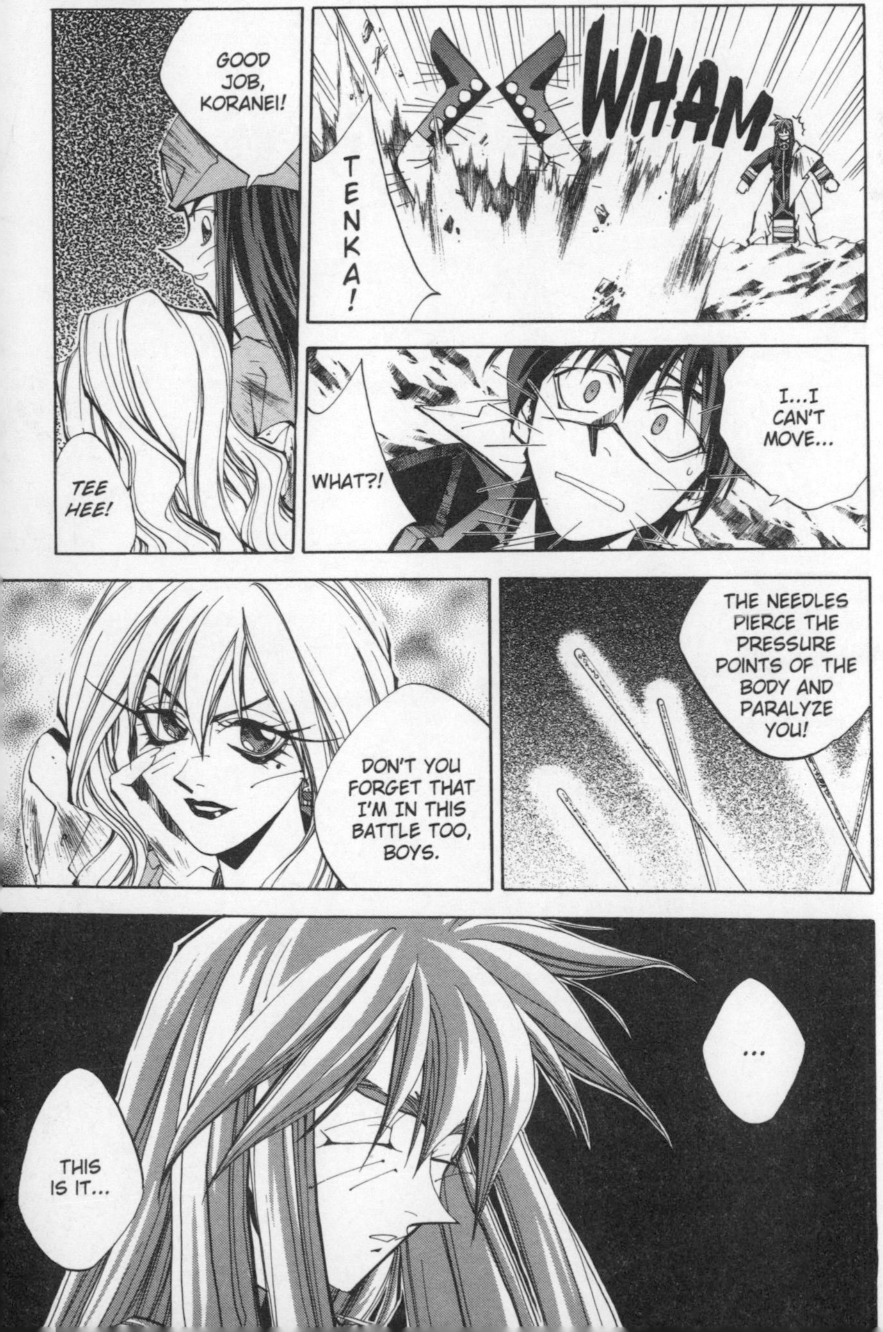
WHAM
TENKA!
I...I CAN'T MOVE...
WHAT?!
GOOD JOB, KORANEI!
TEE HEE!
THE NEEDLES PIERCE THE PRESSURE POINTS OF THE BODY AND PARALYZE YOU!
DON'T YOU FORGET THAT I'M IN THIS BATTLE TOO, BOYS.
...
THIS IS IT...

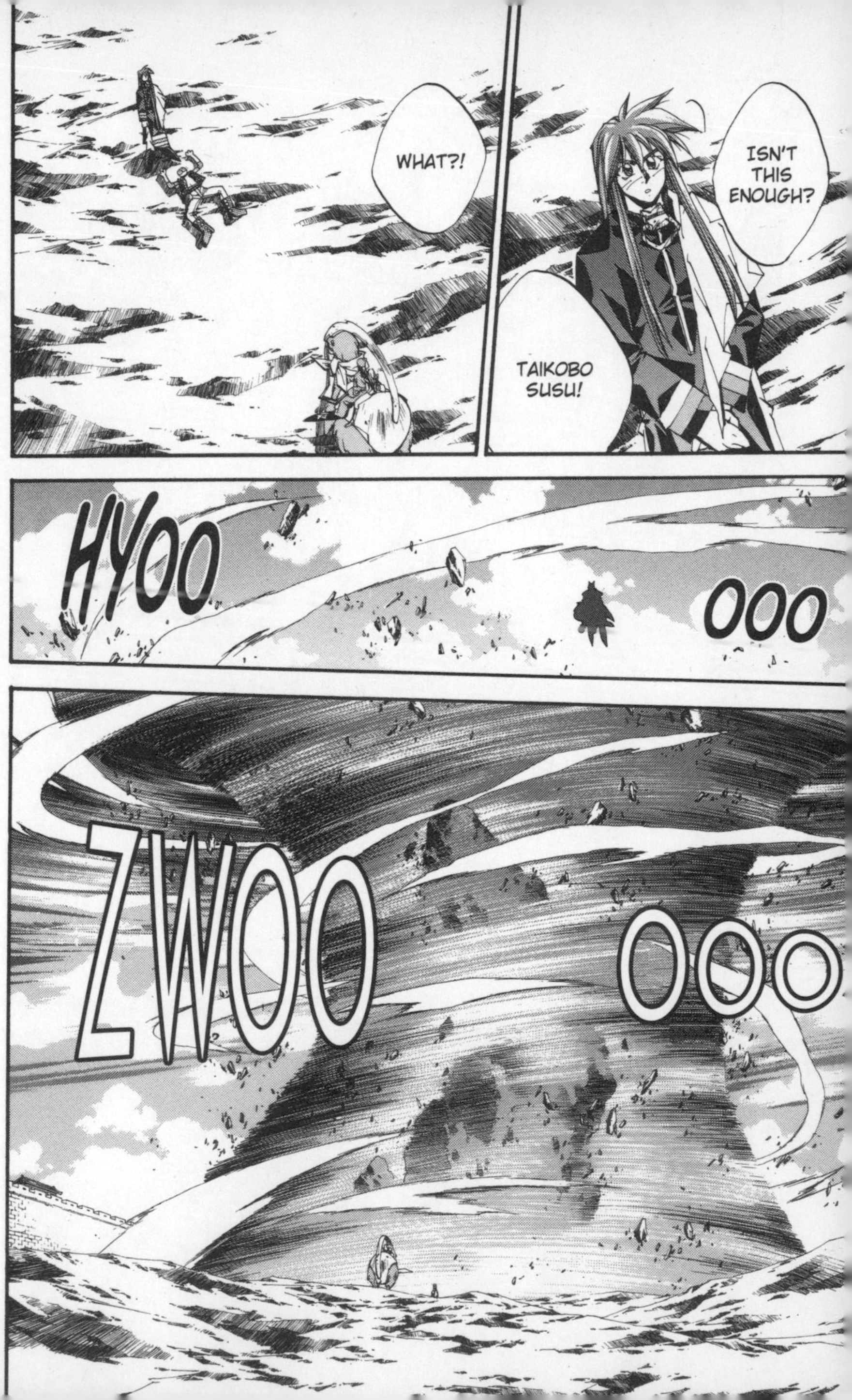
ISN'T THIS ENOUGH?
TAIKOBO SUSU!
WHAT?!
HYOO OOO
ZWOO OOO

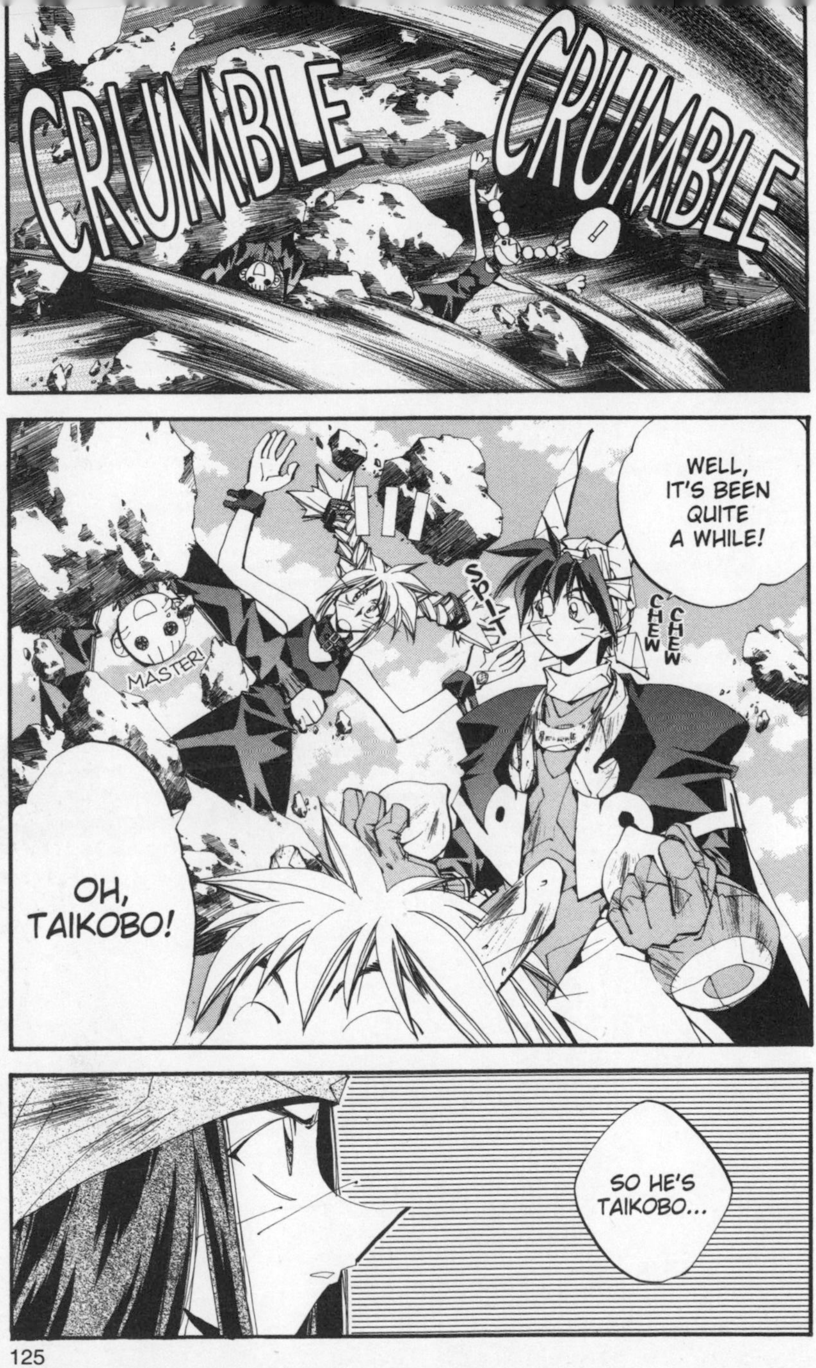
CRUMBLE CRUMBLE
!
WELL, IT'S BEEN QUITE A WHILE!
CHEW CHEW
SPIT
MASTER!
OH, TAIKOBO!
SO HE'S TAIKOBO...

封神演義

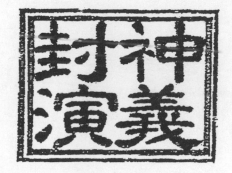

Chapter 158

THE BATTLE OF MENCHI CASTLE, PART 2
THE TEACHINGS OF TAIJO ROKUN

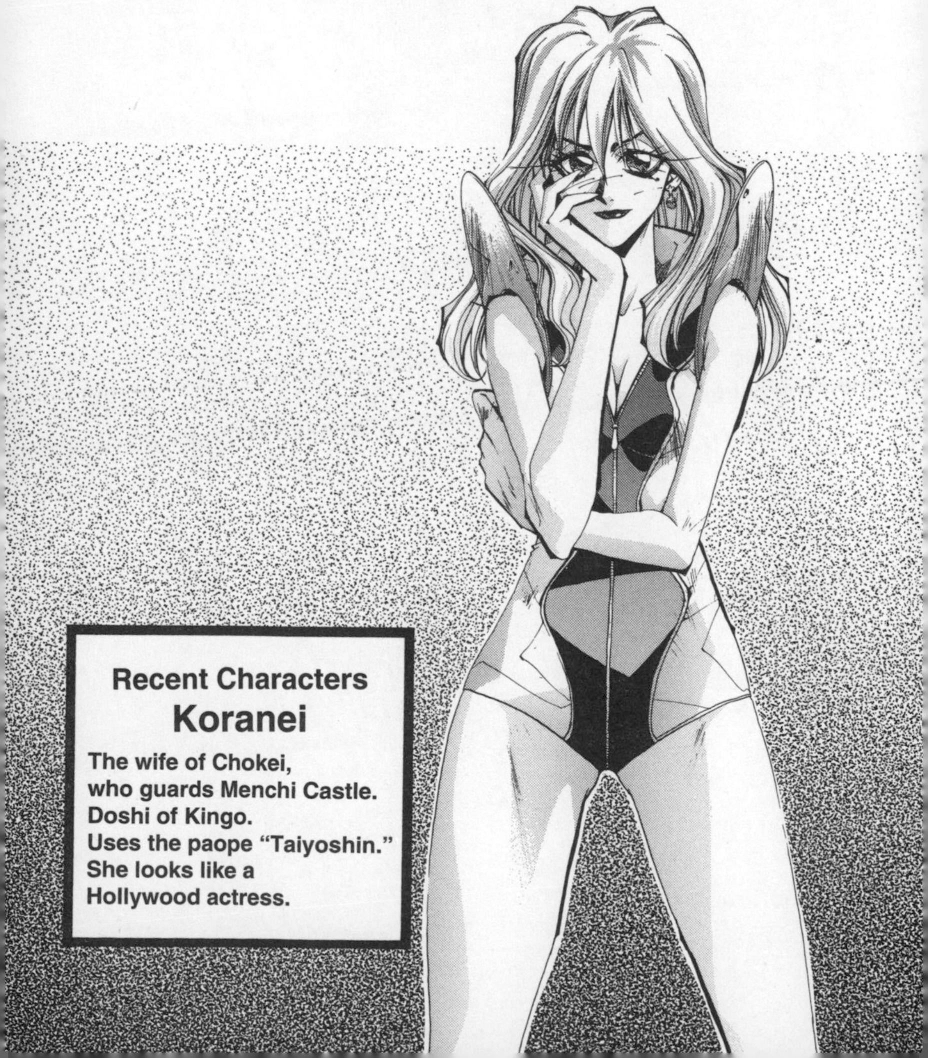

Recent Characters
Koranei

The wife of Chokei, who guards Menchi Castle. Doshi of Kingo. Uses the paope "Taiyoshin." She looks like a Hollywood actress.

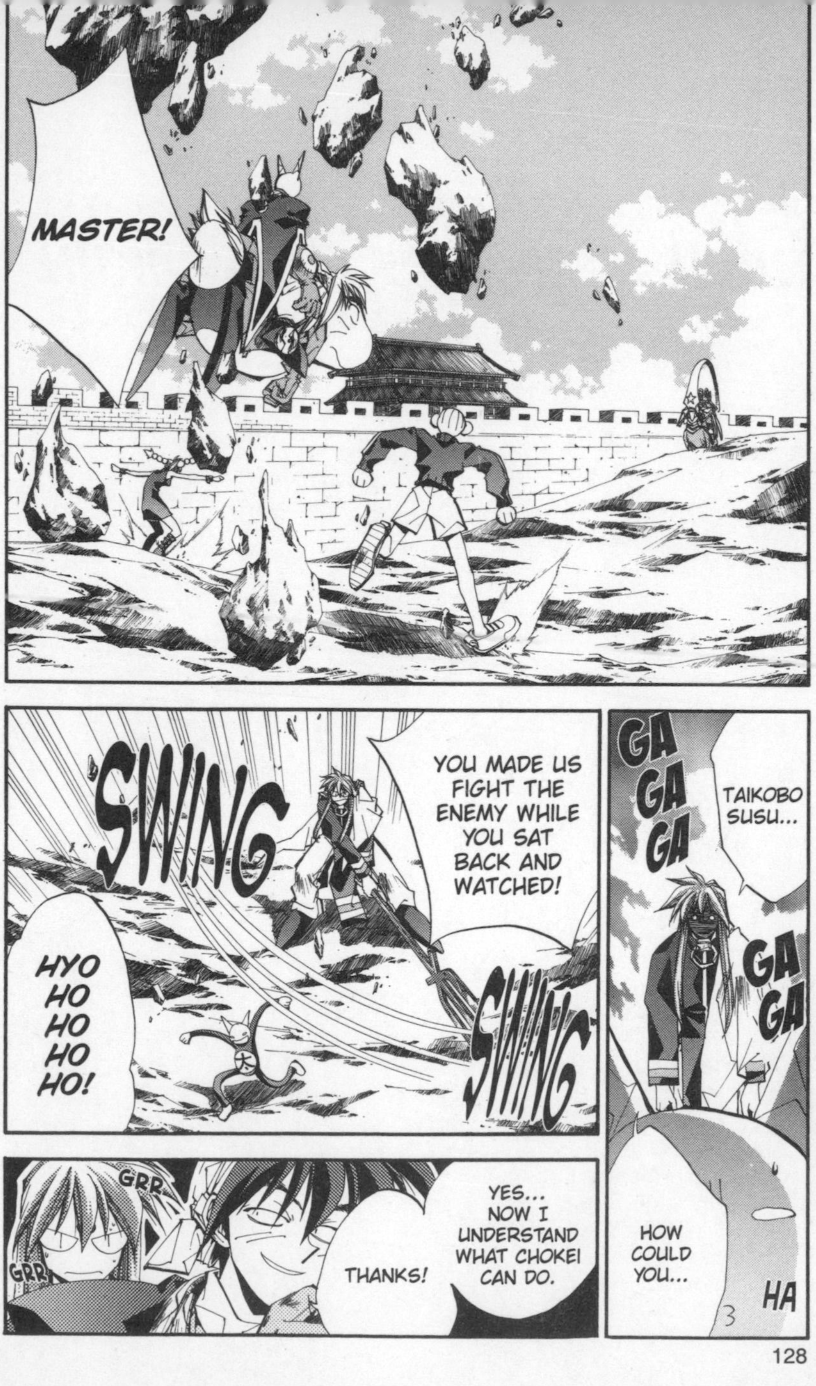

MASTER!
GA GA GA
TAIKOBO SUSU...
GA GA
HOW COULD YOU...
HA
YOU MADE US FIGHT THE ENEMY WHILE YOU SAT BACK AND WATCHED!
SWING
SWING
HYO HO HO HO HO!
YES... NOW I UNDERSTAND WHAT CHOKEI CAN DO.
THANKS!
GRR
GRR

READ THIS WAY

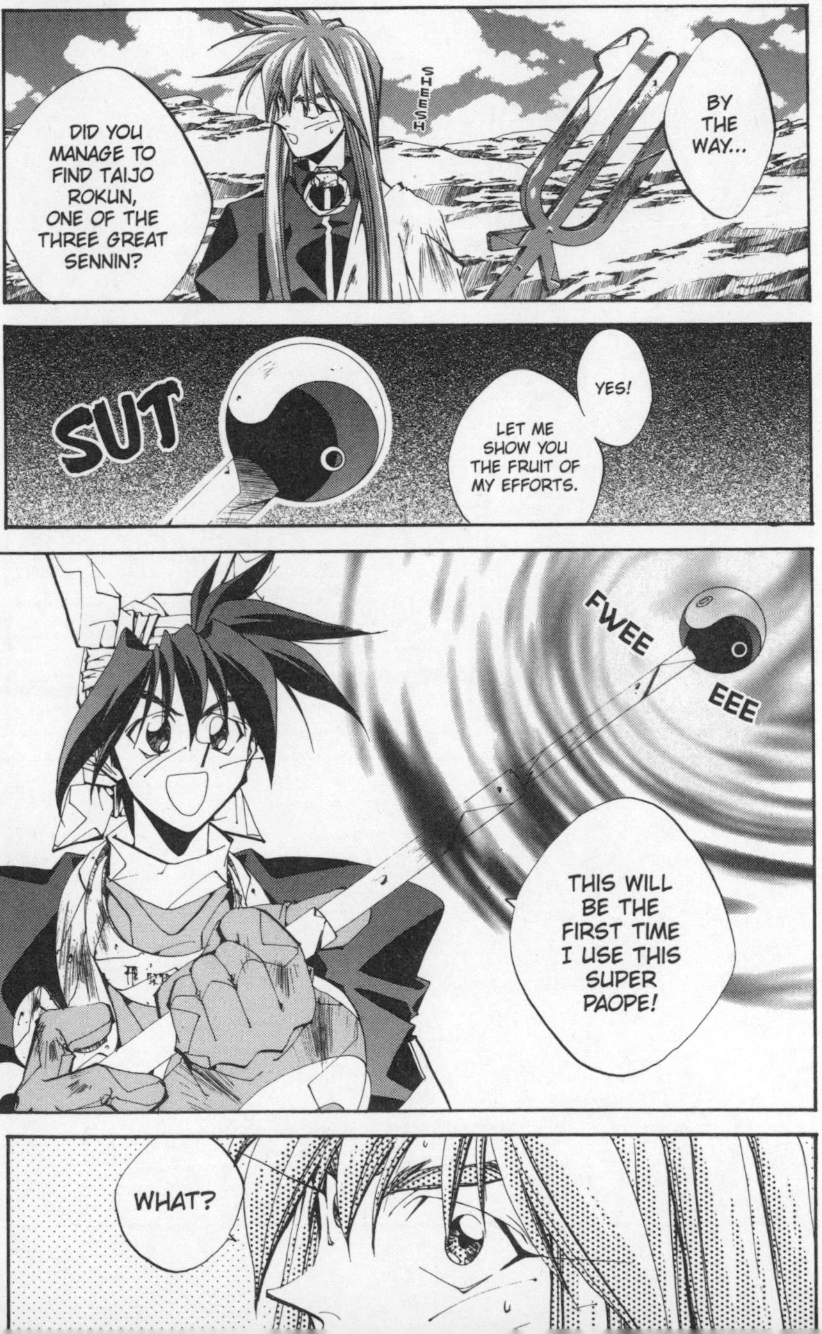
BY THE WAY...
SHEESH
DID YOU MANAGE TO FIND TAIJO ROKUN, ONE OF THE THREE GREAT SENNIN?
YES!
LET ME SHOW YOU THE FRUIT OF MY EFFORTS.
SUT
FWEE EEE
THIS WILL BE THE FIRST TIME I USE THIS SUPER PAOPE!
WHAT?

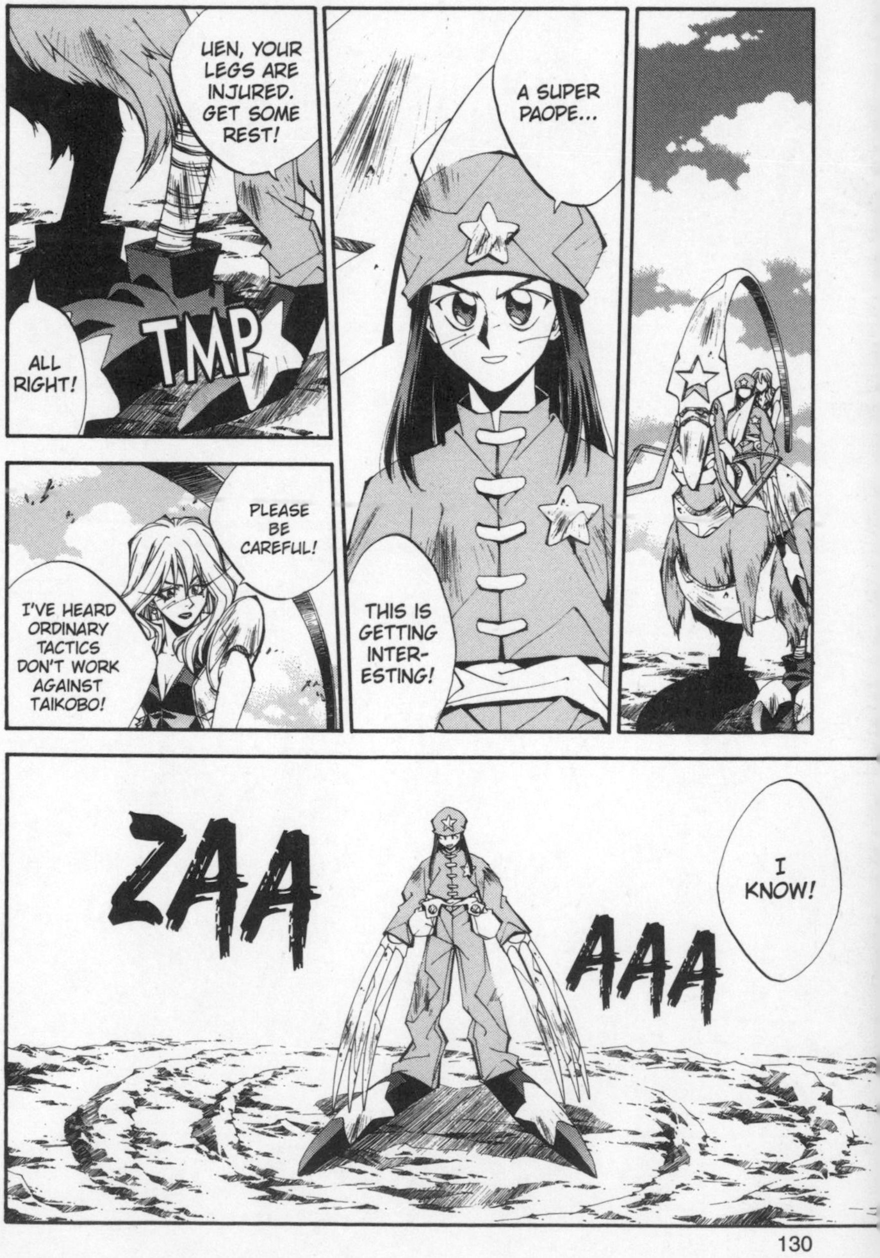
A SUPER PAOPE...
THIS IS GETTING INTER-ESTING!
UEN, YOUR LEGS ARE INJURED. GET SOME REST!
ALL RIGHT!
TMP
PLEASE BE CAREFUL!
I'VE HEARD ORDINARY TACTICS DON'T WORK AGAINST TAIKOBO!
I KNOW!
ZAA AAA

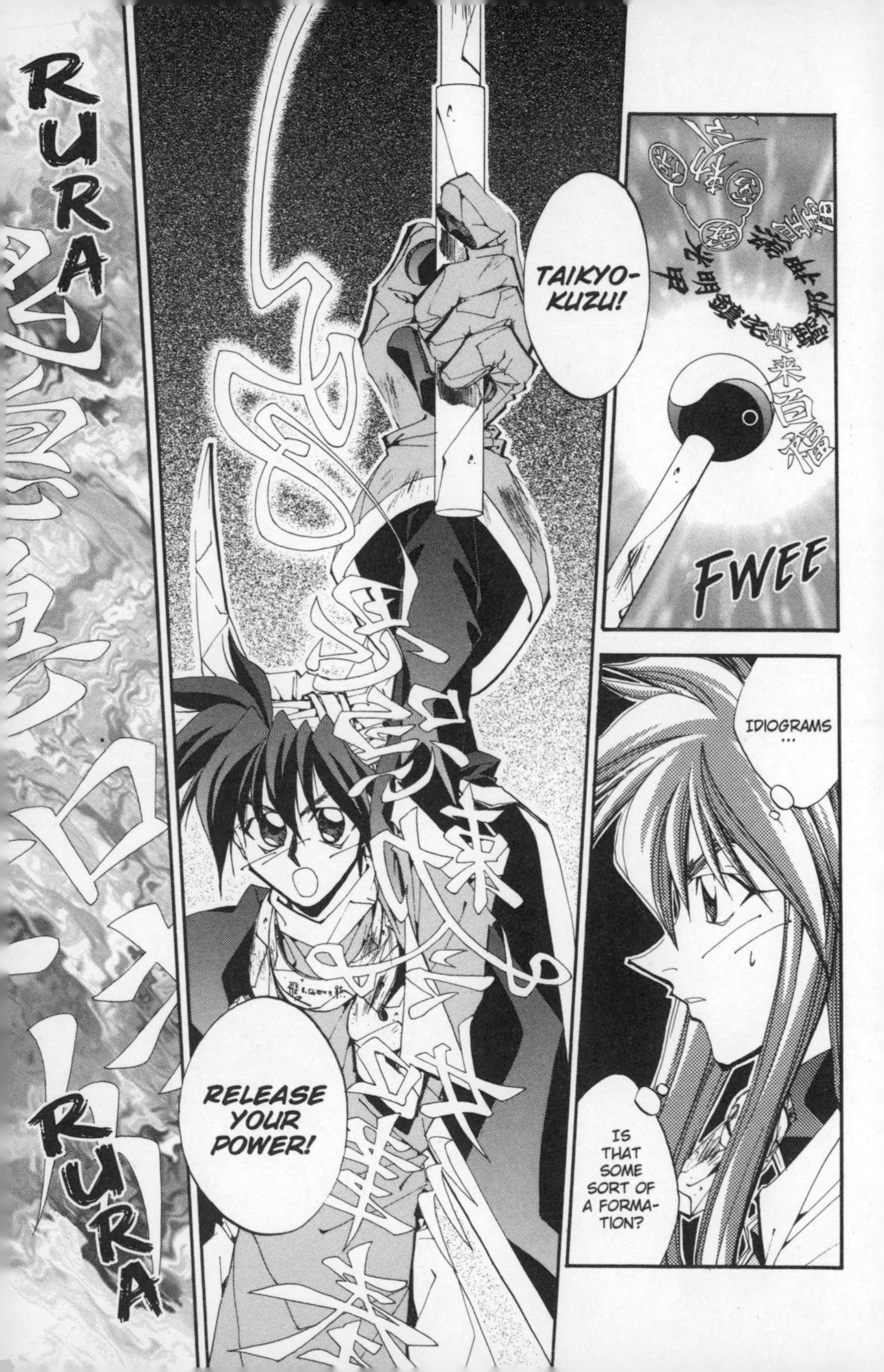
TAIKYO-KUZU!
FWEE
IDIOGRAMS...
IS THAT SOME SORT OF A FORMATION?
RELEASE YOUR POWER!
RURA
RURA

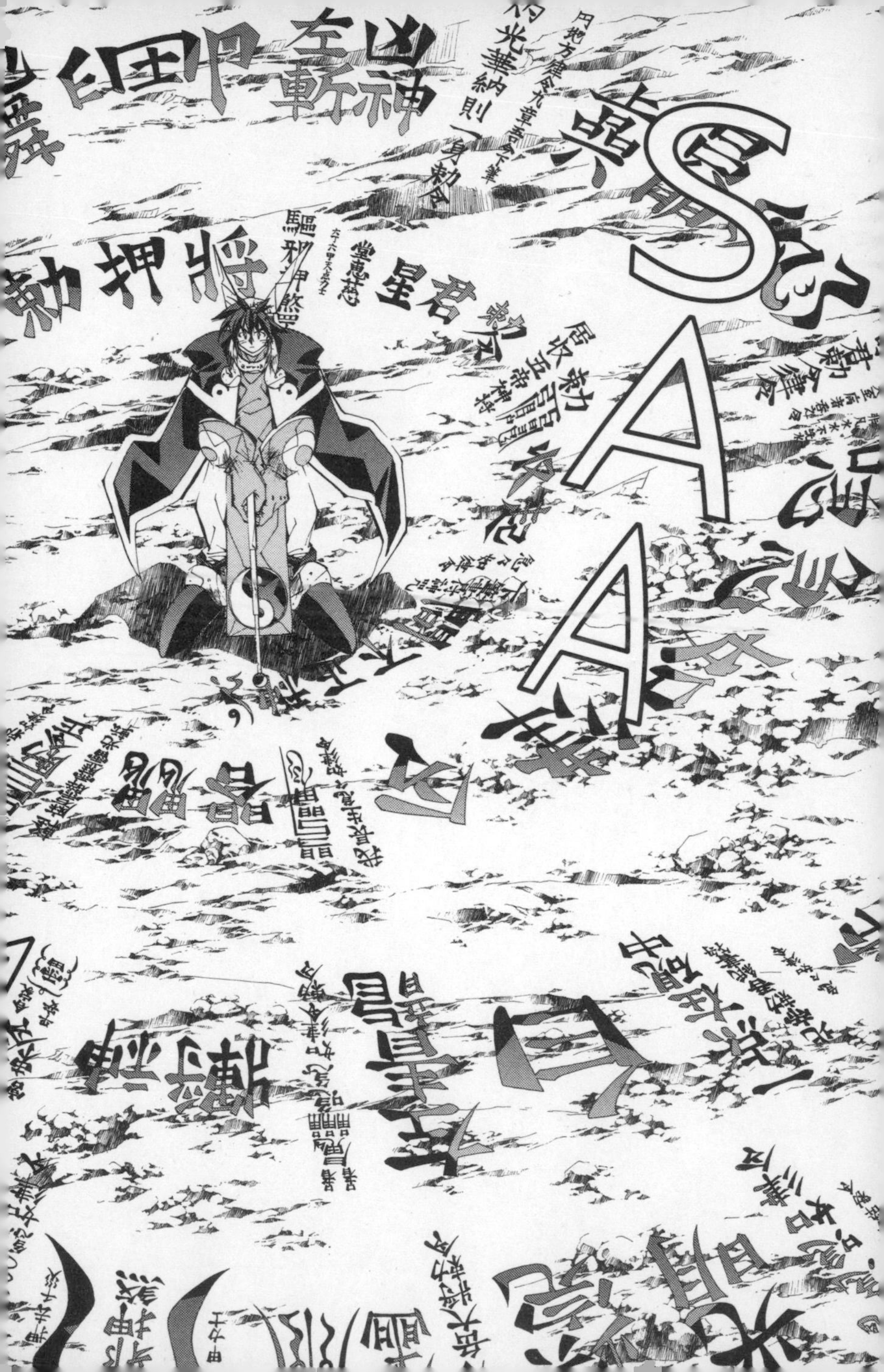
SAA

SUU

?!

SOME-
HOW...

THE AIR
ITSELF IS
CHANGING...

HM

...

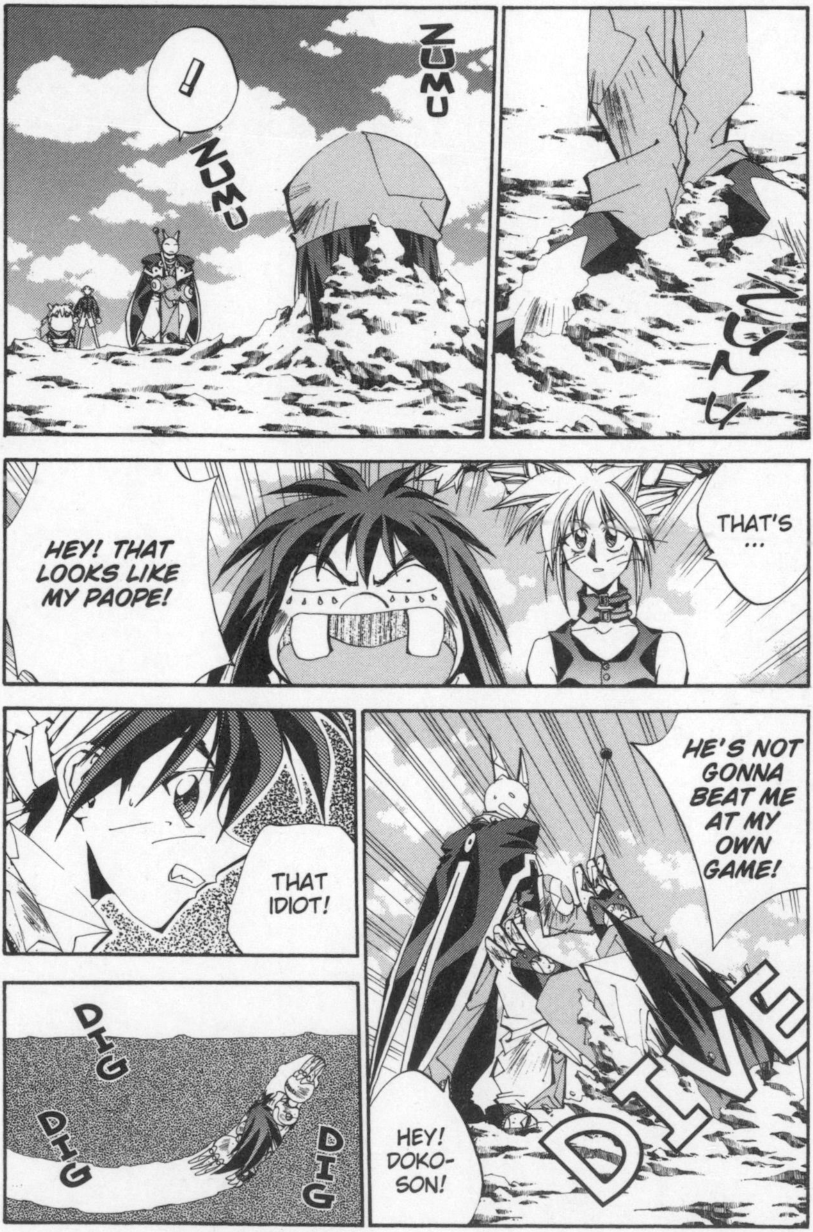
!
ZUMU
ZUMU
THAT'S ...
HEY! THAT LOOKS LIKE MY PAOPE!
HE'S NOT GONNA BEAT ME AT MY OWN GAME!
DIVE
HEY! DOKO-SON!
THAT IDIOT!
DIG
DIG
DIG

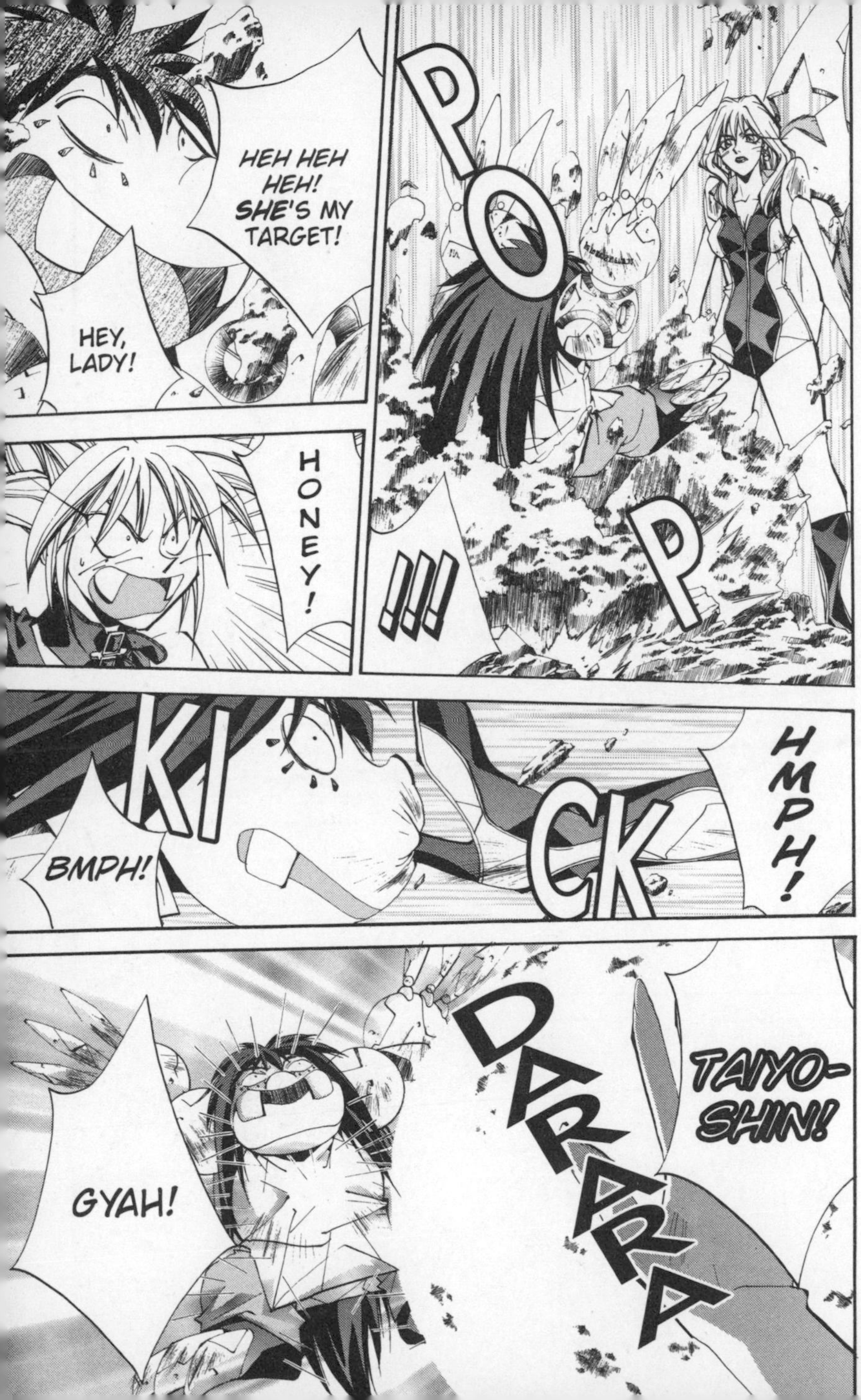
POP
!!!
HEH HEH HEH! SHE'S MY TARGET!
HEY, LADY!
HONEY!
HMPH!
KICK
BMPH!
TAIYO-SHIN!
DARARARA
GYAH!

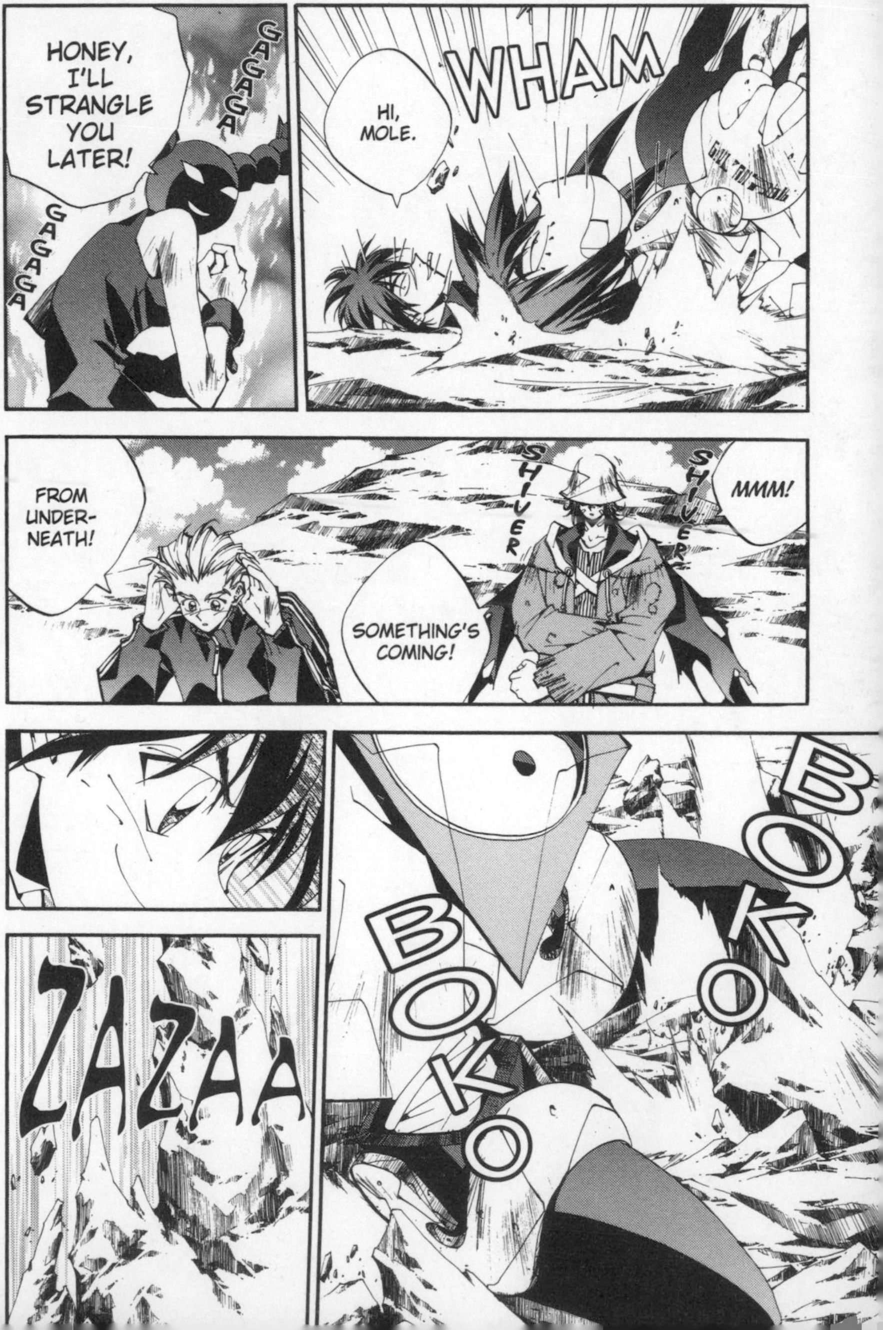
WHAM
HI, MOLE.
HONEY, I'LL STRANGLE YOU LATER!
GAGAGA
GAGAGA
MMM!
SHIVER
SHIVER
SOMETHING'S COMING!
FROM UNDER-NEATH!
BOKO
BOKO
ZAZAA

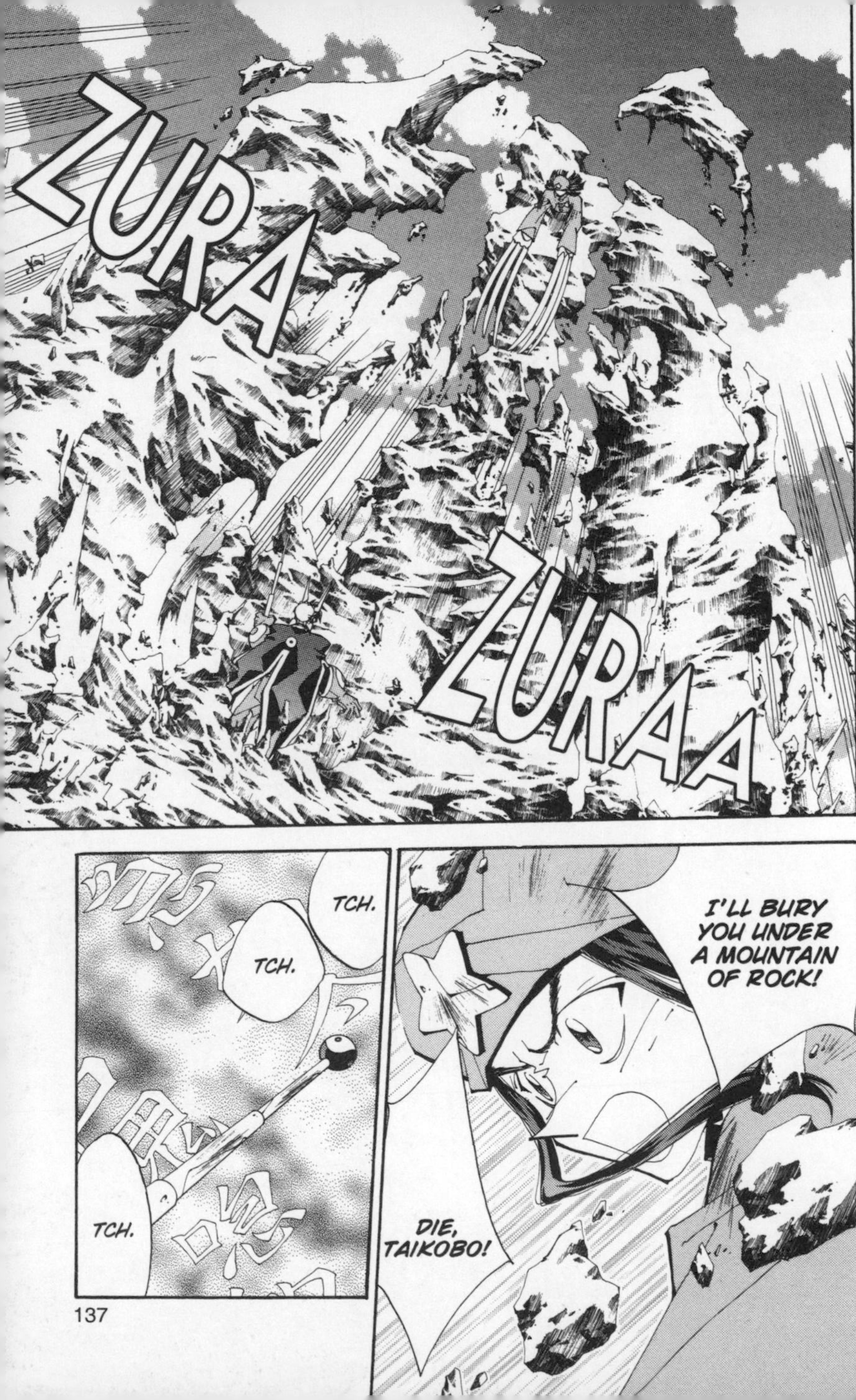
ZURA
ZURAA
I'LL BURY YOU UNDER A MOUNTAIN OF ROCK!
DIE, TAIKOBO!
TCH.
TCH.
TCH.

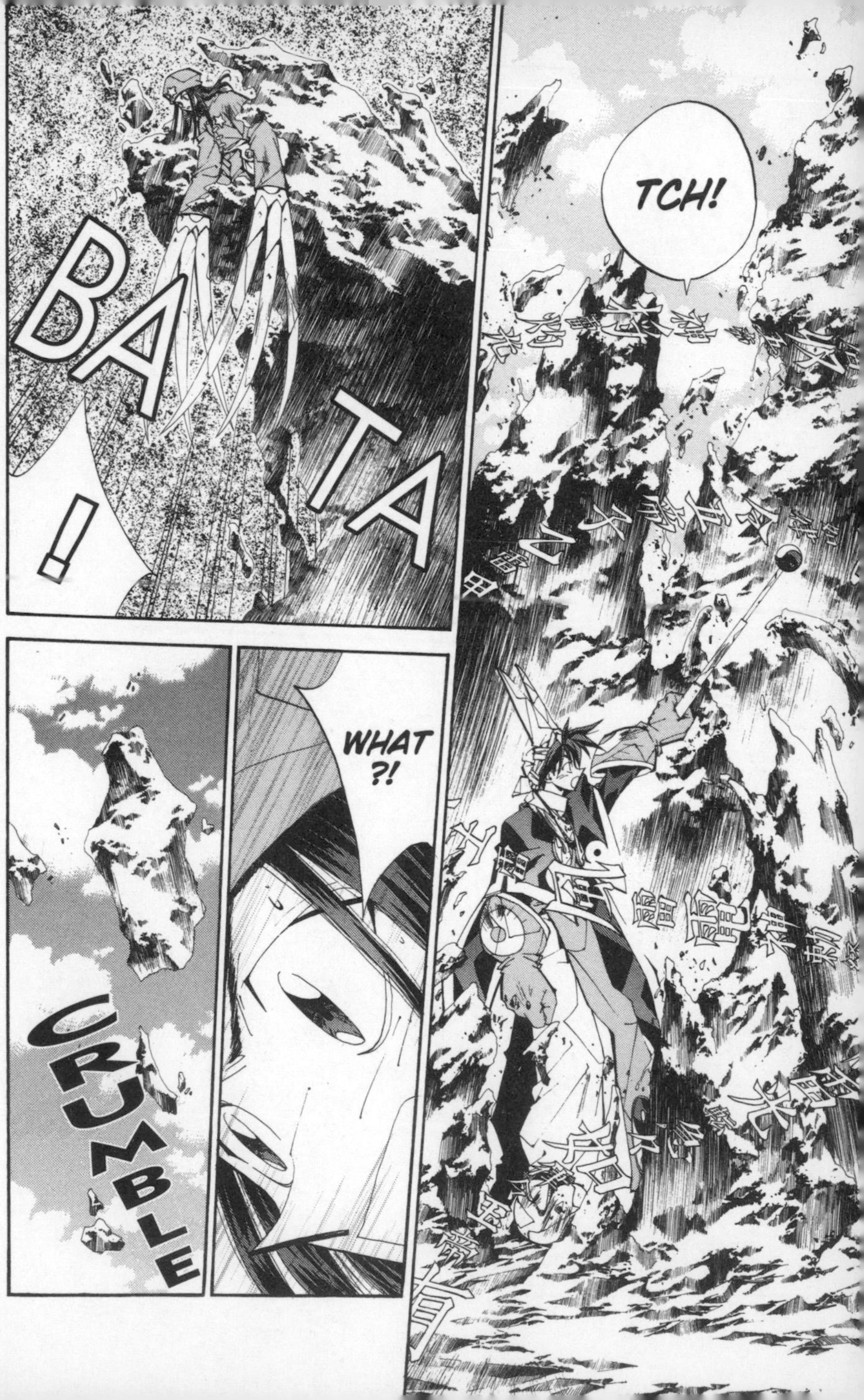
TCH!
BA
TA
!
WHAT
?!
CRUMBLE

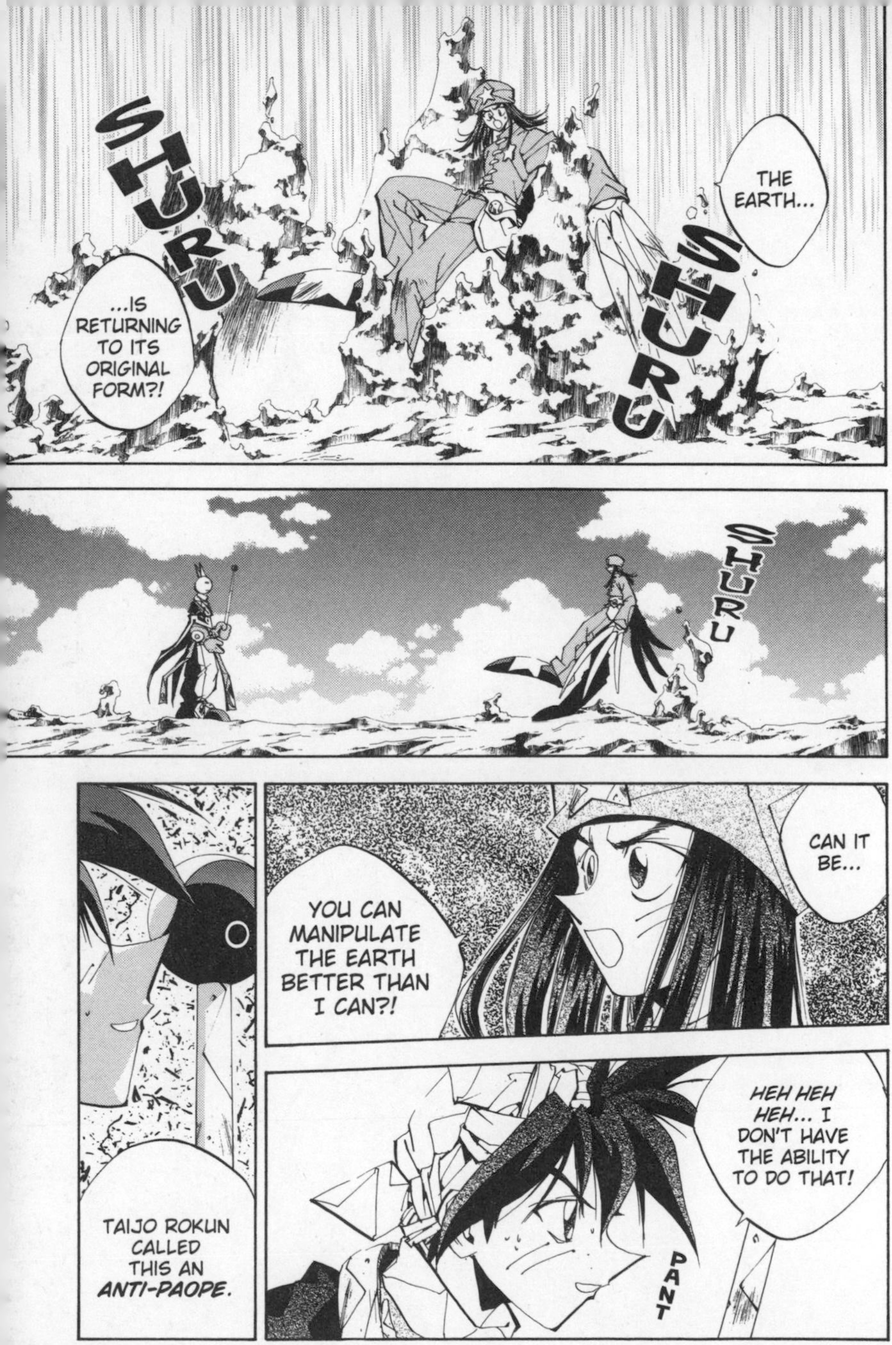
THE EARTH...
SHURU
...IS RETURNING TO ITS ORIGINAL FORM?!
SHURU
SHURU
CAN IT BE...
YOU CAN MANIPULATE THE EARTH BETTER THAN I CAN?!
HEH HEH HEH... I DON'T HAVE THE ABILITY TO DO THAT!
PANT
TAIJO ROKUN CALLED THIS AN *ANTI-PAOPE*.

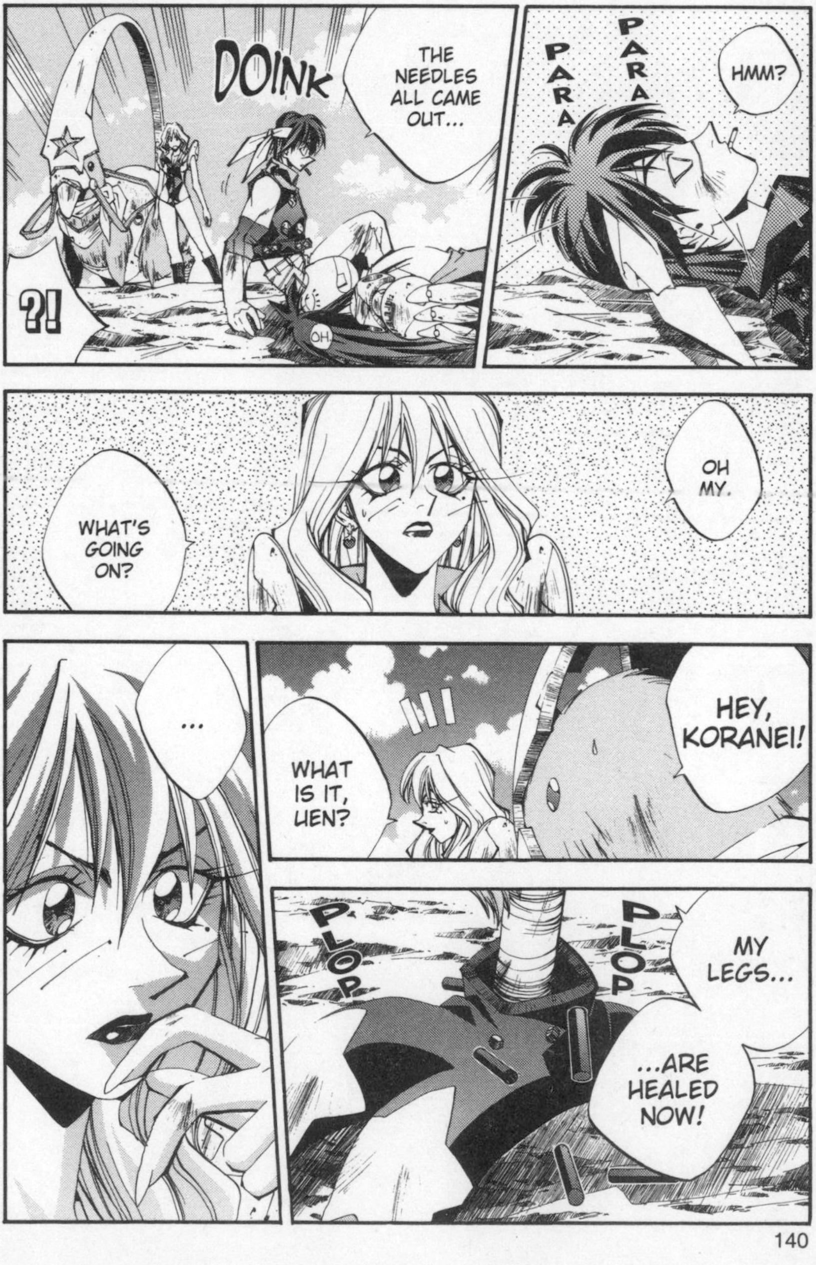

PARA
PARA
HMM?
DOINK
THE NEEDLES ALL CAME OUT...
?!
OH.
OH MY.
WHAT'S GOING ON?
HEY, KORANEI!
WHAT IS IT, UEN?
PLOP
PLOP
MY LEGS...
...ARE HEALED NOW!
...

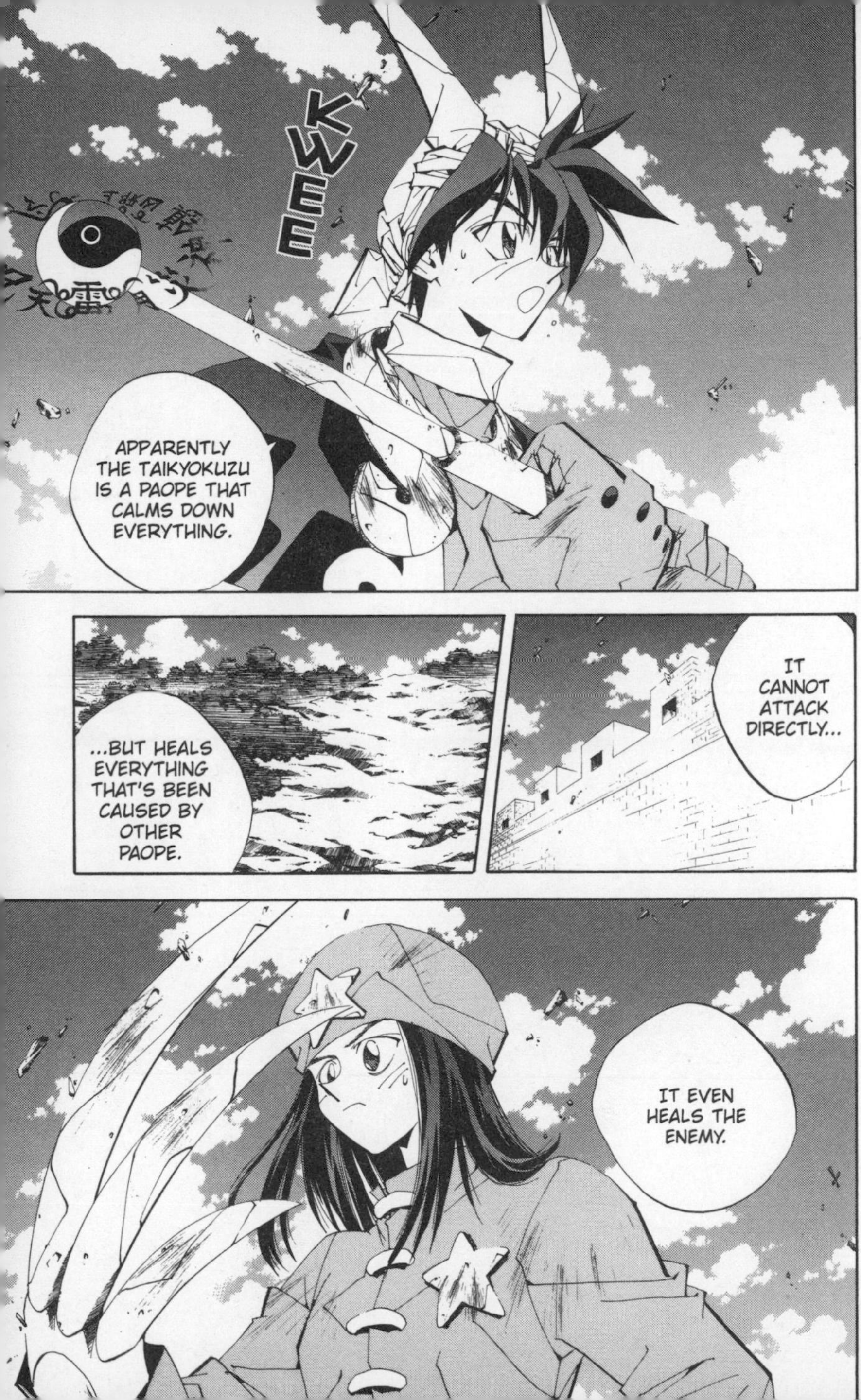
KWEE
APPARENTLY THE TAIKYOKUZU IS A PAOPE THAT CALMS DOWN EVERYTHING.
IT CANNOT ATTACK DIRECTLY...
...BUT HEALS EVERYTHING THAT'S BEEN CAUSED BY OTHER PAOPE.
IT EVEN HEALS THE ENEMY.

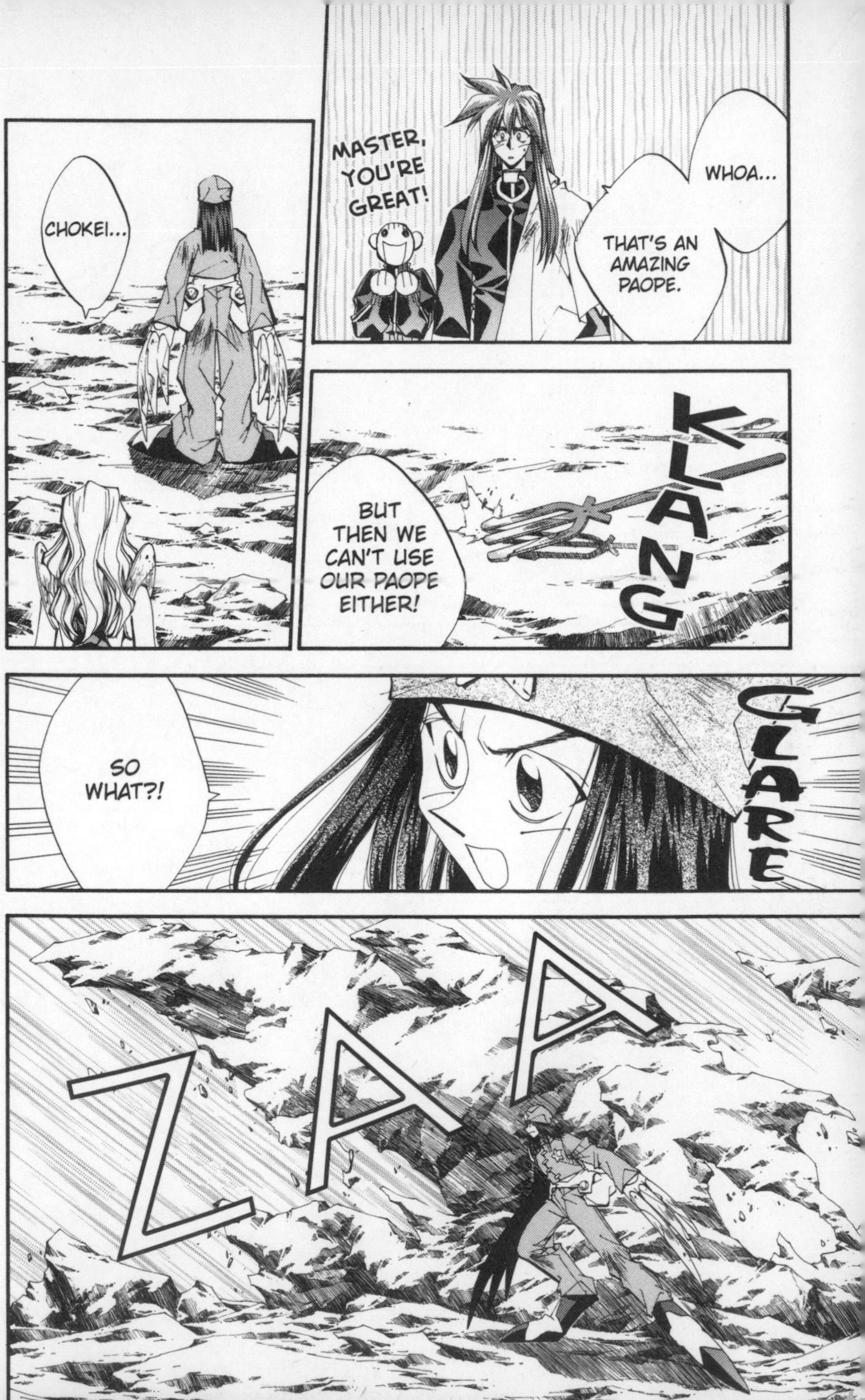
WHOA...
THAT'S AN AMAZING PAOPE.
MASTER, YOU'RE GREAT!
KLANG
BUT THEN WE CAN'T USE OUR PAOPE EITHER!
CHOKEI...
GLARE
SO WHAT?!
ZAAA

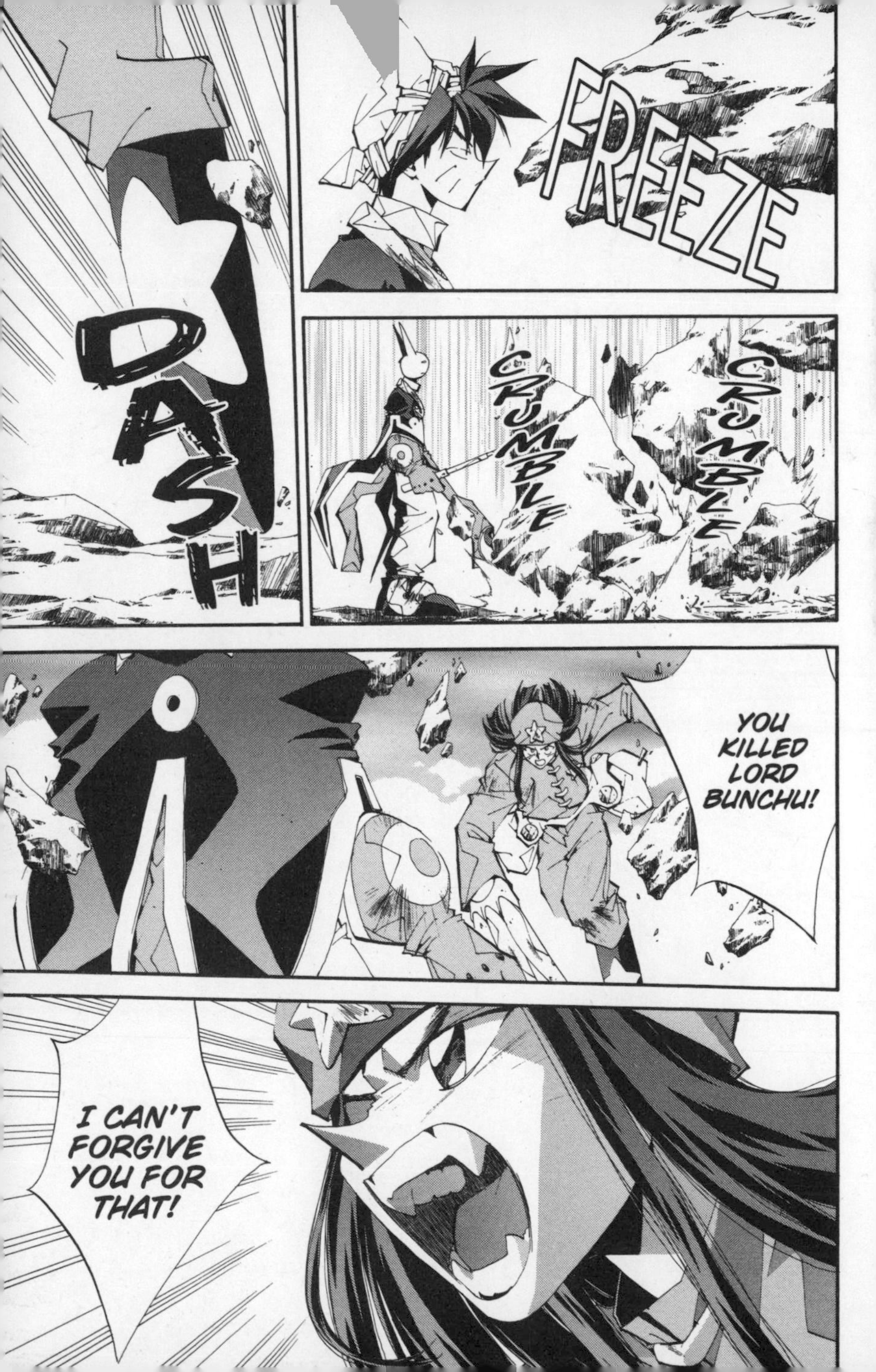
FREEZE
CRUMBLE
CRUMBLE
DASH
YOU KILLED LORD BUNCHU!
I CAN'T FORGIVE YOU FOR THAT!

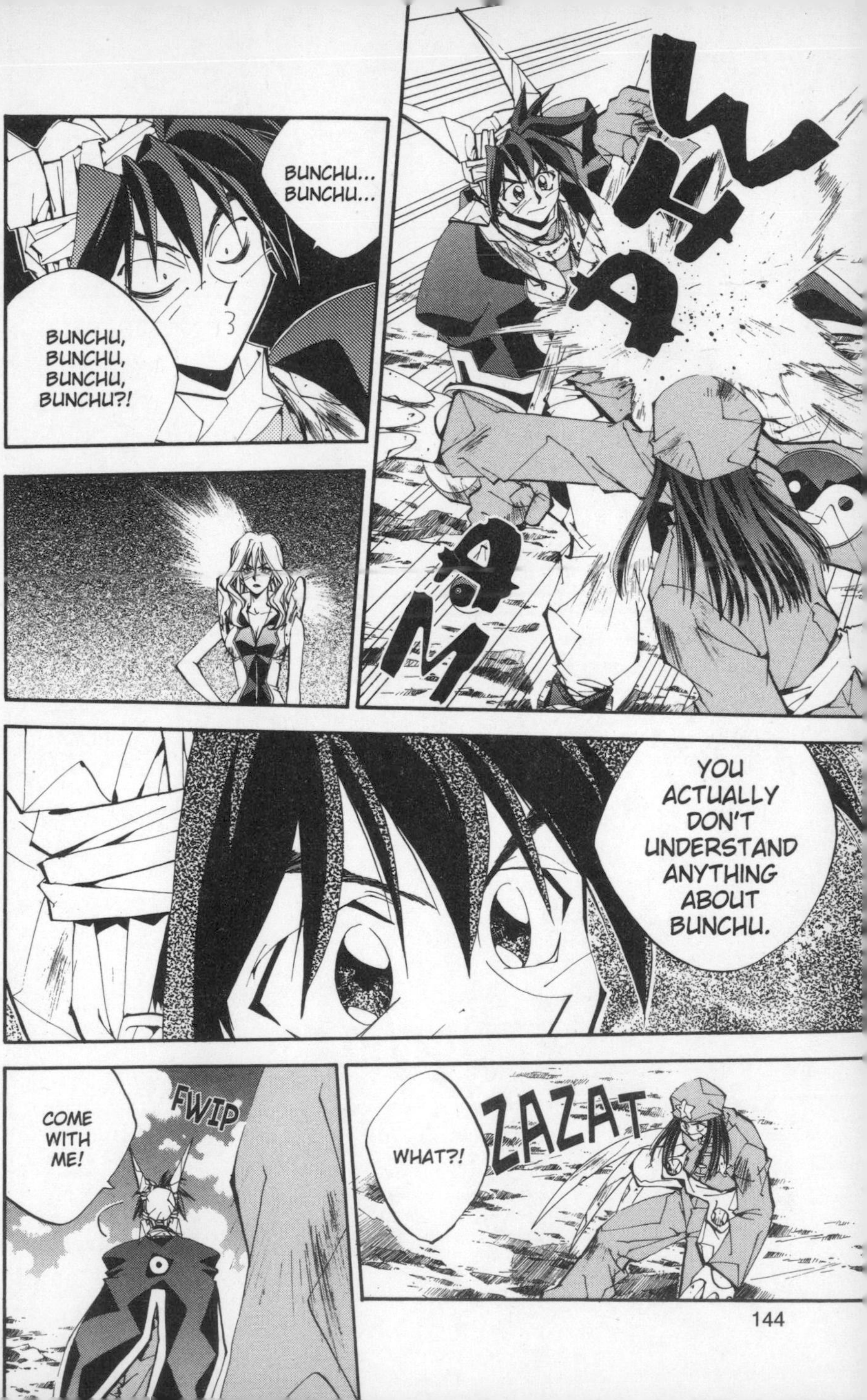
WHAM
BUNCHU... BUNCHU...
BUNCHU, BUNCHU, BUNCHU, BUNCHU?!
YOU ACTUALLY DON'T UNDERSTAND ANYTHING ABOUT BUNCHU.
WHAT?!
ZAZAT
FWIP
COME WITH ME!

READ THIS WAY

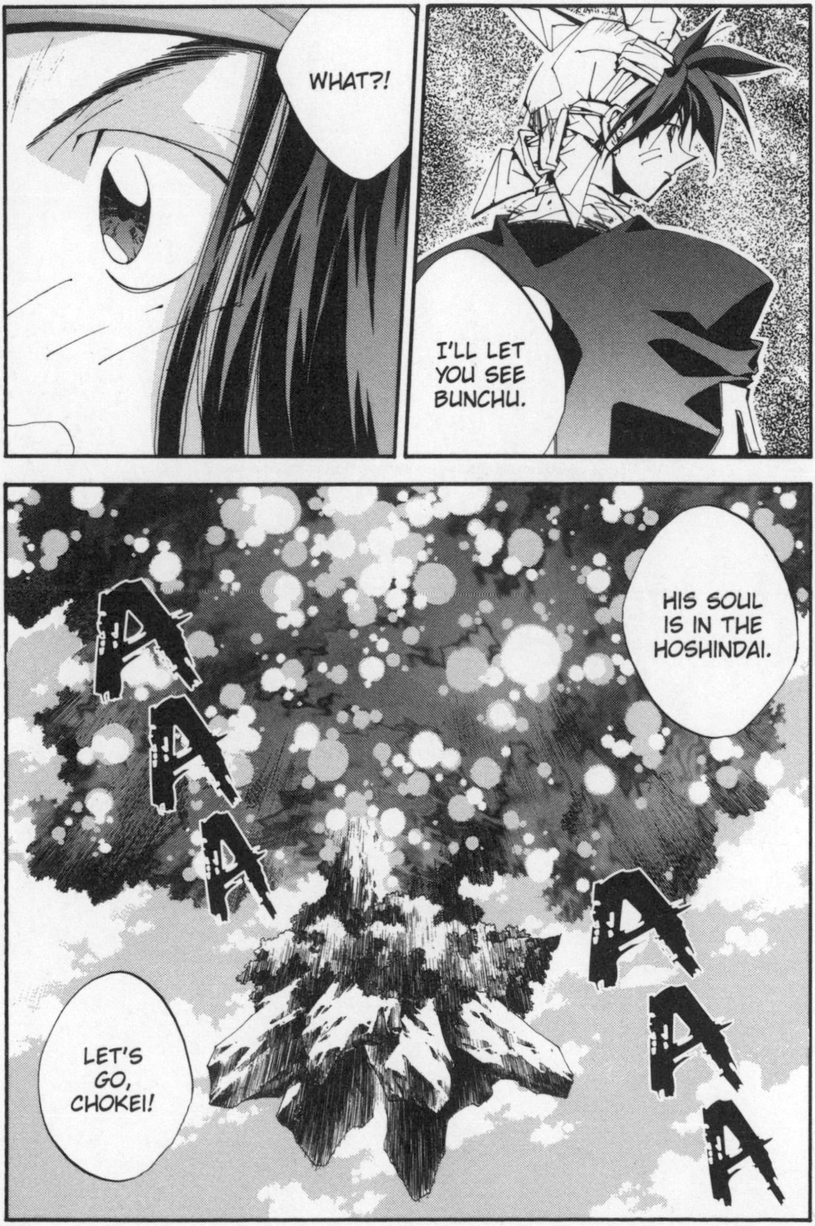
I'LL LET YOU SEE BUNCHU.
WHAT?!
HIS SOUL IS IN THE HOSHINDAI.
AAA
AAAA
LET'S GO, CHOKEI!

封神演義

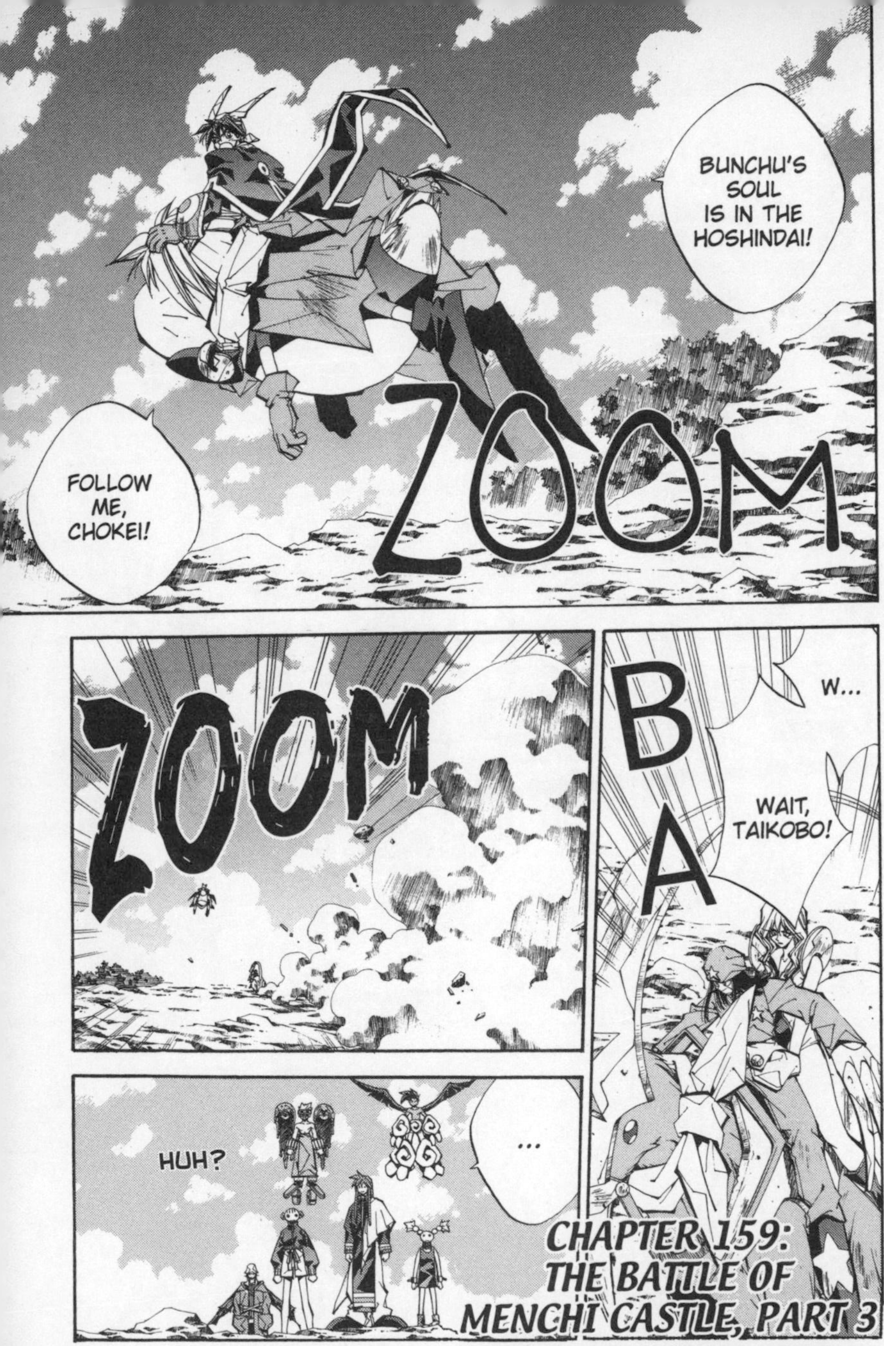
BUNCHU'S SOUL IS IN THE HOSHINDAI!
ZOOM
FOLLOW ME, CHOKEI!
BA
W...
WAIT, TAIKOBO!
ZOOM
...
HUH?

CHAPTER 159: THE BATTLE OF MENCHI CASTLE, PART 3

THE HOSHINDAI

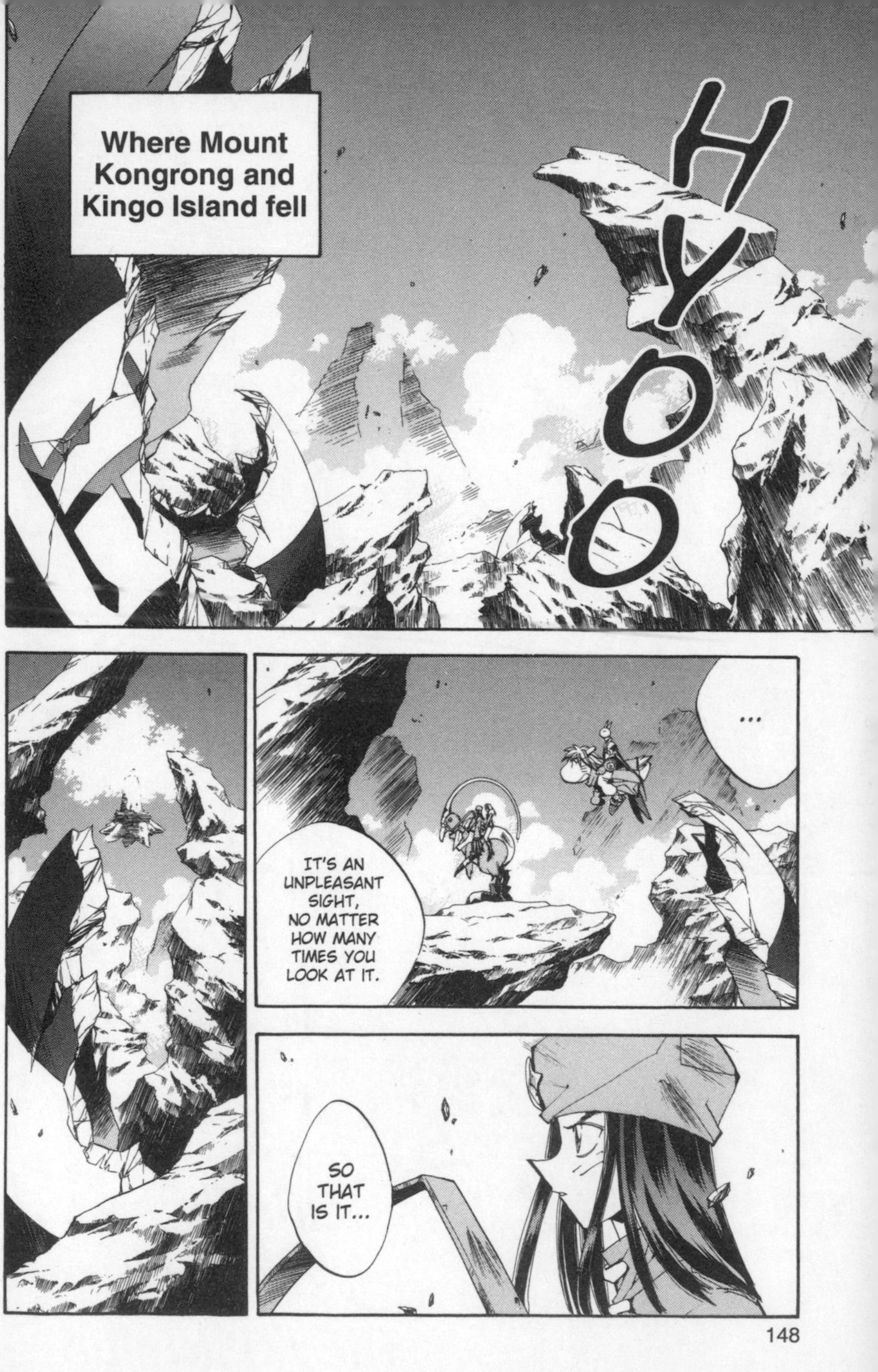
HYOOO
Where Mount Kongrong and Kingo Island fell
...
IT'S AN UNPLEASANT SIGHT, NO MATTER HOW MANY TIMES YOU LOOK AT IT.
SO THAT IS IT...

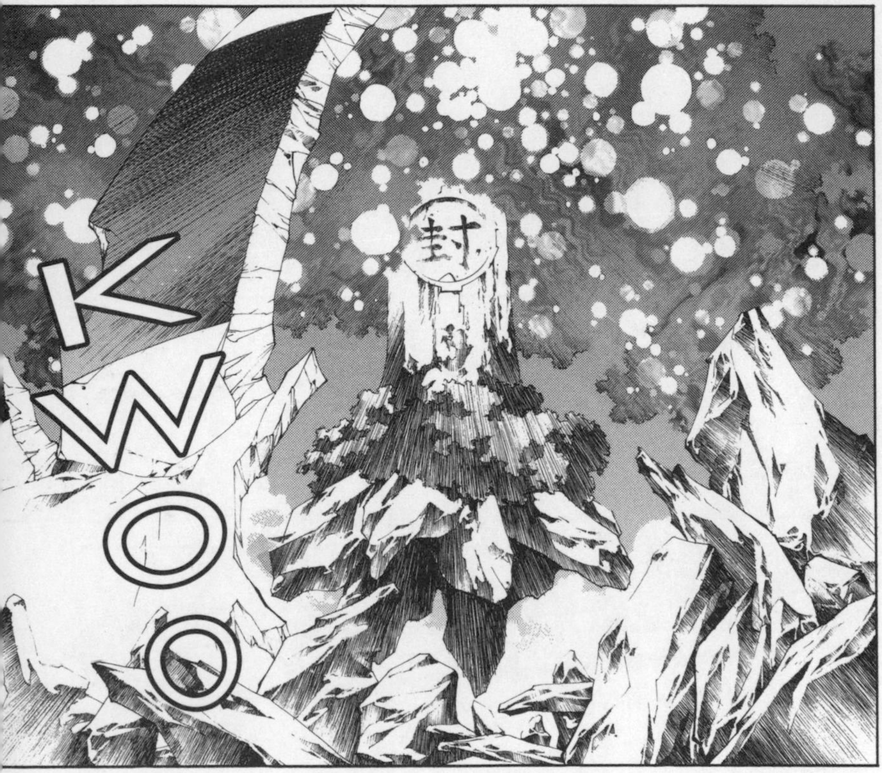
KWOO

Chapter 159

THE BATTLE OF MENCHI CASTLE, PART 3
THE HOSHINDAI

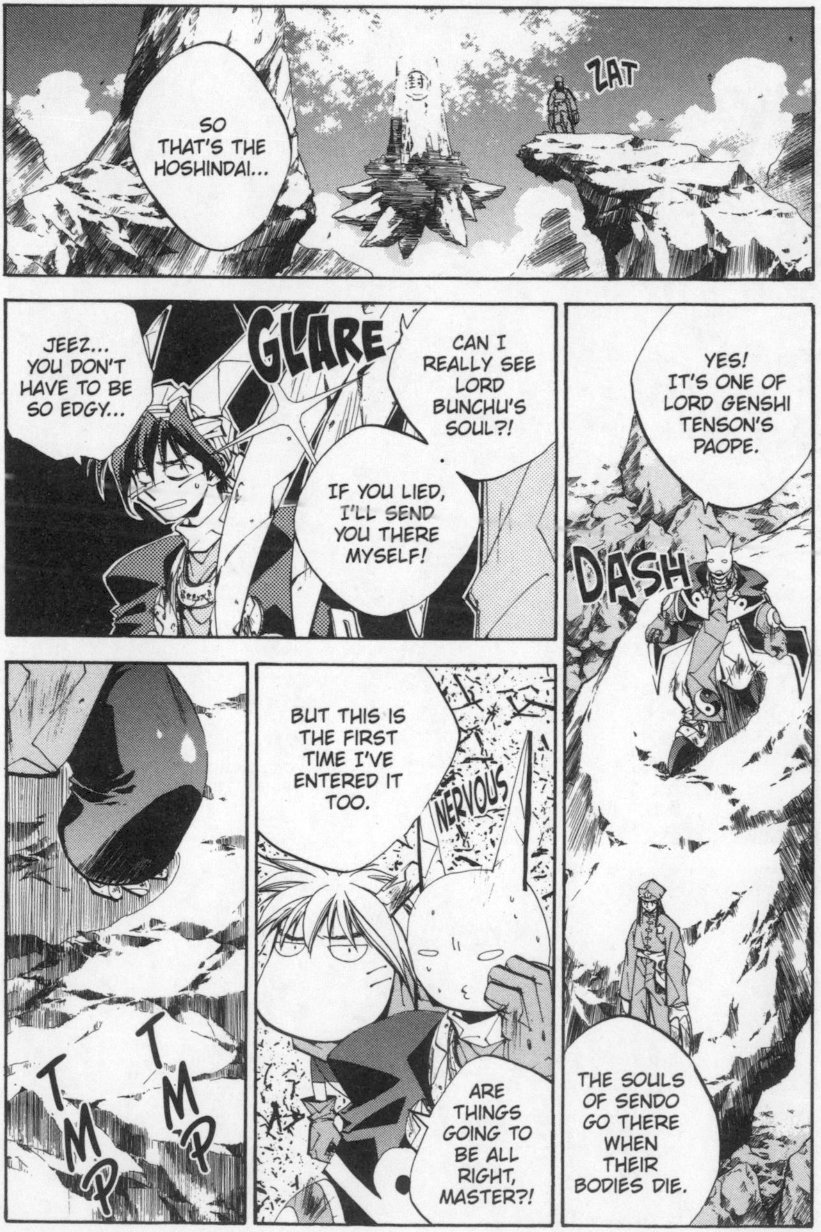
ZAT
SO THAT'S THE HOSHINDAI...
YES! IT'S ONE OF LORD GENSHI TENSON'S PAOPE.
DASH
THE SOULS OF SENDO GO THERE WHEN THEIR BODIES DIE.
CAN I REALLY SEE LORD BUNCHU'S SOUL?!
IF YOU LIED, I'LL SEND YOU THERE MYSELF!
GLARE
JEEZ... YOU DON'T HAVE TO BE SO EDGY...
BUT THIS IS THE FIRST TIME I'VE ENTERED IT TOO.
NERVOUS
ARE THINGS GOING TO BE ALL RIGHT, MASTER?!
TMP
TMP

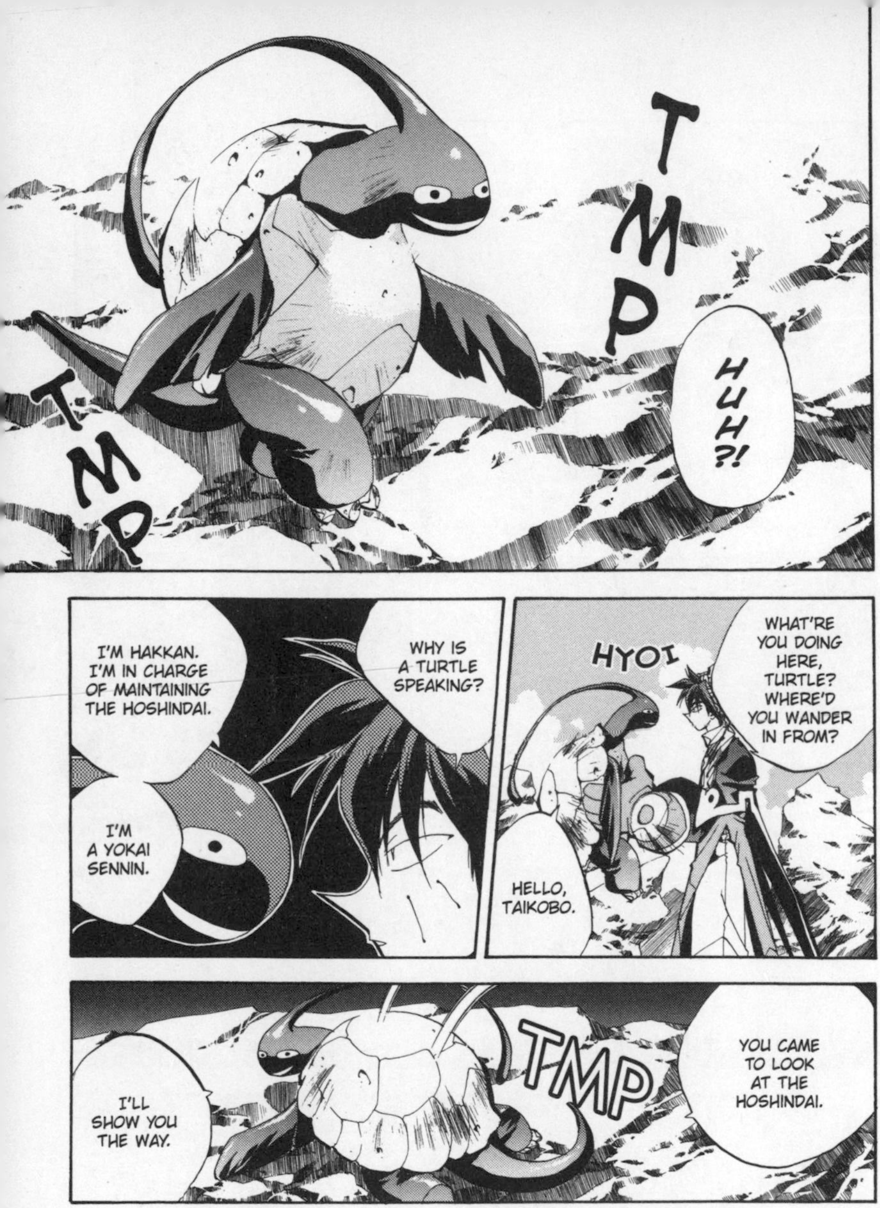
TMP
HUH?!
TMP
WHAT'RE YOU DOING HERE, TURTLE? WHERE'D YOU WANDER IN FROM?
HYOI
HELLO, TAIKOBO.
WHY IS A TURTLE SPEAKING?
I'M HAKKAN. I'M IN CHARGE OF MAINTAINING THE HOSHINDAI.
I'M A YOKAI SENNIN.
YOU CAME TO LOOK AT THE HOSHINDAI.
TMP
I'LL SHOW YOU THE WAY.
...

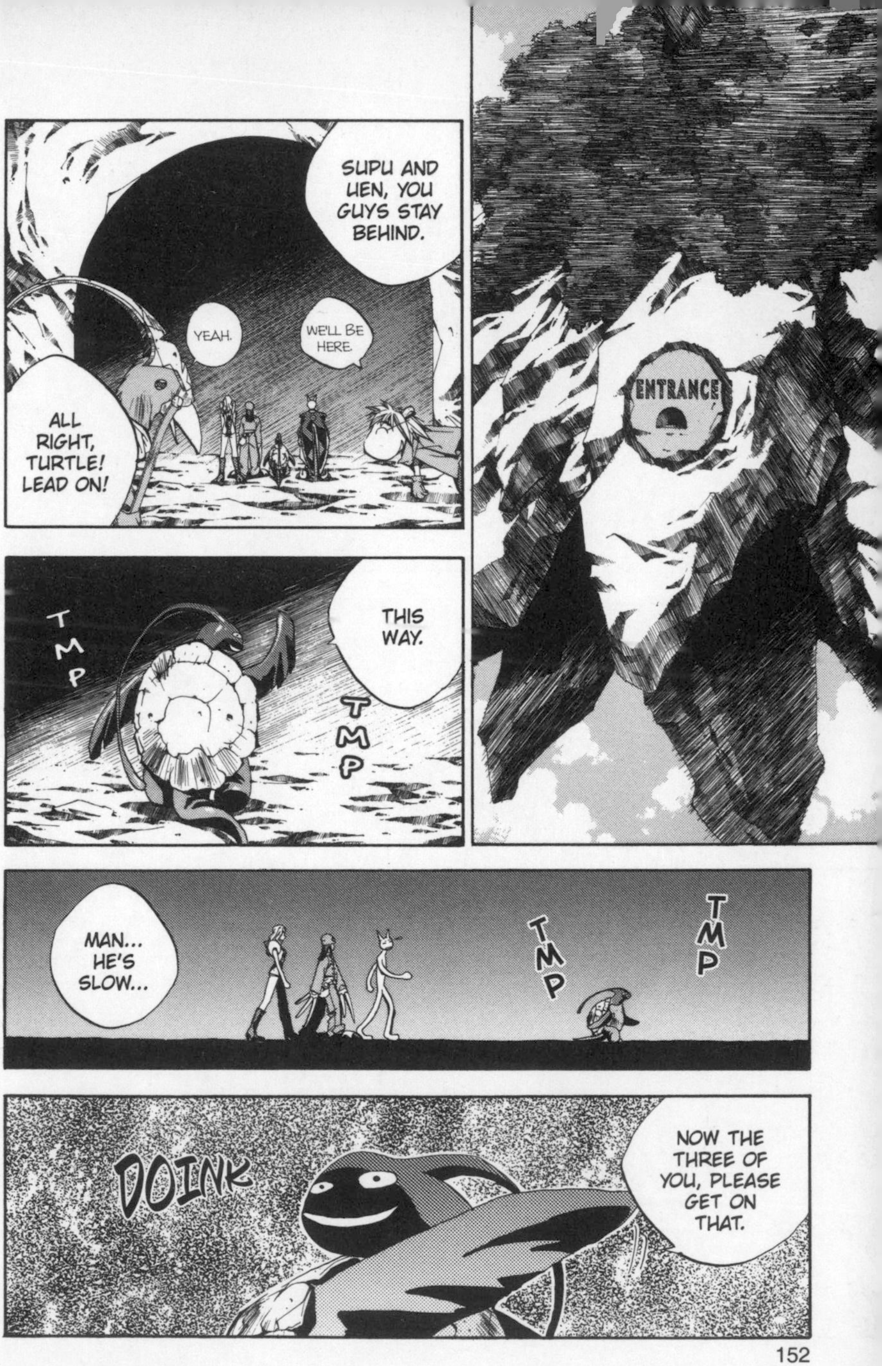
ENTRANCE
SUPU AND UEN, YOU GUYS STAY BEHIND.
WE'LL BE HERE.
YEAH.
ALL RIGHT, TURTLE! LEAD ON!
THIS WAY.
TMP TMP
TMP
TMP
TMP
MAN... HE'S SLOW...
NOW THE THREE OF YOU, PLEASE GET ON THAT.
DOINK

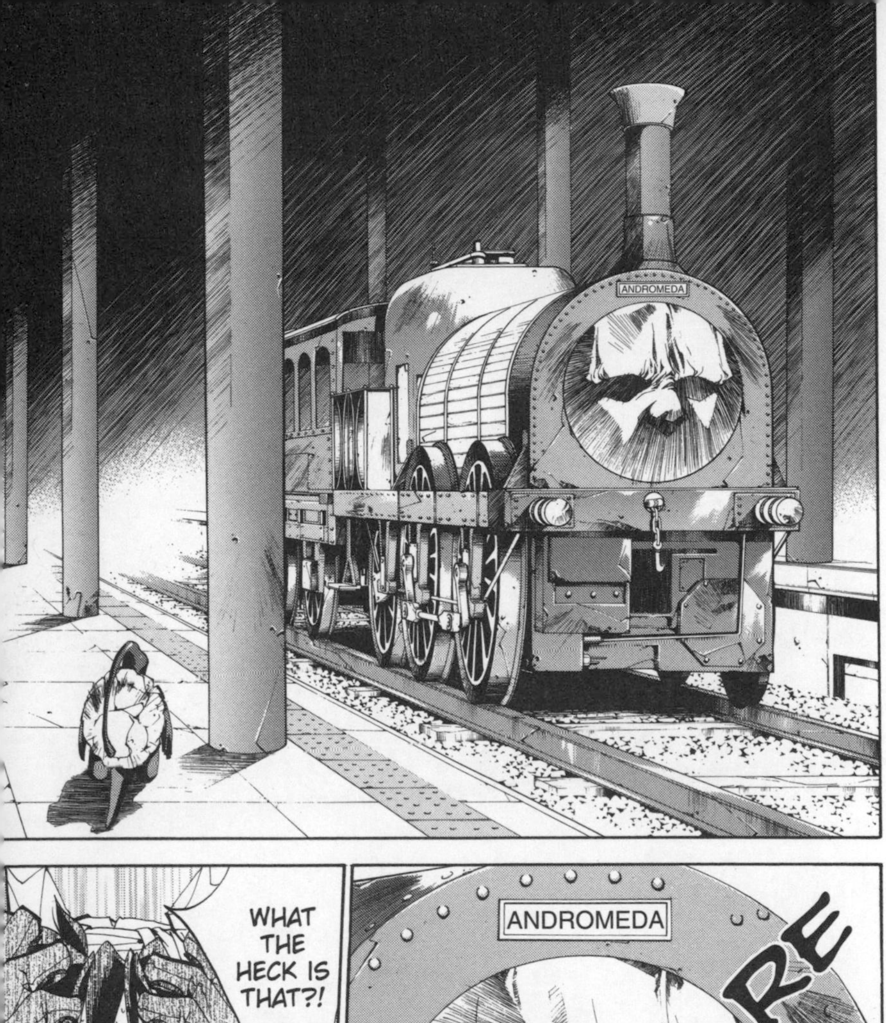
ANDROMEDA

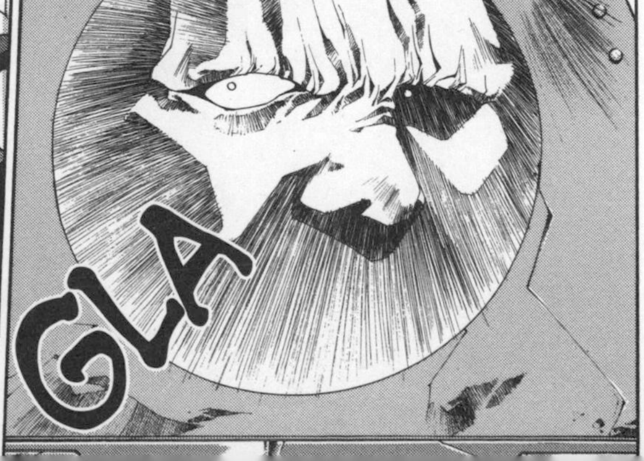
ANDROMEDA
GLARE

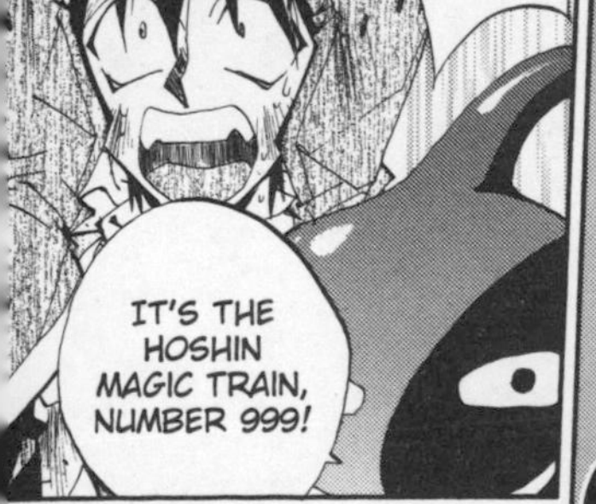
WHAT THE HECK IS THAT?!
IT'S THE HOSHIN MAGIC TRAIN, NUMBER 999!

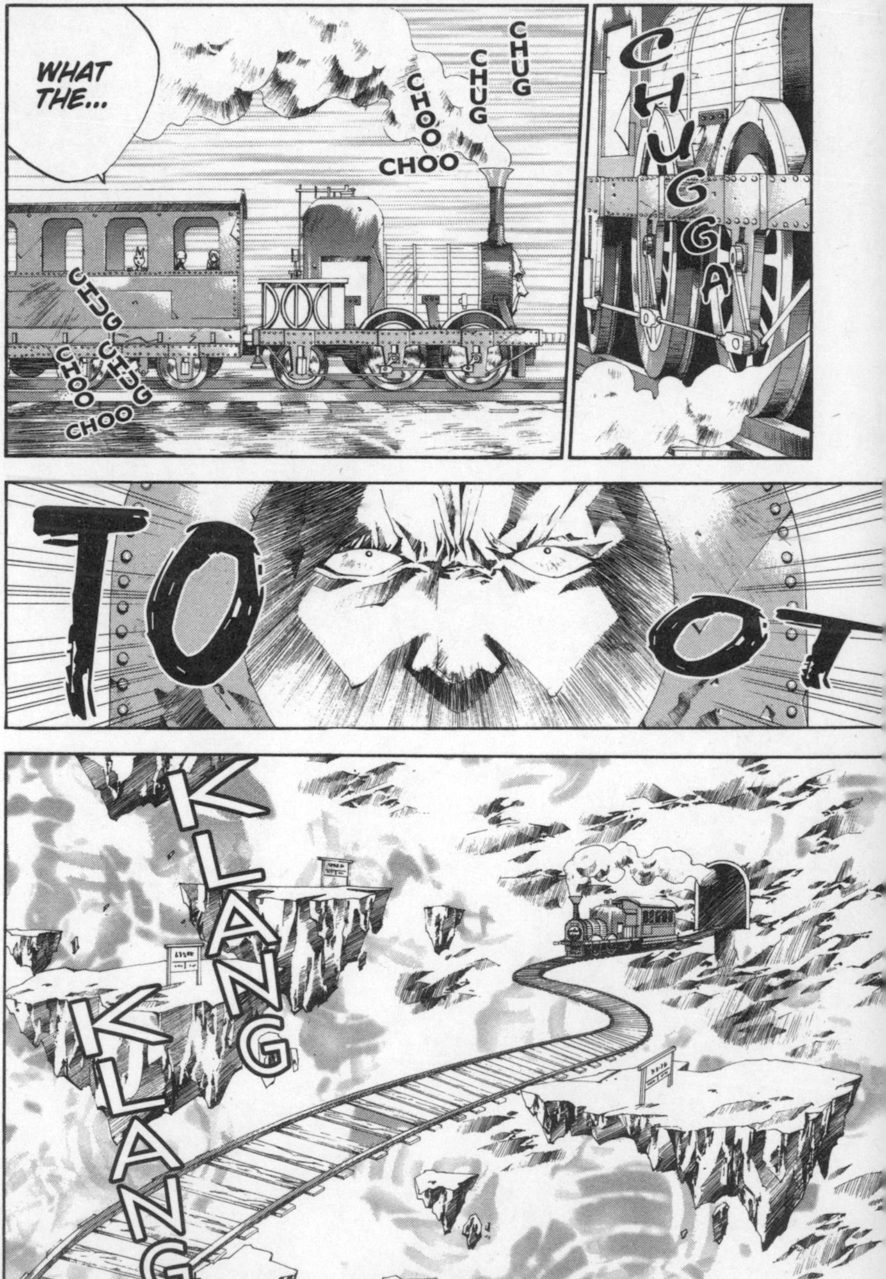
CHUGGA
WHAT THE...
CHUG CHUG CHOO CHOO
CHUG CHUG CHOO CHOO
TOOOT
KLANG KLANG

READ THIS WAY

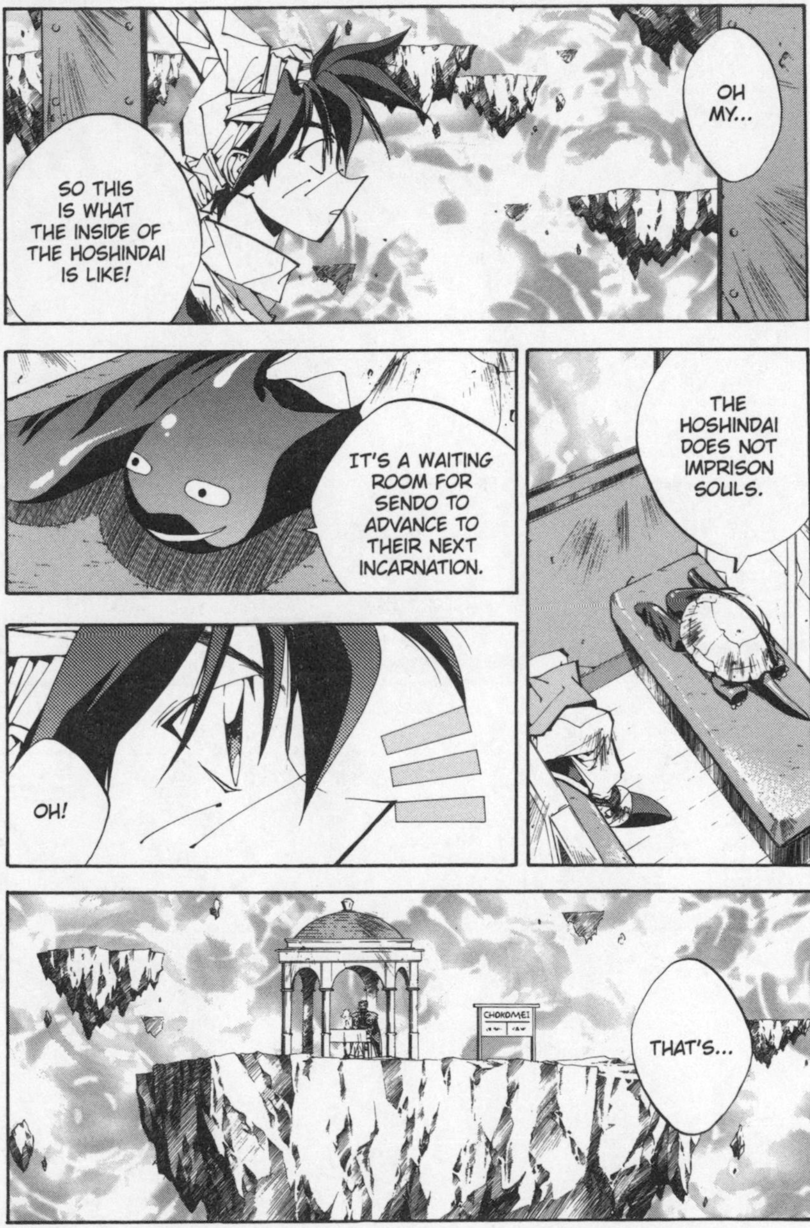
OH MY...
SO THIS IS WHAT THE INSIDE OF THE HOSHINDAI IS LIKE!
THE HOSHINDAI DOES NOT IMPRISON SOULS.
IT'S A WAITING ROOM FOR SENDO TO ADVANCE TO THEIR NEXT INCARNATION.
OH!
THAT'S...
CHOKOMEI

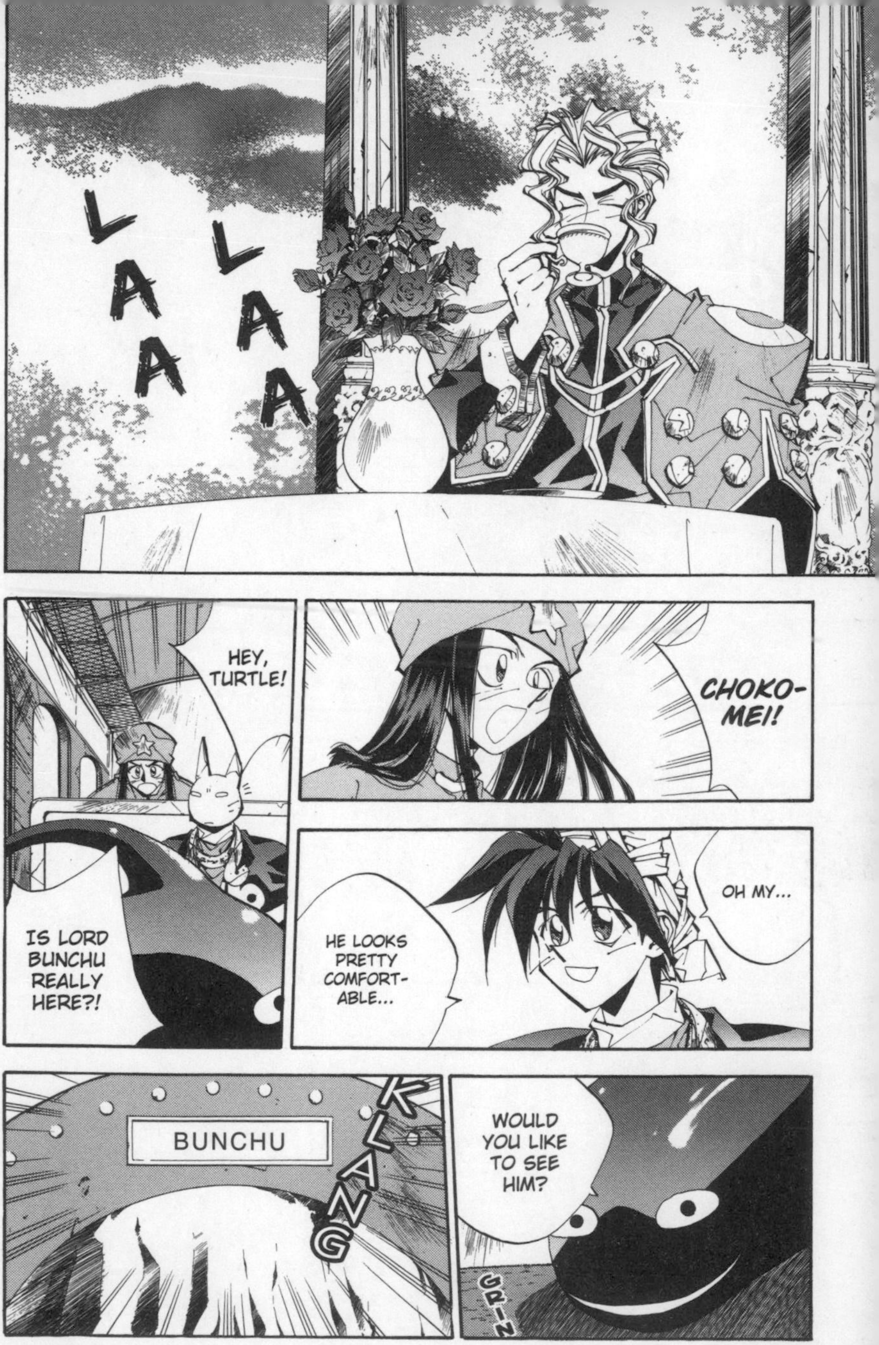
LAA
LAA
CHOKO-MEI!
OH MY...
HE LOOKS PRETTY COMFORTABLE...
HEY, TURTLE!
IS LORD BUNCHU REALLY HERE?!
WOULD YOU LIKE TO SEE HIM?
GRIN
KLANG
BUNCHU

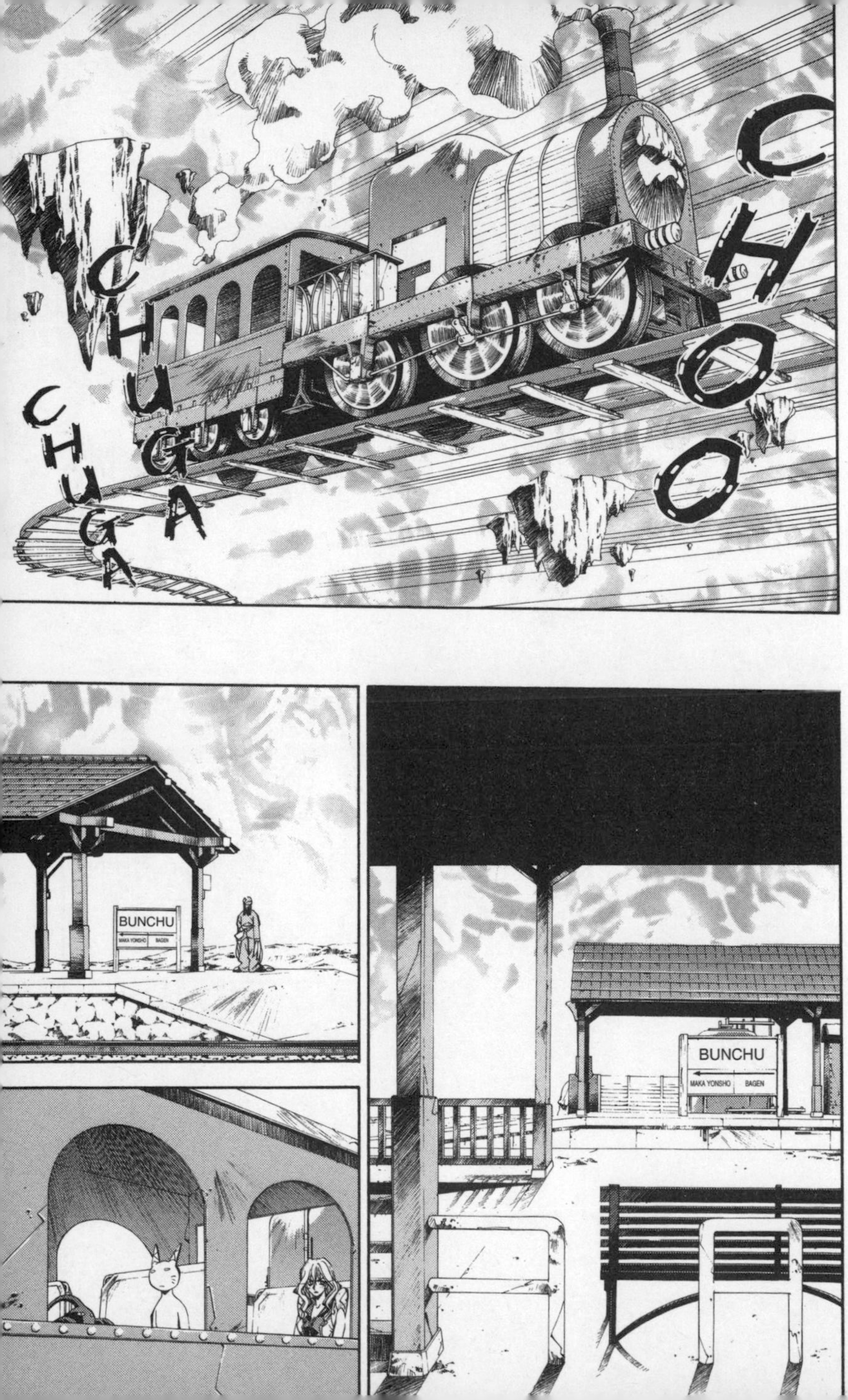
CHOO
CHUGA
CHUGA
BUNCHU
MAKA YONSHO
BAGEN
BUNCHU
MAKA YONSHO
BAGEN

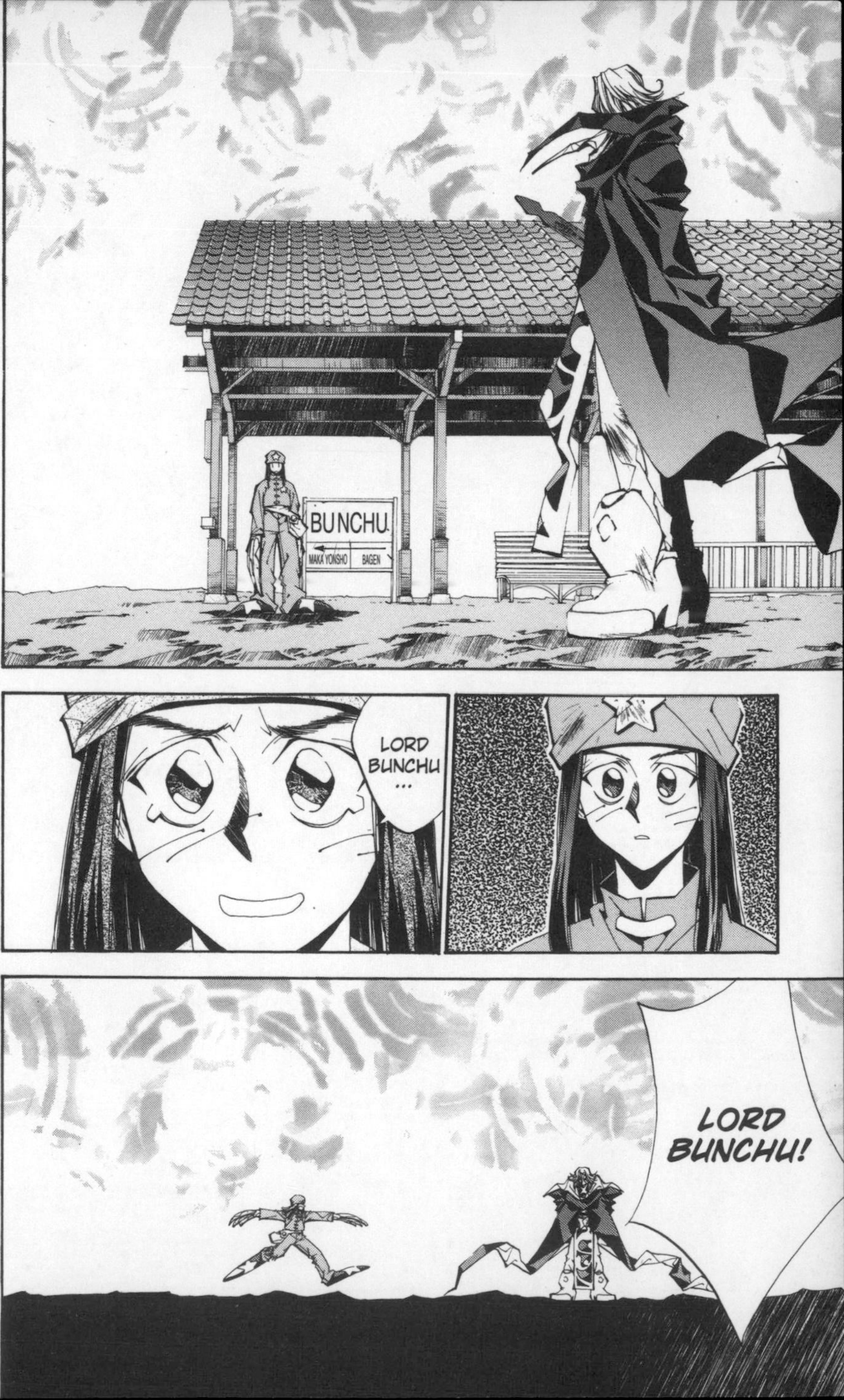
BUNCHU
MAKA YONSHO
BAGEN
LORD BUNCHU ...
LORD BUNCHU!

READ THIS WAY

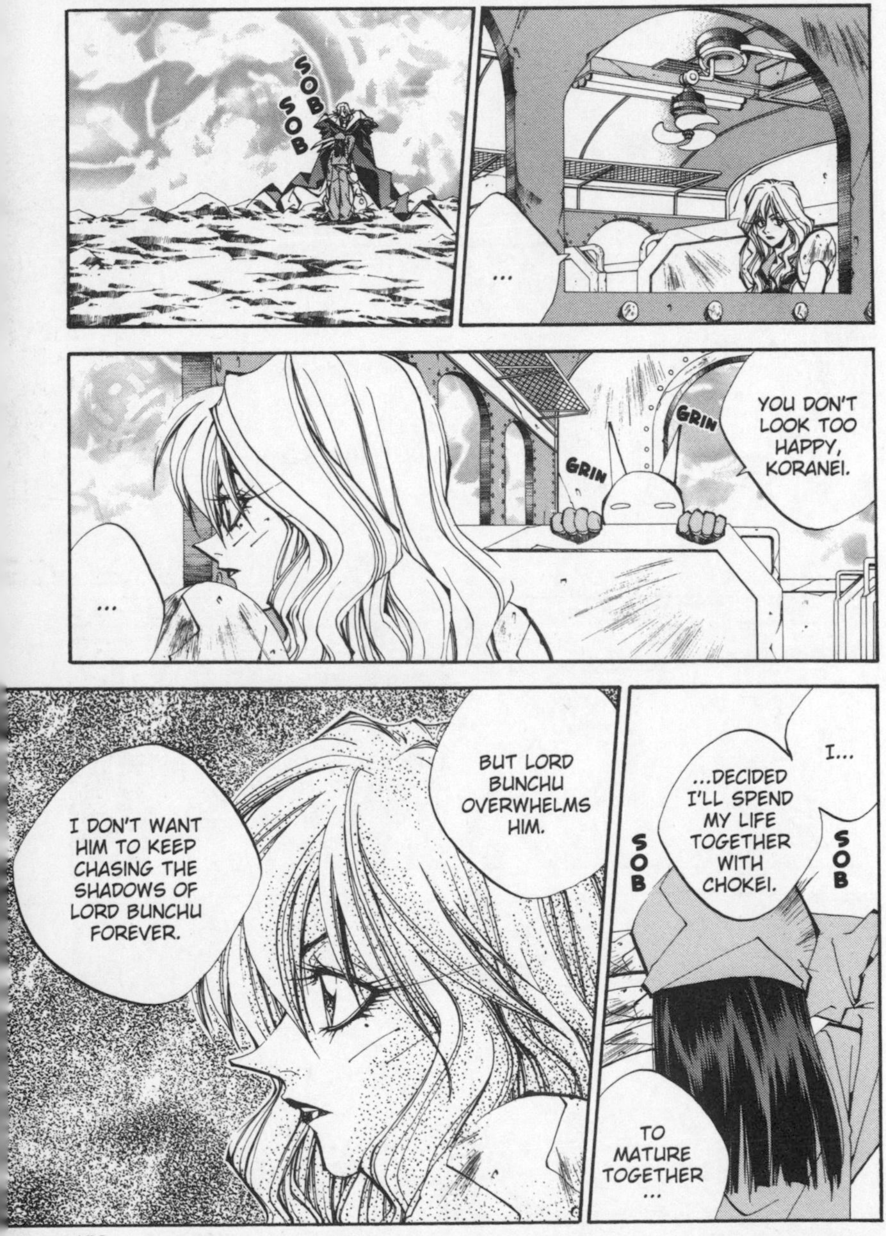
...
SOB SOB SOB
YOU DON'T LOOK TOO HAPPY, KORANEI.
GRIN
GRIN
...
I...
...DECIDED I'LL SPEND MY LIFE TOGETHER WITH CHOKEI.
SOB
SOB
TO MATURE TOGETHER ...
BUT LORD BUNCHU OVERWHELMS HIM.
I DON'T WANT HIM TO KEEP CHASING THE SHADOWS OF LORD BUNCHU FOREVER.

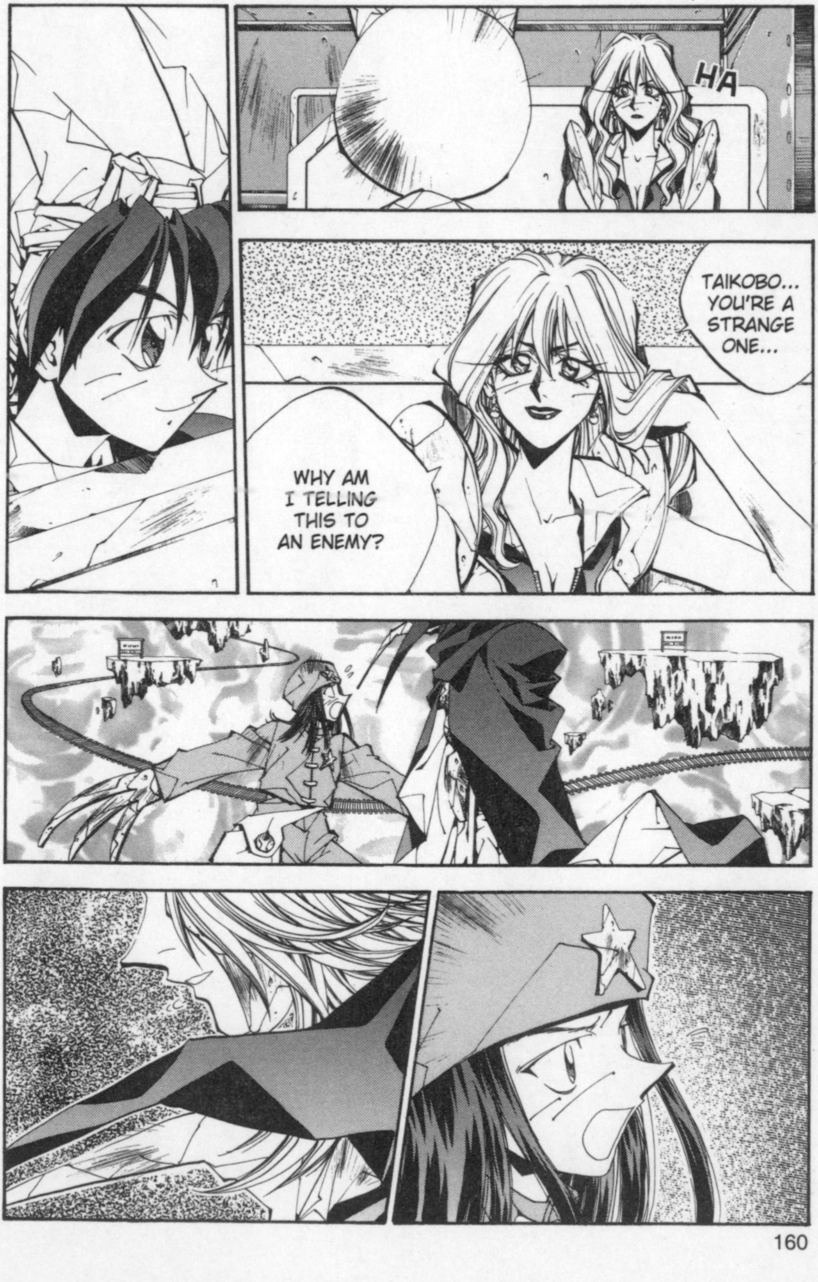
HA
TAIKOBO... YOU'RE A STRANGE ONE...
WHY AM I TELLING THIS TO AN ENEMY?

READ THIS WAY

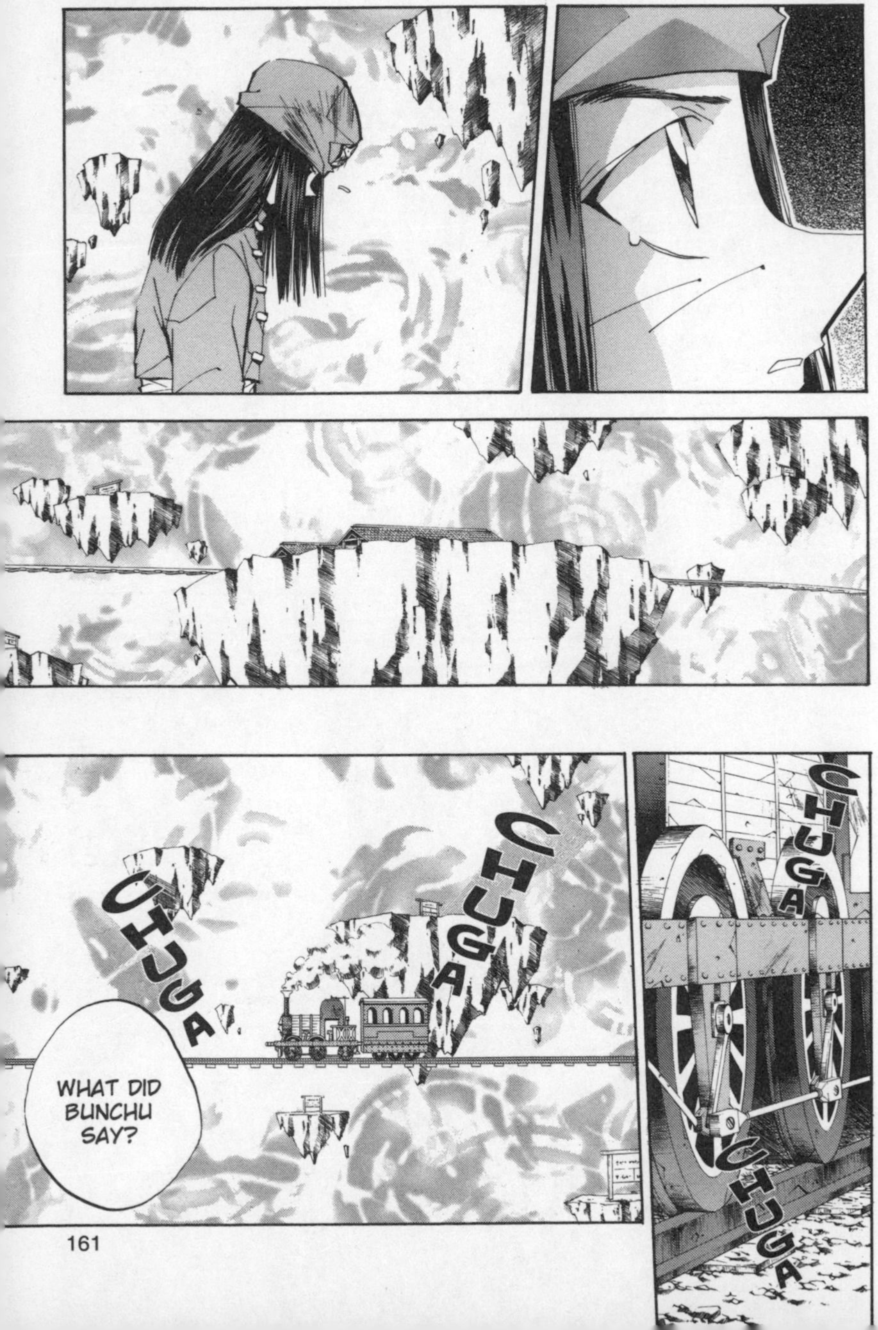

CHUGA
CHUGA
CHUGA
CHUGA
WHAT DID BUNCHU SAY?

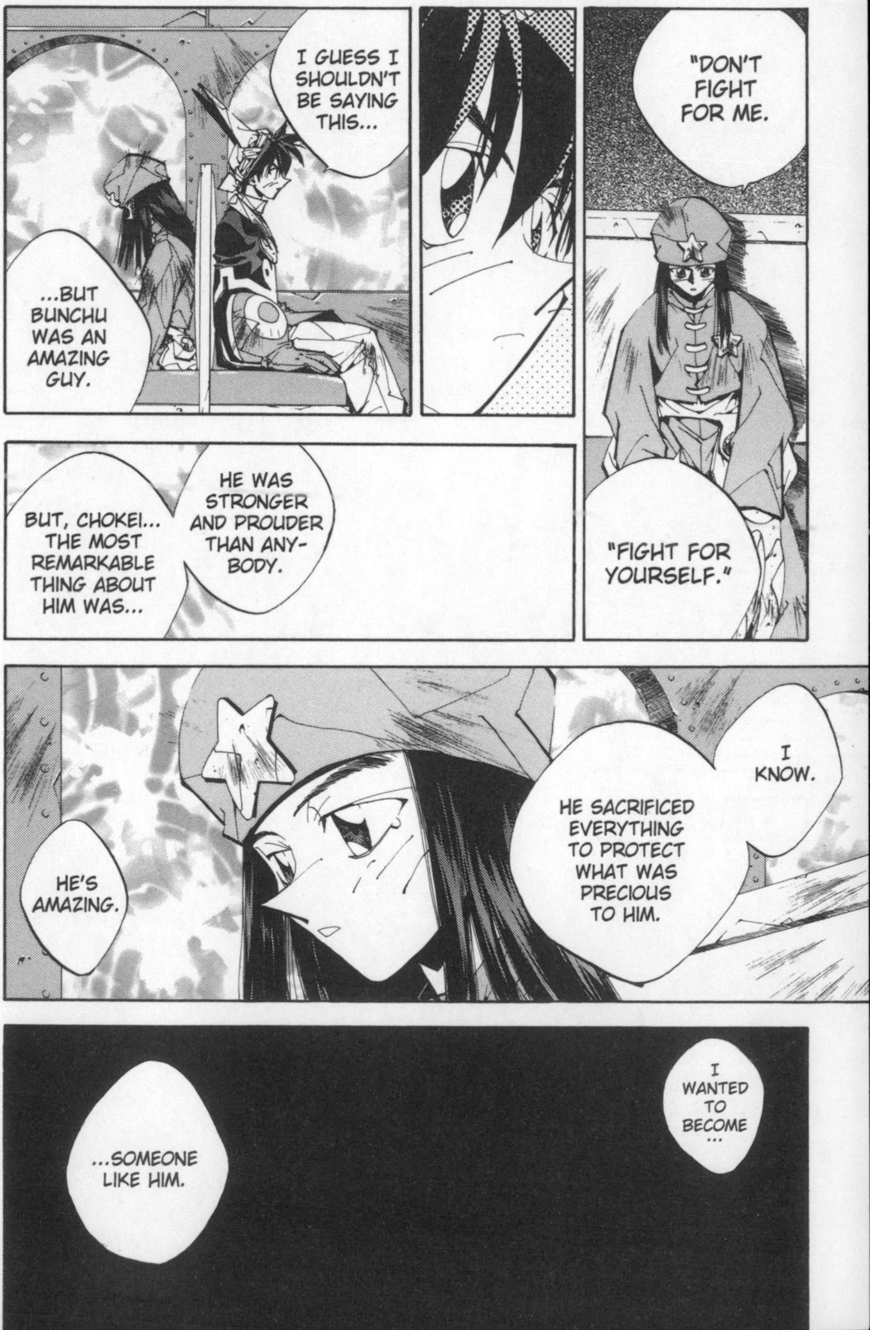
"DON'T FIGHT FOR ME.
"FIGHT FOR YOURSELF."
I GUESS I SHOULDN'T BE SAYING THIS...
...BUT BUNCHU WAS AN AMAZING GUY.
HE WAS STRONGER AND PROUDER THAN ANY-BODY.
BUT, CHOKEI... THE MOST REMARKABLE THING ABOUT HIM WAS...
I KNOW.
HE SACRIFICED EVERYTHING TO PROTECT WHAT WAS PRECIOUS TO HIM.
HE'S AMAZING.
I WANTED TO BECOME...
...SOMEONE LIKE HIM.

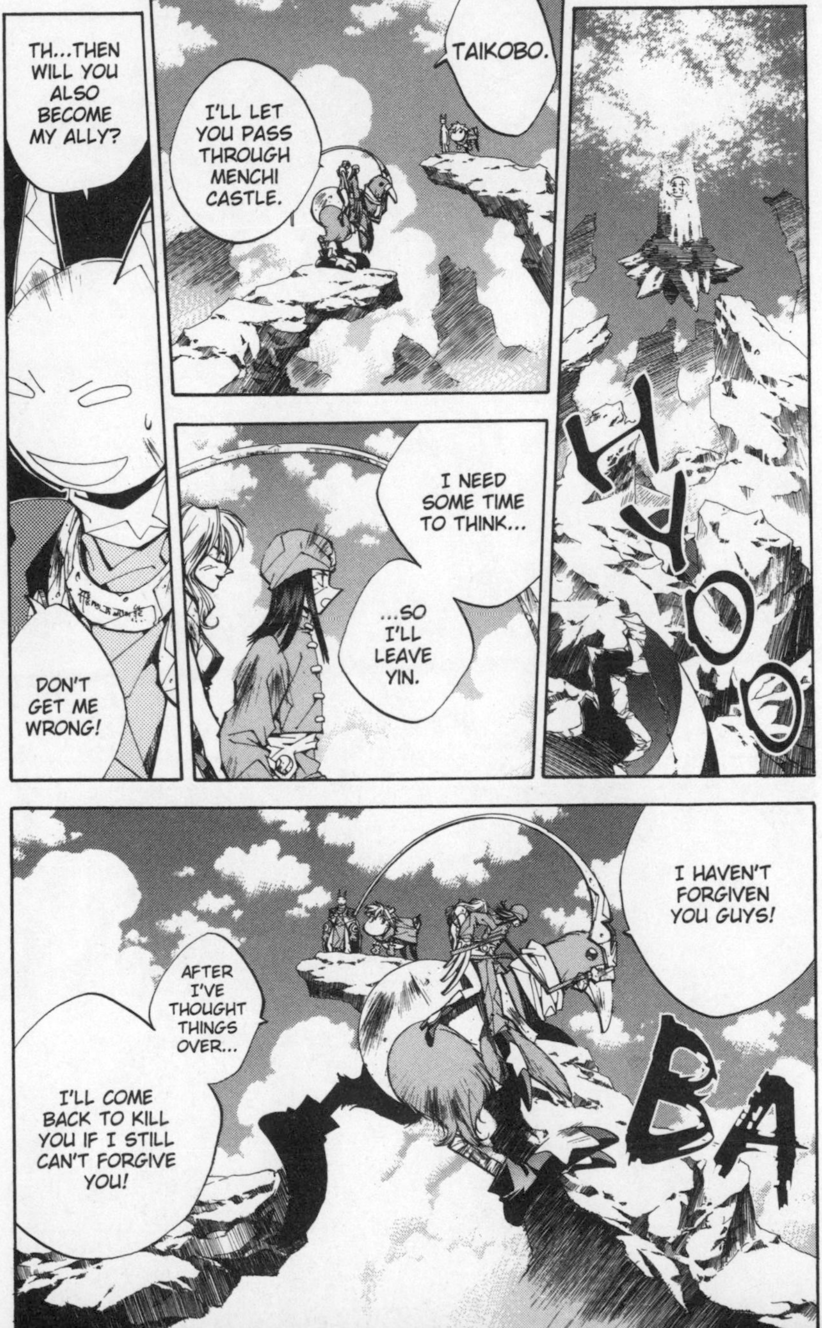
HYOOO
TAIKOBO.
I'LL LET YOU PASS THROUGH MENCHI CASTLE.
I NEED SOME TIME TO THINK...
...SO I'LL LEAVE YIN.
TH...THEN WILL YOU ALSO BECOME MY ALLY?
DON'T GET ME WRONG!
I HAVEN'T FORGIVEN YOU GUYS!
BA
AFTER I'VE THOUGHT THINGS OVER...
I'LL COME BACK TO KILL YOU IF I STILL CAN'T FORGIVE YOU!

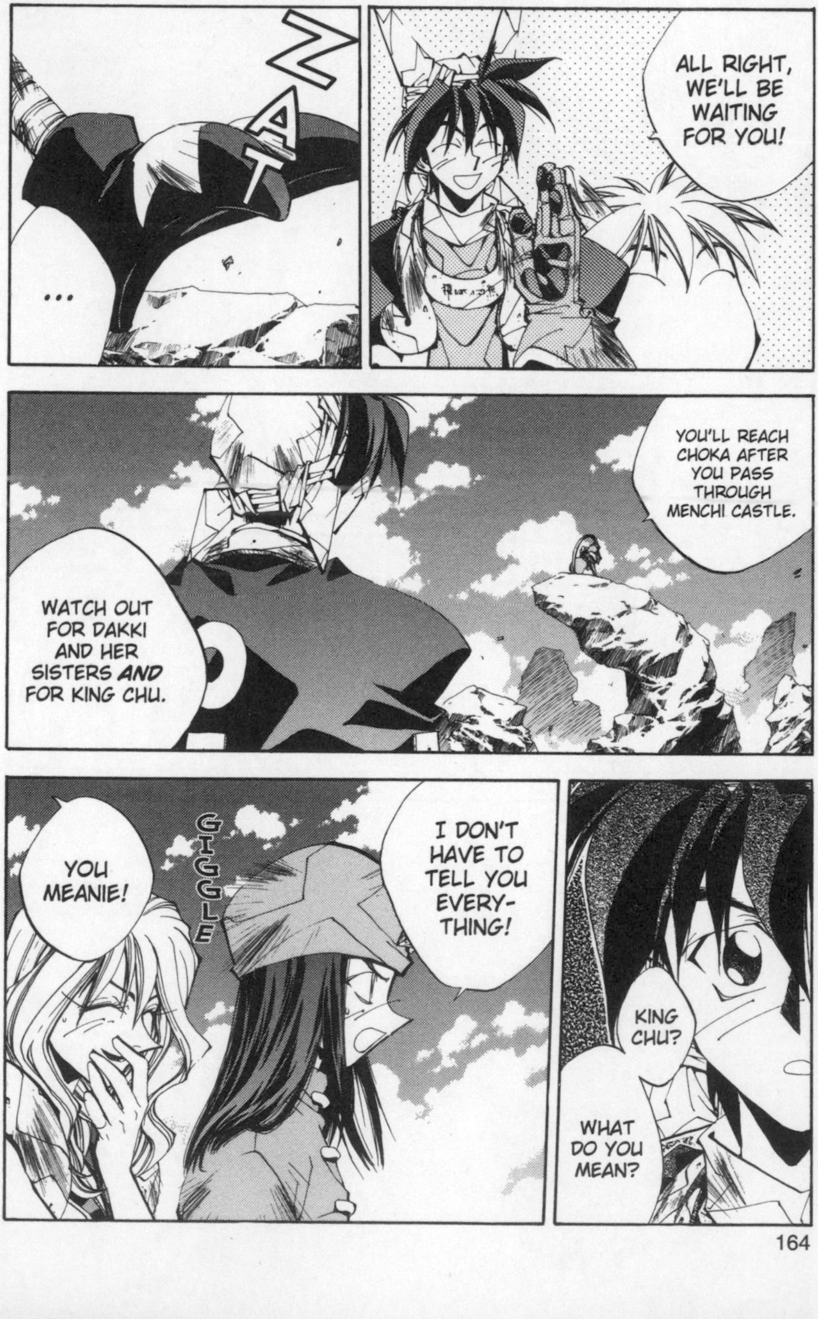
ALL RIGHT, WE'LL BE WAITING FOR YOU!
ZAT
...
YOU'LL REACH CHOKA AFTER YOU PASS THROUGH MENCHI CASTLE.
WATCH OUT FOR DAKKI AND HER SISTERS *AND* FOR KING CHU.
KING CHU?
WHAT DO YOU MEAN?
I DON'T HAVE TO TELL YOU EVERY-THING!
GIGGLE
YOU MEANIE!

READ THIS WAY

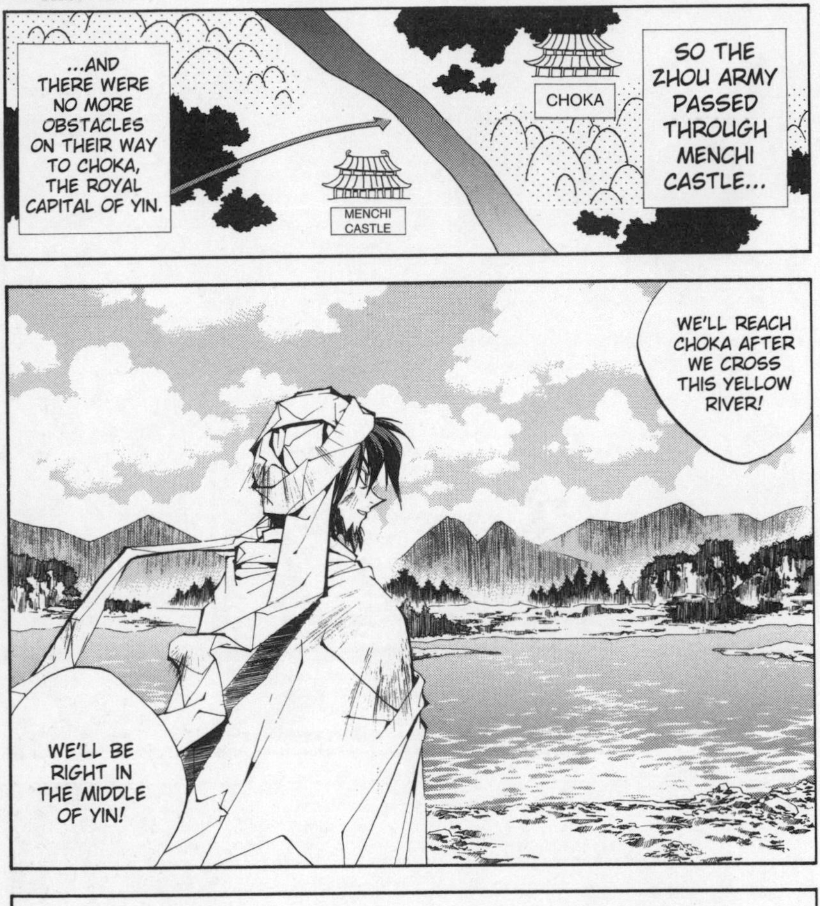
SO THE ZHOU ARMY PASSED THROUGH MENCHI CASTLE...
CHOKA
MENCHI CASTLE
...AND THERE WERE NO MORE OBSTACLES ON THEIR WAY TO CHOKA, THE ROYAL CAPITAL OF YIN.
WE'LL REACH CHOKA AFTER WE CROSS THIS YELLOW RIVER!
WE'LL BE RIGHT IN THE MIDDLE OF YIN!
THE FINAL BATTLE OF THE YIN-ZHOU REVOLUTION WILL BEGIN!
THE FAMOUS HISTORIC "BATTLE OF THE PLAINS"!

封神演義

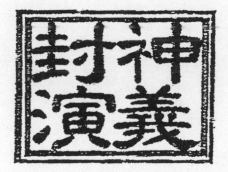

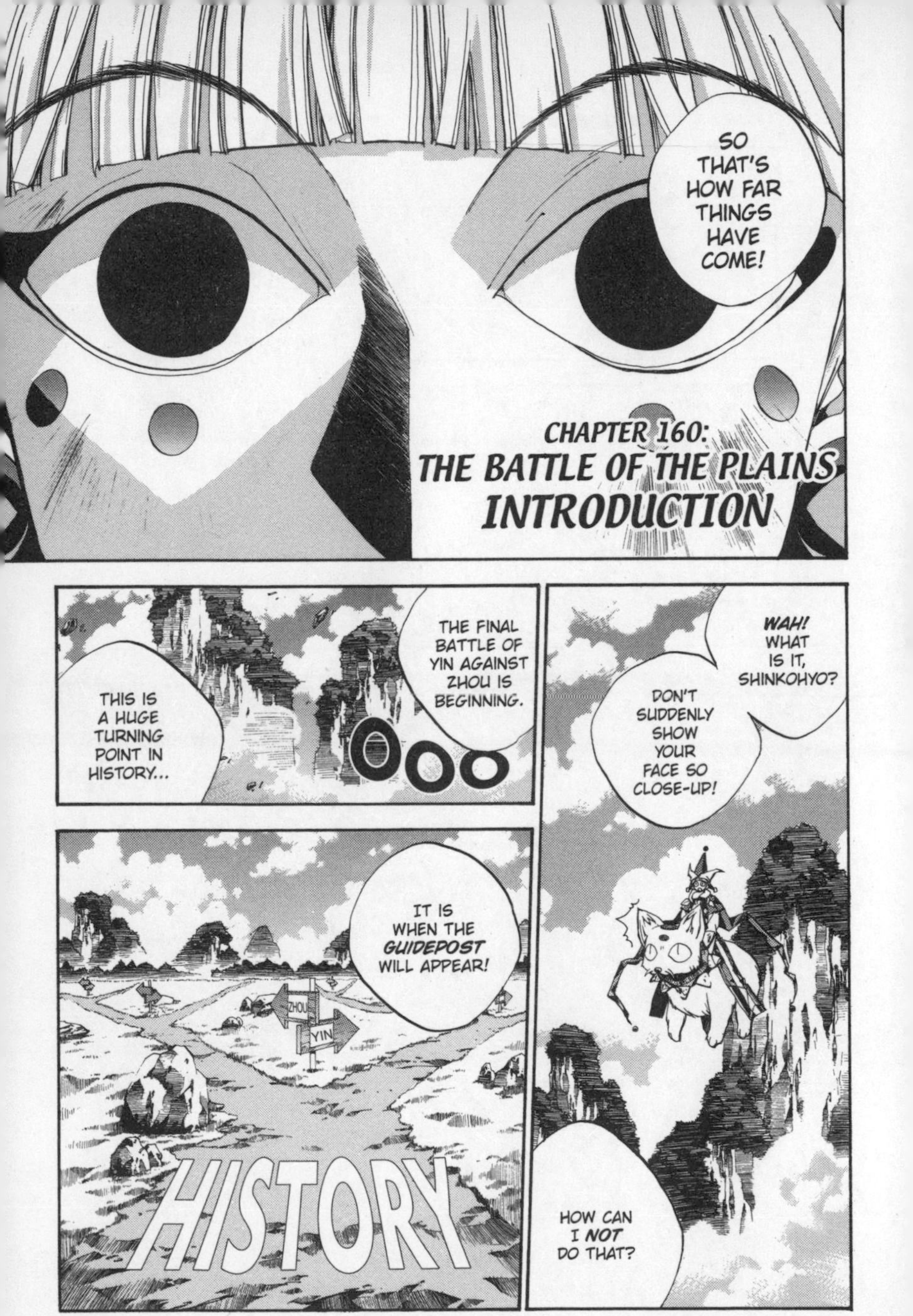
SO THAT'S HOW FAR THINGS HAVE COME!
CHAPTER 160:
THE BATTLE OF THE PLAINS INTRODUCTION
WAH! WHAT IS IT, SHINKOHYO?
DON'T SUDDENLY SHOW YOUR FACE SO CLOSE-UP!
HOW CAN I *NOT* DO THAT?
THE FINAL BATTLE OF YIN AGAINST ZHOU IS BEGINNING.
THIS IS A HUGE TURNING POINT IN HISTORY...
OOO
IT IS WHEN THE *GUIDEPOST* WILL APPEAR!
ZHOU
YIN
HISTORY

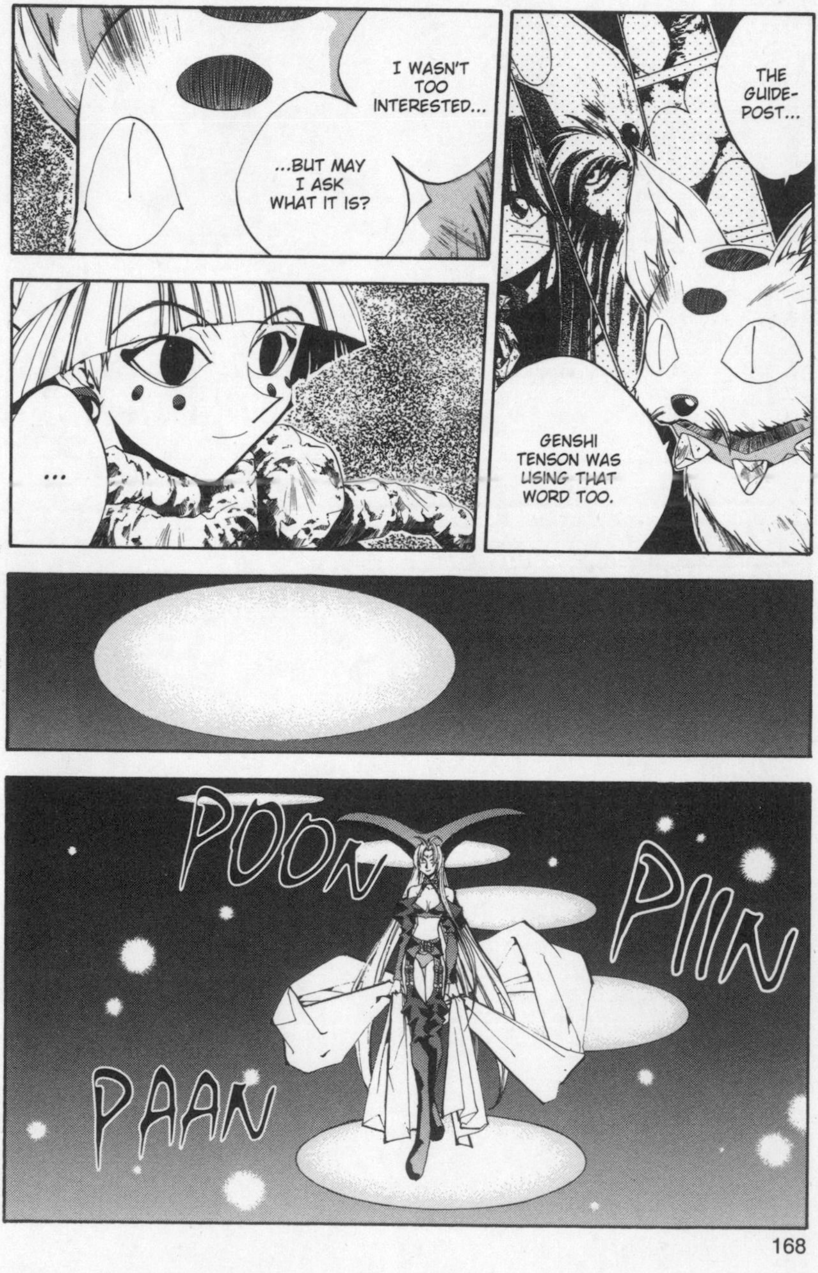
THE GUIDE-POST...
GENSHI TENSON WAS USING THAT WORD TOO.
I WASN'T TOO INTERESTED...
...BUT MAY I ASK WHAT IT IS?
...
POON
PIIN
PAAN

READ THIS WAY

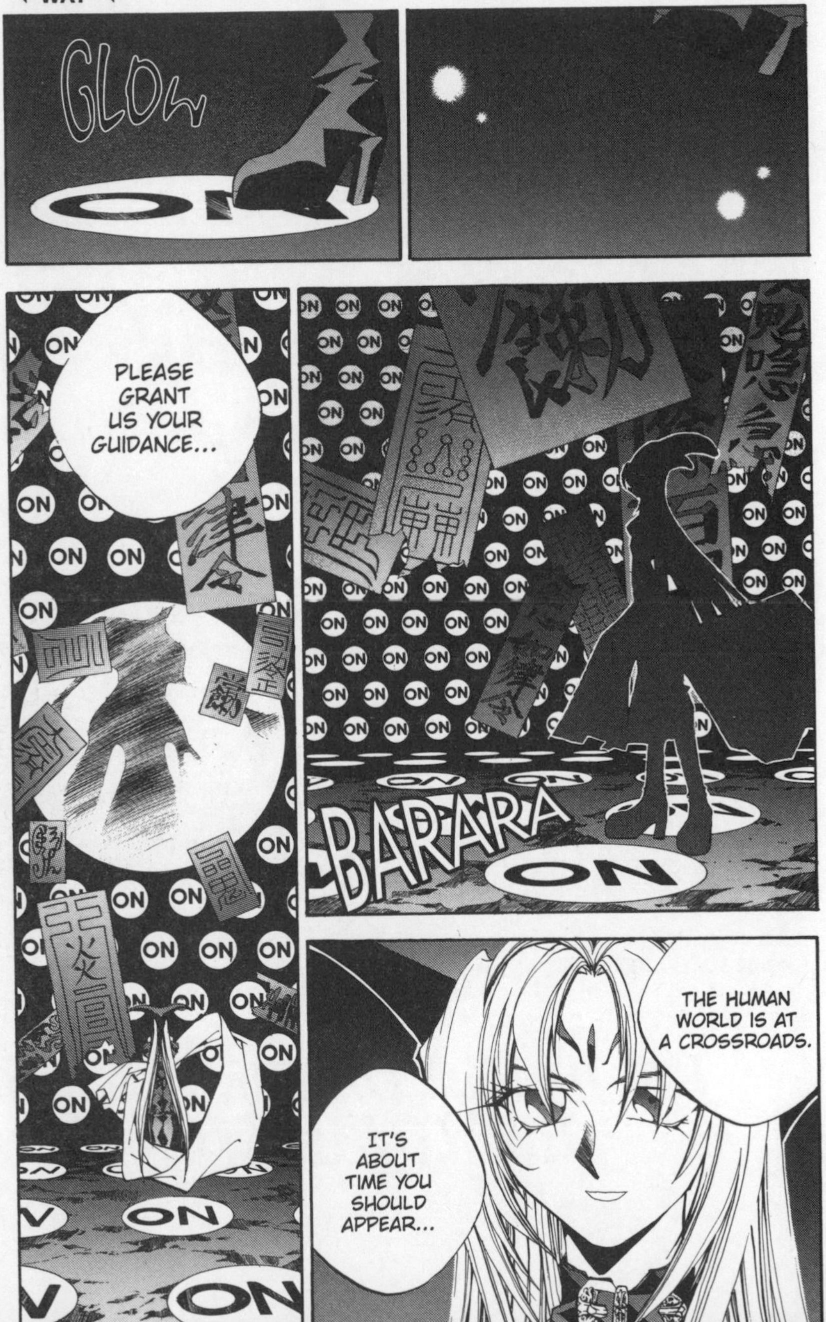
GLOW
ON
BARARA
ON
THE HUMAN WORLD IS AT A CROSSROADS.
IT'S ABOUT TIME YOU SHOULD APPEAR...
PLEASE GRANT US YOUR GUIDANCE...

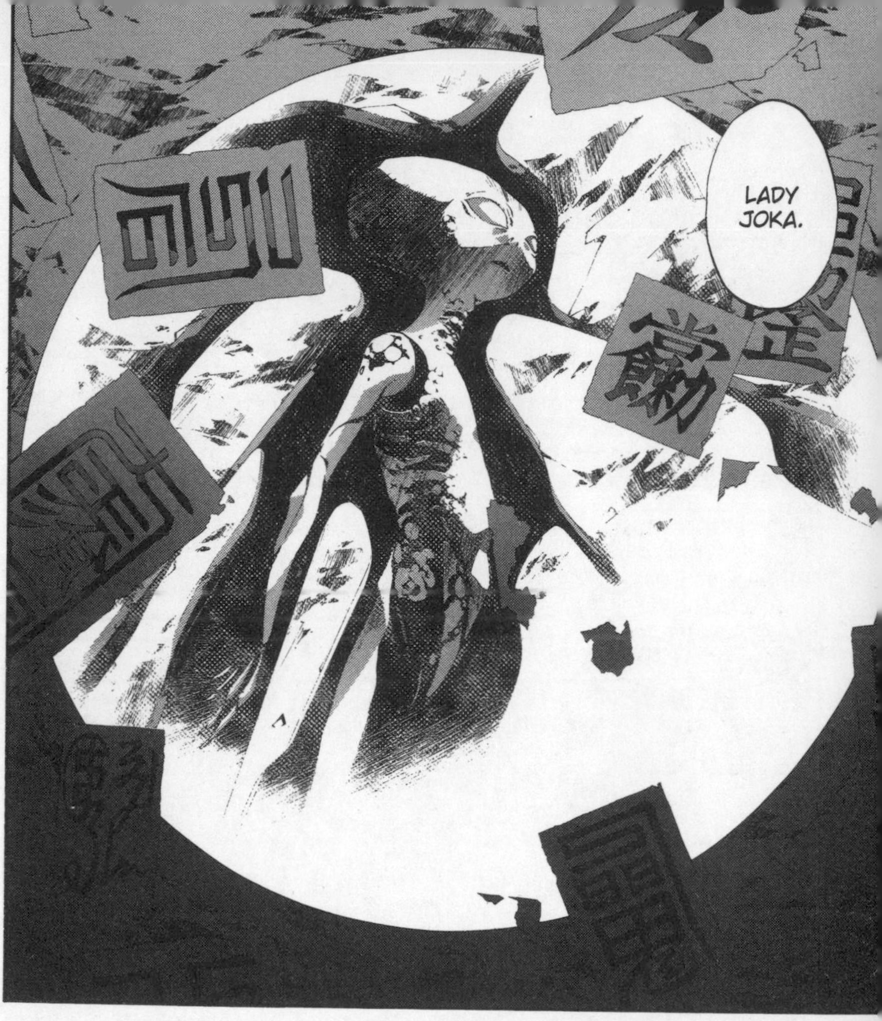
LADY JOKA.

Chapter 160

THE BATTLE OF THE PLAINS INTRODUCTION

READ THIS WAY

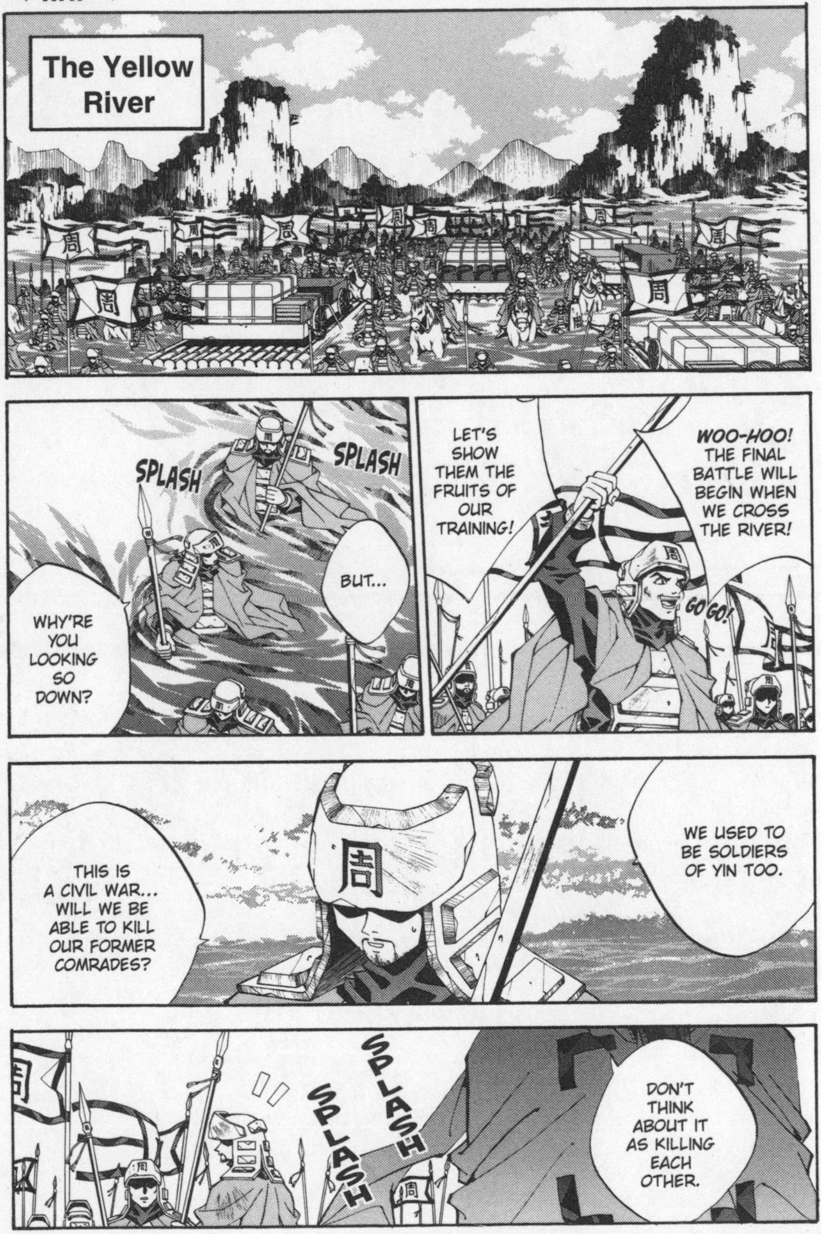
The Yellow River
WOO-HOO! THE FINAL BATTLE WILL BEGIN WHEN WE CROSS THE RIVER!
LET'S SHOW THEM THE FRUITS OF OUR TRAINING!
GO GO!
SPLASH
SPLASH
BUT...
WHY'RE YOU LOOKING SO DOWN?
WE USED TO BE SOLDIERS OF YIN TOO.
THIS IS A CIVIL WAR... WILL WE BE ABLE TO KILL OUR FORMER COMRADES?
DON'T THINK ABOUT IT AS KILLING EACH OTHER.
SPLASH
SPLASH
!!

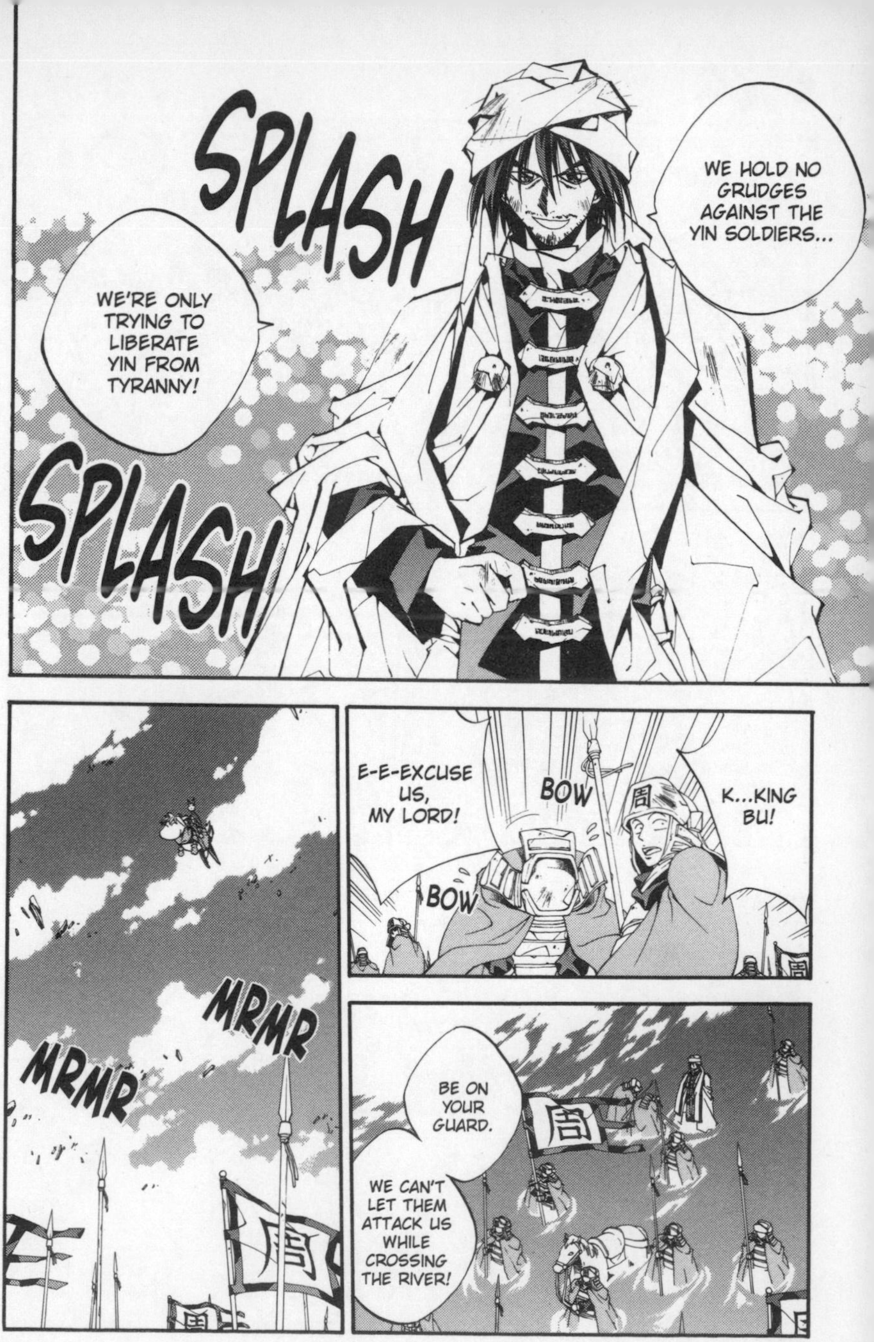
WE HOLD NO GRUDGES AGAINST THE YIN SOLDIERS...
SPLASH
WE'RE ONLY TRYING TO LIBERATE YIN FROM TYRANNY!
SPLASH
K...KING BU!
BOW
E-E-EXCUSE US, MY LORD!
BOW
BE ON YOUR GUARD.
WE CAN'T LET THEM ATTACK US WHILE CROSSING THE RIVER!
MRMR
MRMR

READ THIS WAY

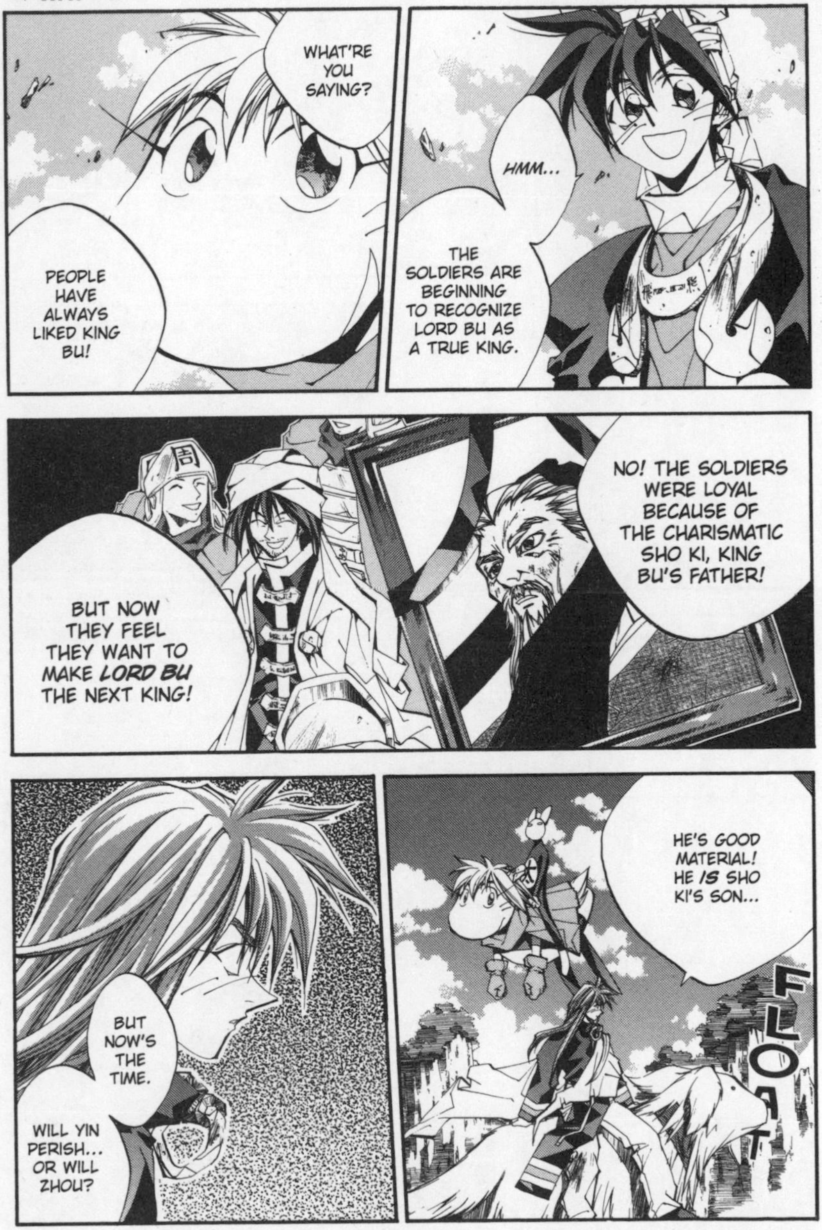
HMM...
THE SOLDIERS ARE BEGINNING TO RECOGNIZE LORD BU AS A TRUE KING.
WHAT'RE YOU SAYING?
PEOPLE HAVE ALWAYS LIKED KING BU!
NO! THE SOLDIERS WERE LOYAL BECAUSE OF THE CHARISMATIC SHO KI, KING BU'S FATHER!
BUT NOW THEY FEEL THEY WANT TO MAKE *LORD BU* THE NEXT KING!
HE'S GOOD MATERIAL! HE *IS* SHO KI'S SON...
FLOAT
BUT NOW'S THE TIME.
WILL YIN PERISH... OR WILL ZHOU?

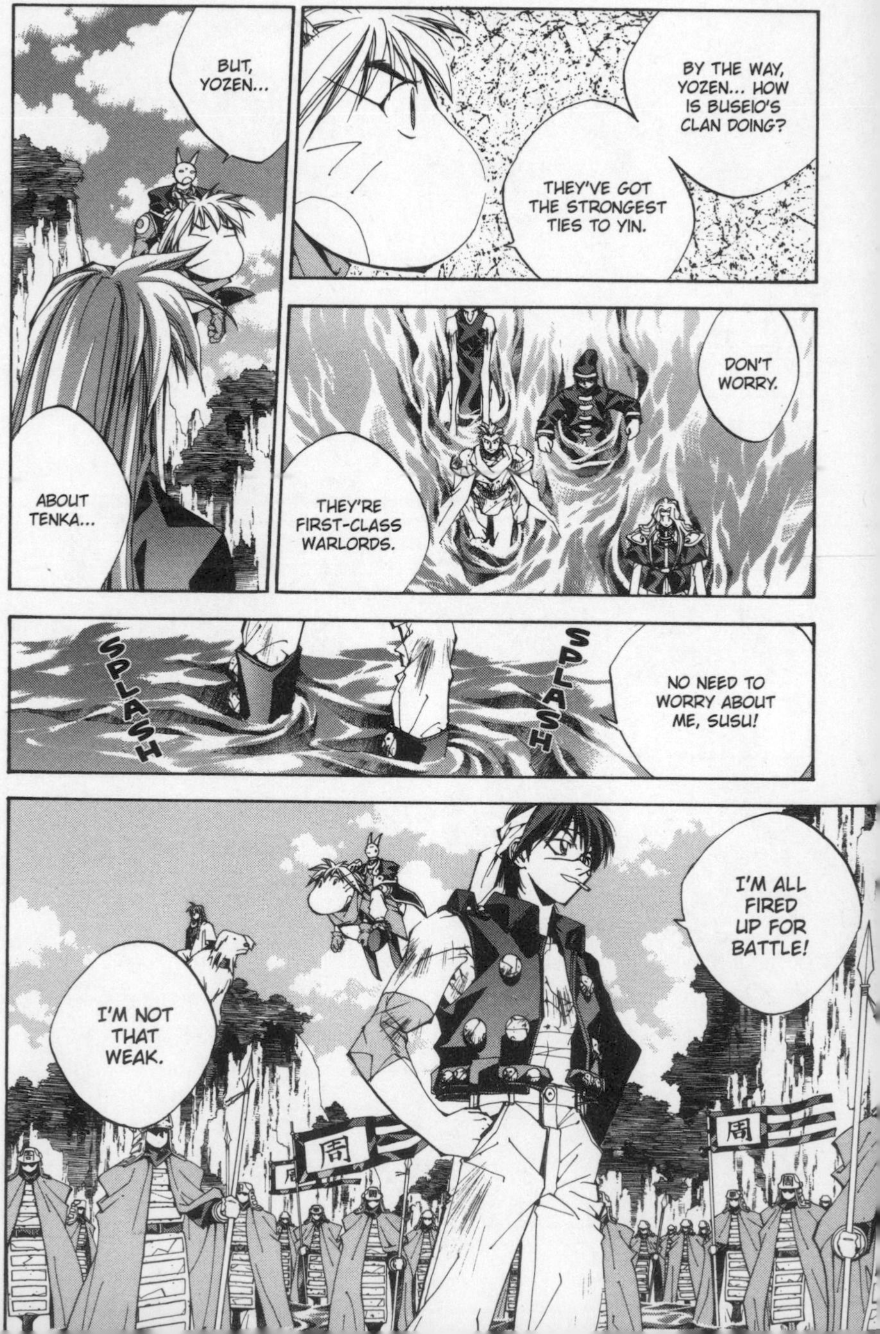
BY THE WAY, YOZEN... HOW IS BUSEIO'S CLAN DOING?
THEY'VE GOT THE STRONGEST TIES TO YIN.
DON'T WORRY.
THEY'RE FIRST-CLASS WARLORDS.
BUT, YOZEN...
ABOUT TENKA...
SPLASH
NO NEED TO WORRY ABOUT ME, SUSU!
SPLASH
I'M ALL FIRED UP FOR BATTLE!
I'M NOT THAT WEAK.
周
周
周

READ THIS WAY

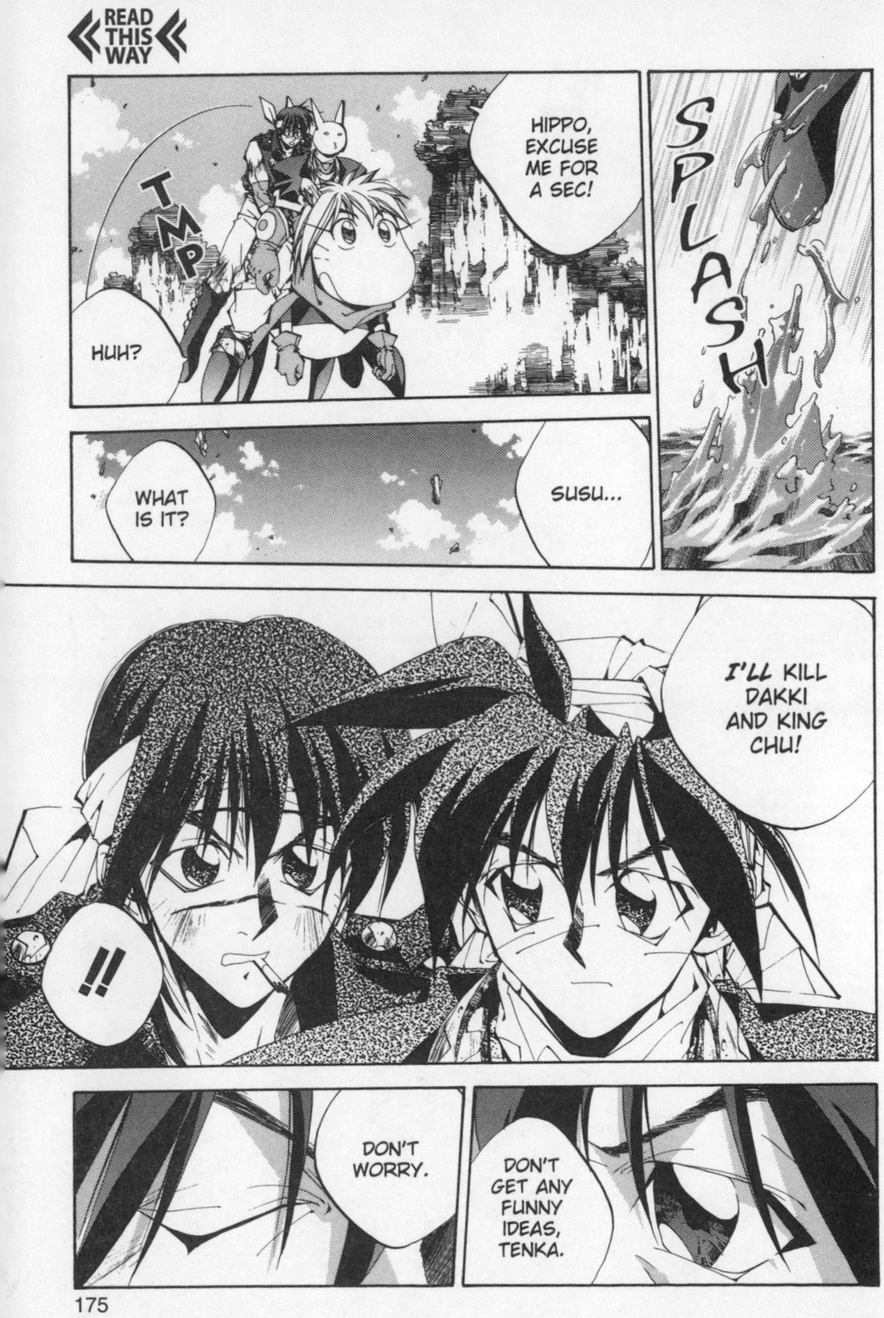
SPLASH
HIPPO, EXCUSE ME FOR A SEC!
TMP
HUH?
SUSU...
WHAT IS IT?
I'LL KILL DAKKI AND KING CHU!
!!
DON'T GET ANY FUNNY IDEAS, TENKA.
DON'T WORRY.

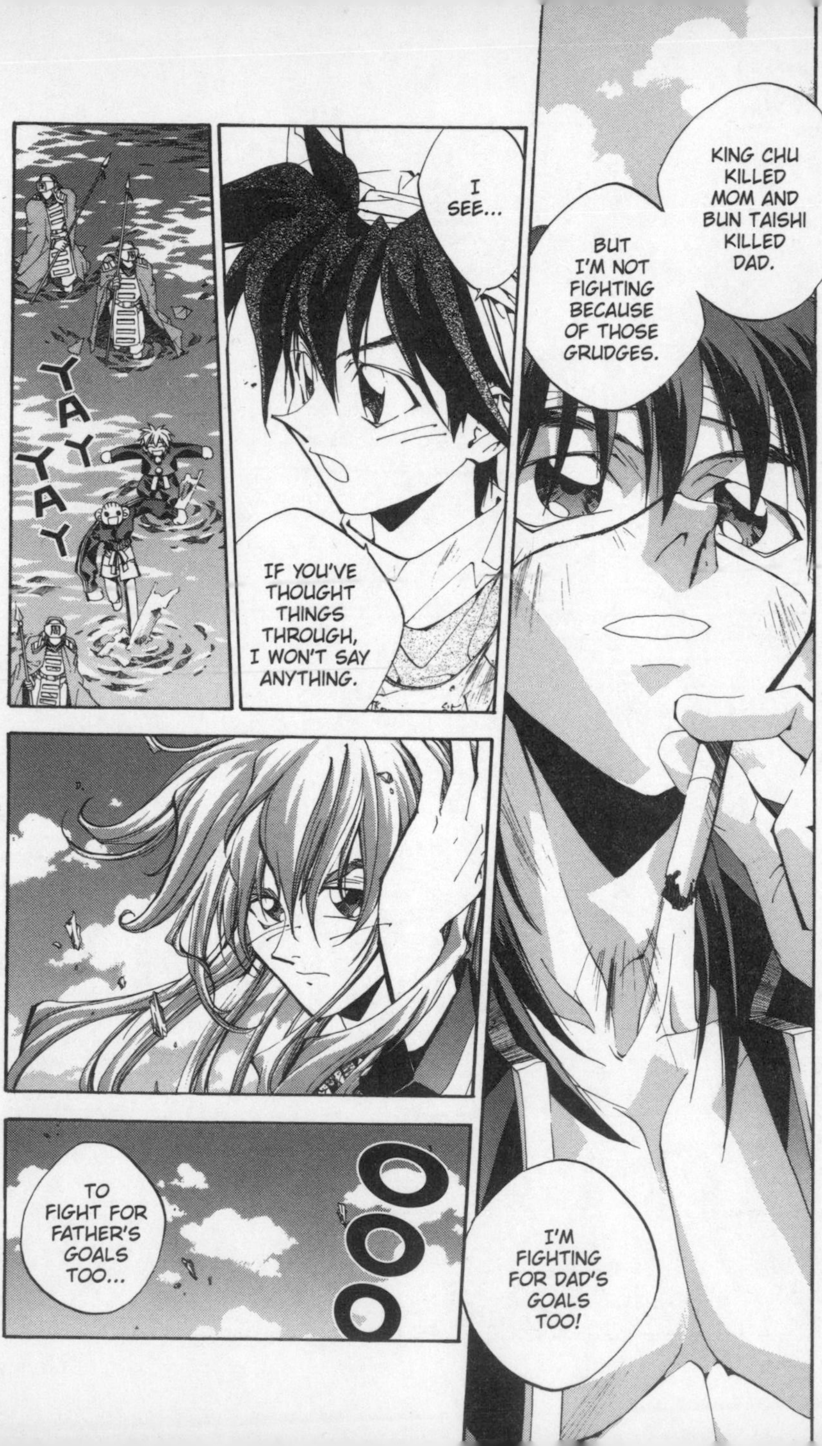
KING CHU KILLED MOM AND BUN TAISHI KILLED DAD.
BUT I'M NOT FIGHTING BECAUSE OF THOSE GRUDGES.
I'M FIGHTING FOR DAD'S GOALS TOO!
I SEE...
IF YOU'VE THOUGHT THINGS THROUGH, I WON'T SAY ANYTHING.
YAY YAY YAY
TO FIGHT FOR FATHER'S GOALS TOO...
OOO

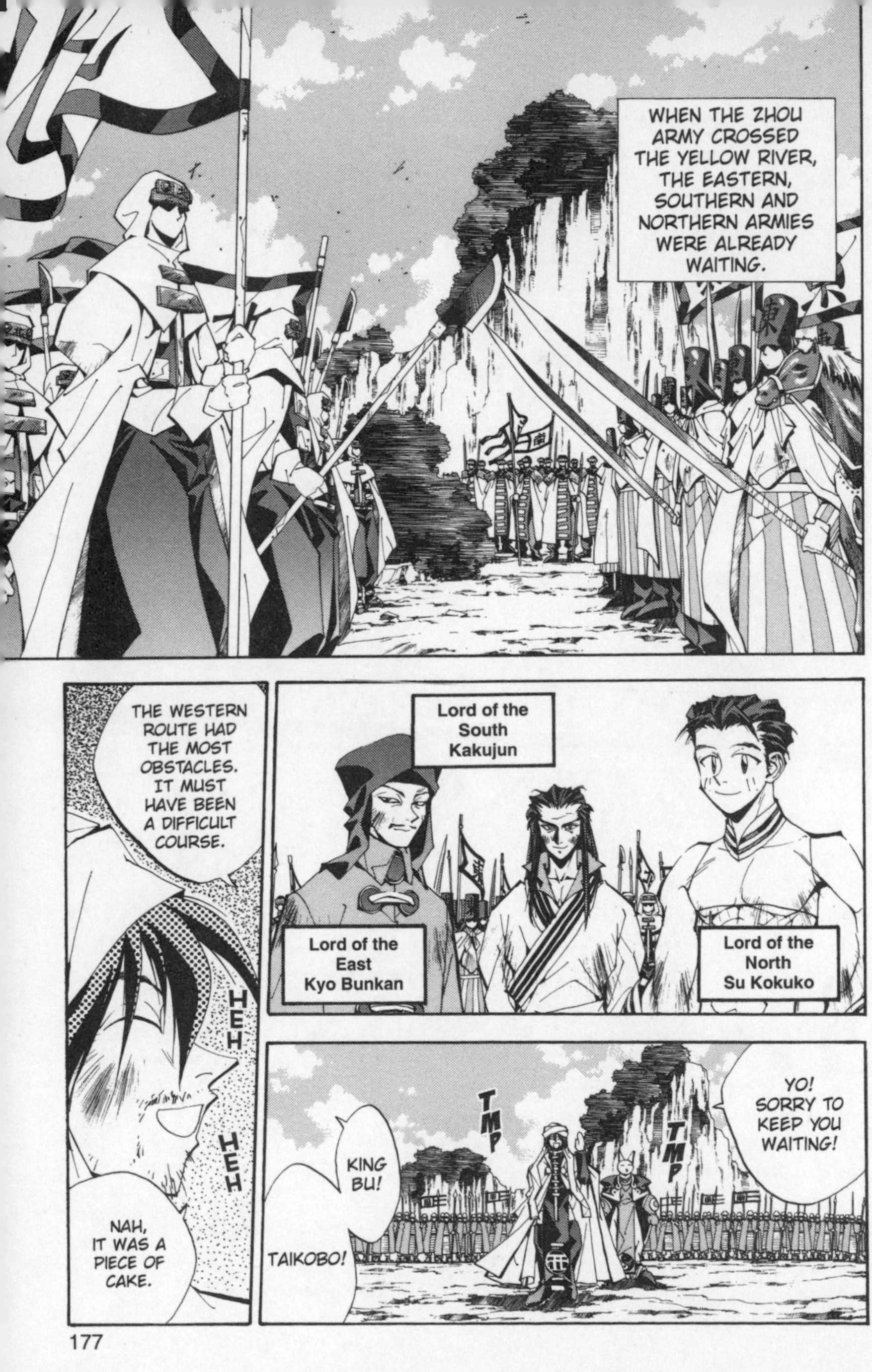
WHEN THE ZHOU ARMY CROSSED THE YELLOW RIVER, THE EASTERN, SOUTHERN AND NORTHERN ARMIES WERE ALREADY WAITING.
Lord of the South Kakujun
Lord of the North Su Kokuko
Lord of the East Kyo Bunkan
TMP
YO! SORRY TO KEEP YOU WAITING!
TMP
KING BU!
TAIKOBO!
THE WESTERN ROUTE HAD THE MOST OBSTACLES. IT MUST HAVE BEEN A DIFFICULT COURSE.
HEH
HEH
NAH, IT WAS A PIECE OF CAKE.

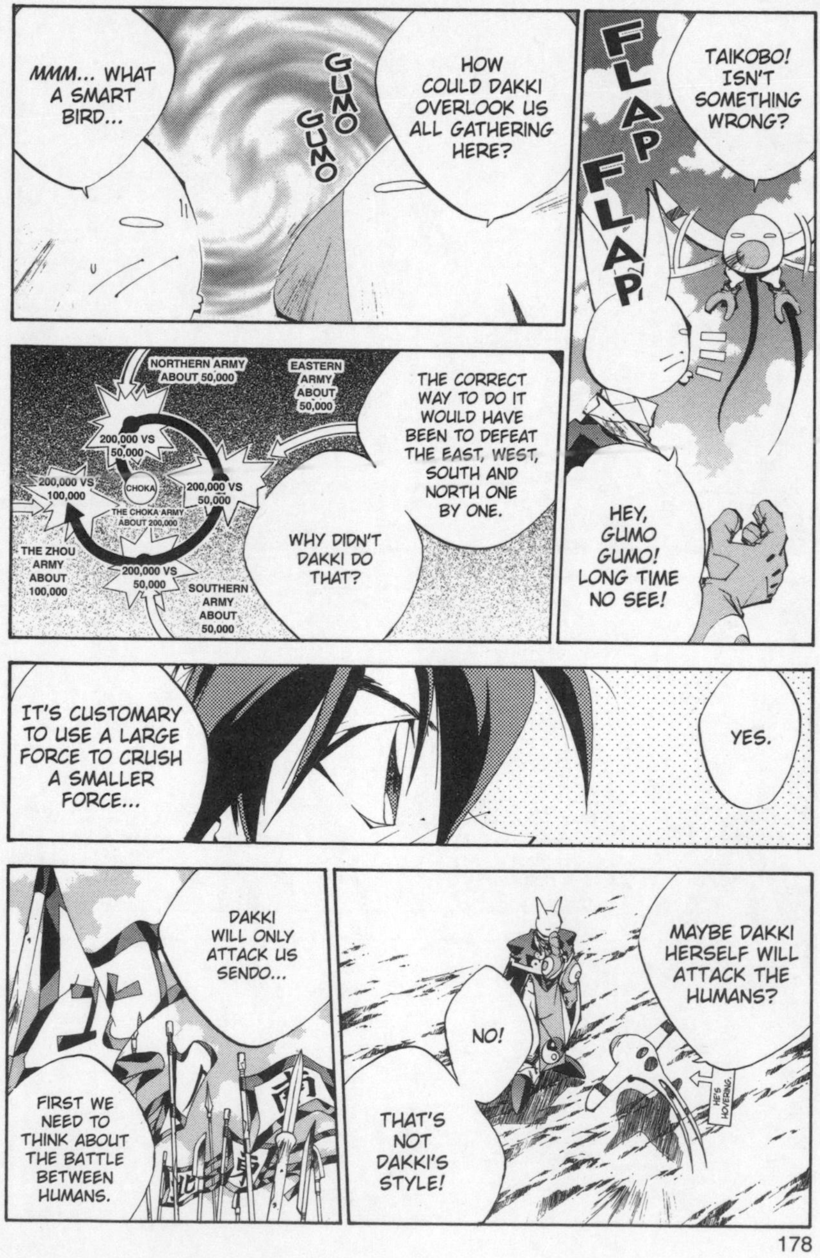

TAIKOBO! ISN'T SOMETHING WRONG?
FLAP FLAP
FLAP FLAP
HEY, GUMO GUMO! LONG TIME NO SEE!
HOW COULD DAKKI OVERLOOK US ALL GATHERING HERE?
GUMO GUMO
MMM... WHAT A SMART BIRD...
THE CORRECT WAY TO DO IT WOULD HAVE BEEN TO DEFEAT THE EAST, WEST, SOUTH AND NORTH ONE BY ONE.
WHY DIDN'T DAKKI DO THAT?
NORTHERN ARMY ABOUT 50,000
EASTERN ARMY ABOUT 50,000
200,000 VS 50,000
200,000 VS 100,000
CHOKA
200,000 VS 50,000
THE CHOKA ARMY ABOUT 200,000
THE ZHOU ARMY ABOUT 100,000
200,000 VS 50,000
SOUTHERN ARMY ABOUT 50,000
YES.
IT'S CUSTOMARY TO USE A LARGE FORCE TO CRUSH A SMALLER FORCE...
MAYBE DAKKI HERSELF WILL ATTACK THE HUMANS?
NO!
THAT'S NOT DAKKI'S STYLE!
HE'S HOVERING.
DAKKI WILL ONLY ATTACK US SENDO...
FIRST WE NEED TO THINK ABOUT THE BATTLE BETWEEN HUMANS.

READ THIS WAY

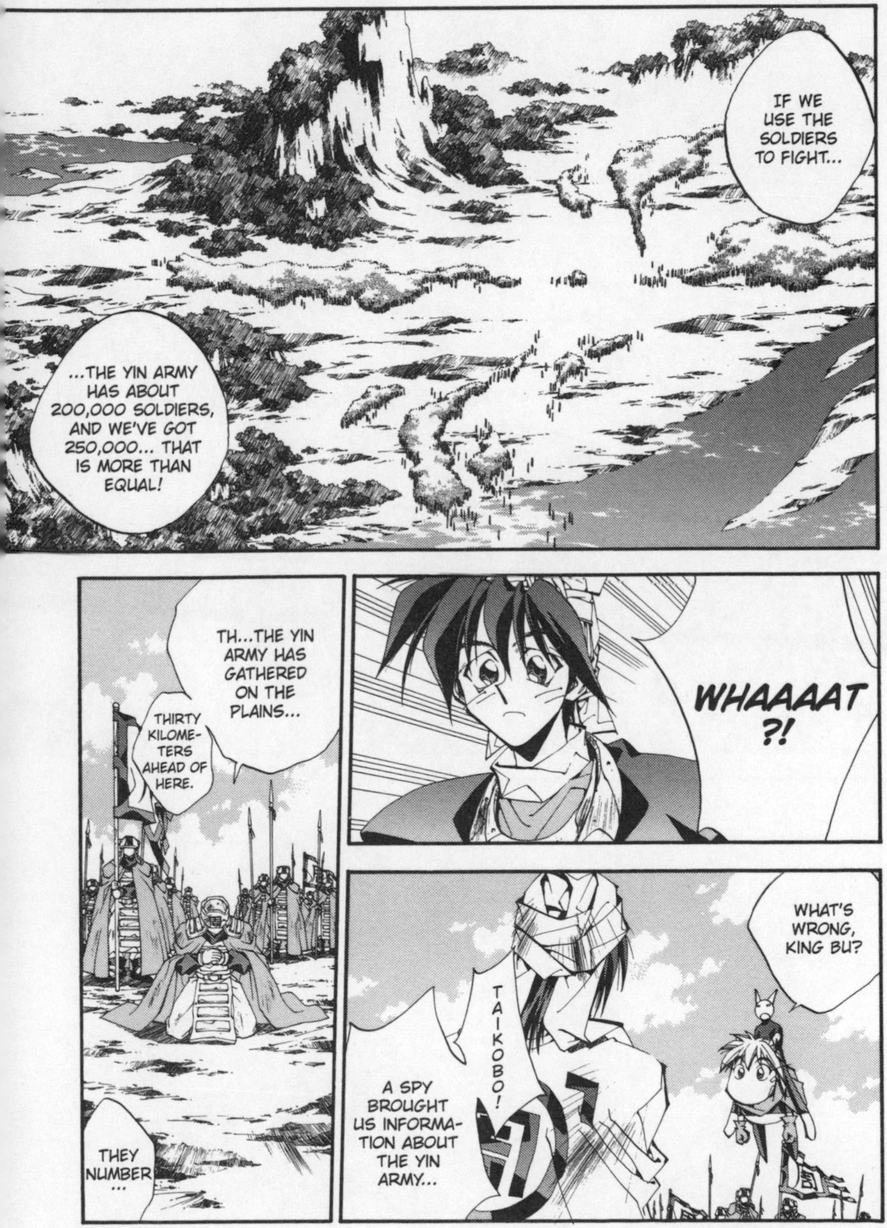
IF WE USE THE SOLDIERS TO FIGHT...
...THE YIN ARMY HAS ABOUT 200,000 SOLDIERS, AND WE'VE GOT 250,000... THAT IS MORE THAN EQUAL!
WHAAAAT ?!
WHAT'S WRONG, KING BU?
TAIKOBO!
A SPY BROUGHT US INFORMATION ABOUT THE YIN ARMY...
TH...THE YIN ARMY HAS GATHERED ON THE PLAINS...
THIRTY KILOMETERS AHEAD OF HERE.
THEY NUMBER...

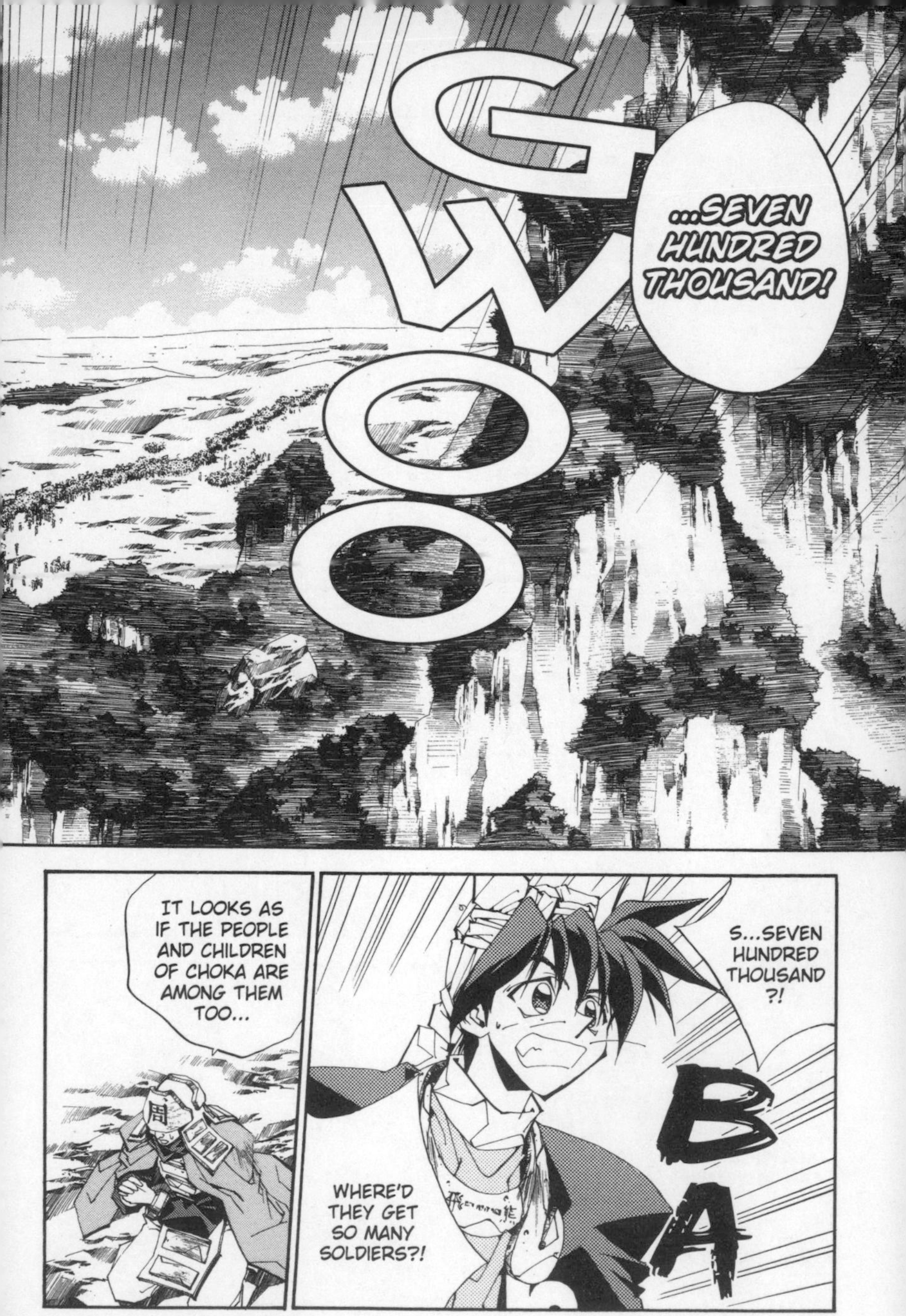
GWOO
...SEVEN HUNDRED THOUSAND!
S...SEVEN HUNDRED THOUSAND ?!
BA
WHERE'D THEY GET SO MANY SOLDIERS?!
IT LOOKS AS IF THE PEOPLE AND CHILDREN OF CHOKA ARE AMONG THEM TOO...

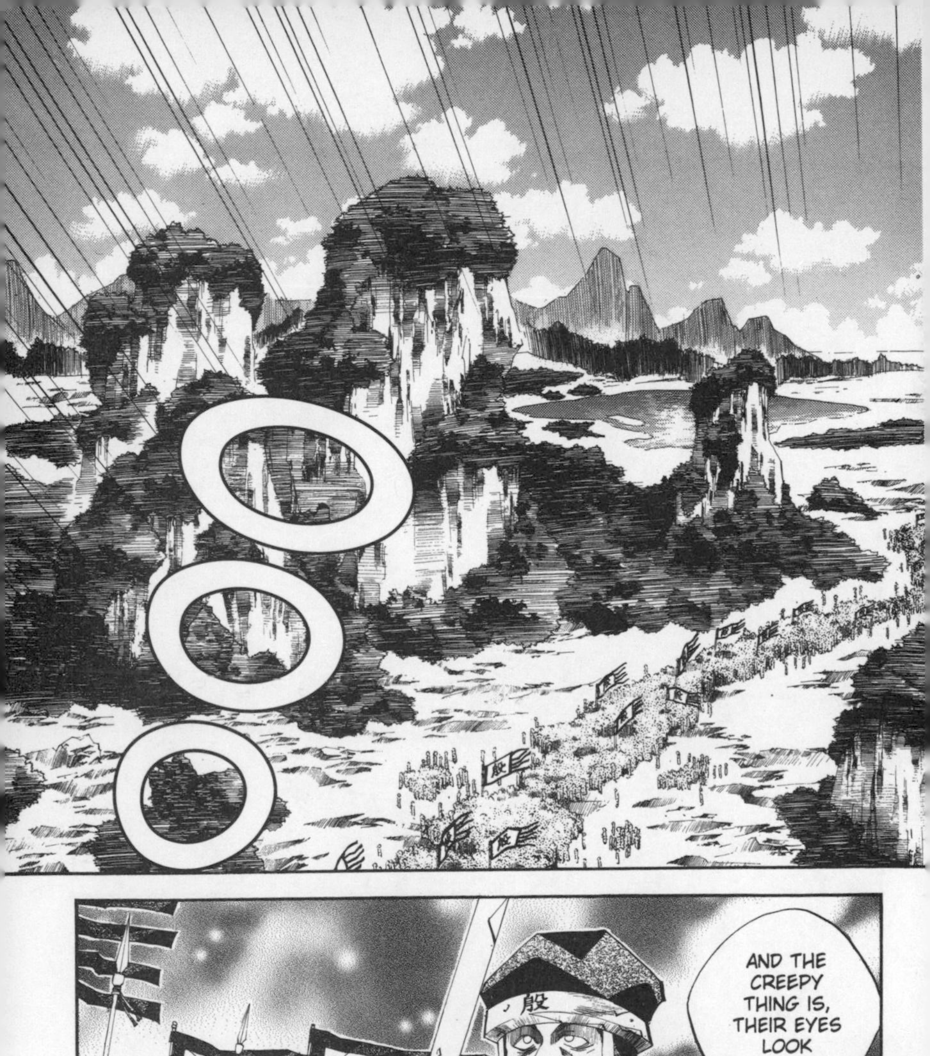

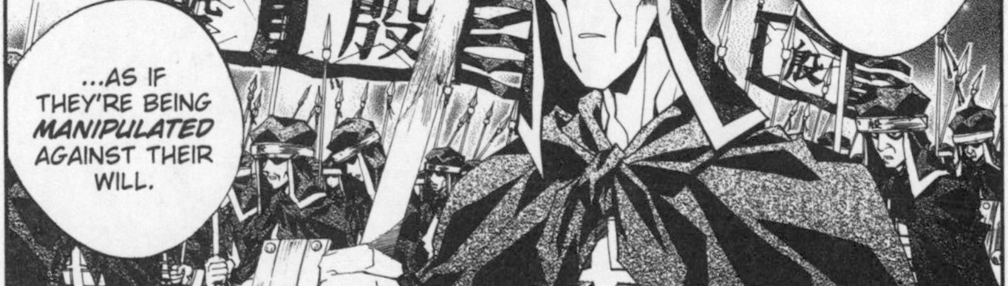
AND THE CREEPY THING IS, THEIR EYES LOOK DULL...
...AS IF THEY'RE BEING *MANIPULATED* AGAINST THEIR WILL.

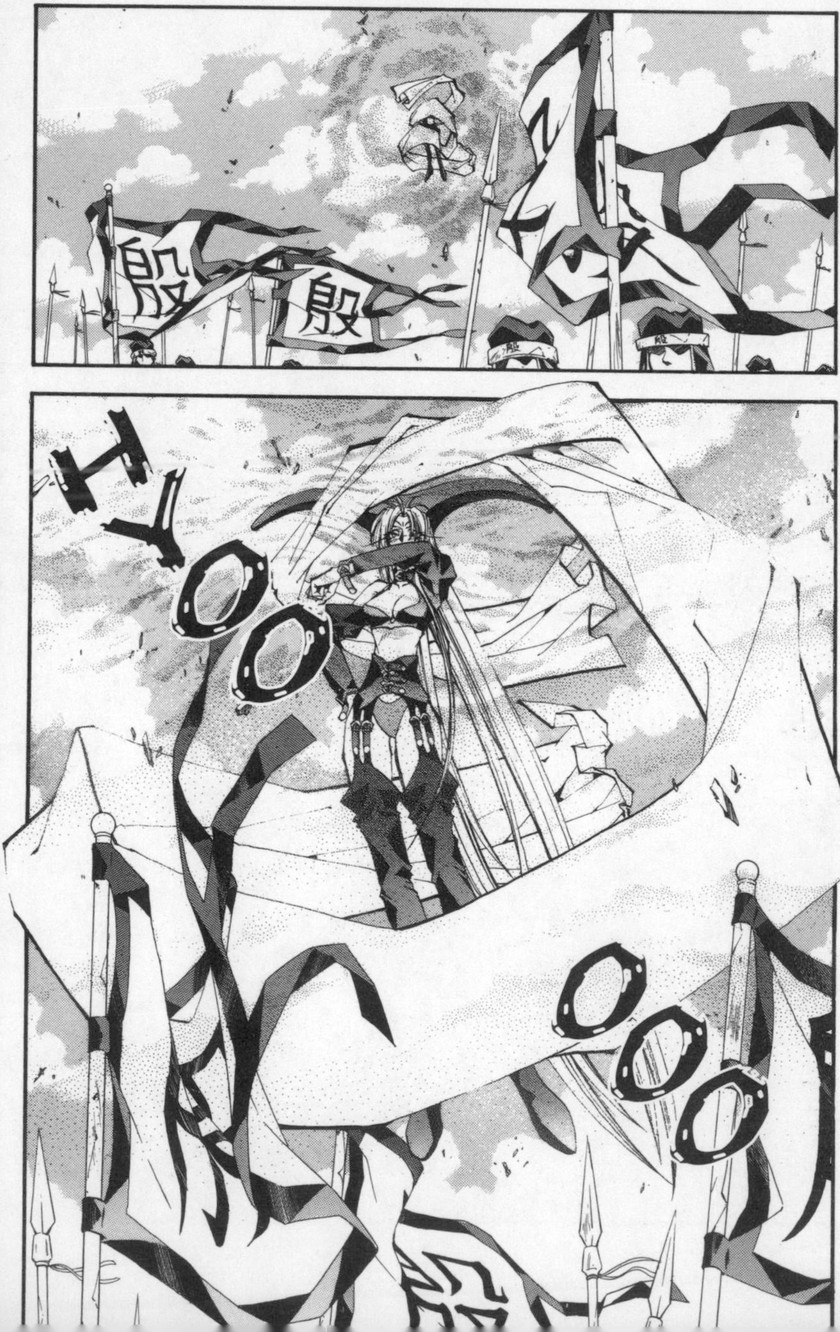
殷
殷
HYOOOOO

READ THIS WAY

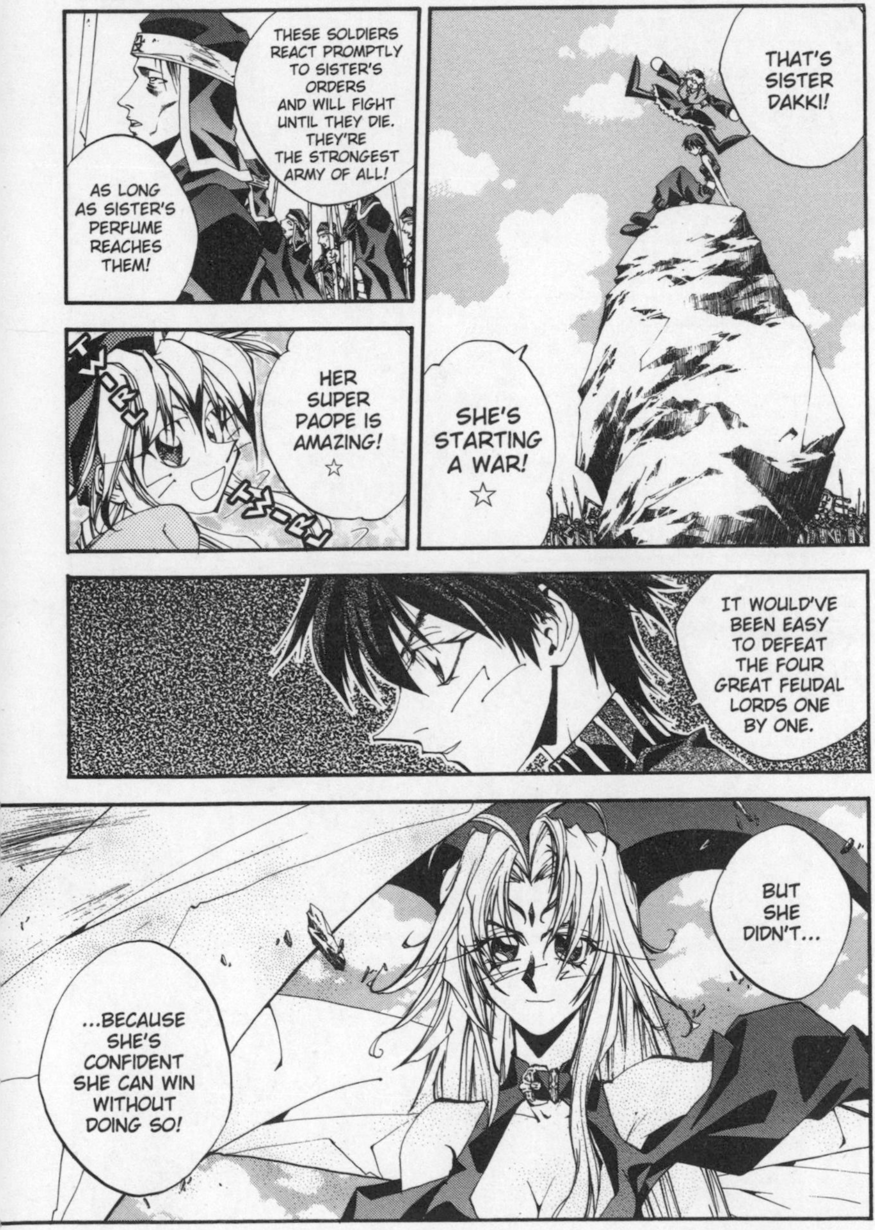

THAT'S SISTER DAKKI!
SHE'S STARTING A WAR! ☆
THESE SOLDIERS REACT PROMPTLY TO SISTER'S ORDERS AND WILL FIGHT UNTIL THEY DIE. THEY'RE THE STRONGEST ARMY OF ALL!
AS LONG AS SISTER'S PERFUME REACHES THEM!
HER SUPER PAOPE IS AMAZING! ☆
IT WOULD'VE BEEN EASY TO DEFEAT THE FOUR GREAT FEUDAL LORDS ONE BY ONE.
BUT SHE DIDN'T...
...BECAUSE SHE'S CONFIDENT SHE CAN WIN WITHOUT DOING SO!

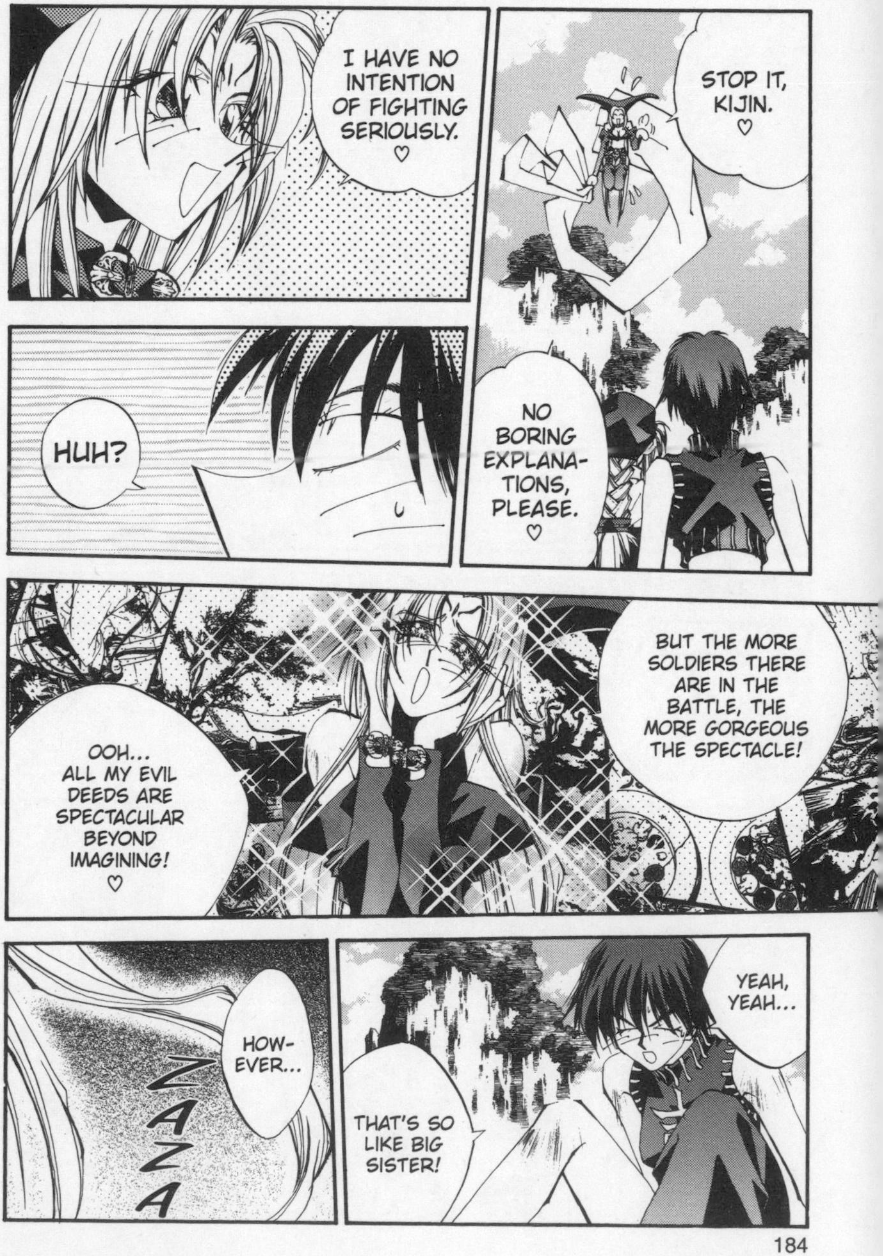
STOP IT, KIJIN. ♡
NO BORING EXPLANA-TIONS, PLEASE. ♡
I HAVE NO INTENTION OF FIGHTING SERIOUSLY. ♡
HUH?
BUT THE MORE SOLDIERS THERE ARE IN THE BATTLE, THE MORE GORGEOUS THE SPECTACLE!
OOH... ALL MY EVIL DEEDS ARE SPECTACULAR BEYOND IMAGINING! ♡
YEAH, YEAH...
THAT'S SO LIKE BIG SISTER!
HOW-EVER...
ZAZA

READ THIS WAY

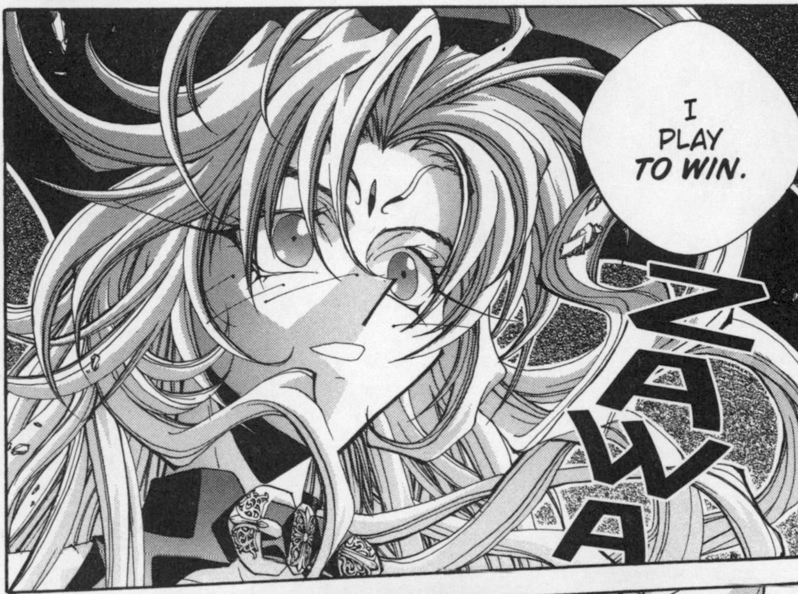
I PLAY TO WIN.
ZAWA

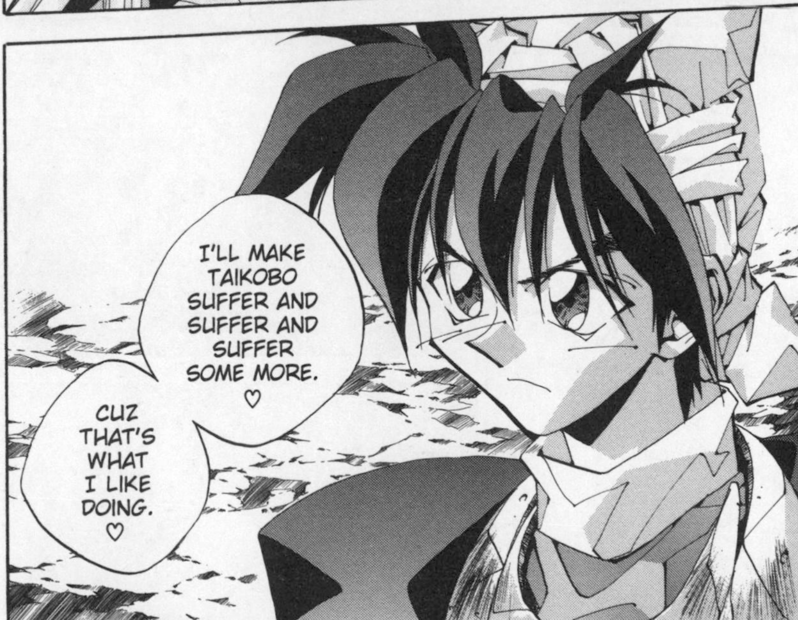
I'LL MAKE TAIKOBO SUFFER AND SUFFER AND SUFFER SOME MORE. ♡
CUZ THAT'S WHAT I LIKE DOING. ♡

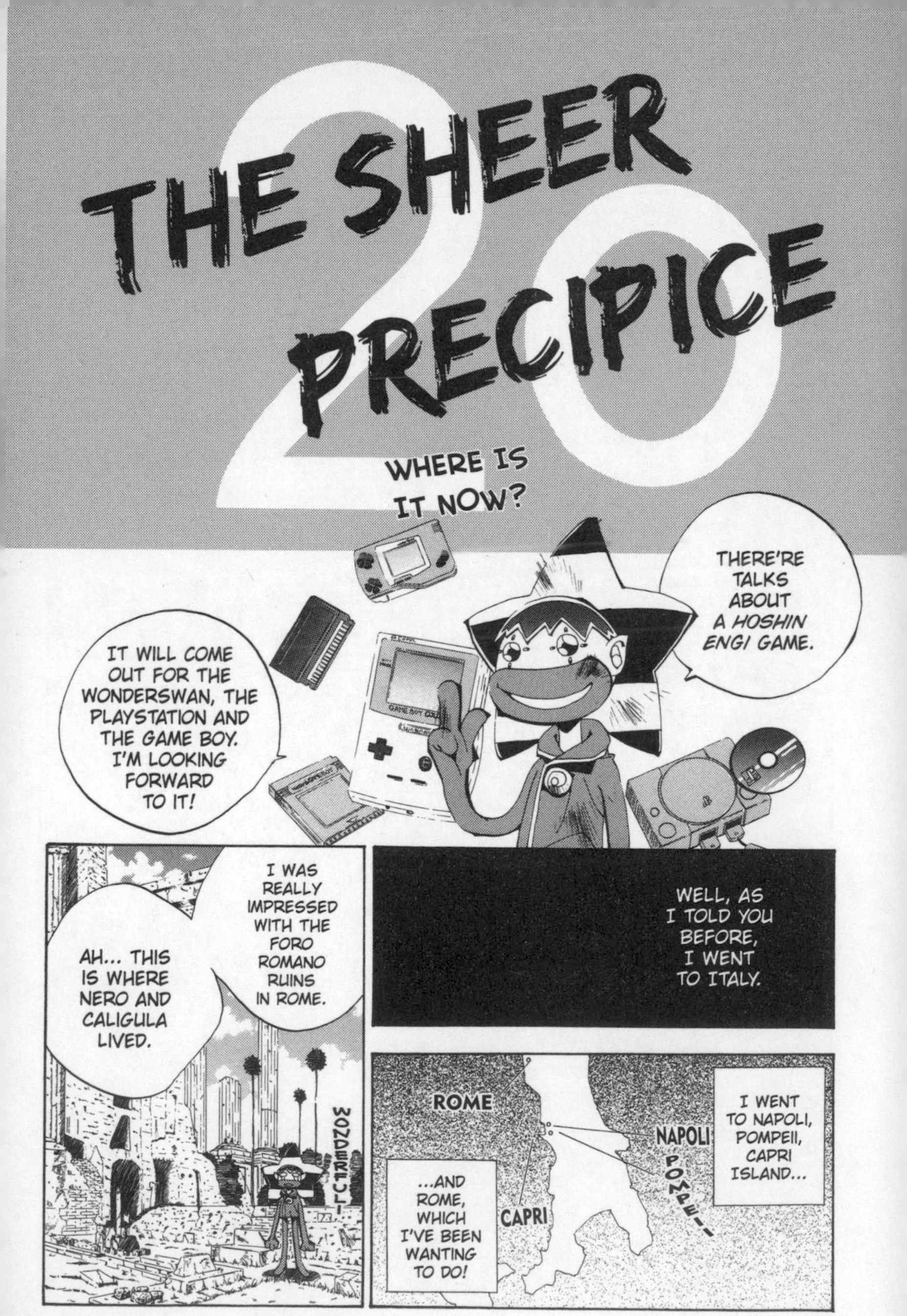
THE SHEER PRECIPICE
20
WHERE IS IT NOW?
THERE'RE TALKS ABOUT A *HOSHIN ENGI* GAME.
IT WILL COME OUT FOR THE WONDERSWAN, THE PLAYSTATION AND THE GAME BOY. I'M LOOKING FORWARD TO IT!
WELL, AS I TOLD YOU BEFORE, I WENT TO ITALY.
I WENT TO NAPOLI, POMPEII, CAPRI ISLAND...
ROME
NAPOLI
POMPEII
CAPRI
...AND ROME, WHICH I'VE BEEN WANTING TO DO!
I WAS REALLY IMPRESSED WITH THE FORO ROMANO RUINS IN ROME.
AH... THIS IS WHERE NERO AND CALIGULA LIVED.
WONDERFUL!

READ THIS WAY

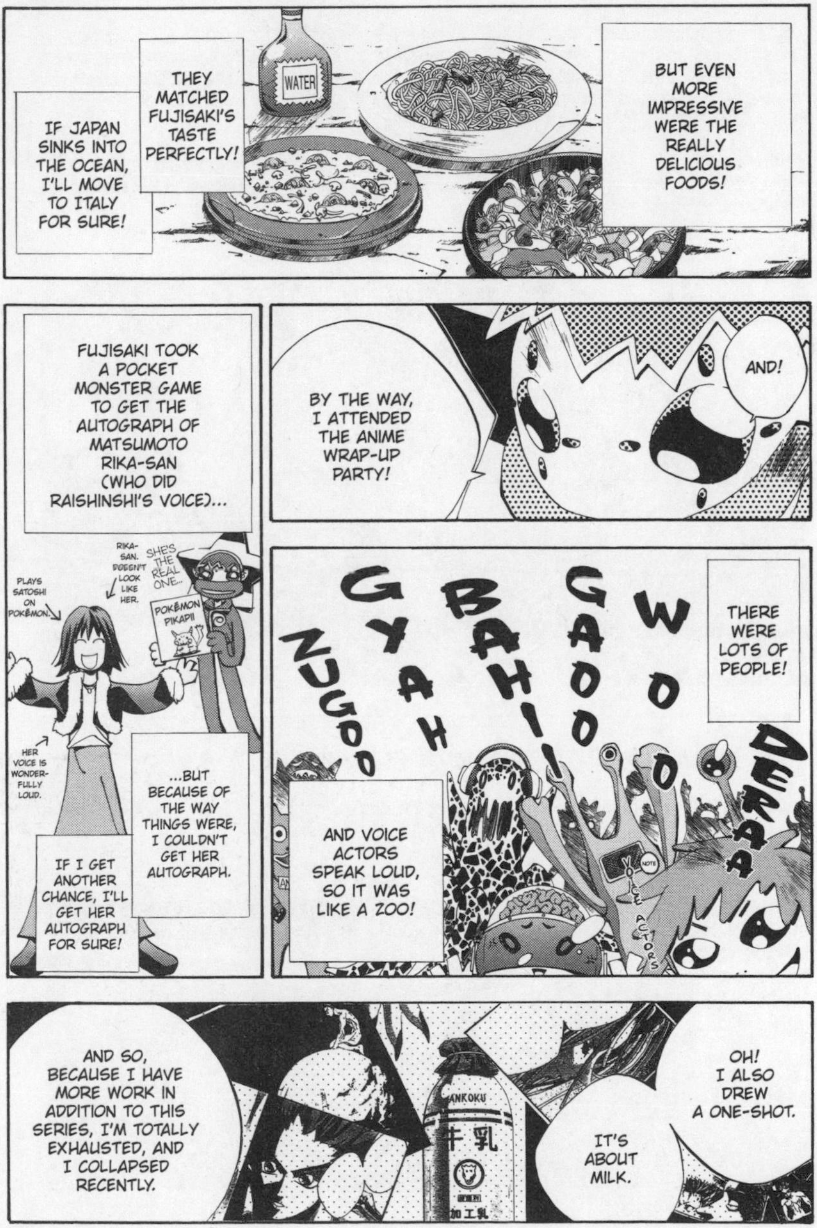

BUT EVEN MORE IMPRESSIVE WERE THE REALLY DELICIOUS FOODS!
THEY MATCHED FUJISAKI'S TASTE PERFECTLY!
WATER
IF JAPAN SINKS INTO THE OCEAN, I'LL MOVE TO ITALY FOR SURE!
AND!
BY THE WAY, I ATTENDED THE ANIME WRAP-UP PARTY!
THERE WERE LOTS OF PEOPLE!
WOO
GAOOO
BAHIII
GYAH
ZUGOOO
DERAA
AND VOICE ACTORS SPEAK LOUD, SO IT WAS LIKE A ZOO!
NOTE
VOICE ACTORS
FUJISAKI TOOK A POCKET MONSTER GAME TO GET THE AUTOGRAPH OF MATSUMOTO RIKA-SAN (WHO DID RAISHINSHI'S VOICE)...
SHE'S THE REAL ONE...
RIKA-SAN. DOESN'T LOOK LIKE HER.
PLAYS SATOSHI ON POKÉMON.
POKÉMON PIKAPI!
HER VOICE IS WONDER-FULLY LOUD.
...BUT BECAUSE OF THE WAY THINGS WERE, I COULDN'T GET HER AUTOGRAPH.
IF I GET ANOTHER CHANCE, I'LL GET HER AUTOGRAPH FOR SURE!
OH! I ALSO DREW A ONE-SHOT.
IT'S ABOUT MILK.
ANKOKU
牛乳
加工乳
AND SO, BECAUSE I HAVE MORE WORK IN ADDITION TO THIS SERIES, I'M TOTALLY EXHAUSTED, AND I COLLAPSED RECENTLY.

Hoshin Engi: The Rank File!

You'll find as you read *Hoshin Engi* that there are titles and ranks that you are probably unfamiliar with. While it may seem confusing, there is an order to the madness that is pulled from ancient Chinese mythology, Japanese culture, other manga, and, of course, the incredible mind of *Hoshin Engi* creator Ryu Fujisaki.

Where we think it will help, we give you a hint in the margin on the page the name appears. But in addition, here's a quick primer on the titles you'll find in *Hoshin Engi* and what they mean:

Japanese	Title	Job Description
武成王	Buseio	Chief commanding officer
宰相	Saisho	Premier
太師	Taishi	The king's advisor/tutor
太金剛	Dai Kongo	Great vassals
軍師	Gunshi	Military tactician
大諸侯	Daishoko	Great feudal lord
東伯侯	Tohakuko	Lord of the east region
西伯侯	Seihakuko	Lord of the west region
比伯侯	Hokuhakuko	Lord of the north region
南伯侯	Nanhakuko	Lord of the south region

Hoshin Engi: The Immortal File

Also, you'll probably find the hierarchy of the Sennin, Sendo and Doshi somewhat complicated. Here, we spell it out the easiest way possible!

Japanese	Title	Description
道士	Doshi	Someone training to become Sennin
仙道	Sendo	Used to describe both Sennin and Doshi
仙人	Sennin	Those who have mastered the way. Once you "go Sennin" you are forever changed.
妖孽	Yogetsu	A Yosei who can transform into a human
妖怪仙人	Yokai Sennin	A Sennin whose original form is not human
妖精	Yosei	An animal or object exposed to moonlight and sunlight for more than 1,000 years

Hoshin Engi: The Magical File

Paope (宝貝) are powerful magical items used by Sennin and Doshi. Sometimes they look like regular objects, like a veil or hat. These are just a few of the magical items, both paope and otherwise, that you'll encounter in *Hoshin Engi!*

Japanese	Magic	Description
打神鞭	Dashinben	Known as the God-Striking Whip, Taikobo's paope manipulates the air and wind.
霊獣	Reiju	A magical flying beast that Sennin and Doshi use for transportation and support. Taikobo's reiju is his pal Supu.
五光石	Gokoseki	A rock that changes the face of whomever it strikes into a "weirdly erotic-looking" face.
莫邪の宝剣	Bakuya no Hoken	Tenka's weapon, a light saber.
蒼巾力士	Sokin Rikishi	Kingo's version of the Kokin Rikishi.
通天砲	Tsutenho	Kingo Island's principal gun.
太極符印	Taikyoku Fuin	A paople that can manipulate physical objects on the elemental level.
仙桃エキス	Sento Extract	A medicine made from sento that helps restore your physical strength.
降魔杵	Gomasho	A mallet-like paope that becomes heavy the moment it hits the enemy. Can change shape as well.
究極黄河陣	Kyukyoku Kogajin	A dimension controlled by the Unsho Sisters. Enemies trapped in the dimension become as weak as insects.
エナジードレイン	Energy Drain	Adults of the Supu clan have the power to drain away paope energy and render the paope useless.
怠惰スーツ	Lazy Suit	An environmentally controlled protection suit that allows Taijo Rokun to sleep undisturbed for years.
特訓くん	Mr. Training	A robot that has the abilities of all the super paope. It allows simulated combat training.
太陽針	Taiyoshin	Needles that paralyze the enemy.

Coming Next Volume:
The Battle of the Plains

The battle continues. Under Dakki's control, King Chu emerges as an unstoppable monster. Shinkohyo reminds the Zhou forces of the legend of King Chu's ancestor, King Toh. Does that legend contain the key to defeating Chu?

AVAILABLE JUNE 2010!

Read Any Good Books Lately?

Hoshin Engi is based on *Fengshen Yanji* (*The Creation of the Gods*, written in the 1500s by Xu Zhonglin), one of China's four classic fantastical novels of adventure, magic and mystery. The other three are *Saiyuki* (*Journey to the West* by Cheng'en Wu, late 1500s), *Sangokushi Engi* (*Romance of the Three Kingdoms* by Guanzhong Luo) and *Shui Hu Zhuan* (*Outlaws of the Marsh*, by Shi Nai'an, mid-1500s).

Want to read these books? You can! They're all still in print, more than 500 years later!

These books are North American in-print editions only.